A Common Law Theory of Judicial Review

The Living Tree

In this study, W. J. Waluchow argues that debates between defenders and critics of constitutional bills of rights presuppose that constitutions are more or less rigid entities. Within such a conception, constitutions aspire to establish stable, fixed points of agreement and pre-commitment, which defenders consider to be possible and desirable and critics deem impossible and undesirable. Drawing on reflections about the nature of law, constitutions, the common law, and what it is to be a democratic representative, Waluchow urges a different theory of bills of rights according to which they are flexible and adaptable. Adopting such a theory enables one not only to answer critics' most serious challenges but also to appreciate the role that a bill of rights, interpreted and enforced by unelected judges, can sensibly play in the constitutional democracy.

W. J. Waluchow is a professor of philosophy at McMaster University in Canada. He is the author of *Inclusive Legal Positivism, Free Expressions: Essays in Law and Philosophy*, and *The Dimensions of Ethics: An Introduction to Ethical Theory*, among other titles.

Cambridge Studies in Philosophy and Law

GENERAL EDITOR: GERALD POSTEMA
(UNIVERSITY OF NORTH CAROLINA, CHAPEL HILL)

ADVISORY BOARD
Jules Coleman (Yale Law School)
Antony Duff (University of Stirling)
David Lyons (Boston University)
Neil MacCormick (University of Edinburgh)
Stephen R. Munzer (U.C.L.A. Law School)
Phillip Pettit (Princeton University)
Joseph Raz (University of Oxford)
Jeremy Waldron (Columbia Law School)

Some other books in the series:

Larry Alexander (ed.): *Constitutionalism*
Larry Alexander: *Is There a Right of Freedom of Expression?*
Peter Benson (ed.): *The Theory of Contract Law: New Essays*
Steven J. Burton: *Judging in Good Faith*
Steven J. Burton (ed.): *"The Path of the Law" and Its Influence: The Legacy
of Oliver Wendell Holmes, Jr.*
Jules Coleman: *Risks and Wrongs*
Jules Coleman and Allan Buchanan (eds.): *In Harm's Way: Essays in Honor
of Joel Feinberg*
R. A. Duff (ed.): *Philosophy and the Criminal Law*
William Edmundson: *Three Anarchical Fallacies: An Essay on
Political Authority*
John Fischer and Mark Ravizza: *Responsibility and Control*
R. G. Frey and Christopher W. Morris (eds.): *Liability and Responsibility:
Essays in Law and Morals*
Steven A. Hetcher: *Norms in a Wired World*
Heidi M. Hurd: *Moral Combat*
Jody S. Kraus and Steven D. Walt (eds.): *The Jurisprudential Foundations
of Corporate and Commercial Law*
Christopher Kutz: *Complicity: Ethics and Law for a Collective Age*
Timothy Macklem: *Beyond Comparison: Sex and Discrimination*
Larry May: *Crimes against Humanity: A Normative Account*
Stephen R. Munzer: *A Theory of Property*
Arthur Ripstein: *Equality, Responsibility, and the Law*
R. Schopp: *Justification Defenses and Just Convictions*

A Common Law Theory
of Judicial Review

The Living Tree

W. J. Waluchow

McMaster University

CAMBRIDGE
UNIVERSITY PRESS

CAMBRIDGE UNIVERSITY PRESS
Cambridge, New York, Melbourne, Madrid, Cape Town, Singapore, São Paulo

Cambridge University Press
32 Avenue of the Americas, New York, NY 10013-2473, USA

www.cambridge.org
Information on this title: www.cambridge.org/9780521864763

First published 2007

Printed in the United States of America

A catalog record for this publication is available from the British Library.

Library of Congress Cataloging in Publication Data

Waluchow, Wilfrid J.
A common law theory of judicial review : the living tree / W. J. Waluchow.
p.   cm. – (Cambridge studies in philosophy and law)
Includes bibliographical references and index.
ISBN 0-521-86476-3 (hardback)
1. Judicial review – Canada.   2. Civil rights – Canada.
3. Common law – Canada.   4. Judicial review.
5. Civil rights.   6. Common law   I. Title.   II. Series.
KE4248.W35   2007
347.71′.012–dc22   2006002130

ISBN 978-0-521-86476-3 hardback

For my mother and father

Contents

Acknowledgements

I am immensely grateful to a number of friends, students, and colleagues who, in a variety of ways, contributed to the writing of this book. Among these are: Dick Bronaugh, Brian Burge-Hendrix, Mark Capustin, Michael Giudice, Les Green, Matt Grellette, Sara Halstead, Grant Huscroft, Aileen Kavanagh, Matt Kramer, David Lyons, Chris Maddocks, Jim Nichol, Denise Reaume, Fred Schauer, Roger Shiner, and Juan Vega. Papers in which my ideas were developed and tested were presented to the Departments of Philosophy at York University and the University of Western Ontario, the Law School at UNAM in Mexico City, the 2003 IVR conference in Lund, Sweden, and to the Analytic Legal Philosophy Conference at New York University. I am grateful for the many helpful comments received on all those occasions. I am also grateful for the role played by the following people: Liam Murphy and Joseph Raz, whose invitation to write an entry for the *Stanford Internet Encyclopedia of Philosophy* sparked my interest in constitutionalism and judicial review; Andrei Marmor and a second, anonymous, referee for Cambridge University Press, whose insights allowed me to improve the manuscript in a number of ways and helped me to avoid many mistakes, of which no doubt far too many remain; Beverley McLachlin, Chief Justice of the Canadian Supreme Court, whom I first met at the IVR conference in Lund and whose interest and encouragement have been an inspiration; and Gerry Postema, for his enthusiasm for the project and his excellent work as an editor. I would be remiss were I not to mention my special debt of gratitude to Jeremy Waldron, whose thoughts on democracy and powerful and probing criticisms of judicial review under charters of rights served as the springboard from which many of my ideas developed. I hope that Jeremy will see, in the sustained effort I make to address his many arguments and criticisms, a testament to the deep respect I have for him as a philosopher and scholar. Finally, I wish to thank Donna for her love and encouragement – and for having the patience and good graces to smile lovingly through the tedious ramblings of an excited husband in the throes of philosophy.

1

A Charter Revolution

A. A Charter of Rights

In the early 1980s Canada experienced a fundamental change in its political and legal structures. A new *Constitution Act (1982)* came into effect, declaring itself to be "the supreme law of Canada." This new *Constitution Act* further decreed that "any law that is inconsistent with [its] provisions . . . is, to the extent of the inconsistency, of no force or effect."[1] In themselves, these statements seem innocuous enough. By its very nature a constitution contains a society's basic law; it is reasonable, therefore, to think that it trumps any subordinate law with which it conflicts. What made the *Constitution Act*'s declarations so momentous and deeply controversial, however, was the inclusion of a new *Charter of Rights and Freedoms*. This specified a number of abstract rights of political morality that federal, provincial, and municipal governments were legally barred from infringing.[2] Among these rights were the right to equality before and under the law; the right to life, liberty, and security of the person, coupled with the companion right not to be deprived of the former except in accordance with the principles of fundamental justice; and the right to freedom of thought, belief, opinion, expression, and association.[3] The adoption of a constitutional Charter incorporating these and other rights of political morality was widely applauded as an important step in enhancing the liberty and self-respect

---

1 Constitution Act, 1982, Schedule B, Part 1, Canadian Charter of Rights and Freedoms, sec. 52 (1).

2 We will assume, for the time being, that many Charter rights – for example, the rights to free expression and equality before and under the law – are a species of moral rights against government. Specifically they are a species of moral rights that governments, in the exercise of their authoritative powers (e.g., to introduce binding legislation), may not validly infringe. In effect, they serve as moral limits to these powers and, consequently, the authority of government. In Chapters 2 and 3 an attempt will be made to ground this assumption in argument. We will also address the question of what kind of moral rights these Charter rights are, together with the question of whose views about their requirements ought to prevail in Charter disputes.

3 Canadian Charter of Rights and Freedoms, sections 15, 7, and 2, respectively.

of Canadian citizens. In adopting the Charter, Canada had clearly heeded the advice of former Prime Minister Lester Pearson, who once commented that "Canadians could take no more meaningful step than to entrench firmly in our Constitution those fundamental rights and liberties which we possess and cherish."[4] Pearson's vision was shared by the principal force behind the Charter's adoption, Prime Minister Pierre Elliott Trudeau: "We must now establish the basic principles, the basic values and beliefs which hold us together as Canadians, so that beyond our regional loyalties there is a way of life and a system of values which make us proud of the country that has given us such freedom and such immeasurable joy."[5] Eventually, and after a sustained series of political debates and a momentous Supreme Court reference,[6] the Charter came into being. Upon its enactment, then–Justice Minister Jean Chrétien assessed the Charter's impact and importance in his introduction to a widely distributed booklet sponsored by the federal government:

In a free and democratic society, it is important that citizens know exactly what their rights and freedoms are, and where to turn to for help and advice in the event that those freedoms are denied or rights infringed upon. In a country like Canada – vast and diverse, with 11 governments, two official languages and a variety of ethnic origins – the only way to provide equal protection to everyone is to enshrine those basic rights and freedoms in the Constitution.

Now, for the first time, we will have a Canadian Charter of Rights and Freedoms that recognizes certain rights for all of us, wherever we may live in Canada.

To be sure, there has been a host of federal and provincial laws guaranteeing some of our fundamental rights and freedoms. However, these laws have varied from province to province, with the result that basic rights have been unevenly protected throughout our country. Now that our rights will be written into the Constitution, it will be a constant reminder to our political leaders that they must wield their authority with caution and wisdom.[7]

As Chrétien states in his introduction, most of the rights included in the Charter enjoyed, in some form or other, recognition in Canadian law before the introduction of the Charter. For example, something *like* the right to equality before and under the law was recognized as far back as *Edwards* (the "Persons Case"), which was decided in 1930 by the Privy Council of the United Kingdom.[8] And many Acts of Parliament and provincial legislatures – for example,

---

4 The Right Honourable Lester B. Pearson, *Federalism for the Future* (Ottawa: Publications Canada, 1968), Introduction cited in *The Charter of Rights and Freedoms: A Guide for Canadians* (Ottawa: Publications Canada, 1982), 1.
5 The Right Honourable Pierre Elliott Trudeau, 1982 (cited in *The Charter of Rights and Freedoms*), 1.
6 *Reference Re Resolution to Amend the Constitution of Canada* [1981] 1 S.C.R. 753, commonly referred to as "The Patriation Case."
7 The Charter of Rights and Freedoms: A Guide for Canadians (supra n. 3), Preface, v.
8 *Edwards v. Attorney General of Canada* [1930] A.C. 124. We will return to *Edwards* later on. It is in this case that the "living tree" metaphor, from which this book takes its subtitle, was introduced into Canadian law.

provincial Human Rights Codes – made reference in some way or another to the notion of equality. Nevertheless, many of the rights to which the Charter makes reference did not, prior to its enactment, enjoy the *kind* of status it accorded them, the status of entrenched, fundamental constitutional rights that no government action is to violate – unless, that is, certain specific conditions are met. For example, an infringement can be justified under Section 1, which specifies that the Charter "guarantees the rights and freedoms set out in it subject only to such reasonable limits prescribed by law as can be demonstrably justified in a free and democratic society." Alternatively, a constitutional impediment can be overcome by way of a Section 33 override, which allows that "Parliament or the legislature of a province may expressly declare in an Act of Parliament or of the legislature, as the case may be, that the Act or a provision thereof shall operate notwithstanding a provision included in section 20 or sections 7 to 15 of [the] Charter." Despite these novel features of the Canadian Charter, its impact was profound. Anyone doubting the significance of Charter recognition rights need only review the sorry history of its predecessor, the *Canadian Bill of Rights*, which had very little impact on the state of Canadian law.[9]

Although adoption of the Charter was applauded by many Canadians, not everyone shared the optimistic views of Pearson, Trudeau, and Chrétien. Many critics pointed to the fact that the Charter's abstract rights were left largely undefined by the political actors whose efforts gave them constitutional status. Canadians were told that they were now guaranteed, in Section 15, an entrenched constitutional right to equality before and under the law. But what exactly that meant in concrete terms was a question that the Charter left completely unanswered. This, together with the fact that the task of answering that question – that is, of determining the concrete meaning and implications of the entrenched rights in specific cases – would invariably fall mainly to the judges, was the source of considerable unease. It was also the source of much vitriolic complaint.[10] This unease found expression in a number of objections, many of which had already been voiced during the long political processes leading up to the Charter's eventual adoption. Perhaps the most powerful objection came in the form of what might be called the "Argument from Democracy." Roughly, the argument is this: Democratic principle is seriously compromised if unelected and politically unaccountable judges are left with the task of fleshing out the

---

9 For an example of a feeble, pre-Charter attempt to use the Bill of Rights to develop a robust jurisprudence of equality, see, for example, *Attorney General of Canada v. Lavell* [1974] S.C.R. 1349. This case is sometimes cited as evidence that a purely statutory, nonconstitutional Bill of Rights is an ineffective tool for the protection of rights.

10 Although Charter rights are usually applied in judging the constitutional status of acts of legislation, their application extends to other forms of government action, including executive and administrative decisions of all kinds. In order to facilitate ease of expression, and unless otherwise stated, I will simply refer to Charter conflicts with legislation, with the understanding that this is only one possible form of conflict.

contours of the moral rights the Charter claims to guarantee, and then applying these rights against legislation duly passed by democratically accountable bodies like Parliament and the provincial legislatures. How could allowing the duly considered judgments of the people's representatives to be trumped by the actions of a small group of judges sitting in appeals courts possibly be reconciled with democracy – with the "free and democratic society" to which Section 1 of the Charter itself makes reference? Not only are the judges empowered by the Charter to thwart the democratic will of Canadians, they seem now able to do so by imposing their own possibly idiosyncratic and biased moral beliefs and ideologies upon the legislatures and, ultimately, the citizens these bodies were elected to represent. Nothing in the Charter specifies precisely what Charter rights to free expression, equality, and liberty mean. And yet judges are empowered to invalidate duly enacted legislation because, in *their* judgment, such legislative acts violate these wholly unspecified moral rights. It seems to follow that legality in Canada is now ultimately dependent on the moral opinions of unaccountable judges.

But there are other, no less serious objections as well. Legal practice under the Charter not only seems to pose a threat to democracy, but it is politically dangerous and fundamentally unfair – indeed, it seems to constitute a threat to the very idea of the rule of law. It is dangerous because considerable political power is now vested in a small cadre of unaccountable judges sitting in appeals courts. They, not the people and their parliamentary representatives, ultimately have been assigned the task of deciding controversial moral issues on behalf of Canadians – and on the basis of these decisions determining what shall be deemed lawful in Canada. This is far too much political power for a small group of unelected judges to wield over an entire population, no matter how learned and wise they might be. It is fundamentally unfair because citizens are, in effect, disenfranchised by this arrangement. Each citizen of voting age has the right, in a democratic society, to contribute to the creation of the laws by which she is governed. This she exercises directly via the ballot box and by whatever contributions to public discourse and debate about controversial issues she chooses to make. She also does so indirectly via the legislative votes of her elected representatives, who are supposed to represent the interests and opinions of constituents. All this has been replaced by subjection to the pronouncements of judges. The duly considered views of citizens and their representatives about the laws by which they are to be governed, arrived at through fair processes of democratic decision making, are, in effect, being set aside in favour of the moral opinions of a handful of judges. The unfairness of this is only compounded by the fact that the judges can almost never demonstrate, to the satisfaction of all concerned, that their decisions are any better at honouring the relevant Charter rights than the democratically chosen decisions they replace. The unfairness is further exacerbated by the undeniable fact that judges on appeals courts often disagree vehemently among themselves about Charter rights and must often, in the end, themselves rely on voting to settle their disagreements. It is not at all uncommon to see split votes when a court deals with contentious issues of moral principle raised by a Charter challenge. And even when the justices are unanimous in their vote, concurring opinions, each in its own distinctive way supportive of the court's decision, reveal deep divisions concerning the precise meaning and import of the relevant Charter rights. Add to this the fact that judges render decisions that all too often appear to conflict not only with views widely shared in the community at large but also with *their own* previous decisions; and what might have appeared like a marvellous idea to Pearson, Chrétien, Trudeau, and many other Canadians – constitutionally guaranteeing moral rights against unwarranted exercise of government power over citizens – is transformed into a living nightmare, a nightmare in which democracy and the rule of law have, in effect, been abandoned and replaced by the rule of a few men and women, by a kind of "judicial oligarchy." And no matter the high esteem in which we tend to hold our judges, this is not a form of government to be eagerly embraced. This was a point noted in the mid–twentieth century by an influential American jurist, Learned Hand, who offered the following analogous warning in relation to the American Bill of Rights and its potential for use by judges to rationalize what is in effect an unadulterated power grab:

> For myself it would be most irksome to be ruled by a bevy of Platonic Guardians, even if I knew how to choose them, which I assuredly do not. If they were in charge, I should miss the stimulus of living in a society where I have, at least theoretically, some part in the direction of public affairs. Of course I know how illusory would be the belief that my vote determined anything; but nevertheless when I go to the polls I have a satisfaction in the sense that we are all engaged in a common venture. If you retort that a sheep in the flock may feel something like it; I reply, following Saint Francis, "My brother, the Sheep."[11]

These initial misgivings about the Charter and the role it appears to assign judges remain unabated, and they flare up from time to time in public discourse when controversial cases are decided in Canadian courts. The list of relevant cases includes *Butler* (obscenity and pornography), *Keegstra* (hate speech), *Egan* (same-sex unions), *Vriend* (discrimination against gays and lesbians), *Sharpe* (child pornography), and *The Montfort* (the threatened closure of Ottawa's only Francophone teaching hospital).[12] An earlier court decision in *Montfort* led the *Globe and Mail* to declare in an editorial that "our courts are amending the Constitution as they will, when they will, spinning principles

---

11 Learned Hand, *The Bill of Rights* (Cambridge, Mass.: Harvard University Press, 1958), 73–4.

12 *R. v. Butler* [1982] 1. S.C.R. 452; *R. v. Keegstra* [1990] 3 S.C.R. 697; *Vriend v. Alberta* [1998] 1 S.C.R. 493; *Egan v. The Queen in Right of Canada* [1995] 2 S.C.R. 513; *R. v. Sharpe* [2001] 1. S.C.R. 45; *Lalone et al., v. Commission de Restructuration des Services de Sante* ("The Montfort"), Ontario C.A., docket no. C33807, December 7, 2001.

into protections with an entrepreneurial fervour with no more than lip service to those who drafted the highest law in the land."[13] Even those who accept the value of the Charter as part of the fundamental law of Canada often object to the way in which it is interpreted and used by Canadian judges. Jeffrey Simpson, in a *Globe and Mail* column, denounced the Supreme Court for opposing legislation restricting the voting rights of prisoners serving two years or more. According to Simpson,

That decision was one of the most aggressive in asserting judicial supremacy over Parliament. It dismissed parliamentary debates on the issue as having offered "more fulmination than illumination." . . . So much for the vaunted but rather tattered notion of the Supreme Court and Parliament engaged in a "dialogue." It's more like diktat from the court.[14]

Often, then, the complaint is that judges substitute their own moral views on the meaning and import of Charter rights for those of the relevant legislature. At other times, the complaint is that the judges, emboldened by their new roles as the nation's guardians of moral rights, have gone so far as to create entirely new rights and read them into the relevant law. In *Vriend*, for example, the Supreme Court was said to have run roughshod over Alberta's *Individual Rights Protection Act* by inventing a completely new legal right against discrimination based on sexual orientation, a right that was nowhere to be found in the Act but that was thought by the judges to be analogous to those that were. Similar complaints were made after the *Montfort* ruling, which recognized an unwritten, general constitutional right to Francophone minority protection based on the more specific minority protections regarding language, religion, and education that are explicitly mentioned in the Charter and elsewhere. In response, the *Globe and Mail* declared:

Think of the Divisional Court of Ontario's Superior Court of Justice not as a body tied to the tedious, written contents of the Constitution, but as a cheerful entrepreneur prepared to expand the document as it deems wise. That is how the court seems to see itself if its astonishing ruling this week on Ottawa's Montfort Hospital is any guide.[15]

Unease over the Charter and the role it seems to assign judges is not, of course, restricted to newspaper commentaries. A parallel academic scholarship has emerged in which the wisdom and legitimacy of the Charter, and of judicial efforts to implement its provisions, have been the subject of scathing critique. Among the principal critics are F. L. Morton and Rainer Knopff, who, in *The Charter Revolution and the Court Party*, offer the following blunt assessment:

---

13 *Globe and Mail*, December 3, 1999.
14 "The Court of No Resort," *Globe and Mail*, Friday, November 22, 2002, A25.
15 *Globe and Mail*, editorial, December 3, 1999.

The Charter does not so much guarantee rights as give judges the power to make policy by choosing among competing interpretations of broadly worded provisions.... In a dazzling exercise of self-empowerment, the Supreme Court has transformed itself from an adjudicator of disputes to a constitutional oracle that is able and willing to pronounce on the validity of a broad range of public policies. Interpretive discretion and an oracular courtroom – these are two of the chief building blocks of Canada's Charter Revolution.[16]

An equally forceful condemnation was proclaimed by Michael Mandel. In summing up his critique of the Charter and its tendency to entrench "legalized politics," Mandel writes:

> ... all I have really tried to do is to reveal the dishonest nature of legalized politics and to show how what has been sold as a democratic movement is actually its opposite.... [I]n every realm, and whether on its best or worst behaviour, the Charter's basic claims have been shown to be fraudulent.... Despite all the heavenly exaltation, the Charter has merely handed over the custody of our politics to the legal profession.... The Charter would be a mute oracle without a legal priesthood to give it life, and the legal profession has shown itself more than willing to play the lead part in the hoax. Canadian lawyers and judges have, for the most part, gleefully and greedily undertaken a job – deciding the important political questions of the day – for which they lack all competence.[17]

Further on the question of the threat posed to democratic ideals, Mandel adds,

> ... we have seen what it means for something to be "constitutionally guaranteed." We have seen that the form makes all the difference in the world. Putting the bare phrase "freedom of association" in a document administered by an unfettered judiciary not responsible to anyone is unimaginable in any society we would call democratic. Nailing down the meaning of freedom of association by specific, concrete, legal (as opposed to constitutional) rights with institutional guarantees that they will be rigorously respected is a different thing altogether. In other words, we do not need "freedom of association" if we have "all it entails." Nor will we have democracy if we are not allowed to make up our own minds about what freedom of association entails, but instead must hand the question over to a few of our betters to decide the matter for us under the pretext of interpretation.... Using the Charter offensively legitimates a form of politics we should be doing everything we can to *de*-legitimate.[18]

So what are we to conclude from all this? Despite the fact that the majority of Canadians seem to share the favourable picture of the Charter and its possibilities enunciated by Pearson, Trudeau, and Chrétien, there remains a significant body of public opinion and scholarship that questions their rosy picture. Many share the view recently articulated by the archbishop of the Roman Catholic diocese of Toronto. In an open letter calling for the federal government to use

---

16 Morton and Knopff, *The Charter Revolution and the Court Party* (Peterborough: Broadview Press, 2000), 13–14.
17 Michael Mandel, *The Charter of Rights and the Legalization of Politics* (Toronto: Thompson Educational Publishing, Inc., 1994), 455.
18 Ibid., 458.

Section 33 of the Charter to override rulings by several Canadian courts that
restricting marriage to heterosexual couples is an unjustifiable infringement of
Section 15, the archbishop wrote:

Some will argue that the use of the notwithstanding clause in the Charter [Sec. 33]
is wrong in principle. I must respectfully disagree. The notwithstanding clause was
inserted to recognize parliamentary supremacy and the need for democratic oversight
for the courts. No Canadian can say that the courts always get things right. Judges
are not elected and are ultimately not accountable for their decisions. Fundamental
social change should only occur with the consent of the people through their democratic
institutions. This understanding of the role of Parliament led to the inclusion of the
notwithstanding clause in the Charter. Its use in the context of same-sex marriage would
be most appropriate.[19]

The arguments put forward on behalf of the archbishop's underlying political
philosophy are not entirely without substance. It *is* difficult to reconcile the
Charter with the view that, ultimately, self-government – arguably, the animating ideal of democracy – demands government by the people and/or their chosen
representatives. It rejects government by a small group of unelected judges who
are not required to answer to the population over whom they exercise considerable authority and who often represent anything but a cross-section of views
on the controversial moral issues arising in Charter challenges. It *is* difficult to
think of the Charter as "guaranteeing" our moral rights, when it is largely left to
judges to figure out what these so-called guarantees really mean. The problem
is only further exacerbated when the judges can seldom, if ever, demonstrate
that their answers are the correct ones, or even come to an agreement on their
proposed solutions. It *is* difficult to reconcile the Charter's "guarantees" with
the suspicion that there really are no "right answers," in either law or moral
theory, to the question of what, in Canada, the rights to equality, free expression, life, liberty, and security of the person really mean in practice. How can
Canadians be guaranteed something about which there is so much controversy?
How can they be guaranteed something that may not even exist? How valuable
is a guarantee when it's only *after* one attempts to act on it that one is told what
the guarantee actually amounts to? Would anyone be prepared to buy a car or a
dishwasher under these circumstances? Surely not. But then why should they
be willing to buy into a Charter that seems, if the critics are correct, to offer
nothing more?

So, in the abstract, and without considering the values and ideals it threatens
to undermine, a Charter or Bill of Rights sounds like a very good idea. But
once one thinks things through a bit more carefully, tough questions emerge
that demand serious attention. It is the aim of this book to contribute to efforts

19 Cardinal Aloysius Amrozic, "An Open Letter: Why the rush on same-sex marriage?"
   Globe and Mail, Wednesday, January 19, 2005, A19.

to satisfy that demand by providing a philosophical exploration of Charters or Bills of Rights and their potential roles in democratic societies such as one finds, not only in Canada, but in the United States, Germany, Mexico, and New Zealand. Many of the issues in play in debates about the value of the Canadian Charter are not unique to that country – and they most certainly did not first arise in 1982. The potential conflict between democratic principle and judicial review of legislation under a Charter or Bill of Rights is one that arises in any country that embraces the idea of constitutionally limited government. This is the idea, often associated with the political theories of Locke and Montesquieu, that government can and should be legally limited in its powers, and that its authority depends on its observing these limits. One way in which government power can be limited is by requiring that its exercise be consistent with a Charter or Bill of Rights that incorporates moral rights against government. This was the avenue taken by Americans more than 200 years ago when they adopted (and later added to) their Bill of Rights. The result has been a long and often impassioned debate about the nature and legitimacy of judicial review – the practice of judges' reviewing acts of government to ensure compliance with constitutional requirements, for example those enshrined in the American Bill of Rights or the Canadian Charter. So the debates are not unique to Canada. And wherever one finds them, the basic themes are roughly the same: Judicial review under a Charter or Bill of Rights threatens democracy, seems fundamentally unfair and politically dangerous, and relies on outmoded views about the nature of moral rights – that there exist "objective" moral rights to which Charters and Bills of Rights make reference, and that judges can sensibly and justifiably be asked to discover and apply against recalcitrant exercises of government power.

Oftentimes, however, the rhetoric surrounding these issues overwhelms the argument. Views are expressed that rely not only on bad arguments but also on a flawed picture of Charters and Bills of Rights and what they promise to provide. One of the more important tasks of this book will ultimately be to explore and defend a conception of such instruments that is radically different from the one normally assumed in the debates to which they give rise. But before we can get to this better conception and appreciate its potential, we will first have to examine the standard conception and the ways in which it underpins many of the arguments, both supportive and critical, that have been advanced in popular and academic discourse. As a result, our investigation will largely divide into two parts. In the first part, we will explore critically some of the strongest and more popular arguments centred on the standard conception; in the second part, we will go on to examine what I believe is a much stronger conception of Charters and Bills of Rights, one that will help us understand better the nature and possibilities of judicial review under such an instrument, and the potentially valuable role some such practice can play within a thriving democracy. With this in mind, our investigations will take the following path.

B. The Structure of the Argument

We will begin, in Chapter 2, with some initial thoughts on the nature of constitutionally limited government. Chapter 3 will explore some of the standard
arguments in favour of Charters and Bills of Rights that one encounters in both
popular and academic discourse. Some of these arguments were mentioned
previously, but we will need to examine them in much greater detail if we are
to assess their force – or lack thereof. In Chapter 4, the case against Charters
and Bills of Rights will be outlined and examined. As we shall see, the rhetoric
employed by critics of Charters and Bills of Rights, and of the practice(s) of
judicial review that arise under them, often outstrips the logic of the arguments
advanced.[20] Much of our effort will be directed towards showing when this is
in fact the case. But equally important will be the task of showing where the
critics have got things more or less right. Oftentimes, and once the rhetorical
flourishes are cleared away, there is a good deal of substance in the criticisms
made. More often than not, the critics have rightly pointed out the considerable
gulf between the reality of life under a Charter and the rosy picture enunciated
by its advocates. The simple fact is that a Charter *cannot* do what its most vocif-
erous advocates often maintain. It cannot, for example, possibly live up to the
ideal of letting citizens know what their rights are, or of representing a society's
guarantee to its members – particularly its minority members – that certain
enunciated rights will be observed and respected in subsequent decisions made
by that society's lawmakers. The critics are correct: One cannot commit to X if
one does not even know what X is. One cannot possibly guarantee that "citizens
know exactly what their rights and freedoms are . . . " if we disagree radically
about what these rights and freedoms actually are. But these are serious problems, I submit, only if we accept the particular picture of Charters and judicial
review presupposed by these comments. And it is *this* particular picture that
underlies much of the current and ongoing debate. But that picture is highly
misleading, and seeing why and to what extent this is so will help us achieve a
better understanding of a Charter and what it can in fact accomplish. Apparently
fatal problems become much more manageable if we reject the standard picture
entirely and accept in its place an alternative conception according to which
Charters represent a mixture of only very modest pre-commitment combined
with a considerable measure of humility. It is the development of this alternative
conception to which we will turn in Chapters 5 and 6.

---

20 We will henceforth use the phrase "judicial review" to refer to any form of judicial
   assessment of the legal validity of government action (typically legislation) under a constitutional Charter or Bill of Rights such as one finds in Canada and the United States,
   or under sections of a nation's constitution that outline basic civil rights like equality
   and freedom of association. We will also simply use the phrase "Charter" to refer to any
   written constitutional instrument, or part thereof, that specifies what appear to be moral
   rights against which government actions are to be measured in assessing their legal force,
   effect, or validity.

The alternative conception of Charters defended in what follows will be called the "common law conception." It accepts the premise that we do *not* in fact know, in advance, what our rights and freedoms are in many cases, and that we do well, in designing our systems of political and legal governance, to set things up so that we can be rationally responsive to this unavoidable feature of our human predicament. As we shall see, one of the ways in which this lack of moral insight can play out in practice is in the largely unintentional violation of moral rights by legislation and other exercises of government power. Often legislators simply do not know when they introduce legislation whether and to what extent their otherwise sensible and justifiable legislative efforts might reasonably be thought later to compromise fundamental rights, values, and social goals. Legal systems are typically sensitive to this feature of our human predicament and employ a host of measures to accommodate it. One measure is to employ abstract terms like "reasonable" and "fair" in general legislation, and then leaving it to the judges who apply that legislation to determine what, in particular situations, is in fact reasonable, fair, and so on. Another way is to rely instead on a common law, case-by-case method of resolving disputes. Instead of having a legislature introduce, in advance, a general rule by which we are expected to abide, legal systems sometimes rely on judges to work things out as particular situations arise. What degree of force is reasonable in responding to a threat to person or property? Given the myriad circumstances in which such threats arise, it would be sheer folly to attempt to define in advance, and for every possible case that might arise, what a reasonable degree of force could sensibly be thought to be. So the system leaves it to people to figure this out for themselves, perhaps with the help of previous judicial rulings in analogous cases. And it then relies on judges deciding such cases to assess a particular citizen's judgment about what was in fact reasonable in his particular set of circumstances. Sometimes this is the only sensible way to proceed, even though a person might reasonably complain that it would have been better to know in advance what would be expected of him. These and other techniques are all used by the law in dealing with our lack of foreknowledge about the situations in which we will find ourselves. The argument in Chapters 4 and 5 will be that the adoption of a Charter is one such technique. A Charter is best viewed as a device for dealing with our epistemic limitations in respect to the effects of government action on moral rights. These are moral rights about whose exact nature we are often undecided or cannot agree on in advance but whose importance has been recognized in the decision to include them within a Charter of Rights and Freedoms. Once we see Charters and judicial review in this very different light, we can not only see our way clear to a better understanding of the disputes between their critics and their advocates, but we can also see why they can be very good things to have – even in a society fully committed to the ideals of democracy and subject to the endless disputes caused by our epistemic limitations. Or so I shall argue.

C. The Scope of the Analysis

As indicated previously, this book aims to provide a general, philosophical exploration of Charters and their potential roles in democratic societies such as one finds in the United States, Germany, Mexico, New Zealand, and Canada.[21] To that end, the analysis purports to be relevant to any democratic country or jurisdiction in which one finds some form of Charter limitation on government action – that is, in which governments are in some way, and to some extent, required or expected, when exercising their (typically legislative) powers, not to infringe on a constitutionally specified set of moral rights. As we shall see, the force of this requirement can vary from system to system and indeed from time to time in one and the same system. It is equally important to stress that the means by which the relevant requirement is enforced can also vary considerably. These can range from the sheer force of moral suasion, which despite its informality can be extremely effective, to a legally specified (either in writing or by way of custom or convention) strong form of judicial review, according to which judges are empowered to nullify the legislative efforts of a Parliament or a Congress. So the relevance of the analysis will, it is hoped, be quite extensive. Despite this, however, a good deal of the succeeding discussion will continue to make explicit reference to the Canadian context. This route has been chosen for a number of reasons.

First, when addressing concepts, arguments, or issues of wide application, it is often useful to focus on a particular example with which one is familiar. To be sure, there is danger in this approach. One can become blinded by special features of the example chosen. One must always be careful not to confuse what is peculiar to a particular instance of X with what is essential to or characteristic of X. But so long as one is cognizant of this potential difficulty and chooses a more or less standard example, concentrating on a particular case or application can enhance the effort to understand concepts and issues that could be only vaguely grasped at a more abstract level. Second, oftentimes discussions of judicial review under a Charter presuppose the American paradigm and proceed as though this example defines the wider phenomenon. It is often assumed, for example, that the decision of a supreme court to overturn legislative decisions is absolute, thus raising and colouring our attempts to answer questions about the consistency of judicial review with democratic principles. Yet as Section 33 of the Canadian Charter illustrates, there is no necessity here. It is possible to have judicial review without granting judges the final say. Focusing on a non-American example, then, should open our eyes to possibilities that might not otherwise appear. Third, the Canadian Charter is in its infancy, and discussions

---

21 We will soon see that there is considerable controversy over what makes a society truly democratic. But for now, we can observe that a minimal, necessary condition seems to be the incorporation of some means of introducing, modifying, and extinguishing laws that are responsive to citizens' wishes, preferences, and views.

of its role in Canadian life are relatively undeveloped. So far as I am aware, no one has attempted an analysis of the sort provided here that uses the Canadian Charter as its primary example. Furthermore, no one, again so far as I am aware, has attempted to provide an analysis of the Canadian Charter that focuses on its philosophical underpinnings and tries to tie contemporary disputes about that particular Charter to more fundamental questions concerning the nature and justification of Charters and judicial review. Much public and academic discourse, both for and against the Canadian Charter, uncritically presupposes the naïve picture of the Charter's aspirations represented in our earlier quotations from Pearson, Trudeau, and Chrétien. Charter advocates seem not to notice, for example, how very much we disagree over the rights whose nature the Charter is supposed to inform us. Charter critics, seizing on facts like this, respond with the claim that the Charter is premised on a politically dangerous naïveté. But is this shared picture the right picture? And if not, why not? What does this show about the many arguments one encounters in public and academic discourse? Are they all off on the wrong track?

So there is, I submit, much to be gained from a philosophical discussion of judicial review that takes, as its focus, the Canadian Charter of Rights and Freedoms. In taking this approach we must, as noted previously, be careful not to generalize in illegitimate ways. We must be careful not to confuse what is peculiar to this particular instance of the phenomenon with what is essential or characteristic of it. But we must also be very careful not to confuse the following two kinds of questions, which, regrettably, have been conflated in many critiques of judicial review: (1) Is a Charter, *at least in principle*, a good thing to have in the context of liberal democratic societies with traditions and institutions such as one finds in Canada and the United States – and if so, why? and (2) How well have particular societies done in implementing judicial review? In particular, how well have their judges done in *applying* their Charters to the many cases in which their terms have been thought to apply? Too often, I submit, criticisms of how the *judges* have, over a period of time, decided cases under their Charter have been confused with criticisms of *that Charter itself,* or with the very *idea* of judicial review. But this is a mistake because it in no way follows from the fact that X has not been implemented correctly that X should be abandoned altogether. Absent a compelling argument to the effect that successful implementation is impossible or highly unlikely, or can be achieved only at a cost that is too high to pay, the answer to such failure might well be better implementation, informed by a better understanding of what is being asked and what is at stake. If the judges have not lived up to their responsibilities, perhaps this is because we – and they – have yet to understand fully what it is exactly that they are being asked to do – and *why*. The answer to the charge that "our courts are amending the Constitution as they will, when they will, spinning principles into protections with an entrepreneurial fervour with no more than lip service to those who drafted the highest law in the land"[22] might not be to abandon judicial review altogether but to foster a better understanding of the nature and role of that practice within a constitutional democracy. If a society's judges seem to be superseding the scope of their licence, then perhaps that society needs a better grasp of why that is so – if indeed it is – and how they might do better. This I hope to provide in the present study.

A final cautionary note. One might be excused for thinking that the foregoing cautions about failing to distinguish what *has* occurred under a Charter from what *should* or *might* occur can lead to error in the opposite direction. What use is an analysis of possibilities that are likely never to be realized – that is, an analysis that is oblivious to the practical realities of life under a Charter? If judges have in fact superseded their authority under a particular Charter, have in fact created new rights with no footing in that instrument, then perhaps there is something in the enterprise of judicial review that inevitably leads in that direction. Perhaps, human nature being what it is, it is sheer folly to have a Charter that places immense power in the hands of a few weathered heads sitting in chambers. If we could ever find Platonic Guardians in whose hands we might entrust the practice, judicial review might be a wonderful thing to have.[23] But in the hands of ordinary mortals, that practice might well prove to be a very bad thing indeed. This is all very true, and our analysis must be sensitive to the worrisome possibilities herein mentioned. Nevertheless, for reasons articulated here, there can be great value in attempting to separate what *has* occurred from what *might* occur, under more suitable, realizable conditions. If we can articulate a conception of judicial review that allows us to understand what it is the judges might well be trying to do and that provides resources with the help of which they might do so better or with a better means of explaining what they are doing and why it is in fact justified, then we will have taken an important and necessary step in the evolution of our understanding of judicial review and the political and legal systems of which it is now such a prominent feature. This is my hope. Whether I will have succeeded in this ambition is a question only the reader will be able to answer.

---

22 *Globe and Mail*, December 3, 1999.
23 But recall Learned Hand's claim that he would reject rule by any such individuals even if he knew where to find them.

Somewhat surprisingly, it is not at all clear on what basis a representative is actually to decide when voting on behalf of her constituents. This is surprising if only because representatives are often criticized for not truly representing the voters, which is puzzling if we have little idea of what exactly they are supposed to be doing for us. Suppose a representative thinks that a proposal before the House of Commons is unjust, but she also knows that the vast majority of her constituents would disagree with her. Should the representative vote her own conscience, or that of her constituents? What does she owe them: *her own* best judgment on the issue, or adherence to what she knows *their* judgment is or would be if they were asked? If the correct answer is the latter, must this be the case even when there is good reason to believe that the constituents have not appreciated all the relevant facts, or that fear or prejudice has clouded their judgment? Perhaps a representative's duty is to vote as constituents would have voted under ideal conditions of deliberation – that is, with full knowledge of all relevant facts, and in the absence of prejudice or other factors that can cloud judgment, and so on. Or perhaps this way of looking at a representative's responsibilities is completely off track. Perhaps the representative's role is not to vote in favour of measures that are *just* but to vote in whatever way is likely to advance the overall *interests* of her constituents. If every representative votes in this way, the result (we will assume) will likely be overall maximization of interests across the relevant constituencies. And perhaps this is the best we can hope for in the way of justice – indeed, perhaps this rough utilitarian justice is all we should be aiming for in this kind of context. Perhaps deeper issues of justice are more properly dealt with in other forums – say, the courts. These puzzles about the nature of democratic representation will be explored more fully in Chapter 3. For now we should note the following feature of indirect democracies: Whatever role is assigned to legislators in an indirect, representative democracy, a kind of "distance" is thereby created between the people and the law-determining decisions by which they are governed. And this does not seem necessarily to disqualify the system from counting as democratic.

So not all law-determining decisions in a democracy are made by the people themselves. Here's another point we should bear in mind: Neither are all such decisions made by *elected* representatives. Many law-determining decisions, even in what clearly appear to be vibrant, fully functioning representative democracies, are made by people who are neither elected by nor accountable to an electorate. To be sure, members of the United States' Senate and House of Representatives are all chosen in national elections. And Canada too has its elected House of Commons. But as in the United Kingdom, the Canadian Parliament partly comprises an unelected second house, in this case a Senate. Many have lobbied for abolition of this body, or for transforming it into an elected Upper House. But few would deny that its presence disqualifies Canada from being counted among the world's thriving democracies. Of equal importance is the fact that legislative bodies, including those that are elected, and in that way fully accountable, often delegate law-determining decisions to administrative bodies such as the Canadian Radio-television and Telecommunications Commission or the United States Food and Drug Administration. When this occurs we have even further distance between the people and the law-determining decisions by which they are governed. Decisions have been delegated to elected representatives, who in turn delegate law-determining authority within a specified domain (e.g., the Canadian Radio-television Telecommunications Commission creates and applies rules governing the licensing of public broadcasters) to unelected administrative officials. So in modern democracies there is considerable distance between the people and *many* of the law-determining decisions by which they are governed. Such decisions may all be made *on behalf* of the people, but it is important to be clear that it is not the people themselves who actually make them.

So democracies come in a number of different forms, each of which (with the possible exception of direct democracies) includes a variety of mechanisms for distancing law-determining decisions from the general citizenry on whose behalf they are made. This aspect of democratic government has enormous significance for our analysis because judicial review also distances the people from law-determining decisions. Judicial review is sometimes said to be inherently undemocratic insofar as it hinders the people's ability to govern themselves – in this view, it is said to stand in the way of the people and their ability to act as they see fit on issues of public importance. How can a people be self-governing, the argument goes, if their current choices, made through their elected representatives and those, like the Canadian Radio-television Telecommunications Commission to whom they have delegated law-determining powers, are curtailed – indeed, often thwarted – by the demand that they be consistent with a Charter? This uncomfortable question becomes even more pressing if we add to the mix the fact that it is typically unelected judges who are left to decide whether a law-determining decision – for example, the decision to enact a statute governing the creation and distribution of child pornography – has lived up to a Charter's demands. How, it might be asked, can this possibly be consistent with democratic self-government?

This brings us to yet another basic fact that must be borne in mind when considering the nature and justification of judicial review. The Charters with which we will be concerned are not only law, they are all part of the *constitutional* law of the societies in which they exist. This means, as we shall see, that they tend to have a kind of built-in inertia or resistance to change that prevents them from being easily modified or eliminated, even in the face of significant change in the people's views about the moral issues typically raised by judicial review. And this in turn is largely because constitutions are meant to provide stable foundations for the everyday business of law and politics. They provide the stable, ongoing framework within which the business of democratic politics is supposed to take place. As a result, Charters characteristically exhibit a number

of crucial features. One of these is "entrenchment." To say that a Charter is constitutionally entrenched is to say, roughly speaking, that it is very, very difficult
to abrogate or modify it. Changing an entrenched Charter might require, for
example, a two-thirds national vote in favour of such a proposal, as opposed to
the usual 50 percent plus one that serves as the rule for making law-determining
decisions in most legislatures. That constitutional Charters are almost always
entrenched serves only to exacerbate the concern of their most strident critics.
Not only do Charters seem to thwart efforts to express the democratic will,
but their entrenchment makes it very difficult – indeed, in some cases practically impossible – to overcome these limitations. In this respect, Charters are
quite unlike ordinary statutes and common law rules, which are usually more
easily altered or overridden by law-determining decisions of the people's representatives. But not so with entrenched constitutions, leading to the inevitable
question: Why should the wishes of "the people-now" be in this way thwarted
by decisions taken by other people, "the people-then," whose views might have
been radically different and who may no longer be living? Take the American
Bill of Rights as an obvious example: The bulk of its provisions were adopted
well over 200 years ago, largely through the efforts of an elite group of white,
male slaveowners. Why should the people of the United States, in their current, ongoing efforts to engage in self-government, be hindered by entrenched
decisions made by such a group of men? Even worse, why should they allow
for the perpetuation of this insult by permitting *democratically unaccountable
judges* to enforce these decisions by applying the Bill of Rights to strike down
what is thought (by the judges) to be recalcitrant legislation? Recall that this
is a document which the current generation did not themselves choose and
which, to some degree, reflects moral beliefs, values, and principles with which
most modern Americans radically disagree. How can such extraordinary limits
on the people's ability to govern themselves possibly be justified? Is there a
way to understand the nature and role of a Bill of Rights that addresses these
concerns?

So in order to appreciate both the nature of judicial review and any role it
might (or might not) justifiably play in a thriving democracy, we need to be
clear on two things: what it means to call a system "democratic" and what
it means to say that a Charter is part of a constitution. In other words, we
need some sense of what it means to say that each of the Charter societies
with which we will be concerned is a constitutional democracy. The democratic element in this equation will be our focus in the next chapter, and later
when we explore the democratic critique, particularly as it is expressed by
its most powerful and persuasive proponent, Jeremy Waldron. In this chapter,
our focus will be on the constitutional element. What exactly is a constitution? What are some of its characteristic features? And how does the fact
that Charters are part of constitutional law affect their justification – or lack
thereof?

B. The Nature of Constitutions

In some minimal sense of the term, a constitution consists of one or more rules or norms constituting, and defining the limits (if any) of, government authority. By the term "authority" we will mean, in this context, the rightful possession of normative powers over some domain. By the term "powers" we will mean Hohfeldian, *normative* powers to alter or otherwise influence existing normative states of affairs, for example by imposing obligations or granting rights and liberties.[1] Some normative powers are legal powers. For instance, when I bring into existence a legally binding will I exercise Hohfeldian legal powers that create this very possibility. By acting in the specified ways I am able to alter the existing legal landscape by creating a new set of rights (of inheritors) and duties (upon my executor and those who now control my assets). Absent the relevant power-conferring legal rules, I could not bring about these normative effects. I could express my wishes about who should have my assets when I die. I might even have a friend promise to see to it that my wishes are honoured. But I could not create a will that legally entitles my inheritors to my assets. Such a creative legal act requires the existence of a legal power to affect such changes in the normative landscape, and this in turn requires the existence of what H.L.A. Hart calls "secondary, power-conferring rules."[2]

Many acts of government – for example, the creation of legislation – are similarly made possible by secondary, power-conferring rules governing the creation, modification, and elimination of legal norms. Absent these rules, there could be no such acts of government legally binding on people, just as without inheritance laws there could be no legally binding wills. A ruthless band of thugs might order people to do certain things and secure compliance through threat of overwhelming force. But they cannot perform an authoritative act of government that creates legal rights, obligations, and so on. For this we need secondary, power-conferring rules that made such acts possible. One of the characteristic functions of a constitution is to specify some such secondary rules. In large part this is what we mean when we say that a constitution consists of one or more rules or norms constituting, and defining the limits (if any) of, government authority.

Given this definition, all states have constitutions and all states are constitutional regimes. Anything recognisable as a state must have an acknowledged means of constituting and specifying the limits (or lack thereof) upon the three forms of state power identified by Montesquieu: legislative power (making new laws), executive power (implementing laws), and judicial power (adjudicating

---

1 See Wesley Newcomb Hohfeld, *Fundamental Legal Conceptions* (New Haven, Conn.: Yale University Press, 1919).
2 See H.L.A. Hart, *The Concept of Law*, 2nd edition (Oxford: Clarendon Press, 1994), 26–49.

disputes under laws).[3] Take the extreme case of an absolute monarch, Rex, in whose person is combined unlimited power in all three domains. Suppose it is widely acknowledged and accepted that Rex has these powers, as well as the authority to exercise them at his discretion or pleasure. Under this simple scenario the constitution of Rex's state could be said to contain one and only one constitutional rule – a secondary, power-conferring rule that ascribes unlimited government power or authority to Rex. He is not *legally* answerable for the wisdom, prudence, or morality of his laws, nor is he bound by procedures, or any other kinds of limitations or requirements, in exercising his powers. Whatever he decrees is constitutionally valid. We might think of Rex's regime as representing a *constitutionally unlimited* form of government. The constitution's secondary rule empowers Rex, but it places no legal restrictions on the exercise of that power.

Most states do not embrace constitutionally unlimited government powers. The closest example is perhaps to be found in the Westminster model of government, according to which (on one traditional theory, at any rate) "the Queen in Parliament" is empowered to rule in whatever way she/it sees fit, unburdened by any substantive legal limits. This was the view of the famous English jurist Sir William Blackstone, who once declared that what Parliament does "no authority upon Earth can undo," implying that Parliament is constitutionally entitled to enact whatever legislation it wishes to enact. But there are at least three points to be made about Blackstone's pronouncement and the theory of the British constitution that underlies it.[4] First, it is not at all clear that the British Parliament ever did possess the unlimited sovereignty he ascribes to it. Though Britain has no written Charter – indeed no written constitution of the kind one finds in the United States and Canada – legal scholars generally agree that it has, for many centuries, contained an "unwritten constitution" arising from a variety of sources. These include longstanding principles of the common law and landmark judicial decisions concerning the appropriate limits of Parliament's legislative authority. These elements of the unwritten constitution serve, in effect, as conditions Parliament must meet if it is to succeed in utilizing the relevant power-conferring rules of the British constitution. They circumscribe or limit the power of Parliament to enact binding legislation. Just as my failure to abide by conditions specified in the relevant secondary, power-conferring rules governing the creation of a will (e.g., I fail to have two witnesses present at its signing) means that I will not have succeeded in altering the legal landscape in the desired way, Parliament's neglect (intentional or otherwise) of the

---

3 See Baron de Montesquieu, *The Spirit of the Laws*, tr. Thomas Nugent (London: J. Nourse, 1977), *passim*.
4 Strictly speaking, one cannot equate Great Britain with the United Kingdom, because the latter includes not only the former but Northern Ireland as well. Because nothing here hinges on the distinction, we will use the terms interchangeably.

incorporated limits upon its power to create valid law means that it will have failed in that endeavour. Its legislative efforts will be "of no force and effect." Second, despite being largely unwritten, the British constitution includes a number of written documents adopted at various stages in its political history, a primary example being the Magna Carta (A.D. 1215). Third, it is arguable that the people of the United Kingdom, by virtue of their membership in the European Community (EC) and the fact that British courts now enforce, as legally binding, EC law, have in fact relinquished unlimited sovereignty within their very own borders. And if the people themselves have relinquished unlimited sovereignty, then something analogous must be true of their elected representatives. If the law of member states (e.g., France, Denmark, and the UK) must now be consistent with EC law, and EC law is immune from legislative change or repeal through the efforts of member governments, then it would appear that the sovereignty of the member states within the EC has been replaced by the sovereignty of "the people of Europe." It further follows that Blackstone's assessment of Parliament's unbridled power, even if once true, is clearly no longer so.

In any event, whether or not the United Kingdom does or ever did embrace constitutionally unlimited government, the fact of the matter is that most states not only grant government powers, but they also limit them in a variety of ways. In other words, most states embrace *constitutionally limited* government. In such states, secondary, power-conferring rules not only create legislative, executive, and judicial powers, but they also impose different kinds of limits on the powers granted. Consider now a second imaginary state in which Regina has all the powers possessed by Rex, except that she lacks authority to legislate on matters concerning religion, and on any day of the week except Wednesday. Suppose further that Regina also lacks authority to implement, or adjudicate on the basis of, any law that exceeds the scope of her legislative competence. We have here the seeds of constitutionally limited government and the adoption of what has come to be known as "constitutionalism."

Constitutionalism is the idea that the powers of government both can and ought to be limited, and that its political, moral, and (sometimes) legal authority depends on its observing these limitations. The limitations imposed by constitutions come in a variety of forms. Some of these are legal, as in a constitutionally entrenched Charter, while others can be a matter of political convention, a matter to be explored shortly. The relevant limits can concern the *scope* of legislative authority, as in the case of Regina, who is forbidden from legislating on religious matters. In modern federal systems, provincial or state governments might have authority over domains such as health care and education, while the federal government's jurisdiction typically extends to areas like national defence, transportation, and monetary policy. Many constitutional controversies arise over questions of jurisdiction, over whether the acts of some particular government within a federation are *ultra vires* – that is, lie outside the enacting body's jurisdiction. Prior to the enactment of the Canadian Charter this was certainly true of Canada, where controversies arose over whether Acts of Parliament actually dealt with matters that the constitution places within the authority of the provinces.[5] Such disputes in the United States often revolve around the idea of "states' rights" – that is, the right of a state and its government to maintain local control over certain matters falling within their jurisdiction.

Another way in which government powers can be limited is in the requirement that certain *mechanisms* be employed in their exercise. These often take the form of procedural requirements governing the form and manner of introducing legislation. In Regina's case, she was prohibited from legislating on any day but Wednesday. She might also have been required to enact her laws in French as well as in English. This particular condition was the focus of a highly controversial Canadian case. In *Manitoba Language Rights*, the Supreme Court of Canada ruled that the vast bulk of Manitoba law was legally invalid owing to a failure on the part of a string of successive Manitoba governments to publish their laws in both of Canada's two official languages. By failing to publish their laws in French, these governments had failed to satisfy a crucial condition of their constitutional power to legislate. As a result, their efforts were, strictly speaking, a nullity, just as my efforts to create a valid will would fail were I to fail in securing the required number of witnesses. Neither I nor the Manitoba governments successfully exercised the powers granted – none of us successfully altered the legal landscape in the desired ways.[6]

Finally, and for our purposes most important, government powers can be subject to *substantive* limits. Some of these are moral in nature. Suppose that, in addition to the requirement that she not legislate directly on religious matters, Regina were bound by the further requirement that her directives respect a right to the free exercise of religion. Here we would have a substantive, presumably moral, limitation upon her legislative powers. We would have to examine the moral substance or content of her enactments to determine whether they infringed upon the moral right to the free exercise of religion. It is perhaps worth noting that this is the kind of limit that can be infringed by legislation that in no way seems to concern itself *directly* with the matter of the relevant right. Suppose Regina were to attempt to enact, in both English and French, and on a Wednesday, a law compelling citizens always to accept standard lifesaving

---

5 For an authoritative discussion of the history of Canadian constitutional law, see Peter Hogg, *Constitutional Law of Canada, 4th edition* (Toronto: Carswell, 1997).

6 *Reference Re. Manitoba Language Rights* [1985] 1 S.C.R. 721. The Court circumvented the problem of having virtually no valid provincial law in Manitoba by invoking rule-of-law principles that, it argued, constituted a fundamental element of Canada's constitution and took precedence over the constitutional requirement to publish in both official languages. On the authority of these more fundamental principles, the Court accorded the impugned legislation temporary validity and granted the Manitoba legislature a short period of time in which to rectify the constitutional deficiency.

medical treatment. Suppose further that standard lifesaving medical treatment sometimes includes blood transfusions, and that these are strictly prohibited by the beliefs of a religious denomination over whom Regina has authority. Regina's legislation violates no procedural requirements, nor does it go beyond any scope requirement. After all, her legislation is *not* concerned with a religious matter: It's about health care, which is clearly within the scope of her legislative competence. Despite this, the content of Regina's directive – its substance – is such that it (arguably) infringes upon the moral right to the free exercise of religion. It does not directly concern itself with a religious matter, but it does have serious implications for such a matter. On these grounds, it might properly be deemed invalid.

Most cases arising under a Charter are concerned with apparent infringements of substantive moral limits upon a government's powers to legislate or otherwise take authoritative action. Consider again the Canadian Charter of Rights and Freedoms, which denies governments the power to create laws that infringe upon the right to freedom of expression – unless, of course, such an infringement can be "demonstrably justified in a free and democratic society" (section 1) or the government has invoked the Section 33 override. Any legislative effort that either directly or indirectly curtails freedom of expression, and that cannot be saved in one of these two ways, is constitutionally invalid: "of no force and effect." Any attempt to exercise the relevant power will have failed, and the legal status quo will not have been changed in the desired way – this despite any efforts made on the part of the government to effect such a change.

In discussing the moral and political foundations of constitutionally limited government, a comparison is often drawn between Thomas Hobbes and John Locke, who are thought to have defended, respectively, the option of a constitutionally unlimited sovereign (e.g., Rex) versus that of a sovereign limited by the terms of a constitution containing substantive limitations on her authority (e.g., Regina).[7] An even better representative of the former view is perhaps to be found in the thinking of the early legal positivist John Austin, who, along with Hobbes, thought that the very notion of legally limited sovereignty is incoherent. "Supreme power limited by positive law is a flat contradiction in terms," Austin wrote.[8] This is because of certain key features of the particular theory of law – the command theory – that he shared with Hobbes. In Austin's view,

---

7 Whether Locke and Hobbes are properly invoked in this way is perhaps open to question. There is reason to believe that Locke's argument defends political, as opposed to strictly legal, limitations upon the Lockean sovereign. But as we shall see, constitutionalism seems to require legal limitation. It might be argued that effective political limitation requires legal limitation as well, but this does not seem strictly necessary. Many argue that the British legal system has, for centuries, operated quite effectively with a Parliament that is both legally unlimited and at the same time politically limited by the terms of a Lockean social contract. More on this in Chapter 3.

8 John Austin, *The Province of Jurisprudence Determined* (New York: The Noonday Press, 1954), 254.

all law is the *command* of a *sovereign*. By this he meant that it is the expression of a wish on the part of a political "superior" (the sovereign) to one or more political "inferiors" (subjects) that the latter should act or forebear from acting in some manner specified, and backed up by threat of sanction should the expressed wish not be fulfilled. It follows from this account of law that the notion that the sovereign's power to legislate could be limited *by law* is nonsense. It requires a sovereign who is at one and the same time both the superior and the inferior in the relationship of sovereignty and who issues self-directed and self-binding commands – that is, who commands him/her/itself to observe prescribed limits under threat of sanction. But no one can sensibly "command" himself, except in some figurative sense of the term. Equally puzzling is the idea that one could somehow threaten oneself with sanction should one not abide by one's own wishes. So the very notion of limited sovereignty is, for Austin, as incoherent as the idea of a square circle. Sovereign power *must* be constitutionally *unlimited*. As Hobbes put it, "For to be subject to laws is to be subject to the commonwealth – that is to the sovereign – that is, to himself, which is not subjection but freedom from the laws."[9]

In any event, this feature of Austin's theory has some surface plausibility when applied to the Westminster model of government, at least as it was conceived by Blackstone, where Parliament is said to be not only supreme but legally unlimited as well. But it faces serious, probably fatal, difficulty when applied to constitutional democracies like the United States and Germany, which clearly appear to embrace legal, constitutional limits on government power. Austin was of course fully aware of such systems, and so he needed a way to reconcile their existence with his thesis that limited sovereignty is an absurdity. Austin's way out was to say that sovereignty does not in fact reside in the government – which is what we normally have in mind when we talk about sovereign powers – but with "the people" themselves. *Governments* can be limited by constitutional law, Austin thought, but the *sovereign* – that is, the people – necessarily remains unlimited. Whether this move provides Austin with an adequate means of dealing with constitutional democracies is highly questionable. For Austin's sovereign must, as he himself notes, be a *determinate* individual or group of individuals (the superior) whose commands *to others* (the inferiors) constitute law. A command, by its very nature, has to issue from some determinate, identifiable source and be directed to some other person(s) who is (are) under threat of penalty. But if we identify the commanders with "the people," then we end up with the paradoxical result identified by H. L. A. Hart – the bulk of the population (hardly a determinate source) obeying, under threat, the bulk of the population. To put it another way, the commanders are commanding the commanders. In short, we lapse into incoherence.[10]

9 Thomas Hobbes, *Leviathan* (Indianapolis: The Liberal Arts Press, 1958), Ch. 29, 255.
10 See Hart, *The Concept of Law,* 71–8. For Austin, see *The Province of Jurisprudence Determined,* Lecture VI. These and other difficulties in Austin's account led Hart to a

C. Sovereign versus Government

The difficulties inherent in Austin's attempt to make sense of constitutionally limited government suggest the need not only to reject his command theory of law, but to distinguish between two different concepts: *sovereignty* and *government*. Roughly speaking, we might define "sovereignty" as the possession of supreme (and possibly unlimited) authority over some domain, and "government" as those persons or bodies by means of which, or through whom, sovereignty is exercised. Once some such distinction is drawn, we see immediately that sovereignty might lie somewhere other than with the government. And once this implication is accepted, we can coherently go on to speak of *limited* government coupled with *unlimited* sovereignty. This is presumably what one should say about constitutional democracies wherein the people's sovereign authority – what is usually termed "popular sovereignty" – is said to be unlimited but the government bodies – for example, Parliament or Congress – through whom that sovereignty is exercised on the people's behalf is thought to be constitutionally limited in the various ways noted above.[11] The constitution is sometimes viewed as the product of a Lockean social contract among a body of citizens inhabiting a particular territory, or between such a body of citizens and their government. Unlimited sovereignty over the relevant territory remains with the people who retain the Hohfeldian power to void the social contract with their government if its terms are flouted. In other words, in a constitutional democracy, government exists at the pleasure of "we the people."[12] Locke puts the point this way:

Though in a constituted commonwealth standing upon its own basis and acting according to its own nature – that is, acting for the preservation of the community, there can be

---

    radically different theory of law that saw commands of a sovereign replaced by rules created in accordance with fundamental secondary rules, some of which are the very secondary, power-conferring rules to which we drew attention above and that we will explore more fully in Chapter 5.

11 Matters are perhaps not so clear-cut as this. It does seem possible for a sovereign people to relinquish unlimited sovereignty by, for example, entering into treaties or accepting the authority of international bodies such as the World Court or the European Parliament. If so, then perhaps the people of nation-states do not necessarily possess unlimited sovereignty. Because these questions do not affect the analysis of Charters and judicial review within nation-states, they can, I believe, be safely set aside.

12 The identity of "we the people" can itself be a controversial question that sometimes figures in debates about the authority of constitutions. It is sometimes said that a constitution gains whatever authority it possesses by being accepted by "we the people." But who are these people? Are they the individuals who lived at the time of the constitution's adoption? Or is it restricted to people who live now? After all, it is these latter individuals who are now expected to comply with its demands. Or are "the people" some sort of temporally extended entity that persists through time across a number of generations? Perhaps it can include those who now live as well as those who are long dead? Here is another question: Does it include those current members who do not wish to be governed by its demands? Take, for example, the many separatists in Quebec who wish to live in a new, independent state governed by something other than the Canadian constitution. These and other related questions will be examined in Chapters 4 and 6.

but one supreme power, which is the legislative, to which all the rest are and must be subordinate, yet the legislative being only a fiduciary power to act for certain ends, there remains still in the people a supreme power to remove or alter the legislative, when they find the legislative act contrary to the trust reposed in them. For all power given with trust for the attaining an end being limited by that end, whenever that end is manifestly neglected or opposed, the trust must necessarily be forfeited, and the power devolve into the hands of those that gave it, who may place it anew where they think best for their safety and security.[13]

Furthermore,

[F]or all the power the government has, being only for the good of the society, as it ought not to be arbitrary and at pleasure, so it ought to be exercised by established and promulgated laws, that both the people may know their duty, and be safe and secure within the limits of the law, *and the rulers too, kept within their due bounds,* and not be tempted by the power they have in their hands to employ it to purposes, and by such measures as they would not have known, and own not willingly.[14]

Though sovereignty and the posession of government power are different properties, it is important to stress that nothing rules out the theoretical possibility of their applying to one and the same individual or body. Indeed, much of Hobbes's argument in *Leviathan* is directed towards justifying a practical need to identify sovereign and government. Hobbes argued that natural law requires a (virtually complete) transfer of all natural rights and powers from sovereign individuals in the state of nature to a political sovereign whose powers of government were, of neccessity, absolute. Were they in any way limited, it would be impossible for him/them to ensure our removal from the wretched state of nature where life is "solitary, poor, nasty, brutish and short."[15] In Hobbes's theory, supreme sovereignty *must* reside in the supreme governmental person or body that enjoys unlimited power and authority to rule the commonwealth. Given human nature and the world we inhabit, anything less than unlimited government power would destroy the very possibility of stable government – the very *raison d'être* of such an institution. So even if "sovereignty" and "the possession of government power" are different properties, this neither means nor

---

13 John Locke, *Two Treatises of Government,* 2nd ed., ed. Peter Laslett (Cambridge: Cambridge University Press, 1967), II, Chap. XIII, par. 149.
14 Ibid., II, Chap. II, par. 137.
15 *Leviathan* Part 1, Ch. 13. Although Hobbes's political sovereign was to be constitutionally unlimited, Hobbes insisted that individuals must retain the right to self-preservation. It would be incoherent, Hobbes thought, for individuals to give up that right the protection of which is the very reason people have for creating a sovereign power in the first place. To give up this right would be to violate the very law of nature by whose authority the commonwealth is created. Although individuals retain the right to self-preservation, it is also true that Hobbes's unlimited sovereign possesses the right to take anyone's life if, in the sovereign's best judgment, this is necessary to preserve the well-being of the commonwealth.

implies that the two could not possibly be possessed by one and the same individual(s). In Hobbes's theory, the individual sovereignty of individual persons in the state of nature must be surrendered to a political sovereign who possesses constitutionally unfettered powers of government. And once the surrender is made, the idea that the power surrendered could be limited by constitutional law is no more sensible, given Hobbes's command theory of law, than it was for Austin. It is as senseless as the notion of a square circle. Again: "Supreme power limited by positive law is a flat contradiction in terms."[16]

D. Constitutional Limitation

The idea of constitutionally limited government involves not only the idea that government (as opposed to sovereignty) can and should be limited in its power and authority. It is usually thought to require something that Hobbes rejected as incoherent: that these limits be imposed *by law*. Neither Austin nor Hobbes would dispute that governments are always required to observe the dictates of reason, morality, and prudence in exercising their powers. Hobbes, for example, was happy to acknowledge that the sovereign is bound by simple prudence not to abuse his powers (lest he risk overthrow by his subjects) and by the wider law of nature (of which the dictates of prudence are a subset). Hobbes also insisted, of course, that the sovereign is answerable to God alone for his political transgressions. It is God's commands that oblige the Hobbesian sovereign to abide by the laws of nature in exercising his government powers, not the commands of the people who have surrendered their sovereignty to him/it, or any "commands" the sovereign might incoherently attempt to impose on him/itself. Austin, for his part, was also perfectly happy to acknowledge a variety of ways in which government power could be curtailed. As we have already seen, Austin thought that the "sovereign people" could cabin government power via constitutional limitations. As we have also seen, it is not at all clear that this option really is open to Austin, largely for the reasons Hart suggests. Yet even if the coherence of this particular form of limitation is rejected, and we restrict ourselves to systems like Rex's, where the sovereign is free from *legal* limit on government powers, there always remains the possibility that a legally unlimited Austinian sovereign could habitually bow to God's will, or even to public opinion. What is incoherent, on Austin's account, is the idea of *legal* limitation upon sovereignty. And once again, the reason is a conceptual one: In his view (and the view of Hobbes), it is the *command* of a sovereign that *determines* the legal. Because X cannot sensibly be bound by X's own commands, it follows that if a "sovereign" were to be *legally* limited, there would have to be yet another determinate individual or group of individuals, Y, whose commands

---

16 Austin, *The Province of Jurisprudence Determined*, 254.

impose these limits on X. But if that were true, Y would in fact be the legally unlimited sovereign, not X.

E. Constitutional Law and Constitutional Convention

These elements in the accounts of law defended by Hobbes and Austin draw attention to a further characteristic feature of constitutionally limited government: nonlegal forms of limitation. Let's begin our examination of this feature by observing, once again, that both Hobbes and Austin were prepared to acknowledge rational, moral, and prudential limitations upon the sovereign. This is a view that no contemporary theorist would reject either, though some might wish to insist, along with Hobbes, that, legally speaking, it should always be up to the sovereign alone to interpret and apply these requirements. But we can go much further than this and recognize additional ways in which government powers are typically limited in constitutional democracies – ways that are neither legal, nor merely the dictates of morality, prudence, and rationality. Government powers can also be subject to specifically *nonlegal* yet *fully constitutional* limitations. These constitutional restraints lack the force of law, but at the same time they are very different from the normal requirements under which all rational creatures labour, to act prudently, rationally, and morally. These requirements are part of a nation's constitution, and yet they are not a part of its constitutional *law*.

Many people will find the idea of nonlegal forms of constitutional limitation puzzling, believing their constitution to be nothing more (and nothing less) than a formal document or set of documents, possibly adopted long ago at a special constitutional assembly, that contains the nation's basic law. But there is a longstanding tradition of conceiving of constitutions as containing more than constitutional law. This is a view associated with Dicey, who proposed that, in addition to its constitutional laws, constitutionally limited systems of government can contain a number of "constitutional conventions."[17] These are informal conventional rules arising within the practices of the wider political community and that often impose important limits on the basic government powers established by constitutional law. The political community observes these conventions and does so with the clear understanding that strict conformity is not only the norm but also mandatory. The violation of a constitutional convention might result in serious *political* costs, for example an absence of cooperation by opposition members in Parliament, or rejection by the electorate in the next election. But it is generally understood that they cannot be enforced in courts. That is, they are not *legally enforceable*. An example of a British constitutional convention is the rule that the Queen may not refuse Royal Assent

---

17 See A. V. Dicey, *The Law of the Constitution,* 10th ed. (London, Macmillan, 1965), Chapters 14 and 15. See also G. Marshall, *Constitutional Conventions* (Oxford: Clarendon Press, 1984).

to any bill passed by both Houses of the UK Parliament, or that the government must resign if it loses the confidence of the House, as is sometimes the case when an important money bill is defeated. These are constitutional conventions, which judges will not enforce in courts of law. Their violation results in no legal costs broadly construed. Such constitutional conventions are distinguishable from constitutional laws by the fact that the latter are indeed legally enforceable.

In Canada, the distinction between constitutional law and convention played a prominent role in the *Patriation Case*. For the first 114 years of its history, the Canadian constitution was (largely) contained in an Act of the British Parliament, the *British North America Act, 1867*. Owing to its unusual pedigree, the *BNA Act* could not be changed except through the legislative efforts of the British Parliament. Wishing to remove this anachronistic holdover from Canada's colonial past, the government of Prime Minister Pierre Trudeau expressed its intention to request formally that the British Parliament "patriate" the constitution – that is, enact legislation relinquishing its control over the Canadian constitution. Once accomplished, the *BNA Act (1867)* was to be replaced by a Canadian-generated counterpart, *The Constitution Act (1981)*, which included the new Charter of Rights and Freedoms. The question arose whether the Trudeau government's request required the assent of the Canadian provinces, and if so how many of them. In deciding this delicate issue, the Canadian Supreme Court drew upon Dicey's distinction between constitutional law and constitutional convention, ruling that (a) provincial assent was not required as a matter of constitutional law; (b) it was required as a matter of constitutional convention – that is, an informal convention existed among the various branches of the Canadian political system requiring provincial assent for any action by the federal government that impinged upon provincial powers; and (c) in some cases – this one included – constitutional conventions are at least as important as, if not *more important* than, constitutional laws.[18] Such conventions are vital to the ongoing implementation of the system of government in which both they and constitutional laws play important parts. If we followed the Canadian court in accepting Dicey's distinction, it would be a serious mistake to identify a constitution with constitutional law. It can include constitutional conventions as well.[19] We must further recognize the possibility that government, though *legally* within its power to embark upon a particular course of action, might nevertheless be *constitutionally* prohibited from doing so. This would be a puzzling result only if one thinks that all there is to a constitution is constitutional law. We must also accept the possibility that the judiciary, which performs its government function(s) courtesy of constitutional rules empowering it to do

---

18 *Reference Re Amendment of the Constitution of Canada*, [1981] 1 S.C.R. 753.
19 Whether all constitutions necessarily contain both constitutional laws and conventions is a question we can safely leave unanswered. For our purposes it is sufficient to note that a constitution is not necessarily restricted to constitutional law.

so, is likewise subject to constitutional conventions. In particular, it might be subject to such restraints whenever it undertakes the important task of applying a Charter in evaluating the actions of other government bodies.

F. Montesquieu and the Separation of Powers

So what have we gleaned thus far? That constitutional democracies come in a wide variety of forms, most of which include institutional mechanisms that in some way distance the people from law-determining decisions. That some of these law-making decisions are not only made by individuals other than the people themselves, they are often made by individuals (e.g., members of appointed administrative bodies) who are neither elected by nor directly accountable to the people. We have also seen that democratic regimes not only include constitutional limits on government powers but that some of these are legal in nature while others are not. The former we identified as the society's constitutional law, while the latter includes constitutional conventions that, though not legally enforceable, are sometimes said to be as vital to a thriving democracy as its constitutional law.

So far, so good. But a number of further questions surrounding constitutions merit our attention. One is whether the possibility of constitutionally limited government power requires, as a matter of either conceptual necessity or practical politics, the kind of *separation of powers* urged by the French political theorist Baron de Montesquieu. Although a defeated U.S. congressman or president may go on later to serve as an American Supreme Court justice, or a judge in Canada might take a leave of absence to run for Parliament, this seldom occurs in practice. And it is certainly the case that these roles are never combined in one and the same person at one and the same time. But is this common feature of constitutional democracies in any sense necessary? If so, why is this the case? And does this fact have any bearing on judicial review wherein, some have argued, judges have too eagerly embraced powers that really ought to reside in the legislative branches of government? In constitutional democracies legislators and members of the executive are not usually thought to be in the business of deciding legal cases. Indeed, they are sometimes chastised for trying to influence the outcome of legal disputes, as when a cabinet minister intervenes in a constituent's legal case by contacting the presiding judge. Likewise, and more important for our purposes, most people believe that judges are not supposed to act as legislators. The business of judging is supposed to be the resolution of disputes according to legal norms *established elsewhere*. According to many critics, however, this is not what is going on. Judges are often inventing new law when they decide Charter cases, thereby wandering into the domain properly reserved for the legislature. Judicial review has, in this view, corrupted the business of judging – it has blurred the separation of judicial and legislative powers that is thought essential to a well-ordered, fully functioning constitutional democracy. In order that we might begin to get clear on how we should deal with these important concerns, let's return to Rex and Regina.

In neither Rex's nor Regina's society do we find the separation of government powers one tends to find in constitutional democracies. Both Rex and Regina combine the role of legislator with that of judge and government executive. Not only do they both create and administer laws in their respective societies, each also applies and interprets those laws whenever called upon to adjudicate disputes. So there is no separation in either case. But does this not raise serious conceptual problems? Perhaps not so in Rex's case because his powers are constitutionally unlimited. To put it bluntly, he can do whatever he wants whenever he wants. And in so doing he can do no wrong, constitutionally speaking. But what about Regina? Recall that Regina's powers are *supposed* to be constitutionally limited in a number of ways. If this is so, then this appears logically to entail the conceptual possibility that she might constitutionally err in observing the prescribed limits. She might, that is, exceed the limits of the normative powers granted her by the constitution. But who, it might be asked, is to judge whether, in some particular case, this has occurred? If Regina alone occupies the judicial role in her society, then presumably it is she who must answer any such constitutional question. But now an important question arises, one that has also arisen in disputes about the role of the courts in conducting judicial review. Can Regina be meaningfully said to be constitutionally limited, if she alone is the one who ultimately determines whether she has lived up to the prescribed limits on her powers? If it is Regina, *qua* judge, who determines whether Regina, *qua* legislator (or executive), has observed prescribed limits, then one begins seriously to wonder whether she can be, in reality, subject to any limits at all. Perhaps, that is, she is really as free as Rex in exercising her constitutional powers. True constitutional limitation may, in the end, require the *separation* of powers that one sees in virtually all constitutional regimes. Otherwise, it might be thought, we end up with one and the same person being judge in her own case – that is, we end up with the *absence* of true limitation, as Hobbes might have put it.

At least two separate questions are lurking here. First is the *conceptual* question of whether it is theoretically possible to combine the roles of prescribing and observing limitations on the one hand, and interpreting and enforcing those very same limitations on the other. Second is the *practical* question of whether it is politically wise to combine government powers in this way, or whether we should always, as a matter of pure practical politics, pursue the kinds of separation we find in modern constitutional democracies. Let's begin with the conceptual question, which is easily answered once we reject the command theory of law.

According to Austin's command theory, the position of Regina represents a conceptual absurdity. If Regina is sovereign, then she cannot command herself, and she certainly cannot enforce self-compliance through threat of sanction. If we try to salvage Austin's theory, as he himself did when he tried to accommodate constitutional democracies, by suggesting that it is the general population, not Regina, that possesses sovereignty, then we descend, for reasons deftly highlighted by Hart, into incoherence. The "bulk" of the population cannot obey the "bulk" of the population. But suppose we reject Austin's command theory in favour of one that distinguishes rules from general commands.[20] If we do this, then perhaps we can conceive of Regina's constitutional limits in a way that avoids the deep difficulties inherent in the Austinian account. The precise nature of rules is, of course, a question about which there is considerable philosophical controversy. H.L.A. Hart's "practice conception," according to which rules can exist as complex social practices of coordination and criticism, has been extensively criticized by Ronald Dworkin in *Taking Rights Seriously*.[21] Dworkin's own theory that rules can be distinguished from principles by the fact that the former necessitate decisions and state conditions for application that apply in an "all or nothing manner," whereas the latter possess "weight" and do not necessitate decisions, has in turn been subject to extensive critique. Joseph Raz, for example, rejects Dworkin's distinction between rules and principles and goes on to offer an elaborate theory according to which rules are a form of mandatory norm that provide "exclusionary reasons for action."[22] Fred Schauer has developed a sophisticated theory suggesting that a rule of conduct is a kind of "entrenched generalization" that is insulated in various ways from its background justifications.[23] And so on. For our purposes, we need not become embroiled in these disputes. We can simply accept, as a working definition, the idea that rules are *prescribed guides for conduct or action*. They set general normative standards for correct behaviour or conduct. There are many types of such normative standards: They can be written or unwritten; conventional in nature or created by deliberate rule-creating acts (e.g., legislative acts); highly specific or very general; absolute or overridable; enforceable or unenforceable; self-imposed or imposed from without; primary and secondary; and so on. They can also serve any number of functions. Two of the more important ones are highlighted by Hart: Some rules impose duties and/or obligations while others create and regulate normative powers.[24] A duty-imposing rule specifies a type

---

20 For a thorough and convincing account of the flaws inherent in command theories of law, see *The Concept of Law*, Chapters II–IV.

21 Ronald Dworkin, *Taking Rights Seriously* (London: Duckworth, 1977), Chapter 3.

22 For Raz's critique of Dworkin, see, for example, "Legal Principles and the Limits of Law," *Yale L. J.*, no. 5 (1972), 823. For his theory of exclusionary reasons, see, for example, *The Authority of Law* (Oxford: Clarendon Press, 1979), 17–33. See also "Authority and Justification," 14 *Philosophy and Public Affairs*, no. 1 (1985), 3.

23 Fred Schauer, *Playing by the Rules: A Philosophical Examination of Rule-Based Decision-Making in Law and Life* (Oxford: Clarendon Press, 1991), 43–52.

24 For a discussion of the wide variety of purposes rules serve in the law, see A. M. Honore, "Real Laws," in *Law, Morality, and Society*, Joseph Raz and Peter Hacker, eds. (Oxford: Oxford University Press, 1977), 112.

of behaviour or conduct in which one is (or is not) required to engage. And important for our purposes, it may not have an attached sanction for failure to comply. A power-conferring rule, as we saw earlier, specifies actions to be undertaken if I am successfully to cause a desired change in the normative landscape. If I have not satisfied the specified conditions, I will not have effected the desired changes. My act will be a "nullity." But whatever form they take, we can conceive of rules generally as prescribed guides for conduct or action.

With this working conception in place, we can now begin to frame our conceptual question about Regina's limitations a bit more clearly. Suppose that we accept something like the theory of basic secondary rules of a legal system as outlined and defended by Hart in *The Concept of Law*. On this theory, Regina's constitutional powers are established – and limited – not by some peculiar type of command but by secondary power-conferring rules. These arise out of the appropriate social practices among those who are directly guided by them (typically the officials of a legal system, in our case Regina) as well as those (the bulk of the general population) who display acceptance of the rules, and of the system of which these rules serve as the foundation, largely by acquiescing in the results of Regina's employment of them in the creation, alteration, interpretation, application, and enforcement of further laws. These fundamental secondary rules enable Regina to engage in acts that can now be identified as official legislative, executive, and judicial acts.[25] Our question now becomes: Does it make conceptual sense to think of Regina as being limited by such rules when it is she herself who has authority to interpret and enforce them? Or does constitutional limitation require that the task of judging whether executive and legislative acts exceed the prescribed limits always be located in some other person(s)? Does constitutional limitation require, in other words, a separate and perhaps independent judiciary to interpret and enforce constitutional limits placed on the powers of other branches of government?

Let's begin with the question of enforcement. Because there is no separation of legislative, judicial, and executive powers in Regina's society, it falls to Regina herself to determine whether she has lived up to the required limits on her constitutional powers. But how can this be? How can Regina be the one (*qua* judge) who determines whether Regina (*qua* legislator and executive) has acted appropriately? Consider the following (invalid) argument. At the time she created the relevant law, T1, Regina either believed that she had honoured her limitations, or she did not. If she believed she had, then presumably Regina (*qua* judge) will not later rule, at T2, that she had failed to do so. If, on the other hand, Regina believed, at T1, that she had not lived up to the required limits, then what possible reason could there be to think that she will later, at T2, accuse herself of violating the constitution? Does this not show that the very

---

25 For further details of Hart's influential theory, see *The Concept of Law*, especially Chapters V and VI. Again, this aspect of Hart's theory of law will be further explored in Chapter 5, where it will be put to use in defending the common law conception of Charters.

idea of being bound by a rule requires at least one other person to determine whether one has lived up to the rule's requirements? And if this is so, does this not demonstrate the conceptual necessity of separating judicial power from executive and legislative power?

Puzzling as this might sound, there is in fact nothing to rule out self-policing of self-imposed rules. We do it all the time. Suppose that I commit to observing a rule that I shall always be polite to strangers, and that I even resolve firmly to deny myself a personal privilege should I for some reason fail to honour this commitment. Suppose now that on some future occasion sheer impatience causes me to engage in road rage while driving to work and that, as a consequence, I decide to deny myself an after-dinner drink. Here we seem to have a clear case of a self-created and self-enforced rule of obligation or duty. There seems nothing incoherent in this situation. Of course if I am *repeatedly* rude to strangers, then it becomes doubtful that I am in fact following a self-imposed rule. But if in the face of a perhaps constant urge to be rude I do manage – at least normally – to resist, then why should we deny that I am following a self-imposed rule? Better yet if I always, or usually, manage to deny myself an after-dinner drink when the urge to be rude overcomes my resolve. Let's now apply all this to Regina. Suppose that, at T1, Regina is overcome by an irrational fear of rising religious fanaticism and responds by attempting to legislate a pre-scribed state religion. Might she not later, at T2, come to realize that irrational fear had caused her impulsively to exceed her constitutional authority at T1, and that her legislative acts are therefore wholly lacking in validity? There is no more reason to deny this possibility, than to deny that I could not later come to realize that I had impulsively ignored my rudeness rule. If this is right, then there seems nothing incoherent in supposing that Regina might honour limits to her constitutional powers that she alone can enforce.

In the preceding paragraph, we assumed a situation in which I later held myself accountable for *impulsively* ignoring the conditions of my self-imposed rule. Once the impulse has run its course, I return to my resolve never to succumb to such forces and to hold myself accountable should I again fail to do so. Holding myself accountable for failure to observe a self-imposed rule is not restricted to this particular kind of case, however. There are many other common types of case. Imagine that I adopt a personal rule according to which I shall always help a friend in need if the cost to me amounts to nothing more than a minor inconvenience. And suppose that I sincerely judge, at T1, that driving my friend to a doctor's appointment would be a major inconvenience and that I am therefore free to turn down his request for assistance. I might later, at T2, come to realize not that I had succumbed to impulse but that I had *misjudged* the situation and had in fact broken my rule. He needed to go to the doctor; I just wanted to go to the bookstore. I might, as a result, decide to deny myself a privilege, or offer to provide my friend with something in the way of compensation. Here we have a "later-self" holding a "former-self" accountable, not for impulsive behaviour but for an *error in judgment*. And, more important, we have yet another kind of case in which there can be self-enforcement of a self-created rule. Why should we think that things are necessarily different if, for my self-imposed rule, we substitute a constitutional rule empowering Regina to legislate within prescribed limits? Why could she not come to realize, at T2, that she had, at T1, misjudged the prescribed limits to her constitutional powers? And why might she not endeavour to correct the situation, perhaps by publicly acknowledging the nullity of her act and providing compensation for anyone adversely affected by her illegitimate conduct?

Perhaps the situation is a bit more complicated than we have been supposing. Here are some reasons for thinking that the idea of self-imposed rule-following just might end up being as incoherent as initially claimed. It is true that I might at T2 come to hold myself accountable for impulsive neglect or misjudgment at T1. But there is still nothing to prevent me from escaping the effect of my "self-imposed, friendly-assistance rule" in at least two ways. I could either ignore the rule, or change it in such a way that it no longer requires me to do something I would really rather not do. Suppose I have a friend, Bob, who needs a ride to the barber shop. Assume further that I'm interested in going to the pub to watch the hockey game, and that the game just happens to be on at the same time that Bob needs his ride. Here we have a friend in need coupled with a minor inconvenience to me should I choose to meet this need. Normally I would lend the required assistance, but let's suppose that I simply choose not to do so on this particular occasion. There is absolutely nothing that prevents me from doing so! So what sense is there in saying that the rule is a self-imposed one? If I can, at any time I wish, choose to ignore it, can I sensibly be said to observe the rule? Suppose now that I don't really want to ignore or abandon my friendly-assistance rule altogether, but I do want to go to the pub. Because I am the one who creates and imposes the rule, what is to prevent me from changing the rule in order to authorize my self-indulgence? Can I not simply modify the rule so that it continues to require self-sacrifice but only for friends who are in *serious* need? Barring highly unusual circumstances, getting oneself to a barber hardly qualifies as a serious need. So I am now free to indulge myself.

We seem to have further reason, then, to question the conceptual coherence of self-imposed rule-following. It would seem that I cannot sensibly be said to be following a rule when I am free to ignore or change it at will. And if this is true, then we seem led, after all, to the following conclusions about meaningful rule-following: (a) There must be an *external mechanism* of some kind to enforce compliance with existing rules, a mechanism whose triggering is independent of the will of the person who is bound; and (b) meaningful constitutional limitation requires a separation of powers. We appear, in other words, to have landed ourselves right back with Hobbes's problem, with the difficulty of imagining that a person can somehow oblige himself to observe a rule. "For he is free, that can be free when he will; nor is it possible for any person to be bound to himself, because he that can bind can release, and therefore he that is bound to himself only is not bound."[26] Limitation by rules (or commands) that one is free to ignore or change is in fact *freedom* from limitation. Or is it?

Let's begin with the freedom to ignore a limitation. One must be careful not to confuse two different senses of the term "freedom." First, there is the *normative* sense according to which to be free of a limitation is to enjoy a Hohfeldian privilege or immunity – that is, one is subject to no relevant duties or restrictions on one's normative liberties or powers. It is this meaning we have in mind when we say that Rex is free of constitutional limitation. But in this sense of the term Regina is not free at all because there *are* normative limits on her power to legislate. The appropriate secondary rules do exist, and these do limit her powers. This remains true even if she sometimes chooses to ignore the incorporated limits. There is, however, a second sense of the term "free" – what we might, for want of a better term, call "*de facto* freedom" – according to which Regina might well be said to be free. It is this second sense of the term, which is invoked whenever we say that there is no one who can coerce, force, or otherwise motivate an individual to act against his or her will. It is true no one can make me drive Bob to the barber shop, and so in this second sense of the term, I am free to ignore my self-imposed rule. The same is true of Regina. No one has the ability, let alone the right, to coerce her into complying with her self-enforced limitations. But the important point is that this in no way diminishes the *normative effect* of the limits under which she is expected to operate. Should she somehow exceed her limits, her legislation *is* invalid. It is as much a nullity as my attempt to create a valid legal will when I have failed to get the required number of signatures. Regina might attempt to legislate a state religion into existence, and there may be no way of preventing her from bringing about compliance with her will. But unless we confuse our two senses of freedom, or accept a dubious command theory according to which valid law exists only when there is the appropriate order from a superior to an inferior backed up by threat of sanction, we are not compelled to say that she has in fact successfully engaged in an act of legislation. She will *not* have created law because she is not free, in the normative, legal sense of the term, to ignore the injunction against legislating on a religious matter.

True enough, it might be replied. But ignoring a rule is not the only way to escape its force. As seen above, if one is free to modify a self-imposed rule so as to avoid its effect, then one can hardly be said to be bound by it. Again, however, we must be careful to distinguish the normative and *de facto* senses of freedom. We must also remember an important disanalogy between

---

26 Hobbes, *Leviathan*, Part II, Chapter 26, 211.

self-imposed rules and the fundamental secondary rules of a legal system. In the case of my self-imposed friendly-assistance rule, it is clear that I am responsible for the creation and enforcement of the rule. It is also plausible to say that I have both normative and *de facto* freedom to ignore or alter the rule whenever I see fit to do so.[27] But none of this is true of Regina, who, we have supposed, is subject to fundamental secondary, power-conferring rules that limit her constitutional powers. If the existence and content of these rules were solely a function of Regina's will, then presumably she would share, in relation to these rules, much the same freedoms that I have in relation to my self-imposed rules. In this scenario one might indeed question the coherence of thinking of Regina as normatively bound by those rules. If Regina is normatively free to change, at will, any incorporated limits upon her powers whenever it suits her fancy, then those powers are, in effect, as unlimited as those enjoyed by Rex. But the fundamental constitutional rules of Regina's society are not entirely a function of Regina's will. On the contrary, they are a complex function of the behaviour, attitudes, and dispositions of the general population. Recall that the fundamental constitutional rules within Regina's society are Hartian social rules whose existence, content, and enforcement are not determined solely by the conduct of the individual – Regina – whose actions they directly authorize and limit. In this scenario Regina is *not* free – in either the normative or *de facto* sense of the term – to create, alter, or ignore the rules empowering her to govern. She is bound by rules whose existence, content, and force are not entirely within her control, normatively or otherwise.

In the scenario just described, Regina might be said to exercise limited government powers on behalf of an unlimited sovereign people who have entrusted her with various responsibilities. As we saw earlier, some such picture underlies the traditional conception of constitutional democracies according to which government power is held, in trust, by the various organs of government that are expected to observe a variety of constitutional limits. Failure to observe the required limits will nullify any attempt to exercise government power. And if we follow Locke's lead, we can add that anything more than an occasional lapse in this regard might justify rescinding the "social contract" on which government power and authority are sometimes said to rest. It might, that is, warrant rebellion or revolution. So the prescribed limits are not ones that the various organs of government choose for themselves and that they are free to disregard or alter at will. On the contrary, they are limits that are *generally* recognized both within the entire population, and even more explicitly by other organs of

---

27 Perhaps things are not as clear as all this. If I conceive of myself as continuing to accept the rule, then sheer consistency and moral integrity require observance. Perhaps I can abandon commitment to the rule, but this is different from ignoring a rule by which I continue to see myself as bound. Moral integrity might also prohibit me from changing a self-imposed rule too often, or whenever it suits my fancy.

government when government power is separated as it typically is within modern constitutional democracies. Whether, for example, legislators abide by the relevant constitutional rules when legislating is *not* entirely a matter of their own choosing. Serious criticism and pressure will be forthcoming from a variety of quarters if such rules are ignored. This will be so whether the rules in question are part of constitutional law or whether they exist as legally unenforceable constitutional conventions. Nor is the power to interpret and apply a constitutional Charter of Rights entirely a function of judicial behaviour and choice. These too are matters governed by fundamental secondary rules whose existence is partly a function of behaviour and attitudes existing within the broader political community. We will have occasion to explore this crucial aspect of constitutional limitation in Chapter 4 when we address the deep concerns of those who believe that the judges have seized powers of decision making to which they are not entitled in a constitutional democracy. Too often, as we shall see, these objections rest on a misguided conception of the kinds of limits under which courts labour in such regimes.

We come now to one final reason for believing that the separation of government powers that is wholly lacking in Regina's regime is, in actual fact, a conceptual requirement of true constitutionally limited government. Let's assume that the fundamental constitutional rules empowering Regina are social rules of the kind described in the preceding paragraph, rules whose existence and normative force are not entirely matters of her own choosing. She cannot simply change, expunge, or ignore her constitutional restrictions at will. Despite all this, it might be objected, she still has a powerful means of escaping their effect. Instead of ignoring or attempting to change or eliminate the rule prohibiting legislation on a religious matter, it is always open to Regina to *interpret* it in such a way that she can achieve that very same effect. She might, for example, interpret the phrase "legislating on a religious matter" as applying only to situations in which legislation *directly* concerns itself with religion. Interpreted in this way, the rule permits Regina to legislate in ways that *indirectly* affect religious observance. On this reading, an attempt to legislate observance of a state religion would violate the constitution, but a law requiring all efforts to preserve life would not do so, even if it indirectly affected the religious practices of those obliged by their religion to refuse lifesaving blood transfusions. As Bishop Hoadly once said (1717) in a sermon before the English king: "Whoever hath an ultimate authority to interpret any written or spoken laws, it is he who is truly the Law-giver to all intents and purposes, and not the person who first wrote or spoke them."[28] If Hoadly is right, then Regina's power to interpret her own limitations really does mean that it is she alone who establishes those limits. She has, in the end, the same degree of normative freedom that I enjoy

---

28 As quoted in John Chipman Gray, "A Realist Conception of Law," *The Philosophy of Law*, 3rd ed., eds. Joel Feinberg Hyman and Gross, 12.

when I choose to interpret a self-imposed rule in such a way as to avoid taking Bob to the barber shop. In other words, she is not truly limited at all.

Despite its initial appeal, Hoadly's position is untenable. To begin, Hoadly's claim is far too sweeping. It is hard to imagine Regina's successfully urging an interpretation of her constitutional limits according to which a decree issued on Wednesday in fact counts as a decree issued on Saturday. As Alice said, one cannot just make words mean what one wants them to mean. Constitutional limits are sometimes of this nature – for example, few questions of interpretation could possibly arise over the provision that restricts the president of Mexico to one term of office. Despite this, many other provisions give rise to reasonable interpretive disagreements – for example, the "due process" and "equal protection" clauses of the U.S. Constitution. In Regina's case, it is easy to imagine her convincing most everyone that a decree requiring all shops to close on Sundays (which just happens to be the common Sabbath) is actually perfectly constitutional, because its purpose is to secure a common day of rest, not impose religious observance of a Sabbath day. Provisions such as this are subject to reasonable disagreements about their proper interpretation. That they are of this nature might lead one to think that, at least with respect to such provisions, Hoadly was in fact correct. So we are still left with an important question: Does the possibility of constitutional limitation on supreme legislative (and executive) power logically entail that judicial power to interpret such limitations must reside in some individual or group of individuals distinct from the person(s) in whom those legislative and executive powers are vested? In modern terms, must Charter limits on a legislative body like Parliament or Congress or an executive body like the president or her cabinet be subject to interpretation and enforcement by a separate and independent judiciary?

Let's return once again to Regina. In what sense could she be said to be bound by the requirement that she not legislate on a religious matter in any case in which that restriction is open to more than one reasonable interpretation? In approaching this question, we should bear in mind that Regina is (presumably) expected to act in good faith when attempting to meet her constitutional responsibilities. We will call this "the good-faith requirement." Leaving aside highly unusual cases in which dishonesty might for some reason be warranted (e.g., to avoid societal unrest or spare the feelings of a dying friend), that one attempts to do so in good faith is part and parcel of what it means to observe normative limits and requirements. If I am under duty to observe rule R, then all else being equal I am under duty always to make a good-faith effort to apply R properly to my behaviour. This ancillary good-faith requirement does not vanish whenever R is subject to reasonable disagreement. It simply means that I must make a reasonable effort to come up with the best interpretation I can – and abide by R thus interpreted. We should expect no less of Regina. She may be free, in the *de facto* sense, to choose an interpretation that she thinks wrong but that serves her purposes. But she is not free in the relevant normative sense. She is constitutionally required, by the good-faith requirement, to interpret her limits honestly in the best way she can and to act on that interpretation. The same is true of judges in modern constitutional democracies – a point to which we will return in later chapters. That they have (if indeed they do have) de facto freedom to adopt interpretations of Charter provisions that allow them to achieve whatever results they wish to pursue in no way entails that they are free, in the relevant normative sense, to ignore the good-faith requirement. For those who continue to insist that Regina and modern judges are free to interpret away their constitutional limitations, because there is no independent party with authority and power to secure observance of the good-faith requirement, we can add the following: The *interpretation* of the rules establishing Regina's constitutional limits is no more exclusively a function of *her* conduct and decisions than is their existence and enforcement. The fact that she governs only at the pleasure of the people she serves is just as relevant when we turn to the duty to observe the good-faith requirement. She is not alone in determining whether she lives up to this crucial responsibility of government. And the same holds true of judges in modern constitutional democracies.

Barring further grounds for thinking otherwise, we seem safe in concluding that Regina's regime, in which legislative, executive, and judicial powers inhere in one person, does not in fact represent a conceptually incoherent attempt to achieve constitutionally limited government. Separation of powers, though perhaps typical of constitutional regimes, is not a conceptual necessity. This brings us to the second basic question with which we began this section. If such a separation is not a conceptual necessity, is it nevertheless a practical necessity? *Marbury v. Madison* settled this question in the affirmative as a matter of U.S. law, and many nations follow *Marbury* (and Montesquieu) in accepting the practical necessity of an independent judiciary with both the normative and *de facto* power to assess the actions and decisions of the other branches of government. The reasons are not hard to find. First, separation of powers allows for a division of labour that, in an increasingly complex world, is necessary if we are to deal successfully with the plethora of problems that inevitably arise. In Regina's very simple world, it might have been sensible to rely on her alone, to ask her not only to create, alter, and eliminate general laws but also to administer and apply those laws to the countless particular cases to which they will eventually apply. No such arrangement could possibly work in the modern world. So we rely on a separation of government powers. We ask legislators to concern themselves with the creation, amendment, and elimination of general laws. We ask presidents and cabinets to administer and implement those laws. And we ask judges to deal with the many disputes, controversies, and uncertainties concerning application that arise under these laws. Separation of powers can facilitate effective government in a complex world.

A second basic reason often given in favour of separating government powers lies in the need to control government abuse and neglect. Human nature and the circumstances of political life being what they are, governments will some-times be sorely tempted to circumvent their constitutional limits, or they will do so impulsively. For a variety of reasons, they will also invariably misjudge or inadvertently misinterpret their constitutional limitations even when attempting to honour the relevant good-faith requirement. In light of these facts of political life, separation of powers is urged as an indispensable feature of any sound instance of constitutionally limited government. We always need someone other than the person(s) whose power is limited to interpret, apply, and enforce those limits. Separation means, for example, that legislators will know that they cannot escape the force of their own enactments by serving as judge in their own case. Knowing that someone else will be in a position to hold one's feet to the fire will lead one to consider a bit more carefully what one is doing in legislating as one does.[29]

Whether, in the end, there truly is a pressing need for a particular form of power separation is an extremely complicated, partly empirical, question. Such questions cannot be answered here, and most certainly not in the abstract in a way that settles the matter for all constitutional democracies. As we shall see in Chapter 4, some nations – for example, New Zealand and the United Kingdom – seem for many years to have found it perfectly acceptable to invest the legislature with the task of interpreting and applying its own constitutional limits. Some theorists go so far as to argue that the supposed advantages of investing this power in a separate, independent judiciary are wholly illusory, and that in actual fact political reality provides more than ample reason to reject the option altogether. Which of these two basic approaches is the more desirable arrangement within a particular constitutional democracy, with its own unique history, character, and traditions? There is no denying that the matter is one upon which there is reasonable disagreement. Yet whichever approach we end up endorsing, one thing seems certain: There is nothing conceptually incoherent in thinking that there could be constitutional limitation – even of the Charter variety – without a separation of powers.

G. Entrenchment

In most constitutional democracies, the rules that create and limit government power are in some way entrenched. In other words, their alteration or elimination requires more than the exercise of normal law-making powers. Many written constitutions contain amending formulae that can be triggered by, and require the participation of, the government bodies whose powers they limit. But they almost invariably require much more than a simple decision on the part of such bodies to invoke the desired change, as occurs when Parliament, in the normal

---

29 On this particular feature of separation of powers, see John Locke, *Two Treatises of Government,* II, Chapter 12, Section 143.

course of government business, introduces a new tax law or amends the Criminal
Code. Sometimes decisions by special constitutional assemblies are required.
At other times, constitutional amendments require super-majority votes, refer-
endums, or the passing of legislation not only by the central government in a
federal system but also by some number or percentage of the governments or
regional units within the federal system. Entrenching a constitutional provision
makes it very difficult – in some instances practically impossible – to change
or eliminate the entrenched limit.

Why would one think it important to entrench a constitution? Two different
sorts of reasons are often advanced to justify this step. First, it might (erroneously) be thought that *the very possibility* of constitutionally limited government demands entrenchment. Suppose that the legislature in a unitary state is
able, through simple majority vote, to change its own constitutional limitations.
In what sense, it might be asked, could these be truly said to *limit* the legislature's powers? As Austin and Hobbes would have insisted, any so-called limits
to one's power of which one can free oneself simply by making the decision to
do so are not really limits at all. On the contrary, unless a legislature's constitutional limits are in some way protected against such decisions, they cannot
coherently serve to limit the legislature's power.

This quasi-Austinian argument rests, however, on the same erroneous
assumption examined in the previous section: that self-limitation is an incoherent notion. There we entertained the idea that whenever we are free to ignore,
change, or creatively interpret a self-imposed rule so as to escape its effect, we
cannot have meaningful rule-following. As we saw, this assumption is false,
once we exchange Austinian commands for rules. It is quite possible to be
meaningfully committed to and governed by self-imposed rules – and there is
no reason to think that things must be different when we turn to a legislature
and its commitment to observe constitutional limits on its own powers. More to
the point, perhaps, the assumption is completely *irrelevant* when one considers
modern constitutional regimes.

This brings us to a second, and for our purposes perhaps, more crucial reason to reject the quasi-Austinian argument. It is a reason to which we will have
occasion to return in later chapters when we consider the complaint that judges
in Charter regimes are making up the rules as they go along. The existence, content, and enforcement of the fundamental secondary rules that create and limit
government powers are not typically, and certainly not *necessarily*, within the
exclusive control of those whose powers are limited. Consider again Regina's
society, in which the fundamental secondary rules empowering her to act were,
we supposed, Hartian *social rules*. As such, their existence and effectiveness
were no less dependent on widespread social acceptance than on any actions
taken by Regina. On Hart's scheme, social acceptance of a society's fundamental secondary rules is not often this simple. One reason is that it is possible for
a system to exist in which acceptance is restricted to officials alone.

There are . . . two minimum conditions necessary and sufficient for the existence of a legal system. On the one hand, those rules of behaviour which are valid according to the system's ultimate criteria of validity must be generally obeyed, and, on the other hand, its rules of recognition specifying the criteria of validity and its rules of change and adjudication must be effectively accepted as common public standards of official behaviour by its officials. The first condition is the only one which private citizens *need* satisfy: they may obey each "for his part only" and from any motive whatever; though in a healthy society they will in fact often accept these rules as common standards of behaviour and acknowledge an obligation to obey them, or even trace this obligation to a more general obligation to respect the constitution.[30]

Whether mere obedience could properly be thought of as a kind of "acceptance" is an interesting analytical question. If so, then perhaps widespread acceptance might well be characterized as a necessary condition of law. But whether this is so need not concern us here. As Hart makes plain, in a "healthy society" citizens do in fact display acceptance of their fundamental secondary rules; and the societies with which we are concerned here – for example, those of Britain, Germany, the United States, and Canada – can all be safely assumed to be "healthy" in Hart's sense of the term. Most citizens in these countries have at the very least a vague notion of what their systems' fundamental secondary rules are – they know, for example, that Parliamentary or Congressional enactment is a legitimate source of law – and they "effectively accept" these rules, and the system those rules help constitute, as being morally and politically acceptable. When citizens in such societies acquiesce in a court's employment of Acts of Parliament or Congress to find against them in legal cases, they also display a kind of acceptance of the fundamental social rules under which their legislature enjoys the normative power to legislate, subject of course to limits that can be written (as in a Charter or other constitutional document) or unwritten (as in an unwritten constitutional convention). But whatever the exact nature of the limits recognized, and whatever degree of knowledge of those limits the individuals in question happen to enjoy, the fact remains that most citizens in these countries are properly characterized as accepting the fundamental secondary rules under which Parliamentary or Congressional authority is established.

So acceptance can be a complicated matter. It can be whole-hearted, thought to be fully warranted morally and politically, or it can be reluctant, begrudging, motivated by fear or by the simple wish to conform. It might even be totally unthinking and result in the sheep (the general population) being led to the slaughterhouse.[31] But whatever its nature, there always *is* acceptance, it *is* required for those secondary rules to exist and to contribute to the bringing into being of a system of law, and it extends well beyond the particular persons whose

---

30 *The Concept of Law,* 116–17.
31 Hart discusses all this, including the possibility of being led to the slaughterhouse, in *The Concept of Law,* 115–17.

powers are defined and limited by the relevant secondary rules. In a "healthy" society, acceptance of the system's fundamental secondary rules will fall closer to the beginning of the scale described above – it will be based on at least a vague knowledge of what the rules actually are, together with a general belief that those rules, together with the rules of conduct whose creation and regulation they make possible, contribute to a system that is morally and politically justified, whatever its particular flaws might be. The modern Charter societies with which we are herein concerned are, as we have noted, in this way "healthy." Despite their many flaws, those who live within such societies generally believe them to be of sufficient value to warrant continued allegiance and acceptance. This is the case even for those – a large majority, I suspect – who have little concrete knowledge of the fundamental secondary rules of their system. To be sure, few citizens in the United States have detailed knowledge of the precise interaction or hierarchical ordering of state law, federal statutory law, state court decisions, federal court decisions, and the federal and state constitutions. But they do have some (if only vague) knowledge of these matters and will draw upon this knowledge if asked to discuss the relative merits of some particular instance of government action. They may also occasionally draw upon this knowledge in expressing dissent to some elements of the system under which they are governed – for example in bemoaning the fact that a Supreme Court's interpretation of a constitutional provision is final. And of course there will be those – for example, some Aboriginal and Quebec Separatist groups in Canada – who have a strong preference for an entirely new system whose fundamental rules and character would be different. But few, even among these groups, believe the society in which they currently exist to be so unjustified, so unjust or corrupt, as to warrant rejection altogether. Perhaps these comments underestimate the lack of detailed knowledge of and depth of disagreement on questions of fundamental legitimacy that exist within modern constitutional democracies. And perhaps "mere acquiescence" or "obedience" better describes the attitudes of many people within modern constitutional democracies. Whether or not this is so, the point remains that in all such communities the fundamental secondary rules empowering and limiting government powers ultimately depend on a range of behaviours and attitudes that extend far beyond the individual persons and bodies whose powers are limited. The relevant attitudes and behaviour extend not only to all those persons and bodies occupying offices in other branches of government, whose knowledge of and attitudes towards their system's fundamental secondary rules perhaps best exemplify the notion of "acceptance." They also extend to the people at large. The existence and effectiveness of the fundamental secondary rule(s) under which the Canadian Parliament is both recognized and accepted as possessing limited power to enact valid legislation are *not* the creature of Parliament alone. They are dependent on a complex array of practices and attitudes among the Canadian people and their political and legal organs of government, all of which are premised on some form of recognition of Parliamentary legislation as a source of valid law in Canada. When Canadian courts enforce duly passed Parliamentary legislation as valid law, they thereby contribute to the existence of rules empowering Parliament to act. The same is true when they rule against Parliament's efforts by declaring its legislation invalid owing to a Charter violation. They display acceptance of Parliament's normative power and authority by applying limits to them. When I recognize and observe a legal duty to pay my taxes on time, I too contribute in my own way. If the courts and other government bodies did not in these ways recognize the normative power and authority of Parliament, or if Canadians came generally to ignore or disregard their enactments, the existence of Canada's fundamental secondary rules would be threatened. So too would be the system of law of which they serve as a critical foundation.

So entrenchment does not seem to be a conceptually necessary feature of constitutional limitation on government powers. Meaningful limitation seems possible absent such a feature, as seems to be the case in some jurisdictions. Many constitutional norms containing limits to governments powers – for example, the British *Statute of Westminster* of 1931, which provided in section 4 that no statute of the United Kingdom would extend to a commonwealth nation "unless it expressly declared in that Act that the dominion has requested, and consented to, the enactment thereof" – are ordinary statutes amenable to introduction and change by ordinary legislative procedures. Indeed, some constitutions are in fact wholly statutory, for example the 1848 Italian Constitution and the constitution of New Zealand.[32] Despite this, it must be more than mere coincidence that entrenchment is no less characteristic of modern constitutional arrangements than separation of government powers, leading to the question of why this is so. Given that it clearly has a choice in the matter, why would a society opt for entrenched constitutional limits? What reasons of politics or political morality might motivate the embracing of this particular option? A full answer to this question must await later discussion, in Chapters 5 and 6, of the role of judicial review in constitutional democracies. But for now we can identify two main reasons thought to justify entrenchment. The first has to do with the perceived need for stability, over time, in the basic ground rules of law and politics, the second with the need for extra protections against government abuse of power.

Entrenched constitutional rules are said to fix the ground rules for the spirited, disputatious, and rough and tumble, day-to-day workings of law and politics. They are as necessary to stable, ongoing governments as Robert's Rules of Order are for orderly debates in town hall meetings and faculty senates. If these rules were not fixed by being entrenched, there would be nothing to prevent

---

32 For further discussion of this particular point, see Thomas Grey, "Constitutionalism: An Analytic Framework," in *Constitutionalism* (Nomos XX), ed. R. Pennock and J. Chapman (New York: New York University Press, 1979), 189.

the government from changing them on the fly if this appeared necessary to secure a desired result. Don't like the result? Just change the rules of quorum retroactively, thereby invalidating the vote taken. Of course, significant social and political costs often accompany blatant attempts to circumvent rules in this way. We must also remember that a system of law depends on an acceptance of its fundamental secondary rules that extends beyond those whose powers are directly affected. But the need for continued acceptance will not necessarily be enough to counteract the actions of a government intent on having its way, especially in a society in which acceptance has come dangerously close to sheeplike acquiescence. There might not be sufficient involvement or interest on the part of society, or even the other organs of government, to thwart the efforts of a legislature intent on achieving its objectives. Entrenchment helps to prevent such end runs around the basic ground rules governing the practices of government.

A second reason a society might opt for entrenchment involves a perceived need to secure *extra* protection from government abuses of power, particularly those affecting the fundamental interests of minorities. Recall our earlier discussion of self-enforced rules. We saw how I could, for any number of reasons, abandon or misjudge my commitments under the friendly-assistance rule, or be led, by overwhelming impulse, to break my rule against rudeness to strangers. It is possible for governments to do much the same. All else being equal, governments in representative democracies are expected to act as relevant majorities deem appropriate. And they can be held accountable for failure to do so – if not through the ballot box, then through rebellion in the streets. Yet majorities can sometimes place untoward pressure on their governments. Just as rage can lead me to violate my rudeness rule, fear can lead mobilized majorities to demand that their democratically accountable governments act in ways that violate minority rights. One need not look far to discover relevant historical and contemporary cases involving deep-seated fears arising from perceived threats to national security. Serious violation of the rights of Japanese North Americans by both the U.S. and Canadian governments during World War II serves as one obvious example. History will likely come to much the same judgment about analogous post–September 11 violations, by these same governments, of the rights of Muslims living in North America. Entrenching important moral rights of such minorities in a constitutional Charter, as limits upon the valid exercise of government power, is often heralded as one way in which we can at least make an attempt to overcome these unfortunate tendencies. As we shall see in Chapter 4, however, such a move has also been roundly condemned as an irrational, insulting, immoral, and ultimately incoherent constraint upon the democratic right of a people to effect meaningful self-government. Whether, in the end, this is truly the case is a question that will be dealt with in some detail later when we examine the cases for and against judicial review in Chapters 5 and 6.

H. "Writtenness"

When one thinks of a constitution, it is perhaps natural to think of a written document, such as the Canadian *British North America Act* of 1867, since replaced by the *Constitution Act (1982)*, or the *American Constitution* with its famous and influential *Bill of Rights*. Yet as we have already seen, many (if not all) constitutions contain much more than law, and certainly more than *written* law.[33] They contain constitutional conventions that, despite immunity from legal enforcement, can be as crucial to the effective working of a political society and its organs of government as its constitutional law. In the view of the Canadian Supreme Court, constitutional conventions can be even *more* important than constitutional law. In the *Patriation* case the Court ruled that the need for national unity and consensus in a diverse federal state such as Canada can compete with the requirements of constitutional *law*. This particular need warrants continued recognition of an established convention prohibiting the federal government from acting unilaterally to change the constitution in a way that significantly affects provincial powers. It is an important constitutional fact, the Court ruled, that constitutional law empowers the federal government to act unilaterally in this regard. It is an even more important constitutional fact that any such action would be unconstitutional because it would violate the consensus convention, a crucial, nonlegal constitutional norm that imposes limits on the exercise of this legal power. In short, what law makes legitimate may yet be wrong – not just morally or politically, but *constitutionally*. In coming to these conclusions, the Court acknowledged the vital contribution of unwritten constitutional norms like the consensus convention to the effective working of a democratic system of government. Even at the deepest of levels – the constitutional level – much more is required for the achievement of democratic self-rule than strict compliance with law, even constitutional law. It is important that the organs of government observe the unwritten, nonlegal norms of the constitution as well.

The *Patriation* case involves the interplay of written constitutional norms – those contained within *The British North America Act* – with an unwritten constitutional norm: the consensus convention. Unless the Supreme Court was deeply confused about the fundamentals of its own legal system, we are safe in concluding that there clearly can be more to a constitution than written law. But this leads to a further question: Is there anything to rule out the possibility that a society's constitution might be *entirely* unwritten? Or is it essential to constitutionally limited government that some part of the constitution, perhaps its "constitutional law," be written down in the form of a canonical legal text? As before when we examined the issues of entrenchment and separation of

---

33 Whether a constitution necessarily contains more than written law is a question that we can safely leave aside. It does not affect our analysis one way or the other.

powers, it is important to distinguish between two different questions. First is the question whether, as a matter of conceptual necessity, it is essential that constitutional law be written. Second is the question whether this is practically necessary or, on balance, desirable, as a matter of practical politics. We can quickly dispense with the former question before going on to consider the latter in more detail.

Some scholars believe that constitutional rules cannot exist unless they are in some way expressed in written form. "Writtenness," it is said, is no less a defining feature of constitutional law than entrenchment.[34] It is difficult to see why this must be so, however, given that many laws exist in unwritten form, as evidenced by the longstanding practice of appealing to unwritten common law principles and customs in common law jurisdictions like the UK, Canada, New Zealand, and the United States. If much of law is unwritten, what possible reason could there be for thinking that constitutional law is necessarily different in this regard, that it must be enshrined in written form? This was certainly not the case in the imaginary societies of Rex and Regina, where the relevant constitutional norms were all *social* rules of the kind analyzed by Hart in *The Concept of Law*. We viewed them as Hartian, secondary social rules empowering Rex and Regina to act as judge, legislator, and executive, and in the case of the latter limiting those powers in a variety of ways. Regina was required to legislate on Wednesdays and was barred from creating laws that dealt with religious matters. There seemed nothing incoherent in these examples, simple as they might have been, and despite the many differences that distinguish them from modern constitutional democracies that often contain far more complex rules and limitations, some written and some not. Yet any such differences should not blind us to the fundamental similarities. Anyone uneasy about the validity of conclusions based on analogies with such simple, imaginary examples might well consider the example of the United Kingdom, which is often claimed to possess an unwritten constitution. One must be careful here, however. Though the UK has nothing resembling the *American Constitution* and its *Bill of Rights*, it does nevertheless contain a number of written instruments that arguably form a central element of its constitutional law. The *Magna Carta* (A.D. 1215) is perhaps the earliest document of British constitutional law, while others include *The Petition of Right* (1628), the *Bill of Rights* (1689), the *Act of Settlement* (1701), and *The Statute of Westminster*. Despite all this, the fact remains that Britain's constitution largely comprises unwritten laws and conventions, lending further support to the idea that writtenness is no more a defining feature of constitutional law than it is of contract law or the law of torts.[35]

---

34 See, for example, J. Rubenfeld, "Legitimacy and Interpretation," in L. Alexander, ed. *Constitutionalism* (Cambridge: Cambridge University Press, 1998), 194.

35 Constitutional norms in the United Kingdom can also be found in a number of basic principles of the common law, particularly those explicitly cited in landmark legal cases.

We come now to our second question. It must be more than mere coincidence that heavy reliance on written constitutional norms is highly characteristic of modern constitutions, leading one to wonder why this is so. Given that it clearly has a choice in the matter, why would a society opt for written constitutional norms? As before, a full answer to this question will have to await later discussion (in Chapters 5 and 6) of the role of judicial review in constitutional democracies. But for now we can make do with the following preliminary observations.

Unlike their written counterparts, unwritten rules are sometimes said to possess a kind of fluidity and imprecision that often make them unsuitable for the purposes of constitutional law. They tend to be far less precise and identifiable, and far more open to "creative interpretation," gradual change, and hence avoidance than written rules. Written rules, it is said, have a kind of *clarity* and *fixity* that arise from the fact that they enjoy authoritative statement in canonical form. Their identity is seldom, if ever, in dispute because they are written down for all to see and apply, and their meanings are far less likely to suffer from lack of clarity. People who disagree on all kinds of things at least have something – the written text – upon whose identity they can all agree and focus and in the light of which they can conduct the controversial affairs of law and politics. Compare the written rules of chess, which clearly define legitimate moves in the game, with unwritten contemporary social norms governing displays of respect and courtesy. No one disputes the existence and meaning of a rule that prohibits a player from moving a chess rook diagonally, and no one would consider attempting to change the rule mid-game. None of this applies, however, when we turn our attention to social rules governing displays of respect and courtesy. Here the norms are constantly evolving in complex ways as social practices and expectations change. As a result, one is often uncertain what the currently accepted norms require – indeed, whether there are in fact any such norms to be followed. Surrender one's seat on a bus to an elderly person, and one might just as easily be accused of condescension as thanked for one's courtesy. In light of such examples, it is tempting to say that a constitution must contain legal rules that assume canonical, written form if it is to set effective ground rules for the everyday business of law and politics. Only in this way, it might be said, can we all agree on what the ground rules actually are and require. Written constitutional laws may not be conceptually necessary, but they are highly desirable nonetheless. They may, in fact, be a practical necessity if we are to achieve the benefits of a workable constitutional democracy.

These are perhaps in some sense "written" given their appearance in written case reports. But the fact remains that they enjoy no canonical form of expression of the kind reserved for legal norms authoritatively adopted in legislatures or founding conventions. And it is the latter which is being contemplated when addressing the question of whether constitutional laws must be written.

Though they are clearly related to one another, it is possible to distinguish, in the argument described above, three different properties on which the stated preference for written rules is based: (a) identity, (b) resistance to change, and (c) clarity. It is on the relative possession or absence of these properties that the argument hinges. In each case, however, the contrast being drawn is misleading at best. Let's begin with (a), the question of identity. The foregoing observations notwithstanding, the identity of many social rules and conventions is beyond reasonable dispute. It may be unclear whether there is a rule of courtesy requiring one to surrender one's seat on the bus to an elderly person, but one can hardly deny the existence of a conventional rule requiring that one respond to a friend's formal invitation to dinner, or that one dress in an appropriate fashion when attending the opera.

Moving on to (b), resistance to change, we once again see an exaggerated contrast between written and unwritten rules. Social norms governing relations between the sexes, or between various racial or age groups, are often more rigid and entrenched than written ones. This is because their elimination, alteration, or reinterpretation typically requires widespread changes to long-standing attitudes, beliefs, and behaviour on the part of a very large group of people. Countless people, even those not generally resistant to change, may be highly resistant to the particular changes being urged. Many otherwise liberal-minded people of the past few decades have been highly resistant to changes in social norms governing, for example, driving while under the influence of alcohol. Campaigns to encourage abstinence and designated drivers have had their effect. But traditions like the casual after-work drink at the local pub or faculty club are deeply entrenched in our social practices and work against changes that threaten them. Whether, in the end, drunk driving campaigns could have succeeded on their own in modifying the relevant behavioural patterns, there is little doubt that success in this regard would have taken a considerable period of time. In contrast, legislated changes to these very same practices – for example, those imposing much stiffer penalties for driving while under the influence, and the elimination, in some jurisdictions, of after-work "happy hours" – took effect very quickly and efficiently. This despite much grumbling and continued resistance, and despite the fact that the legislation's effectiveness was no doubt helped by – indeed, might have depended on – concurrent underlying changes in social attitudes. Laws that work against highly entrenched social attitudes and practices often fail, as witnessed by the ultimately unsuccessful battle to implement legal prohibition in the United States. So the assumption that informal social rules lack the fixity of written rules seems questionable at best. In many instances it's the other way round.

This brings us to (c), the issue of clarity. Consider the following argument, which would have us begin by comparing the consensus convention upon which the Canadian Supreme Court relied in the *Patriation* case with the *British North*

America Act.[36] Suppose that we accept as incontestable that the consensus convention did exist, that it was part of the constitution of Canada, and that it would have taken a Herculean effort to have it changed or eliminated. In this respect it might be quite like many written laws, including the *BNA* Act. The fact remains, it might be added, that the convention's requirements were unclear and hotly disputed. The content of the consensus convention was itself a matter upon which there was lack of consensus! In the *Quebec Reference Case* (the disposition of which came only after the constitution had been successfully patriated), the Supreme Court of Canada was asked to decide whether the convention required the agreement of Quebec.[37] It was unclear whether substantial agreement among the provinces demanded the agreement of a uniquely situated province like Quebec. By way of contrast, no one disputed the meaning of the *British North America Act*, in particular the fact that it contained nothing which legally prohibited the Trudeau government from acting unilaterally. The *Patriation case* illustrates the importance of writtenness when it comes to the norms of constitutional law.

Again, there is exaggeration lurking here. The *Patriation* case notwithstanding, the meaning of unwritten constitutional norms can be as clear as those that are written. Compare, in this respect, the clear constitutional convention prohibiting the British monarch from refusing Royal Assent to any bill passed by both houses of the UK Parliament, with section 15 of the Canadian Charter according to which "Every individual is equal before and under the law and has the right to the equal protection and equal benefit of the law without discrimination and, in particular, without discrimination based on race, national or ethnic origin, colour, religion, sex, age or mental or physical disability." Is the former any less clear than the latter? Perhaps the examples will be thought to be rigged in favour of the objection, because this particular unwritten convention is fairly determinate whereas section 15 seems deliberately abstract and open-ended, and therefore in need of interpretation. But the point remains: Nothing in the sheer fact that one norm is written while the second is unwritten makes it more likely that the meaning of the former will be any more clear and incontestable than that of the latter. For every relatively indeterminate unwritten constitutional norm – for example, the convention that the government must resign if it loses the confidence of the House – one can cite a relatively indeterminate written norm: – for example, section 15. And for every relatively determinate written norm – for example, section 3 of the U.S. Constitution, which specifies that

---

36 Although the consensus convention was not, the Court said, a legal norm, it still functioned as a constitutional norm and can safely be used for purposes of illustration.

37 The Court ruled that there was no such requirement, but the question was moot at that point anyway. See *Re: Objection by Quebec to Resolution to Amend the Constitution* [1982] 2 S.C.R. 793.

"The vice-president of the United States shall be president of the Senate, but shall have no vote, unless they be equally divided" – one can cite a relatively determinate unwritten norm, for example the rule that British monarch may not refuse assent to a bill passed by both houses of Parliament.

So it is far from clear that choosing written over unwritten norms always secures the practical advantages trumpeted in their favour. Equally important is the point that written constitutions sometimes carry significant costs. These are often ignored or underplayed in arguments for adopting Charters and judicial reviews. In addressing Ronald Dworkin's argument that written Charters encourage a higher form of public debate on contentious moral, political, and social issues, Waldron cites a few of the pitfalls of their written form:

> My experience is that national debates about abortion are as robust and well-informed in countries like the United Kingdom and New Zealand, where they are not constitutionalized, as they are in the United States – the more so perhaps because they are uncontaminated by quibbling about how to interpret the text of an eighteenth century document. It is sometimes liberating to be able to discuss issues like abortion directly, on the principles that ought to be engaged, rather than having to scramble around constructing those principles out of the scraps of some sacred text, in a tendentious exercise of constitutional calligraphy. Think of how more wisely capital punishment has been discussed (and disposed of) in countries where the debate has not had to centre around the moral reading of the phrase "cruel and unusual punishment," but could focus instead on broader aims of penal policy and on dangers more pressing than "unusualness," such as the execution of the innocent. It is simply a myth that the public requires a moral debate to be, first of all, an interpretive debate [about a written constitutional norm] before it can be conducted with any dignity or sophistication.[38]

We will have occasion to explore this argument in greater detail later (in Chapters 4, 5, and 6) when we consider arguments for and against judicial review. But for now, Waldron's concerns, together with those that arise from the analysis provided in the preceding pages, should be enough to make us pause in thinking it obvious that a written constitution is desirable politically, let alone a practical necessity.

I. Constitutional Interpretation and Constitutional Theories

There is, then, often more to a constitution than constitutional law. There is also little reason to believe that constitutional norms must always be expressed in writing. Despite these important observations, two facts must be acknowledged: (1) The vast majority of constitutional cases hinge on questions of constitutional law; and (2) modern constitutions are predominantly of written form. Consequently, constitutional cases often raise theoretical issues concerning the proper

---

38 Jeremy Waldron, *Law and Disagreement* (Oxford: Oxford University Press, 1999), p. 290.

approach to the interpretation of written instruments – coloured, of course, by the special role of a constitution in defining and limiting the powers of government. One's views on the latter can dictate an approach to constitutional interpretation that differs dramatically from the approach one wants to take in an ordinary nonconstitutional case involving, say, the interpretation of a tax statute. Judge Ronnie might, in a run-of-the mill tax case, be perfectly prepared to pay considerable deference to the explicit intentions of legislators, assuming, of course, that these can be ascertained and even if he thinks that the legislators acted unwisely. But if he believes that the principal point of a Charter in a constitutional democracy is to protect minorities against majority excesses, then he might be more inclined towards (though by no means necessarily committed to) a theory that grants him considerable leeway in striking down legislation that, in his view, seriously infringes upon constitutionally protected minority rights. And this will be so even when such an action would clearly thwart the clear intentions of those very same legislators, who, we may suppose, had a very different theory of the constitution and the limits it enshrines. It would defeat the very point of constitutionally limited government, on Ronnie's understanding of this notion, were he required to display deference to the will of a legislature that, presumably, represents the will of the majority against which the constitution largely serves as protection. Judge Antonin, on the other hand, who believes that the very point of a constitution is not to protect minorities from majorities but to protect all citizens from arbitrary government power – including the arbitrary judicial power that, he believes, Ronnie's decision represents – might be inclined to pay considerably greater deference to the will of the legislature when tackling Charter cases. He might, as a result, be far less inclined in such cases to strike down legislation presumably expressive of the people's will. Rampant and arbitrary judicial activism is of greater concern in Antonin's view than any threat there might be to minority rights if judges respect the will of the legislature and the people it represents. We will return to these points in Chapters 4, 5, and 6. The crucial point to be made here is simply this: Theories of constitutional interpretation, and hence Charter interpretation, are not easily separated from theories concerning the very nature, point, and authority of constitutions.

Although theories of constitutional interpretation are many and varied and cannot, as we have just seen, be divorced from views concerning the nature and authority of constitutions, they all seem, in one way or another, to ascribe importance to a select number of key factors. These factors are: meaning, intention, precedent, and theory.[39] Whatever its nature, a plausible theory of

---

39 Although different theories ascribe different roles and/or weights to these factors, none seems to ignore them entirely. Even Ronald Dworkin, according to whose theory constitutional interpretation involves determining the principles of political morality underlying the settled law, would agree that the plain meaning of constitutional words must be factored

constitutional interpretation has something to say about these four factors and provides answers to questions like the following: Are interpreters bound by plain meaning, to the extent that this is discernible, in determining the scope of constitutional provisions? Must they always attempt to divine the intentions of those – the so-called "framers" – who created the relevant constitutional provision?[40] What should be done if some of the particular applications of a constitutional provision clearly intended by its framers turn out to conflict with what it is reasonable to think must have been the framers' more general intentions in choosing the provision they did? Suppose they intended to prohibit punishments that were excessively cruel, believing this to cover torture but not hanging. Suppose further that we come to learn, in light of modern scientific developments, that hanging often causes a lengthy period of excruciating pain to the person executed and is, for that reason, excessively cruel? Which intentions are to govern, the general or the particular? Should judges be required to respect the particular *applications* intended by the framers, or the *general aim or principle* (wrongly) thought by them to entail or encompass those applications? What is to be done if construing a constitutional provision in accordance with plain meaning, or with the undisputed intentions of the framers, would lead to a manifest absurdity owing, perhaps, to some radical change in technology that could not possibly have been contemplated by the framers? What if such a reading would result in the violation of a fundamental moral principle as it is presently understood in contemporary society? These are all examples of questions with which a fully developed theory of constitutional interpretation must in some way grapple.

If one views a constitution as a foundational document whose existence, content, and authority are fixed by the acts and intentions of its authors and/or those they represent(ed), then one will be inclined towards an interpretive theory that accords pride of place to factors like framers' intentions, whenever these are clear and consistent with one another (as they would not be in the case of hanging described above), or perhaps plain, original meaning insofar as it is considered the most reliable guide to framers' intentions. On such views, which we will refer to as "fixed views," such factors combine to establish fixed points of constitutional limitation. The content of the constitution and the limits on government power it establishes are fixed by factors like the plain meaning or intentions of the framers. One who takes this kind of approach will

---

into their interpretation. And as we shall see, even those who believe that the most important factors in constitutional interpretation are "original intent" or "plain" or "original" meaning will admit that these must sometime be overridden if they lead to "absurd" results.

40 By "framers" we will mean all those people through whose actions a constitution or constitutional provision comes into existence. This will include not only those individuals who drafted and proposed the relevant provision(s). It will also include all those individuals whose acts of legislation and/or ratification (perhaps in a general plebiscite) were necessary for the provision(s) to come into effect.

think it wholly inappropriate for judges to depart from the framers' meaning or intention, even when doing so would allow them to avoid results that some of us now find unacceptable for moral or other reasons.

If, on the other hand, one views a constitution as a "living tree" that grows and adapts to contemporary circumstances, trends, and beliefs and whose current and continued authority rests on its justice or on factors like the consent, commitment, or sovereignty of the people-*now*, not the framers or the people-*then*, then one will be far less likely to find such appeals conclusive, or even particularly relevant.[41] One who adopts a living tree approach will be inclined to spurn appeals to framers' intentions as attempts to impose the dead hand of the past upon contemporary society and practice. But then a living tree theorist will face his own tough questions: Is viewing a constitution as a living tree, malleable in the hands of contemporary interpreters, consistent with its status as foundational law, and with the entrenchment and stability that many see as essential aspects of the very idea of constitutionalism? The framers of the U.S. Constitution (at least most of them) would likely have approved of "separate but equal" educational opportunities among different racial groups, and they would likely have been shocked to discover their constitution interpreted and applied in such a manner as to render segregated schools unconstitutional. This, they would likely have said, is not what we meant or intended; it is clearly not what we had in mind in adopting the constitution we did. It is not, they might have said, what our constitution allows. If so, does this mean that the U.S. Supreme Court in *Brown* violated its judicial duty to respect the Constitution in arriving at its decisions? Did it in effect rewrite the constitution in deciding that case? A living tree theorist will want to avoid such conclusions, and so he owes us a better explanation. He owes us an explanation that allows us to say that the decision in *Brown* was – or at least could have been – correct even though it seems clearly at odds with what the framers would have found acceptable. Was it because the constitution, interpreted properly in terms of the moral principles incorporated into American law in the eighteenth century but developed over the centuries in light of an increasingly better – or at the very least different – moral understanding on the part of courts, legislatures, and the community at large warranted the decision in *Brown*? If so, then by what factors should courts be guided in developing their better moral understanding? These and other such interpretive questions are crucial both to constitutional practice and to a theoretical understanding of the nature, role, and authority of Charters in constitutional democracies. So once again, we see that questions concerning how constitutions should be interpreted cannot be divorced entirely from questions concerning their nature and authority. And we shall not attempt to do so in what follows.

---

41 As noted earlier, the notion of a constitution as a "living tree" was introduced into Canadian law in *Edwards,* now referred to as the Persons Case.

With the foregoing observations in mind, and with the usual cautions uttered about the dangers associated with oversimplification, we might, at this stage in our analysis, usefully divide theories of constitutional interpretation in terms of the four key factors listed above: meaning, intention, judicial precedent, and theory.

i. Fixed View 1: Original Meaning

No one denies that the actual meanings of the actual words chosen in drafting a Charter play a key role in determining its impact upon decisions. Despite factors such as vagueness, open texture, essential contestability, indeterminacy, and the like, the semantic content of a constitutional provision, as a rule or norm intended to convey meaning through the use of words, sets limits to its proper interpretation. As Alice said, words can't just mean whatever one wants them to mean. They can be stretched, but there is a limit to their elasticity. It follows that any interpreter, respectful of her good-faith requirement to apply the constitution according to her best understanding of its requirements, will factor in the plain or obvious meanings of the words actually chosen.

So meaning must be allowed to play a role in constitutional interpretation, just as it does in the interpretation of statutes, wills, consent forms, and any other kind of written (or unwritten) legal instrument. But the precise nature of its role is subject to considerable difference of opinion. Views on the role of meaning cover a broad range. On one end of the spectrum one finds theorists like William Rehnquist and Antonin Scalia (and our imaginary judge, Antonin), who equate the meaning of a constitutional provision with "the original understanding" of a constitutional provision – that is, what people of that time would have understood the words plainly to mean. In their view, original understanding or meaning should always govern whenever possible.[42] At the other end are those, like Ronald Dworkin (and our imaginary judge, Ronnie), who argue that the typical constitutional case turns on "concepts" whose meaning each succeeding generation must interpret by providing its own "conceptions" of them.[43] In the view of the original-meaning theorist, historical understanding should govern whenever it is clear what it is, which in his view is often the case. For a theorist like Dworkin, original understanding merely helps frame the initial (but revisable) terms of an ongoing debate about the inherently contestable meaning of the moral principles of justice, fairness, and due process underlying

---

42 See William Rehnquist, "The Notion of a Living Constitution," 64 *Texas Law Journal* (1976), 695; and Antonin Scalia, "Originalism: The Lesser Evil," 57 *U. Cin. L. Rev.* (1989), 849. See also Scalia, *A Matter of Interpretation* (Princeton, N.J.: Princeton University Press, 1996).

43 See Dworkin, *Taking Rights Seriously,* 134–6. Dworkin borrows the distinction from John Rawls, *A Theory of Justice* (Cambridge, Mass.: Harvard University Press, 1971), 5–6, who in turn borrows the distinction from Hart's *The Concept of Law,* 159 ff.

typical constitutional cases. And as our understanding of these principles develops and improves, the meaning or content of the constitution's provisions develops and improves. What was considered "equal protection of the laws" in eighteenth-century America (separate but equal facilities and opportunities) is now considered in clear violation of the U.S. Constitution. We will return to Dworkin's theory below.

The original-meaning theory will appeal to many, but especially to those who see their constitution as a foundational document whose authority derives from the authority of its framers. This will be especially true for those who also see their constitution as, principally, a device through which "we the people" are able to protect ourselves from arbitrary state power, including, though not exclusively, arbitrary judicial power. Requiring that judges and legislators interpret constitutional provisions in light of historical, original understanding respects the role of the framers in setting, on behalf of the community, a fixed framework of government and the limits within which state power is to be exercised. Political decisions about that fixed framework and its constituent limits have, on this particular theory, already been made in a proper forum by those in whose hands such decisions were properly placed. Their decisions have been communicated via the semantic content of the provisions chosen to figure in the constitution and should not, lest legitimacy and stability be threatened, be subject to continual revisiting and review. In particular, those decisions should not be subject to continual revisiting and review by unelected judges who lack the authority enjoyed by the framers to settle controversial questions concerning the proper limits of government power. Insisting that judges be restricted to original, plain meaning helps prevent them from abusing their powers by placing fixed limits on them. The discovery of historical, original understanding is a largely factual matter, requiring none of the contentious moral and political reasoning appropriately undertaken by the framers. If constitutional change is required – that is, if the constitutional norms set by the original understanding of the framers' constitutional provisions require change or elimination – the constitution itself sets procedures through which such changes can be effected. Should these prove ineffective, and yet change be clearly warranted, then the people themselves, as the sovereign power underlying constitutional democracies, have the authority to abandon their constitution, through revolution, peaceful or not, and to substitute something else. But so long as the constitution remains in force, the original meaning of its rules must be taken as governing all matters of constitutional law. Interpreters must always remain within its "four corners."

... the constitution, though it has an effect superior to other laws, is in its nature the sort of "law" that is the business of the courts – and enactment which has a fixed meaning ascertainable through the usual devices familiar to those learned in the law. If the Constitution were not that sort of a "law," but a novel invitation to apply current societal values, what reason could there be to believe that that invitation was addressed to the courts rather than the legislature? One simply cannot say, regarding that sort of novel enactment, that "[it] is emphatically the province and duty of the judicial department" to determine its content.[44] Quite to the contrary, the legislature would seem a much more appropriate expositor of social values, and its determination that a statute is compatible with the Constitution should, as in England, prevail.[45]

Despite its obvious appeal to many, the original-meaning theory faces serious difficulty on a number of fronts. First, it is not at all clear that plain, semantic content will get one very far when the words in question are abstract and evaluative in nature. Words and phrases like "equality," "due process of law," "fundamental justice," "free and democratic society," "freedom of religion," and so on lack the determinate semantic content of words and phrases like "tree," "one mile," or "five-year term." Proper application of the latter seems a good deal more fixed by common practice and usage than the former, though even here we must be careful. Meanings can change over time, prompted by factors like advances in our knowledge of the phenomena with which the relevant words deal.[46] We seldom, except when doing science or philosophy, disagree about what counts as a tree, and we seldom face the need to chose among different criteria, reasons, or theories in making decisions about whether something is or is not a tree – though it is easy to imagine special cases where such a choice would be both necessary and appropriate.[47] But none of this is true of the evaluative terms and phrases listed above. We very often have occasion to argue about the proper application – "the meaning," if you will – of phrases and words like "due process of law," "equality," and "freedom of religion." This is part and parcel of the circumstances of politics. The evaluative concepts expressed by such words are highly contestable, perhaps even "essentially contestable" in modern pluralistic societies.[48] The criteria, reasons, or theories employed in applying them to concrete cases are not fixed by anything like common usage. Adopting the terminology of Hart, Rawls, and Dworkin alluded to above, we might say that such words set concepts, not conceptions. That is, they set basic concepts

---

44 Citing Marshall, in *Marbury v. Madison* 5. U.S. (1 Cranch.) 137, 177 (1803).
45 Scalia, "Originalism: The Lesser Evil," 854.
46 Theories about semantic content vary enormously among philosophers. Some claim that there are criteria of application that constitute the meaning of descriptive terms like "table" and "tree." These criteria, when not obvious, can usually be ascertained through careful philosophical analyses. Others opt in favour of a theory according to which the referents of such terms set their meaning, not any set of necessary and sufficient conditions of application – and so on.
47 Is a magnolia a bush or a tree? An answer to this question might be necessary for a community competition to see whose garden has the most attractive trees. Is a whale a mammal or a fish?
48 See William Gallie, "Essentially Contested Concepts," 56 *Proceedings of the Aristotelian Society* (1965), 167. Dworkin draws on Gallie's theory in *Taking Rights Seriously,* 103 and Chapter 10.

defined (in part) by paradigms of their application and require, for their interpretation and application to nonparadigmatic cases, a theory that best explains and justifies those applications and the actions they licence and justifies a variety of inferences typically made through use of those concepts. To interpret a phrase like "due process of law" is to develop a contentious moral theory or conception of the concept that consists mainly in a set of principles that explains and justifies (a fair number of) the paradigmatic decisions and inferences taken in its name and that explains away those that it rejects as mistaken. This process is a far cry from factual investigation into original meaning.

So on this Dworkinian understanding of the meaning of abstract constitutional terms, historical, original meaning plays a severely limited role. But one needn't adopt Dworkin's understanding to see the limitations of original meaning as a resource for deciding typical constitutional cases. Even when the original, plain meaning of a word or phrase employed in a constitution is plain for all to see, it is not always the case that that meaning is considered dispositive. For example, taken in terms of both its historical and contemporary meaning, the First Amendment of the U.S. Constitution is clearly violated by a whole host of American laws, for example those proscribing incitement, perjury, and libel. Taken literally in terms of the plain meaning of the terms used, both then and now, the First Amendment would seem to render unconstitutional *any law* that in *any way* restricts freedom of speech. If so, then it is unconstitutional in the United States to punish untruthful witnesses, prevent primary school teachers from uttering vicious racial slurs against their minority students, or convict those who incite crowds to violence. But such actions neither were nor are now understood to violate the American First Amendment, leading to the inevitable conclusion that more than the meaning of the terms chosen – original or contemporary – governs its interpretation and application. And this is generally, if not universally, true of modern states and their constitutions. But if more than original meaning governs the interpretation of constitutions, what else counts? The most obvious choice, especially for those who continue to look for fixed points, is the intentions of the framers. In response to the suggestion that the American First Amendment prohibits laws against perjury, one can easily imagine a fixed-view theorist replying, "But that can't possibly be what the framers had in mind – what they intended – in choosing the words they did." This suggests a second type of fixed view: one that focuses not on original meaning but on the intentions of those by whose actions the constitution's various provisions came into existence.[49]

---

49 Most theories of meaning ascribe some kind of role to "intention" in fixing the meaning of a term. This suggests that my attempt to separate original meaning and original intention theories is perhaps misguided – that the original meaning of the First Amendment never did prohibit libel laws because this can't possibly be what the framers intended. There may be some truth in this charge – at the very least it signals the need to be very careful in separating meaning and intention. But it remains analytically useful to pursue this route

ii. Fixed View 2: Original Intent

Perhaps the plain meaning (original or contemporary) of the First Amendment invalidates perjury laws; but this, one imagines, could not possibly have been what the authors of the First Amendment had in mind, what they intended.[50] They must have intended their restriction to apply only to things like censorship of the press and denials of platforms upon which to express political opinions. This fact must figure in any plausible interpretation of the amendment. But how? Like theories that focus on historical meaning, original-intent theories can come in a variety of different forms. These can range from theories that identify the content of a constitutional provision with the applications, goals, and values its authors actually had in mind when they chose the words they did to theories according to which such intentions play a secondary role only when original meaning is indeterminate or uncertain. Alternatively, an original-intent theory might claim that the original intentions of the framers are what really count in all cases, and the reason original meaning is so important is that in most cases it is by far the most reliable guide to original intentions. After all, the framers may be presumed to have known and had in mind the then-current, standard applications of the words they used and to have intended the results suggested by those applications, as well as the goals and values those applications were best suited to achieve. But when original meaning for some reason fails, some other means of discerning original intent will be necessary. In all cases, however, the ultimate aim is to respect original intentions.

Whatever its precise contours, an original-intent theory, like an original-meaning theory, almost certainly rests on the fixed view of constitutions. It sees the latter as a set of (normally entrenched) standards fixed by the historical decisions of political morality made by its authors. To be sure, the standards are fixed by the authors' intentions in deciding as they did, and not by the semantic content of the words chosen to communicate those intentions. But they are fixed nonetheless and must, as a result, not be revisited and revised by judges lest the authority and stability of the constitution be threatened. The intentions of those by whose authority a constitution is made must always govern its interpretation, not the new value judgments and decisions of contemporary judges (or other interpreters) asking the very same questions the founders' intentions were supposed to have settled.

---

if only because no plausible theory of meaning will identify the meaning of a term with the intentions of a person who, on some occasion, uses it. Owing to sheer ignorance or carelessness, I could, for example, intend to include my cat when using the term "dog" in describing my pets. This does not mean that the word "dog" means both dogs and cats. It is likewise possible for the meaning of a constitutional provision to be different from what its framers might have intended to include (or exclude).

50 One might also say that the "original understanding" of these phrases did not encompass such cases, that understood in their proper historical (and contemporary) contexts the words "freedom of speech" do not extend to acts of incitement and libel.

Original-intent theories face many difficulties, some of which they share with historical-meaning theories. For example, original intentions are notoriously unclear, if not completely indeterminate, leaving the interpreter with the need to appeal to yet further factors. Take, for example, a typical constitutional provision entitling all citizens to "equality before and under the law." The intentions plausibly ascribed to its authors can vary enormously, with nothing in the historical record, including the record of debates leading up to the adoption of the provision or in later commentary on its content, that could help us to settle on any particular intention(s). And we must remember: On the original-intent theory, the *actual* intentions of the framers are what counts, not idle, counterfactual speculation about what someone back then *might have* intended *were* she to have entertained the question or thought as we do. So the question for an original-intent theorist is always *historical*: What did the founders actually have in mind when they chose what they did? Yet the possible answers to this question can vary enormously, depending on a host of factors, not all having to do with the fact that some constitutions will have been created centuries ago and the intentions of long-dead legislators can often be difficult to discover.

Among the relevant difficulties in discerning original intentions is deciding on the appropriate level of generality at which to pitch the investigation. At one end of the spectrum of possible answers to the question "What did the framers intend?" are the very general *goals* and *values* they wished to further in creating what they did. In the case of a clause guaranteeing equality before and under the law, these might have included such things as equality in the *administration of laws*, equality in the administration *and substance* of laws, *justice itself*, or an even more general and abstract goal like the *general good*. Different framers might have intended to further all, some, or none of these goals and values when they chose to include the particular equality provision in question. But this variety of possibilities raises serious difficulties for an original-intent theory, if only because these goals can be inconsistent with one another. For example, suppose that one framer believes that the general good sometimes permits overall utility to trump considerations of justice, say when it comes to the state funding of Catholic schools in situations where equivalent funding is denied to all other religious groups. The defenders of such differential treatment sometimes acknowledge that it creates injustice for some but counter with the claim that the injustice of the arrangement is outweighed by its contribution to the greater good of the greater number. Suppose, however, that there is another framer who believes that the overriding value protected by the equality provision is justice, and that the injustice of differential school funding cannot be outweighed by the general good of society. Unless we can ascribe one of these two underlying value orderings – justice over the general good, or vice versa – to the framers, we have no basis for deciding, on the basis of original intention, whether differential school funding is constitutional. The problem is compounded by the fact that one and the same individual might, if asked, have claimed to have supported both values, not realizing the potential conflict they pose with one another. Yet if historical intentions are incompatible with one another in some cases and we must make a choice among them, then that choice will have to be made in terms of something other than original intent.

So at one end of the spectrum of original intentions are the various, and sometimes conflicting, goals and values the authors of a provision intended their creation to further. At the other end of the spectrum are the very specific *applications* they might have had in mind when they chose the provision they did. Did the intended applications of the equality provision encompass *equal access to the legal system* by all groups within society? Or only something more specific like equal access to *fairness at trial*? Did they perhaps include *equal economic and social opportunities* for all groups within society? Again, different framers might have intended all, none, or some of these applications when they chose to support the equality provision. And as with the general goals and values underlying a provision, there is room for inconsistency and conflict. Some framers might have intended their provision to apply only to the workings of the legal system in courts of law. They might have been concerned to ensure that no one would be denied access to the court system because of her race, gender, ethnicity, or social class. Other framers might have intended the provision to apply to the substance of laws. Equality before and under the law for these individuals might have meant a guarantee that the law will step in to ensure economic and social equality by, for example, striking down legislative attempts to ensure the continued dominance of a privileged class. Again, we might have a conflict of intentions, in this case as to applications, and no historical basis for ascribing one particular intention to "the framers."

Owing to the many different intentions often ascribable to framers of a constitutional provision, an obvious question will inevitably arise for one who insists that constitutional interpretation should always be governed by original intent: Which intention(s) should govern constitutional interpretation? The answer was supposed to be: the actual intentions that the framers actually had in mind when they created the provision they did. But as we have just seen, it is quite possible that different individuals whose actions combined to create a constitution, or even a small part of it like a particular Charter provision, did not share the same intentions – that is, did not have the same general and specific goals in mind and did not intend that the same things be done (the same applications) to achieve those goals. Constitutional authors, no less than legislators, union activists, or the members of a church synod, can have different goals and applications in mind *and yet settle on the same set of words*. In light of this fact, it can be unhelpful to rely on original intentions for help in interpreting a constitution.[51]

51 For further critique of fixed views, see Dworkin's analysis in *Law's Empire* (Cambridge, Mass.: Harvard University Press, 1986), Chapters 9 and 10.

iii. Fixed View 3: Hypothetical Intent

Yet another difficulty faced by original-intent theories is that contemporary life is often very different from the life contemplated by the authors of a constitution.[52] As a result, many intended applications may now seem absurd or highly undesirable in light of new scientific and social developments and improved moral understanding. Hanging may not have been viewed as cruel in the seventeenth century; it would be so characterized were sufficient evidence gathered to show that it causes prolonged suffering to its victim. Even more important, perhaps, is the fact that modern life includes countless situations that the framers of a constitution created long ago could not possibly have contemplated, let alone intended to be dealt with in any particular way. The right to free speech, which found its way into the U.S. Constitution, could not possibly have been intended by its defenders to encompass, for example, pornography on the Internet. In response to such difficulties, original-intent theorists sometimes appeal to what we will call "hypothetical intent." The basic idea is that we should always consider, in such instances, the hypothetical question of what the original authors *would have intended* to be done in the case at hand had they known what we now know to be true. We are, on this view, to put ourselves imaginatively in the authors' shoes and determine, in light of their intended goals and values, and possibly by way of analogy with their intended applications, what they would have wanted to see done in the particular circumstances in question. In other words, we are supposed to try to discern what new applications they would have intended had they been made aware of the information we now have at our disposal.

The hypothetical-intent theory also faces a number of difficulties, some of which it shares with its original-intent cousin. First, the theory presupposes that we can identify a single, consistent set of values, goals, and applications attributable to the authors and in terms of which we are to ask the question: What would they have wanted to have done given these (intended) values, goals, and applications? But as we have already seen, the authors of a constitution almost invariably have different things in mind when they agree on a constitution. It is highly unlikely, then, that we could, with any degree of confidence, gather the appropriate set of intentions from which our hypothetical inquiry could proceed. Second, even if we could somehow single out, at some appropriate level of generality, a set of goals, values, and applications from which our hypothetical inquiry could reasonably proceed, we are still likely to face indeterminacy. There will seldom be a uniquely correct answer to the counterfactual question of what the authors would have intended with respect to situations they did

---

52 This is a problem for original-meaning theories as well because, as noted earlier, sometimes an improved understanding of a phenomenon (e.g., the physiology of whales) can lead to a change in the very meaning of words associated with that phenomenon.

not anticipate and could not even have imagined. What would an eighteenth-century framer, firmly in favour of freedom of the expression, have thought about child pornography on the Internet? What would a framer who agreed to a provision against cruel and unusual punishment have thought about the electric chair, or about allowing someone to languish for years on Death Row contemplating the moment of his own execution? At best, there is a range of possible answers to these questions and no reasonable means of choosing among them within the terms of the exercise. Any such choice could amount to little more than pure speculation. Third, and perhaps most important, we are left with the question of why it much matters what a long-dead group of individuals might have wanted to see done were their circumstances different or were they made aware of what we now know. The main appeal of fixed views like the original-intent theory is that they appear to tie constitutional interpretation to *historical decisions actually made* by individuals with authority to make these decisions – that is, with authority to decide questions concerning the proper limits of government power. If we are now to consider not what they *did* decide but what they *might have decided* had things been different, or had they known what we now know, then the question naturally arises: Why should we not just forget this theoretically suspect hypothetical exercise and make the decisions ourselves? There may be some measure of plausibility in the claim that the decision we make should respect the very abstract goals and values probably intended by the authors – if, that is, one can discover what these are and if they can be rendered reasonably consistent with one another. But why should we perpetuate their particular views about the appropriate, concrete ways in which to secure these goals and values? Had we apprised the framers of the U.S. Constitution of the wonders of modern travel, they might well have considered a law requiring members of racial minorities to sit at the back of airliners perfectly consistent with a constitutional guarantee of equality before and under the law. But contemporary Americans, who now view such treatment as anything but equal, should not be tied to this particular moral understanding. Unless we reject completely the idea that there might be moral progress, or the idea that any such progress must be dismissed for the sake of adhering to framers' intent, there seems little reason to believe that they should be so tied. To think otherwise really would be to allow the dead hand of the past to govern the affairs of today. It would be to engage in what one author has aptly described as a "misconceived quest" for an original understanding.[53]

True enough, it might be replied. But the only available options are ones that would undermine the very point of having a constitution. If we do not view a constitution as fixed by factors like plain or original meaning, or framer's intentions, but as a living tree whose limitations are constantly open to revision

---

53 Paul Brest, "The Misconceived Quest for the Original Understanding," 60 *Boston U. Law Review* (1980), 204.

in light of changing times and improved moral/political understanding, then how can it possibly function as an instrument whose very point and purpose is to set a stable framework that limits government power and curbs its excesses? Arguments of political morality may be necessary to *frame* a constitution, but if judges and other modern interpreters are later allowed continually to reframe it in light of how *they* choose to understand its limits, then the whole point of a constitution is lost. But is it? In later chapters we will be developing in some detail a theory of constitutional Charters – the common law conception – that seeks to avoid this consequence. But for now, let's look briefly at one established living tree conception that attempts to do much the same: the theory of Ronald Dworkin, whose work represents one of the most powerful contemporary alternatives to fixed views.

iv. Dworkin's Interpretive Theory

According to one who adopts a fixed view, historical intentions and/or plain meaning should always govern the interpretation of constitutions whenever it is clear what these are. Otherwise both legitimacy and stability are lost. For Dworkin, such historical factors, though always important, are in no way dispositive. They in no way *fix* the limits of government power until such time as an amendment passes or a revolution occurs. On the contrary, constitutions frame the initial terms of ongoing political and legal debates about the moral principles of justice, fairness, and due process underlying a community's constitutional limits on government power. And as the community's understanding of these principles develops and improves, the very content of the constitution develops and, it is hoped, improves along with it. Again, what might have been considered "equal protection of the laws" in the eighteenth century (separate but equal facilities and opportunities) is now considered in clear violation of the U.S. Constitution – just as what might have been considered perfectly responsible behaviour in nineteenth-century America would now, following cases like *Rylands v. Fletcher* and *MacPherson v. Buick Motor Co.*, be considered paradigmatic cases of negligent behaviour.[54]

A crucial element in Dworkin's constitutional theory is his general claim that the law of a community includes more than any explicit rules and decisions authoritatively adopted in accordance with accepted procedures. It does, of course, include many such rules and decisions, and these can be found, paradigmatically, in statute books, judicial decisions, and, of course, written constitutions. These Dworkin is happy to characterize as "positive law." But the positive law in no way exhausts the law, according to Dworkin. Most important for our purposes, it in no way exhausts that part of law we call "the constitution."

---

54 *Rylands v. Fletcher* [1866] L.R. 1 Ex. 265, aff'd (1868) L.R. 3 H.L. 330; *MacPherson v. Buick Motor Co.*, 217 N.Y. 382, 11 N.E. 1050 (1916).

In Dworkin's view, the latter includes the principles of political morality that provide the best explanation and moral justification – that is, interpretation – of whatever limits have been expressly stated in positive law. Hence, constitutional interpretation must always invoke a theory of political morality. One concerned to interpret the limits upon government power and authority imposed by a constitution must look to the theory that provides positive constitutional law with its morally best explanation and justification. But how are we to discover this theory? And what will such a theory look like?

According to Dworkin, a constitutional theory includes a constellation of moral principles, of varying scope, weight, and subject matter, all of which bear on issues raised in constitutional cases. For any particular constitutional case or set of cases, there will invariably be several competing theories, and some of these may justify different readings of the relevant constitutional provision(s) and the different decisions taken under it (them). In picking the one that is best, an interpreter will choose the one that, in his view, ascribes the most value to the constitution. This follows from Dworkin's general theory of constructive interpretation, according to which to interpret an object, whether it be a work of art, a body of scientific data, or a constitution, is to attempt to make the object of interpretation "the best that it can be." It is to construct a theory that ascribes the most value possible to the object of interpretation. The type of value in question will depend on the type of object in question. When it is an artistic object, say *David Copperfield* or a painting by Picasso, then the value of relevance is *aesthetic* value. An interpretation of *David Copperfield* is an account of that novel which best displays its aesthetic value – that is, which puts Dickens's literary achievement in its best possible aesthetic light.

When we turn to law, on the other hand, the justification in question is one of political morality. "In the case of law, of course, the justification in question is one of political morality. Showing positive law in its best light means showing it as the best course of statesmanship possible."[55]

So constitutional theories are attempts to show the constitution and the history of previous decisions taken under it in their best moral light, and the best theory is the one that does this better than all its rivals. Competing theories are to be judged along two dimensions: fit and political morality. In explaining the dimension of fit, Dworkin writes:

No interpretation of the positive law can be successful unless it can justify, broadly, the ... decisions that have actually been reached; otherwise it cannot claim to show *these* decisions in their best light. ... The first requirement tests a proposed interpretation by asking whether [a] single [author] guided by the principles set out in the proposed interpretation could have made those decisions.[56]

55 Ronald Dworkin, "Law's Ambition for Itself," 71 *Virginia Law Review,* no. 2, 173, 178.
56 *Ibid.*, 177–8.

An interpretive theory of the French constitution according to which there are no legal rights to private property in France could not be thought of as a theory of *the French constitution*. Such a theory would not fit the system that exists and could be, at best, a pure political theory of how, in the judgment of the theorist, that system ought to be replaced or changed in some fundamental way. So a constitutional theory is, for Dworkin, a moral theory, but it is a moral theory that must fit existing and historical constitutional practices. It must, that is, fit positive constitutional law.

Often, Dworkin notes, more than one theory will fit constitutional practice more or less equally or adequately. And even if one theory, T1, fits the practice better than a second theory, T2, the latter may nevertheless surpass a minimum threshold of fit and remain a candidate for the best interpretation. In other words, it may fit constitutional practice *well enough* to warrant our counting it as a valid interpretation. In each instance, Dworkin suggests, the choice between T1 and T2 will have to be made in terms of his second dimension: value or justification. If T1 and T2 each passes the minimum threshold of fit, the best theory of the constitution is the one whose explanatory principles are superior on the dimension of true political morality – that is, that morality of government and political society which is most justified, independent of whether or not it is in fact endorsed by anyone, including the interpreter. It is the one whose principles accord the constitution most value, that puts the constitution in its best moral light. And, most important, it is the theory whose principles are, for this reason, actually implicit in the words of the constitution and its history of interpretation. These principles, not historical (or hypothetical) intentions or original meanings, are what set the pre-existing limits upon state power truly contained within the constitution.

The development and application of an interpretive theory of the constitution is, Dworkin acknowledges, an extremely difficult task, and people of good will and integrity will reasonably disagree about which theory is best and what it requires in a particular case. There is no mechanical, morally neutral test to apply, only the competing interpretations of those whose task it is to interpret. This does not mean, however, that the pursuit of the best constitutional theory is foolish, or that there really is no such thing as the correct theory because there is no mechanical way of determining what it is. The presence of disagreement, controversy, and uncertainty in constitutional cases does not suggest that there are no right answers to the questions posed, and no uniquely correct theory that determines what those answer are and hence what the constitution actually requires.[57] The presence of such factors suggests only that interpreters must, as they must in all interpretive enterprises, including the arts, the sciences, and the

---

57 As we shall see, similar points can be made in response to a Critic's charge that judicial review licenses rampant judicial discretion owing to the non-objectivity of morality. See Chapter 4 (vi).

law, exercise judgment in fashioning their interpretive theories. Dworkin goes so far as to argue that in a mature legal system there almost always will be a best constitutional theory, and judges are duty-bound to try their best to discern and implement its requirements in making their decisions. He asks how plausible it is to believe that, in any particular case, a judge will not be able to discover some reason to prefer one interpretive theory over its competitors, some reason that tips the balance in favour of that theory over the others. Dworkin is confident that we will see the implausibility of supposing that this can happen in any but the most unusual of cases.[58] So the absence of a mechanical test and the corresponding presence of controversy and uncertainty in deciding among rival interpretive theories of the constitution do not, in Dworkin's view, establish that there can be no right answer to the question of which theory is best and what the constitution therefore establishes. They do not, in other words, establish that a judge must exercise strong discretion and just pick a theory for whatever reason she happens to choose. It establishes only that a judge must inevitably exercise judgment in coming to decisions about the relative merits of the rival constitutional theories concerning the proper limits of government authority. Such judgment is required by the very nature of interpretation.

There are, for our purposes, three important implications of Dworkin's living tree theory of constitutional interpretation. First, historical intentions and plain or original meaning do not fix the limits of government power and authority; they only set the stage for the debates in political morality that constitutional cases, by their very nature, both require and licence. They seldom settle matters, except perhaps in highly unusual cases, such as when historical analysis yields an emerging consensus about the intentions behind a particular provision, and these are for some reason thought dispositive. Second, constitutional cases require the kind of decision making that is, on fixed-view theories, properly undertaken only by those whose decisions have already established the limits contained within the constitution – that is, its authors or framers. The kind of morally neutral decision making, under standards set by other responsible agents, to which fixed-view theories aspire is simply not possible. In Dworkin's view, phrases like "equality before and under the law," "due process," and "freedom of religion" set concepts, not particular conceptions. That is, they set basic concepts whose interpretation requires the development of a moral theory or conception that explains and justifies paradigms of their application. Many, though perhaps not all, of these paradigms lie in constitutional decisions courts have made in the past. To interpret a phrase like "due process of law" is to develop a moral theory or conception of that concept that consists mainly in a set of principles that explains and justifies the vast majority of these paradigmatic decisions and that explains away those it rejects as mistaken. On this view, constitutional decisions

---

58 This particular claim has been challenged by several authors. The first to have done so is John Mackie in "The Third Theory of Law," 7 *Philosophy and Public Affairs*, no. 1 (1977), 3.

cannot possibly be morally neutral, factual investigations into original meaning, understanding, or intention. If the authors of a constitution chose to frame their creation using such essentially contestable terms and phrases, they deliberately chose *not* to fix the limits to be observed in the name of the constitution. Rather, by using such terminology, they set the terms of an ongoing legal/moral/political debate about the proper limits to government authority and power. In Dworkin's particular take on this, they set the terms of a debate about the best conceptions – that is, the best interpretations – of the relevant concepts as they play an ever-evolving role in limiting government power. A constitution is not a finished product handed down in a form fixed until such time as its amending formula is invoked successfully or a revolution occurs. Rather, it is the blueprint for a work in progress requiring continual revisiting and reworking as our theories about the limits it establishes are refined and improved. It is, in short, a tree that is very much alive.

A third important implication of Dworkin's theory of constitutional interpretation is this: Given the contestable nature of the moral reasoning employed in constitutional cases, judges are not merely agents of the framers in carrying out their explicit wishes and decisions. On the contrary, they are partners with the framers in an ongoing project, one that requires participants, both then and now, to engage in the kind of moral decision making that, according to fixed-view theories, was appropriate only at the time that the constitution and amendments to it were adopted. The limits to government power are, on Dworkin's alternative theory, essentially contestable, perhaps ad infinitum. The only way we could possibly escape this consequence is if we were somehow able to discover a correct moral theory of the principles underlying a constitution that somehow provided answers in all conceivable cases. Of course, were the discovery of such a theory possible, it would require a mind capable of exercising superhuman powers of moral, political, and legal reasoning. It would require, in other words, Dworkin's Hercules.[59] But Hercules is a product of Dworkin's imagination. And even if he were not, the fact is that social, technological, and political changes in his society would require even Hercules to continually develop his theory of the constitution to meet those changing circumstances. So the project of interpreting the contestable terms of constitutions is an ongoing one, even for Hercules. It requires each and every judge, and each and every generation, to provide its own best, and undoubtedly imperfect, interpretation of the limits placed upon government by its particular constitution.

v. Critical Theory

That it seems to require the skill, acumen, and insight of a Hercules is seen by many theorists as a serious drawback of Dworkin's particular living tree

---

59 Hercules is first introduced by Dworkin in "Hard Cases," reprinted as Chapter 4 of *Taking Rights Seriously*, and reappears in subsequent writings, most notably *Law's Empire*.

conception of constitutional interpretation. Ordinary judges lack Hercules' intellectual and moral qualities, and it is therefore highly unlikely that their attempts to emulate him could ever prove successful. If ordinary judges, with their limited skill, integrity, and objectivity, are at liberty to decide in terms of their own, highly contestable, imperfect moral theories of the constitution, then the inevitable result is the kind of unbridled judicial decision making alluded to in the previous chapter and that we will explore more fully in Chapter 4. It is an undisciplined kind of activism that threatens the legitimacy and stability of constitutional Charters and the limits on government power and authority they supposedly represent. Instead of limitations properly fixed and settled by apolitical factors like historical meanings and intentions, we have so-called "limitations" continually in flux and subject to different interpretations by different judges with their own theories of political morality – or, as some will say, their own political agendas and biases. Those who adopt the fixed view will see in such consequences sufficient reason to reject Dworkin's theory in favour of alternative approaches that accord pride of place to factors like plain meanings and original intentions. But for many critics of judicial review, originalism and its fixed-view cousins are as problematic as Dworkin's interpretive theory. In their view, plain meaning, historical intentions, and Herculean interpretive theory all fail, in their own distinctive ways, to fix meaningful limits upon government power. The result is that reliance on such factors in judicial review serves only to licence arbitrary political decisions by judges pursuing, consciously or not, their preferred political agendas. A further consequence is suppression of those – women, minority racial groups, the poor, and so on – whose interests are not supported by these agendas. Instead of the curbing of arbitrary government power for which the idea of constitutionalism is supposed to stand, we have political suppression disguised in a cloak of false legitimacy.

Critical theorists come in a variety of forms, the most prevalent being those who espouse critical legal studies and feminist jurisprudence.[60] Despite their many differences, however, critical theorists of all persuasions have at least one thing in common: They doubt, for reasons such as those canvassed above, that the fixed view is plausible or attractive politically. They doubt, for example,

---

60 On critical legal studies, see, for example, Mark Tushnet, *Red, White and Blue: A Critical Analysis of Constitutional Law* (Cambridge, Mass.: Harvard University Press, 1988); "Constitutional Interpretation, Character and Experience," *Boston U. Law Review*, Vol. 72, no. 4; *Taking the Constitution Away from the Courts* (Cambridge, Mass.: Harvard University Press, 1999); Roberto Unger, *The Critical Legal Studies Movement* (Cambridge, Mass.: Harvard University Press, 1986). On critical feminist theories, see, for example, Catherine MacKinnon, *Feminism Unmodified: Discourses on Life and Law* (Cambridge, Mass.: Harvard University Press, 1987); *Toward a Feminist Theory of the State* (Cambridge, Mass.: Harvard University Press, 1989); *Only Words* (Cambridge, Mass.: Harvard University Press, 1993). For a critical theory of the Canadian Charter of Rights and Freedoms, see Michael Mandel, *The Charter of Rights and the Legalization of Politics in Canada* (Toronto: Thompson Educational Publishing, Inc., 1994.)

that it is ever possible to settle on *the* historical intentions of the framers of a constitution. Different framers had different intentions at different levels of generality or specificity, and there is seldom if ever a means of cobbling together one such consistent set of intentions. They also agree that more than plain historical meaning or understanding is always involved in interpreting provisions like the First Amendment to the U.S. Constitution. Appeals to so-called plain historical meaning of a constitutional provision are really nothing more than attempts to rationalize readings chosen for political reasons of some other kind. As for Dworkin's mythical judge Hercules, the point made is that he is just that: a myth. There is no objectively best theory of the constitution, only competing theories serving the political interests of some dominant group or other. That the U.S. Constitution is now interpreted as prohibiting separate but equal treatment when such treatment would, in earlier centuries, have been considered a paradigmatic instance of equality in no way shows that American constitutional law now rests on a *better* conception of equality. Nor does it show that it rests on a better understanding of what the framers really meant or intended. It shows only that the relevant political forces were successful in bringing about a different reading of the U.S. Constitution, one that served whatever interests they then had. The relevant factor was increased political *power*, not increased moral understanding or knowledge of framers' intentions or meanings. And as power bases shift, views on what the constitution "really means" shift along with them.

So critical theorists are all highly skeptical of constitutional practice. They are highly skeptical of theories that applaud constitutions and constitutional Charters as bulwarks against oppression. As we have seen, a key element in the notion of constitutionalism is the idea that government can/should be limited in its powers and that its authority depends on its observing these limitations – limitations concerning scope of authority, the mechanisms used in exercising power, and the nonviolation of important rights of political morality. We further noted that the authority of constitutions in liberal democracies is generally thought to lie in "we the people." One important claim of critical theorists is that the concept of "we the people" is as much a fabrication as Dworkin's Hercules. Instead of "we the people," Western societies are composed of various interest groups competing either for domination (e.g., white males and the wealthy) or for recognition and the elimination of oppression (e.g. the poor, women, and racial minorities). Legal practice, including judicial review, is a powerful tool utilized by the dominant groups in society to secure and maintain their superior status. As such, a constitution is anything but the protection from arbitrary power that its champions have heralded over the centuries. What is taken to be the plain meaning of the word "equality" is what the dominant group defines it to be. What is taken to be the obvious historical intentions or understandings of the framers is whatever intentions serve the contemporary interests of the dominant groups. What is taken to be the best moral theory underlying the constitution is nothing more than a rationalization of current social structures, all of which systematically oppress the interests of women, minorities, and the poor.

So critical theories represent a serious challenge not only to conventional theories and practices of constitutional interpretation but also to the very idea of constitutionalism itself – the idea that government can and should be limited in ways that serve to protect us from arbitrary power. According to most fixed-view theorists, the constitution protects us from judges and other government officials by restricting them to a morally neutral determination of the plain meaning or intentions of the framers of the constitution, whose role it was to make, on behalf of a sovereign people, the decisions of political morality the constitution was meant to incorporate. According to Dworkin, it is Hercules' moral theory of the constitution that serves as the bulwark against oppression, as it did, according to Dworkin, in a variety of constitutional decisions in the United States, for example *Brown* and *Roe v. Wade*. One crucial feature of Hercules' theory is that it is often at odds with received opinion, in particular with the convictions and prejudices of the various dominant groups within society. Following *Hercules'* moral theory of the constitution may lead a judge to protect the rights of oppressed groups from the arbitrary power of dominant groups, especially when that power has the sanction of legislation. But as we observed earlier, no ordinary judge is identical to Hercules. On the contrary, he is more often than not a member of the dominant group (e.g., wealthy white males) and shares the social background, education, perspective, and values of that group. As a result, his conceptions of the relevant contested concepts (e.g., equality and freedom of expression) will be their conceptions – that is, conceptions which serve the interests of the dominant groups against which a constitutional Charter is, in theory at least, meant to serve as protection. But if plain or original meaning, intentions, and Hercules' best theory are all potentially destructive myths, at the mercy of political agendas, then the kind of protections represented by the very idea of constitutionalism are themselves myths, and harmful ones at that.

So what is the solution according to critical theorists? The proffered solutions vary considerably from one critical theorist to the next, depending on how radical or skeptical the theorist tends to be. One critic motivated by Marxist thought might advocate wholesale rejection of Charters, while another motivated by feminist thought might be content to work within an extant system of judicial review to eradicate the vestiges of patriarchy inherent in the law.[61]

---

61 A prime example of the first kind of theorist is Michael Mandel, whose views will be discussed in Chapter 4. An example of the second kind of theorist is Catherine MacKinnon, who develops a radical critique of existing American laws on freedom of expression. See, for example, *Only Words*. For a less critical assessment of American law on free expression and pornography, one rooted in a more liberal feminist perspective, see Nadine Strossen, *Defending Pornography* (New York: Scribner's, 1995).

Yet others, such as Jeremy Waldron, recommend that we do away with Charters of Rights altogether and allow constitutional limits on government to be established by a more flexible discourse of politics in which the people play a more active role. But whatever their particular angle, critics all agree that progress can be made only if myths surrounding constitutional protections – that these can (and should) be discerned in plain meaning, original understanding, framers' intentions, or objective moral theory – are all exposed, and that the true political forces at work in constitutional practice are acknowledged and dealt with openly. Whether the very idea of constitutionalism can survive the lessons of critical theory is a question we will continually have to bear in mind in our exploration of the case for judicial review.

3

Why Charters?

A. Taking Stock

In the preceding chapter we reached a number of conclusions about constitutions and constitutional democracies. We saw (a) that constitutional democracies come in a wide variety of forms. In particular, we found (b) that they embrace a number of different ways in which law-determining decisions – that is, those which result in the creation, alteration, or elimination of legal norms – are "distanced" from the people on whose behalf and authority they are made. For example, modern democracies are all fundamentally representative, not direct, in nature. Furthermore, they also typically contain a number of practices and institutions (e.g., unelected assemblies and regulatory bodies) that combine to create even greater distance between law-determining decisions and the general citizenry. We also saw (c) that there can be more to a constitution than constitutional law; it can contain constitutional conventions that regulate constitutional powers and that are sometimes said (as in, e.g., the *Patriation* case) to be at least as important as the fundamental constitutional laws with which they act in tandem. We discovered (d) that constitutional norms need be neither (e) entrenched, nor (f) written, despite the undeniable fact that modern constitutional systems characteristically contain norms possessing both properties. We further discovered that a separation of legislative, executive, and legal powers is neither conceptually necessary nor always thought to be practically essential or desirable in modern constitutional democracies. This despite the fact that, once again, such systems characteristically embrace some form of separation, at least to some degree. Even those parliamentary systems in which executive and legislative powers are largely combined in the office of a prime minister and his cabinet, find it essential to have a separate and independent judiciary. The regimes of Regina and Rex, though certainly imaginable and (I hope) useful for the purposes of conceptual analysis, are hardly typical of modern constitutional democracies.

With these conclusions in mind, we turn now to the following question: Why, among the numerous possibilities open to it, would a democratic society choose a system of government in which the powers of government are limited by an entrenched, written Charter of Rights? And why would it then call upon one of the parties whose powers are created and regulated by constitutional law and convention – the judiciary – to apply this Charter in ways that can sometimes thwart the will of the legislature and, arguably, the people upon whose authority the legitimacy of the entire system rests? What could possibly justify the taking of such a monumental step?

In answering these vexing questions, we will sketch and examine what will be called "the Standard Case" for Charters. This is a case that represents an amalgam of views historically associated with a diverse group of individuals all of whom in some way or other defend the adoption of entrenched, written Charters in constitutional democracies. These people we will call "the Advocates." Not all Advocates argue on the same grounds, and some are highly critical of views held by fellow Advocates. For example, "democratic process" Advocates such as John Hart Ely criticize those who wish Charters to be used for more than simply guarding the integrity of the democratic process.[1] According to other Advocates, Charters should also be used to protect minorities against encroachments on substantive moral rights that have little to do with the proper functioning of democratic procedures. Despite the ever-present dangers of over-simplification, and hence distortion, inherent in any such effort, we can, if we are careful, distill from the widely divergent positions on offer, the essentials of a case for Charters and the practices of judicial review with which they tend to be associated. And with all due caution, this is what we will mean when we refer to "the Standard Case."

In the course of presenting the Standard Case we will also have occasion to note a corresponding set of views advanced by an increasingly large group of people who are highly critical of Charters and judicial review. This group of individuals we will refer to as "the Critics." Charter Critics, like Charter Advocates, in no way form a uniform group. Some Critics – for example, Jeremy Waldron, whose views will be a principal focus of Chapter 4 – argue that the Standard Case rests on conceptual confusions about the very possibility of limitation. Others, for example, Canadian legal scholars Michael Mandel and F. L. Morton, restrict their attack largely to the claim that Charters are politically dangerous, indeed subversive of democratic practice, a view shared by Waldron but on very different grounds. Some Critics are dismissive of cases made by fellow Critics. The arguments of those who argue that Charters falsely presuppose that moral rights are in some sense "objective" are, for example,

---

1 John Hart Ely, *Democracy and Distrust: A Theory of Judicial Review* (Cambridge, Mass.: Harvard University Press, 1980).

rejected by Waldron, who bluntly states that objectivity is completely irrelevant when it comes to considering the wisdom of judicial review.[2] What binds Critics together may be little more than their mutual rejection of Charters and the Standard Case made in its favour. Despite this, and once again with all due caution, it is this group of individuals to whom we will be referring when we speak of "the Critics."

B. From Regas to Demos

Let's begin by returning once again to Regina. Recall that Regina combines legislative, executive, and judicial powers. Recall as well that Regina is no tyrant: She acts "at the pleasure of her people." She is generally accepted by the members of her community as entitled to exercise these combined powers on their behalf and in any way that she believes will advance their interests. A few notable exceptions, however, distinguish her from Rex. She is required to legislate on Wednesdays and must not interfere in religious matters. This was enough, we said, to introduce the idea of constitutional limitation. It is also arguably enough to establish Regina's system, which we will henceforth call "Regas," as one that at the very least takes an important step towards the democratic. Though there is, to be sure, considerable distance between citizens, on the one hand, and Regina's law-determining decisions, on the other, her authority does rest on popular acceptance, on the authority of "we the people." It rests, in other words, on popular sovereignty. This is perhaps not enough to qualify Regas as fully democratic in nature, because "democracy" is almost universally understood as requiring direct or indirect voting by the general population – and where government is effected through representatives that these representatives be generally accountable to the general public through the polls. Yet to the extent that Regas combines popular sovereignty with limited government power, it at the very least approaches modern forms of constitutional democracy. To be sure, the latter contain elected, representative assemblies, not benevolent, unelected rulers. But we must remember that they also contain a wide range of distancing mechanisms that, in combination, also create *significant* separation between law-determining decisions and the citizens on whose behalf they are made. So it is not altogether implausible to view Regas as at least lying on the fringes of the democratic.

Suppose now that citizens in Regas come to the conclusion that Regina's law-determining decisions are not adequately meeting their needs. In particular, her decisions are not adequately representing their considered views about how their society should be structured and governed. Her views differ from theirs far too many times and on far too many issues. The situation has developed to such a point that serious doubts are emerging about whether the system

---

2 See *Law and Disagreement*, Chapter 8, "The Irrelevance of Moral Objectivity."

in Regas can truly be said to rest on popular sovereignty. How might this situation be rectified? One relatively simple way would be to alter the basic constitutional rules of Regas so as to require the following: Before she makes a law-determining decision, Regina must always directly consult citizens to determine their interests or wishes about the matter in the question – at the very least, they must be consulted to a greater degree than is now the norm. Consultation can of course come in a wide variety of forms. It can range from informal chats with a random or select group of citizens to something more akin to modern forms of political polling wherein a systematic, scientific effort is made to determine the pulse of the nation on specific issues of interest. One immediate objection to this arrangement is this: There is no guarantee that Regina will factor such consultations into her deliberations. As things now stand, nothing prevents her from simply ignoring what she finds. We must be careful here. Recalling the distinction drawn in the previous chapter between normative and *de facto* freedom, we can admit that Regina might have the *de facto* freedom to ignore the results of required consultations, though if her power truly does rest on popular sovereignty, it is difficult to see how she could do so with any degree of regularity. It would be a serious mistake, however, to confuse this *de facto* freedom with normative freedom. She might be able to get away with ignoring citizens' input, at least on occasion, but it would nevertheless always be wrong of her to do so. Add to this the ever-present good-faith requirement that she always act on her best understanding of what her duty demands, and we have significant normative constraint. Her hitherto largely unbridled power to legislate now has two further conditions. Regina's legislation is valid not only if (a) it is declared on Wednesdays, and (b) it is not concerned with a religious matter. It must also be (c) preceded and influenced by the required level of consultation; and (d) the product of a good-faith attempt to meet the previous three conditions. In particular, it must result from an attempt to ensure that the results of the required consultation are reflected in whatever legislative measure is ultimately chosen.

The foregoing observations notwithstanding, there may yet be serious problems with the constitutional change under consideration. Suppose that Regina always attempts to meet her new responsibilities. In particular, she always consults and she always introduces legislation that she honestly believes reflects the community's wishes and interests. There is still no guarantee that she will succeed in her efforts. Regina is, after all, but one person – a human one at that, with all the usual limitations. She is not a Platonic Guardian with a pipeline to eternal verities and with the objectivity, impartiality, and strength of will required of such individuals. Nor is she George Gallup. So even with all these important changes, citizens may be left believing that their needs, interests, and wishes are still not being adequately reflected or represented in Regina's law-determining decisions. What further improvements to the constitutional structure of Regas should be contemplated?

A possibility that comes readily to mind is to replace Regina with a legislative assembly that has a better chance of reflecting, in an ongoing and systematic way, the interests and wishes of the general population. As a rule, two heads are better than one, and many heads better than two, whenever attempts are made to answer difficult questions. Furthermore, whatever biases and other such limitations one finds in individual legislators will often be counterbalanced, at least to some degree, by biases and strengths found in other members of a largish representative assembly. If X is biased in favour of proposal P, then there will likely be a Y whose biases incline him in the other direction. When the questions that need answering are questions like What does the community wish to be done in this situation? or What is the fair way to apportion the benefits and burdens of a cooperative social enterprise? such considerations provide us with the basis of a potentially powerful argument in favour of a multi-member legislative assembly. It provides an attractive reason – what we'll call the *multiple heads principle* – to opt for a radical change in the government mechanisms through which popular sovereignty is expressed in Regina's community. Let us suppose that members of the community see the wisdom in the multiple heads principle and decide, perhaps in a rudimentary constitutional gathering, that Regina should be replaced with a legislative assembly comprising many members. Instead of relying on Regina alone to act on their behalf, decisions will now be made by an assembly each member of which will be elected by a group within the general community identified geographically. Legislative decisions will be made on the basis of majority votes among these elected representatives. Each representative will be expected, when voting, to reflect the interests and wishes of citizens. It might even be expected that the focus of each member will not be the interests and wishes of the entire population but only those who live within his or her electoral district. It is expected that each member will be an advocate for these particular people, much as a trial lawyer is an advocate for her client's interests. Each member is supposed in this way to represent the people who elected her – and will be held accountable to her constituents on that score. Let's suppose that further rules requiring periodic elections are adopted to help ensure that the views, interests, and wishes of constituents are truly being reflected in votes taken by elected members. If a representative fails to do her job, she faces likely defeat in the next round of elections. Regina will still retain her executive and judicial powers in the new arrangement, but she will be expected to administer and apply only laws adopted by members of the assembly. Finally, suppose that it is no longer thought necessary to impose constitutional limits on legislative power in Regas. In particular, it is no longer thought necessary to require that legislation avoid dealing with a religious matter. Now that legislative decisions are to be made by an elected assembly, they are, it is supposed, more likely to reflect the views, interests, and wishes of the general population. If the latter do not wish to see legislation on a religious matter, elected members will be more attuned and responsive to this fact and loath to introduce any such measure.

With these simple yet fundamental changes in place, there is little question that Regina's community has embraced a rudimentary form of democracy. Any qualms there might have been about viewing their constitutional arrangements as at least approaching the democratic have presumably been laid to rest. Instead of being expressed via the decisions of one person, popular sovereignty is now expressed through the decisions of an elected, representative assembly. This fundamental change, which we will mark by renaming Regina's reconstituted society "Demos," is still one in which there is distance between citizens and law-determining decisions – it is, after all, a *representative* democracy, not a direct one. But that distance appears to be have been significantly reduced. We will see shortly that appearances can be deceiving, but for now we can agree that a reduction has taken place. We can also add that Demos has a constitutional arrangement in which one form of government power – the power to legislate – has been separated from all the others, which continue to reside in Regina's person. The questions we will now address are: How might things still go wrong in Demos? What might lead Regina's people to institute still further changes to their constitutional arrangements? In particular, what might lead them to adopt a Charter of Rights together with some form of judicial review, and perhaps an even further separation of government powers? In answering these questions, we will see the emergence of the Standard Case.

C. Representation

Let's begin by asking why, precisely, Demos represents an improvement over Regas. At first blush, the answer seems obvious. Demos is an improvement because it is more democratic, and it is more democratic because legislative decisions are more likely to reflect the needs and interests of the people on whose behalf those decisions are made. In actual fact, however, it is not at all clear why, from the point of view of democracy, Demos is an improvement over Regas. A good deal depends on what exactly elected members are supposed to be doing when they vote in a legislative assembly, and whether they actually succeed in doing so with any degree of regularity. In order to achieve a modest degree of clarity on these matters, we need to address, at the institutional level, what exactly it is that makes a form of government a representative democracy. At the individual level, we need to ask what exactly it is for an elected member of a legislature to act *as a representative*.

Let's begin with the second of our two questions. What is it to be or act as a representative? Consider the following attempt to answer this question:

Answer A: Y serves as X's representative when Y is chosen by X to act on X's behalf.

Answer A has some appeal. In thinking about the notion of representation, it is quite natural to think of one person's choosing another person to act in his stead. Mark acts as my representative at a department meeting when I ask him to substitute for me. He voices my concerns and casts a vote in my name. The opinions he voices are taken as those that I would have voiced had I been present, and the vote he casts is my vote – the one I would (likely) have registered had I been physically present. Turning now to Demos, we see that members of the legislature are also chosen, via elections, to act on behalf of their constituents. They are expected to voice the concerns of constituents, and when a member casts his vote, it is natural to think of him as casting *their* votes – the votes each one of them (or at least most of them) would have registered had he (or they) been physically present in the assembly. In other words, a representative acts as his constituents would have acted had their system of government been a direct democracy. Under this description, one naturally thinks of a legislative member as one chosen to act on behalf of his constituents. He is, in this way, their representative.

Despite its initial appeal, Answer A is actually quite unhelpful and somewhat misleading. First, it runs together two very different things: acting on X's behalf and being chosen to do so by X. Parents in PTA meetings act on behalf of their children when they participate in decision making and might even be said to represent their children by promoting their needs, interests, and wishes when they do so. This despite the fact – a no doubt regrettable one in the view of some teenagers – that parents are neither elected nor in any way chosen by their children to take on these roles. One possible reason for running the two conditions together – acting on X's behalf and being chosen by X to do so – is that the latter is typically a necessary condition of the *legitimacy* of the former. In some circumstances – for example, when X is involved in a real estate transaction and hires a lawyer, Y, to act as his agent – Y could not legitimately act on X's behalf unless she were chosen by X to do so.[3] But this is not always the case. Being chosen by X is not always a condition of legitimately representing him. Once again, parents in PTA meetings act legitimately when they represent their children, but they are not chosen by their kids to do so. The same is true in many other situations, for example, when, in an emergency situation a patient advocate acts on behalf of a comatose accident victim who is himself unable to consent to lifesaving surgery and whose family is unavailable to do so on his behalf. The patient advocate legitimately represents the patient under these circumstances, even though she is not chosen by the patient to serve this role. Of course it is possible that these latter cases are anomalous. The first involves children, the latter incapacitated adults. It may yet be true that legitimate representation *in the case of competent adults* always requires choice on the part of the one represented. But whether or not this is in fact true, the point remains that the notion of representation does not itself seem to require any such choice.

---

3 We will leave aside unusual cases where, for example, an agent is appointed by a Court.

So the key to representation cannot lie in being chosen by the party represented to perform this task because this does not seem to be necessary. This is a crucial point to bear in mind later when we address in Chapter 5 reasons for thinking that the representation and protection of minority interests are one of the major roles a judge can play in judicial review. The latter is often promoted as a mechanism by which minorities can achieve a level of representation that is simply not possible in a constitutionally unbridled legislative assembly. Majorities, it is said, are naturally inclined to favour majority interests, resulting in failure of minority representation. An independent judiciary can help ensure that minority interests are duly represented in law-determining decisions. This line of argument would face serious difficulty if a condition of representation were choice on the part of those represented, because judges are, for the most part, unelected. They are most certainly not elected by the minorities whose interests they often help to represent.

A second reason why Answer A is unhelpful is that it introduces but leaves unexplained the equally puzzling notion of acting on someone else's behalf. In particular, it leaves us asking what exactly a representative member of a legislative assembly is supposed to be doing when she acts on behalf of her constituents. The answer to this question is also not at all obvious. So Answer A, which substitutes one puzzling notion for another, is not of much help. We need to look elsewhere. Perhaps we can begin to get a handle on these questions by looking at analogous cases in which the representative role is better understood. With this in mind, let's return to the example of patient advocacy. What exactly is it to be a patient advocate?

D. An Analogy: Patient Advocacy

A patient advocate serves a role analogous to the one Mark serves when he acts on my behalf at the department meeting. Just as Mark's voice stands in for my voice, and just as Mark's vote stands in for my vote, the patient advocate speaks and acts for the incapacitated patient. She makes decisions that, in law, stand in for the patient's own decisions. All else being equal, her decisions are treated as identical to the patient's, identical to what the patient's decisions would have been had she been able to make them on her own. When the advocate consents to surgery, the patient is taken to have consented, and to have thereby granted medical staff the right to proceed – a right they would not otherwise have had. To act as a patient advocate is to act under secondary, power-conferring rules that enable the advocate to alter the legal status quo – a status quo in which performing surgery absent consent would amount to a battery. All these features of patient advocacy are marked by the terminology used in describing such decisions: They are said to be "surrogate decisions" or "substituted judgments," and patient advocates are correspondingly referred to as "surrogate decision makers," ones empowered to make decisions on the patient's behalf. With this in mind, we might replace Answer A with the following:

Answer B: Y serves as X's representative when Y is empowered to make decisions and/or take actions that stand in for X's decisions and/or actions.

Answer B is quite an improvement over Answer A, but questions still remain. Among the most difficult questions are those having to do with the kinds of reasons to which a representative may properly appeal in reaching her decisions. In other words, things get very tricky, very quickly, when one asks about the *basis* on which a patient advocate is to exercise her power to decide – that is, when one asks about the *grounds* to which she should appeal in making decisions on the patient's behalf. The answer we end up giving to these important questions turns crucially on how we deal with the interplay between two key factors that such cases almost inevitably bring to the fore: the patient's *expressed wishes* versus the patient's *best interests*. These figure in almost all cases of patient advocacy, but none more so than in dramatic cases involving religious convictions that preclude standard lifesaving measures.

Suppose that the patient is an accident victim who, being found unconscious and in urgent need of care, is transported to a hospital emergency room. Suppose further that the unconscious victim is known to be a member of a religious group that is itself well known for its official ban on blood transfusions, even when these are required as routine lifesaving measures. Let's even suppose that a card officially declaring allegiance to this policy, duly signed and witnessed by the patient, is discovered in his wallet.[4] On the assumption that no family member is available for consultation, either the attending medical staff or a legally sanctioned patient advocate will end up in the unenviable position of having to make decisions on behalf of the unconscious accident victim. In particular, they or she will have to decide whether to honour what would appear to be the victim's previously expressed wishes, even though doing so will almost certainly result in death. Ordinarily, a patient's expressed wishes with respect to medical treatment must be respected. This is the very basis of the doctrine of informed consent: that no medical treatment may be undertaken without the expressed consent of the patient. But in this particular instance, a case can be made that the victim's fundamental interests conflict with his expressed wishes and are sufficient to override the latter. Furthermore, it is not altogether unreasonable to question whether we can be absolutely sure that the signed card truly does express the victim's wishes, or those he would continue to have were he now able to express himself on the matter. Can one really assume that commitments made in the abstract, well before a life-threatening situation arises and forces one to consider

4 Many legal jurisdictions have had to deal with this kind of case. For a Canadian example, see *Malette v. Shulman* [1990] 72 O.R. (2d) 417 (Ontario Court of Appeal).

the validity and strength of one's commitments, would always be maintained in this kind of situation? There are, as they say, few atheists in foxholes. And even if we could, or legally must, presume that the victim's commitment would be maintained in the present circumstances, is it obvious that such commitments must always trump all other considerations? There is a strong tendency to think that they must: X's expressed wishes concerning what shall be done to his body must always be accepted as overriding all other factors. Let's call this the "bodily integrity principle." As it stands, however, the bodily integrity principle is far too strong. Compulsory immunization against highly infectious, life-threatening diseases can sometimes be justified in the interests of public safety. Here third-party interests clearly and easily outweigh any expressed wish not to be immunized. Suppose we weaken the principle in such a way that it applies only when no third-party interests are at stake. We might, that is, prohibit interference when the only relevant interests are those of the person whose expressed wishes are at issue. Yet even in these cases it is not at all clear that expressed wishes always trump best interests. One cannot, for example, validly consent to becoming a slave, or to being killed for the sheer pleasure of another. If so, then is it not entirely possible that, in the kind of situation under consideration, where lifesaving measures are declined for highly contentious religious reasons, the autonomy right of a victim to control over his own life and body is properly overridden by what is in X's best interests?[5]

So it is not at all clear that the bodily integrity principle, even when limited to cases in which no third-party interests are at stake, must always be followed in medical emergencies. It is not altogether unreasonable to think that in at least some cases the patient's best interests might well trump his expressed wishes, thus leaving the patient's representative with some very difficult choices. But the difficulties don't end there: Precisely what, it might be asked, actually are in the victim's best interests in this kind of case? Most human beings have a deep and abiding interest in physical self-preservation. And some are prepared to say that this interest overrides all others, as evidenced by the appeal of the bodily integrity principle and the fact that the right of self-defense is widely recognized, both morally and legally, as being all but absolute. It is presumably this particular interest that would morally justify imposing the blood transfusion.

---

5 We have here waded into the treacherous waters of legal paternalism. I am in no way arguing that paternalism in these contexts is warranted. My aim is merely to show how complex the issues are and the types of questions that arise in cases of representation. For a discussion of the perils of defining and defending legal paternalism, see Gerald Dworkin, "Paternalism," in R. Wasserstrom, ed., *Morality and the Law* (Belmont, Calif.: Wadsworth, 1971), and "Paternalism: Some Second Thoughts," in Rolf Sartorius, ed., *Paternalism* (Minneapolis: University of Minnesota Press, 1983). See also Joel Feinberg, *The Moral Limits of the Criminal Law, Volume 3: Harm to Self* (Oxford: Oxford University Press, 1989).

But physical self-preservation is not always thought to be of paramount or overriding importance. Setting aside suicide, allowing oneself to be killed for the sheer pleasure of another, and perhaps even dying patients who often willingly decline treatment that would result only in prolonging an unwelcome dying process, people are willing to sacrifice themselves for all kinds of reasons. Soldiers will throw themselves on live grenades to save their comrades. Others will volunteer for suicide missions in order to advance what is believed to be a just cause. Indeed, many religious individuals see their most fundamental interest as resting in the fulfillment of their moral duty to obey God's word, which word is sometimes thought to demand self-sacrifice. And even those among this group whose weakness of will would prevent them from bravely facing this (perceived) duty to God without an additional source of motivation might be sufficiently motivated by fear of divine sanction. Or they might find sufficient motivation in the prospect of the eternal happiness promised to those who obey God's law under the most trying of circumstances. How does one compare the loss of a few mortal years, on the one hand, with the avoidance of God's displeasure coupled with the prospect of a rapture-filled eternity, on the other? To such individuals, the desire for physical self-preservation pales in comparison with these more fundamental interests. So judging that the victim's best interests are found in a lifesaving blood transfusion is an exercise fraught with peril in many cases. One could justify confidence in any such judgment only if one were to discount the patient's convictions as based on foolish, irrational religious belief. But is anyone, patient advocates included, entitled to make this particular call?

So representation in the case of patient advocacy and surrogate decision making can be, and often is, a highly complex matter. Though most cases are not as complex as the one just described, a sufficient number of questions emerge even when we restrict ourselves to less dramatic cases. These should make us pause before assuming that we have a firm grasp of the practice, or of how we would solve the many riddles and dilemmas that arise in some cases from the interplay between expressed wishes and best interests. Some of the more vexing questions are the following:

1. Should a surrogate always attempt only to honour the patient's expressed wishes, or can the patient's best interests ever enter into the equation and possibly override expressed wishes?
2. May a surrogate discount a patient's expressed wishes if, in the judgment of the surrogate, they were based on faulty or irrational beliefs?
3. Or must the surrogate always take the patient's expressed wishes as a given, whenever it reasonably clear what these are (or were)?
4. Is it ever safe to assume that the patient's previously expressed wishes are different from what they would be now were the patient able to speak for himself? Recall the maxim: There are no atheists in foxholes.

5. On what basis *does* one judge what is in the patient's best interests?
6. In judging what is in the patient's best interests, should the surrogate assume the role of a "reasonable person" and attempt to determine what would be in the best interests of such a person?
7. Or, in judging what is in the patient's best interests, must a surrogate always assume the role of a reasonable person *in the patient's circumstances* – that is, with all the beliefs, values, and convictions of the patient? Must she do so even if some of the relevant beliefs, values, and convictions would be rejected as irrational by the surrogate and by the vast majority of reasonable people in the general population?
8. What must a surrogate do if a situation arises that is, arguably, significantly different from the ones contemplated by the patient when his wishes were expressed? Is it ever reasonable to assume that the patient might have said: "Well, if I knew at the time that it's *this* to which I was agreeing when I consented to X, I would never have done so!"?
9. What must a surrogate do if a completely novel situation arises – that is, a situation about which the patient has expressed no wish or opinion, about which, in fact, he might never have even entertained a thought? Should the surrogate somehow attempt to decide what the patient would have wished, *given his basic values, commitments, and beliefs?*[6]

This set of questions is by no means exhaustive. There are many others. Are competent family members always entitled, morally and legally, to act as surrogates whenever they are available to do so? At what stage should (or do) children acquire the power to decide for themselves instead of having medical decisions made for them by their parents? And so on. But we will leave these aside because they concern matters that have no direct bearing on the analogous context in which our interest mainly lies: decisions made in legislative assemblies by democratically elected representatives. Things are complicated enough without considering these further case-specific complexities.

E. Authenticity and the Doctrine of Informed Consent

Before returning to Demos, let's take one further detour and consider in a bit more detail the doctrine of informed consent. This doctrine, a cornerstone of the ethics of modern medical practice, will be used to introduce the notion of "authenticity," a concept we will use in developing the Standard Case.

With the exception of emergency cases in which it is truly impossible to obtain, valid consent to medical treatment must, legally, always be secured in

---

6 There is a striking parallel here between this particular set of questions and ones that interpreters of legislation and constitutional provisions are supposed to be asking according to original-intent theories. There is also a striking parallel between the immense difficulties inherent in attempts to answer such questions.

advance. If the patient is physically unable to provide consent, then a surrogate decision maker is called upon, in ways described above, to act on the patient's behalf. Let's concentrate here on non-emergency situations in which the patient is in fact physically able to provide the required consent. Exactly what is it to provide consent to treatment, and under what conditions is consent considered valid?

Among the things one does in providing consent to treatment is to express the wish that relevant procedures be undertaken on one's person.[7] But there is much more to the act of giving valid consent than simply expressing such a wish. In giving consent one also exercises a legal power. In consenting to a medical procedure, one alters the legal status quo by relieving medical staff of their otherwise standing duty not to "touch" (or the duty *to* touch, depending, again, on circumstances) one's person. But not all attempts to exercise this power are valid. As noted earlier, powers always come with conditions of their valid exercise. Three conditions of valid consent are (a) that the agent is *legally competent*, (b) that consent is *freely given or voluntary*, and (c) that consent is *informed*. Condition (a), the competency condition, rules out young children and those whose mental capacities prevent them from satisfying conditions (b) and (c). Condition (b), the voluntariness condition, rules out consent given in the face of coercion or other undue influences, while (c), the epistemic condition, rules out cases in which the agent lacks knowledge or understanding of relevant information. For example, the patient might not be aware that there is only a tiny chance that the procedure will succeed but a very large chance that it will mark his remaining days with immense suffering. If this information is kept from the patient, or if he fails to appreciate what he is being told when an attempt is made to convey it to him, then he suffers from an "epistemic deficiency" and his consent is invalid. That is, his failure to meet the epistemic condition means that the legal power through which valid consent occurs will not have been successfully exercised. And those who failed to provide him with the required information could be held liable, if it is found that their failure was intentional, reckless, or negligent. Because the patient did not validly consent, the patient did not successfully exercise the power to relieve medical staff of their otherwise standing legal duty not to touch his person. That duty remains. And having violated this important duty not to touch, they could be held to have committed a battery.

So the competency, voluntariness, and epistemic conditions must be met if the expression of a wish amounts to valid consent. It is not clear, however, that this list of conditions is exhaustive. Questions can still arise over whether the

---

7 One can also consent to withdrawal of treatment or to non-initiation of what is standard treatment in the circumstances. We will leave these complications aside and focus on consent to treatment, with the understanding that what is said about this particular form of consent applies *mutatis mutandis* to the others as well.

expressed wish is "genuine" or "authentic." If it is not, then consent may yet be invalid. Lack of authenticity can occur for any number of reasons, some related to the foregoing three conditions. It might arise, for example, if the patient appears not to have met the epistemic condition, as in the case in which he doesn't know that there is only a slim chance that the procedure will succeed but a very large chance that his remaining days will be marked by immense suffering. The absence of this highly relevant information means that the patient does not fully appreciate what he is doing – does not, as it were, appreciate the nature and consequences of his act – when he expresses his wish to be treated. His expressed wish might, for this reason, be described as unfounded or inauthentic.

In the foregoing case we have a rather straightforward failure to meet the epistemic condition. But epistemic deficiencies are not always so uncomplicated and uncontroversial. A more complex kind of case involves a different way in which the epistemic condition might be breached. Authenticity might be questioned not only when there is doubt whether the patient knows or fully understands some relevant medical fact but also when there is doubt that she understands or appreciates the extent to which her expressed wishes are radically at odds with her own fundamental beliefs, values, commitments, and settled preferences – those features of her personality that, in a sense, make her the person that she is. Consider a situation in which, for example, a daughter is moved to declare: "I know what she just said, but that can't be my mother talking! She says she wants to die, but she has always firmly believed in a duty to God to preserve one's life at all costs. To surrender to death in this way would be, in her eyes, to insult God – something she would never, ever wish to do." In such a case, the patient might be described as speaking or acting out of character. One might go so far as to say that in such cases of "evaluative dissonance" it is "her condition" speaking, not her. If so, then one might be inclined to say that her consent cannot possibly be valid because it is inauthentic.

Evaluative dissonance cases are admittedly controversial. Recall our earlier observation that there are few atheists in foxholes. Can we ever really rule out the possibility that the one who has expressed a seemingly inauthentic wish has actually experienced a change in her fundamental beliefs, values, commitments, or preferences? Perhaps when faced with the prospect of imminent death, the mother now chooses to violate her duty to God, or no longer believes in a God who would require one to prolong a dying process marred by immense suffering. There may be few atheists in foxholes, but there are also some theists who change their minds when confronted with unbearable demands. It is admittedly very difficult in some instances to distinguish between true evaluative dissonance, on the one hand, and genuine changes of heart on the other. And it may be good policy to forbid medical staff, surrogates, and caregivers from ever assuming that a competent patient's currently expressed wishes are anything but authentic. In other words, there may be good reasons to reject a fourth condition of valid consent – (d) that the patient's expressed wish that the relevant measures be taken is *authentic*. Perhaps the immense epistemic difficulties encountered in judging authenticity are enough to rule out such an option, especially when these are coupled with the potential for abuse that could arise because of it if authenticity were added as a fourth condition of valid consent – "I know that's what my mother said, and I know that I stand to inherit a whack of cash which I could really use right now. But she really does not want that blood transfusion!" Nevertheless, we should not allow the practical complexities of these cases to obscure the important point they are intended to illustrate: Expressions of wish can sometimes be inauthentic. If so, then it is not altogether inconceivable that, under the right conditions, they can or should be ignored or discounted.

Those still hesitant to accept the idea that expressed wishes can be inauthentic might consider the many, far less controversial cases that serve to illustrate the point further. Suppose I express the wish that no one throw me a party on my upcoming birthday. My friends, knowing me all too well, readily conclude that I didn't really mean what I just said. I express the wish not to have a party, but I really do want one and would be deeply disappointed were one not thrown in my honour. I might know this about myself and expect my friends not to take my words literally, not to take them as constituting a sincere expression of my wishes. Alternatively, I might lack this self-knowledge and be perfectly sincere in my pronouncement. My friends, on the other hand, know me much better. They know that "deep down" I really do want the party and that I will later come to regret not having one if my expressed wishes are followed. I will come later to see that my words do not reflect my *genuine* wishes. In this latter instance, we once again see a failure to meet the epistemic condition.

Cases involving deficiency in knowledge, including self-knowledge, or where words are used to convey something other than what they are normally taken to mean, are not the only ones in which expressed wishes can be inauthentic. Another range of cases arises when there is doubt over whether the expression of a wish is fully voluntary. Suppose I express the desire to drive home after a long night in the pub, even though it is well known that I deplore drunk driving and morally condemn those who engage in it. Despite my long-established moral commitment, I insist, in an act of sheer bravado, that I'm perfectly capable of driving myself home. In fact, I am so insistent that my friends have to struggle to separate me from my car keys. In this case my expressed wish is clearly not genuine or authentic; it conflicts with my fundamental moral beliefs and commitments. We say that it's the drink – or the machismo – talking, not me, just as it was the mother's condition talking when she asked to be let go. What's lacking in this kind of case isn't self-knowledge but the willingness or ability to act in accordance with one's deepest moral commitments and settled preferences. This temporary deficiency is one that renders my expressed wish to drive home inauthentic – and my friends are surely right to discount or ignore it.

So, what is it, in the end, for the expression of a wish to be authentic or genuine? A full analysis would take us too far afield, but certain conclusions can be drawn from the preceding discussion. In order for the expression of a wish to be authentic, at least three conditions must be met. First, the means chosen to express my wish must be employed with the intention that they be understood, or taken to imply, what they are normally taken to mean and imply in that particular kind of context. Sometimes the means chosen are verbal in nature, as when I say "Give me my keys!" or the mother says "Let me go!" But wishes can also be expressed nonverbally, for example, by the very stern look I give my children when they attempt to switch the television from the ball game to the music video. In both cases, the means chosen to express my wishes are chosen with the intention that they be understood, or taken to imply, what they are normally taken to mean and imply in that particular kind of context. On the other hand, when I say that I don't want a party but expect my friends to read my words as expressing something other than what they would normally be used to say, my expressed wish is not genuine. I expect them to understand me as saying that I really do want the party even though I use words which clearly imply that I do not. In this particular case it isn't my *wish* that's inauthentic. I truly do want the party and know this about myself. It's my *expression* that is inauthentic. It doesn't reflect what I know my true wishes to be. In a false display of modesty, I use words which imply that I'm above wanting such trite things as birthday parties – when this is really what I want and expect to receive.

A second condition of authenticity is that the wish be based on adequate knowledge and understanding. In this case it is not the expression that is authentic or not, but the wish itself. The level of knowledge and understanding required to meet the condition will presumably vary with the context. If we're talking about consent to medical treatment, then presumably that level is very high. If we're talking about throwing a birthday party, it's presumably much lower. As we did when we looked at the special case of consent to medical treatment, we can refer to this as "the epistemic condition."

A third critical condition of authenticity is what we will call "the evaluative dissonance condition." This is the requirement that the wish expressed be consistent with the basic beliefs, values, commitments, and settled preferences of the agent. It is possible that an evaluative dissonance case involves a failure to meet the epistemic condition, in which case it falls under the second condition as a special case. The relevant deficiency resides here in a deficiency in self-knowledge. It resides in a failure to understand or appreciate the extent to which the measures about which the wish has been expressed conflict with fundamental beliefs, values, convictions, and settled preferences. This can happen when, for example, the agent has failed to draw the moral implications of the measures

he wishes to see pursued and would alter his expressed wishes if these implications were brought to his attention. But not all cases of evaluative dissonance
involve lack of self-knowledge. A patient might be fully aware of the evaluative dissonance but be temporarily overcome by profound fear or some other
emotional disturbance. The same was true of me in my drunken state. I was
fully aware of the risks involved in drunk driving and the extent to which such
conduct violates my fundamental convictions and settled preferences. What
prompted me to make my demand was not an absence of self-knowledge but a
temporary, drink-enhanced, macho preference or impulse to get myself home
under my own steam. This temporarily ascendant preference led me impulsively – but knowingly – to pursue a course of action that violates not only my
convictions but also my settled preferences and wishes. As a responsible moral
agent, I presumably had, and continue to have, a settled wish never to allow
temporary, far less worthy preferences to override my fundamental moral commitments. If so, then my drunken situation can be described as one in which a
currently expressed, but inauthentic, wish conflicted with an authentic, settled
wish always to act as a responsible moral agent. The latter I will have expressed
either verbally or, as is more usually the case, through my conduct. That is, my
settled wish always to act in accordance with my fundamental commitments is
illustrated by my living my life, as best I can, according to them. In living my
life this way, I express the wish to live as a responsible moral agent according to
those commitments. And this authentic wish is temporarily overridden by my
inauthentic, drink-induced wish to drive myself home. There is no epistemic
deficiency here. On the contrary, the deficiency lies in the fact that the action is
not fully voluntary.

These reflections on the authenticity of expressed wishes are in no way
intended to be exhaustive. They are meant only to illustrate the importance
of thinking about the authenticity of expressed wishes. They force us to ask
whether some expressed wishes should be discounted or overridden in situations in which normally they must – and would – be honoured. One situation
in which this question can arise is, I suggest, that of the modern legislature. A
legislative representative might find herself in the unenviable position of having
to ask whether or not the expressed wishes of her community are truly authentic or genuine. Perhaps they introduce an unsatisfactory level of evaluative
dissonance when measured against the community's previously expressed fundamental beliefs, values, commitments, and settled preferences. Yet another
situation in which questions of authenticity could arise is when a court has
been charged with the responsibilities associated with judicial review. Are the
wishes of the community, as expressed in legislation adopted by its representative assembly, consistent with its basic beliefs, values, convictions, and settled
preferences as expressed in the Charter it has adopted? Judges and legislators
who find themselves in such situations will inevitably be forced to address moral
questions at least as difficult as those faced by the daughter whose mother asked

for measures that seem to violate the mother's every moral fibre. We will have occasion in Chapters 5 and 6 to explore these questions in some depth.

F. Representation in Assemblies

Let's use what we have just learned about the practice of patient advocacy, the doctrine of valid consent, and the concept of authenticity of expressed wishes to deepen our understanding of the role of a representative who finds herself in an elected legislature. We can begin with the observation that our elected representative will often have to grapple with the same basic dilemmas as those faced by our patient advocate. In particular, she will sometimes be faced with the dilemma of choosing between *expressed wishes* and *best interests*, or between expressed wishes that she considers *genuine* and those that she judges to be *inauthentic*. And these moral dilemmas will in turn give rise to a number of analogous questions. On what basis should a representative make her decision when called upon to vote in the legislature? Should she always attempt to honour the expressed wishes of the electorate, whenever these are known? Or may she at least factor in what she considers to be their best interests? Following the parallel a bit further: Is it ever legitimate for her to override or ignore the clearly expressed wishes of constituents in order to promote their best interests? If so, under what conditions would this be permissible? And finally, should legislative representatives be barred, morally, from ever judging constituents' currently expressed wishes to be inauthentic? Should they be barred from doing this, even though slavishly adhering to the inauthentic expressed wishes of the community might actually lead representatives to undermine their more genuine wishes? It might lead them, in other words, to acts that contribute to a harmful state of evaluative dissonance at the social level. Is this what we want them to be doing? If not, then we will have to face up to the consequences of what we are asking them to do: We will be requiring them, on occasion, to refuse to do what we have demanded that they do! We will be asking them, in effect, to tell us that we have got things wrong. In Chapter 6 I shall provide good reasons for accepting this seemingly paradoxical result. In so doing, I no doubt run the risk of being labeled an elitist and paternalist – of assuming that our representatives sometimes know better than we do and are justified morally in forcing us to do the right things. This is a risk assumed by anyone who argues that a community must sometimes be protected against its own excesses. In seeing why these labels do not, in the end, apply we will begin to see not only the basis for a much more nuanced conception of the role of legislative representative but also the emergence of a central argument for Charters and judicial review. In other words, we will begin to see one of the fundamental planks in the Standard Case.

Intuitively, most people think that a representative should always attempt to honour the expressed wishes of voters, whatever these might happen to be. After all, the role of a legislative member is to *represent* those by whose authority she holds office. And is it not the role of one who represents X to do what X wishes him to do? Consider how you would respond to a lawyer who ignored your instructions in drafting a contract on your behalf. The response would likely be: "Your job is to do what I tell you to do, not what *you* think you should do." This view of the legislator's role is one that was often expressed in the impassioned public debates that recently took place in Canada over the issue of same-sex marriages. Eventually, this issue found its way into Parliament, where each legislative member was required to stake his or her position one way or the other.[8] For each Member of Parliament the question that arose was: On what basis should I, as a representative member of this assembly, vote on the issue of same-sex marriage? One Canadian MP, Conservative Member of Parliament for Clarington-Scugog-Uxbridge, Beverly Oda, was happy to declare publicly what her answer to that question was going to be. According to one press report, Ms. Oda, who was herself very sympathetic to the recognition of same-sex marriages, announced that she would nevertheless not be moved by her own convictions when voting in the legislature. On the contrary, she reportedly "pledged to poll her constituents on how to vote" adding that "her vote [would] reflect the views of her constituents regardless of what she [thought]."[9] According to Ms. Oda, it would seem, the job of a representative is to ascertain, and act in accordance with, the expressed wishes of the electorate – even when, in her sincere judgment, the best interests of the electorate lie elsewhere, or are for some reason ill informed, inauthentic, or just plain wrong.

In the very same issue of the *Globe and Mail* in which one finds Ms. Oda's declaration, Conservative Party leader Stephen Harper expressed a position that is a bit more complicated. Upon chastising Prime Minister Paul Martin for his plan to "whip" members of his cabinet into voting in favour of same-sex-marriage legislation, Mr. Harper went on to declare that

... MPs are free to vote according to their *consciences* or *the wishes of their constituents*. This is the approach that the Conservative caucus will follow. While I support the traditional definition of marriage and will vote against the government bill as currently drafted I respect the freedom of my MPs – including my shadow cabinet – to disagree with me.[10]

---

8 The result was *Bill C-38: The Civil Marriage Act*, Statutes of Canada 2005, Chapter 33 (passed, 158–133, by the House of Commons on June 28, 2005, receiving Royal Assent on July 20, 2005). According to the Official Summary of the Act, it "extends the legal capacity for marriage for civil purposes to same-sex couples in order to reflect values of tolerance, respect and equality, consistent with the *Canadian Charter of Rights and Freedoms*."

9 *Globe and Mail*, December 14, 2004, A4. Emphasis added. Ms. Oda's decision was to vote against passage of the legislation.

10 *Globe and Mail*, December 14, 2004, A25.

From Mr. Harper's comments it is possible to discern the following. First, he objected to whipping Members of Parliament into voting for or against same-sex-marriage legislation: He wanted a "free vote" in the House. Second, he was himself opposed to legal recognition of same-sex marriages (though he was not opposed, he had repeatedly said, to same-sex civil unions conferring legal rights "equivalent" to those enjoyed by married persons). Third, it is clear that Mr. Harper did not himself share Ms. Oda's rather simplistic view of the representative's role. In his view, MPs should be "free to vote according to their consciences *or* the wishes of their constituents." Beyond this it is not clear what Mr. Harper thought. In particular, he left unanswered the difficult question of which of his two bases for decision is to be chosen in the event that they provide inconsistent guidance – as they did in the case of Ms. Oda. In other words, he did not say what he thinks a Member of Parliament's moral responsibility is when her own conscience pulls in one direction on the issue and her constituents' wishes pull in the other. It is not much help to be told that a representative can legitimately vote either way. A choice has to be made, and Mr. Harper's stated position provided the unfortunate Member with little help in making this difficult moral choice.

Let's see if we can make some further progress. There is good reason to think that Ms. Oda's position does not bear careful scrutiny. As our earlier discussion strongly suggests, overriding expressed wishes is precisely what is sometimes demanded of a morally responsible legislative representative, just as it is sometimes required in the case of a good friend, a loving daughter, or a patient advocate. It is perhaps here more than anywhere else that I run the risk of being labeled an elitist and paternalist. I seem to be assuming that a representative might sometimes have superior moral knowledge, or at least superior knowledge of her constituents' interests and authentic wishes – that she might know their interests and wishes better than they do – or that she might be better equipped to ensure that they act in accordance with them. In other words, I seem to be assuming that she is morally entitled to violate the autonomy rights of those whom she is supposed to be representing by acting on her superior knowledge and/or resolve. But how can this be the role of a representative? She is supposed to be representing their wishes, not telling them what those really are or should be – and, in effect, forcing them to act against their will when she acts on their behalf. Remember that the acts of a representative are supposed to be the acts of the represented – the former stand in for the latter.

So why would I risk calumny by suggesting that the representative's role is not always to respect the expressed wishes of constituents, even when it is clear what these are? There are a number of different reasons. Let's begin by returning briefly to the concept of representation and highlight a crucial aspect of that concept that we have hitherto left unexplored. As we have already seen, a representative is one who acts on behalf of someone else. When X acts as Y's representative, X's actions stand in for Y's – his actions are treated as identical, in the relevant ways, to Y's. In light of this key feature of representation, it is correct to insist that X's decisions and actions should normally reflect what Y wishes to be decided or have done. They are, after all, Y's decisions and Y's actions. But we can take this thought only so far. We must not underplay or ignore the fact that X is, himself, a responsible moral agent who, though he acts on Y's behalf, is morally responsibility for what *he*, X, does. This is a responsibility that *all* responsible moral agents bring with them in whatever role they are asked to serve. And in this particular instance, it is a role that X does not automatically fulfill by doing whatever Y wishes him to do. After all, Y's wish may be that X do something that is morally reprehensible. X may be required to heed Y's demand that A be done even if X thinks that B is the more prudent course, or if he thinks that Y's choosing B over A would be a better moral choice. He might also be required to heed Y's demand even if he thinks that choosing B would reveal Y (and perhaps, derivatively, X) to be a morally better person. But there are limits to the moral duties associated with the role of representative. It would be ludicrous to suppose that X is bound in his role as a representative to bring about the death of a third party if that is what Y demands. A representative cannot be required to check his other moral duties at the door when he assumes that role. He can no more escape his overall duties as a responsible moral agent in this way than a soldier can escape *his* overall duties as a moral agent by always following orders. The moral duty of a soldier to follow orders must give way to other duties if he is ordered to engage in a war crime. Among these other duties is the basic moral duty he shares with any responsible moral agent, in any context: the (*prima facie*) duty to avoid inflicting unnecessary harm on others. "I was only following orders" is often a strong defense – but it's a limited one. Analogously, "I was only doing what my constituents (or my client) wanted me to do" is a legitimate basis for decision – but it too is limited.

A second reason representatives are not always required to follow the expressed wishes of constituents is that the former sometimes *do* have superior knowledge. This is not because they are elite Platonic Guardians, or smarter, or better at reasoning than their constituents. It's because matters coming before a legislature are often highly complex, requiring a background knowledge that the average citizen simply does not have, and an attention to detailed facts and arguments that he has little interest in displaying. The reason citizens are generally lacking in these respects is more often than not that they are genuinely not interested in pursuing the relevant matters to the degree necessary for the responsible exercise of legislative power. Either that, or they lack the time and energy required for informed reflection and responsible decision making. We prefer, generally, to get on with the business of leading our day-to-day lives, leaving it to our elected representatives to sort things out for us – just as we leave it to our financial advisors to handle our investments, within agreed general guidelines and with periodic updating and vetting. That's their job; that's what we pay them for. Of course, the public's attention is drawn to the relevant issues on some occasions – if only at election time and if only via intervention by the media – and informed public debate ensues. Under conditions such as these, our representatives may not be in a better epistemic position than we are, and so superior knowledge could not be invoked to justify radical departure from expressed wishes. But it would be a mistake to push this point too far. Often the devil is in the details. Public debate tends to take place at a very general, sometimes superficial level. It is only when less abstract, concrete measures are contemplated that the full nature of the problems addressed, in all their gory detail and with all implications and consequences fully considered, becomes evident. Only then can informed decision making take place. This, we hope, is what occurs in legislatures – or at least in meetings of legislative committees where a good deal of legislation is hammered out before making its way to the full legislature. In light of all this, it is apparent that much goes on in the legislative process that does not rise to an adequate level of popular awareness and involvement. People have only a partial understanding of the issues at stake. In such instances, a responsible representative will no doubt consult with constituents and, if necessary, attempt to persuade her constituents that her view is the correct one and theirs is wrong. But in the end her efforts may prove unsuccessful. If so, then a representative may be entitled – indeed required – to act on her superior knowledge in supporting measures that conflict with the ill-informed expressed wishes of her constituents. This is especially true if the measures in question have the potential to cause serious harm to some members of the community – perhaps a minority group. It is here that the second of Stephen Harper's two bases of decision – voting one's conscience – takes effect, and it is here that one must always remember that legislative representatives are, themselves, responsible moral agents who cannot always escape moral accountability for their actions by appealing to their duty to honour the wishes of those whom they represent. Expressed wishes – the other of Harper's two bases – are not always well grounded in reason, fact, and sound moral philosophy. And the duty to follow orders is no more absolute for a representative than it is for a soldier.

A third – admittedly more controversial – reason for denying that expressed wishes must alone guide a responsible representative's decision is based on what we have been calling the authenticity, or lack thereof, of expressed wishes. There is nothing to rule out the possibility that a legislator might both intelligibly and legitimately judge that the community's expressed wishes on some issue are *inauthentic*. She can do so if only because a community's expressed wishes are sometimes inconsistent with the community's own basic beliefs, values, commitments, and settled preferences. These are expressed via, for example, the community's basic laws and political institutions, as well as through its many and varied social practices. Recall the case of the daughter who says "That's not my mother speaking!" Such declarations are prompted by the sincere belief that expressed wishes do not always reflect the agent's basic beliefs, values, commitments, and settled preferences. The mother always believed deeply that life is a divine gift and that it would be nothing short of an insult to God were not every possible effort made to sustain that life. But her suffering causes her to ask for termination. The daughter's sincere belief is that it's the pain talking, not her mother. And so as one who represents her mother in the making of medical decisions, she is faced with a moral dilemma. Does she decide in accordance with current and perhaps inauthentic expressed wishes and run the risk of causing her mother great harm? Or does she honour what she judges to be her mother's previously expressed, genuine wishes? Something analogous to this can occur in the case of a political community. As we shall see in more detail in Chapter 6, communities sometimes demand courses of action that are as "out of character" as the mother's expressed wish to die. They can do so for any number of reasons, not least of which are the prejudice and rampant fear that sometimes grip communities in the face of perceived threats to their security. Such fear sometimes leads them to demand courses of action – for example, the internment of citizens of Japanese descent during World War II – that introduce deep evaluative dissonance. The same is true in respect of the ongoing march of gays and lesbians towards equal status in Western societies. Much, though certainly not all, opposition to such measures as same-sex marriage is prompted by nothing more than a deep, visceral dislike of gay and lesbian sexual practices. As with the fear that sometimes grips a community, prompting a demand for measures that violate minority rights, such visceral reactions can prompt a demand for measures that discriminate unfairly against gays and lesbians. As we shall see shortly, phenomena such as these provide the basis for one of the strongest arguments in favour of judicial review: protection of minority rights and interests. But we should not get too far ahead of ourselves here. Our concern at the moment is restricted to seeing that the authenticity of expressed wishes can be challenged at the social as well as at the individual level. Under what conditions representatives are, in the end, entitled to issue and act on such challenges is not an easy question to answer, and certainly not in the abstract without attention to the intricacies of the system of representative government in place and the wider social and political context in which it is situated. Yet enough has been said, I believe, to show that this is at the very least a question well worth asking.

One final point of clarification, before we return to Demos and the reasons why it might want to adopt some version of judicial review. The argument made in the preceding few paragraphs was decidedly not in favour of the claim that representatives should sometimes override a community's expressed wishes on grounds of *best interests*. Though promoting best interests is indeed an important part of a representative's role in cases in which no serious moral issues arise, or in which there is little public interest or no wishes have been expressed, arguing in support of this proposition has not been my aim. Rather, it has been the much more modest one of arguing that a representative's role can sometimes require overriding one set of expressed wishes – the inauthentic ones – for the sake of honouring other expressed wishes, the genuine ones. Again, this is not to rule out, *a priori*, its ever being part of a representative's role to make judgments about the electorate's best interests, or even to balance these against expressed wishes when the latter are known. This proposal would come much closer than mine to a kind of paternalism that many will find inconsistent with the basic principles of representative democracy, and so it has been left out of the analysis. A case can be made for Charters and judicial review that rests on the less contentious ground that they represent a vital means by which a society can strive to honour *its own* basic beliefs, values, commitments, and settled preferences – that is, its own authentic wishes. If this is to promote paternalism, then it is a form of that practice which is perfectly acceptable within a democratic community.

G. Problems in Demos

Let's return to Demos and begin, with the foregoing discussion of representation in mind, to construct the Standard Case for Charters and judicial review. Remember that we are constructing a case that represents an amalgam of views held by Charter advocates. And recall that this case is one to which a number of serious objections have been raised, objections to which we will turn our attention in subsequent chapters. At this stage, our aim is get the Standard Case out in the open, warts and all. We have pursued this strategy so that we can (a) see why Charters are generally thought to be good things to have, (b) understand why certain critics think that they are terrible things to have, (c) determine how one might construct a better conception of Charters and a better case for adopting them, and (d) answer the many objections to Charters and the Standard Case that one finds scattered about in public and scholarly discourse. So if our Standard Case seems oblivious to obvious objections and complexities, bear in mind that this is quite deliberate.

Recall that Demos is a fictional democracy carved up into constituencies each of which elects one representative to a general legislative assembly. How might things go badly in this simple, representative democracy? One way might be in a failure of the system adequately to accommodate the concerns, interests, and wishes of minority members. Instead of looking at Demos as a whole, let's focus for now on one constituency, Athenia, and its elected representative, Atticus. Assume that Athenia contains a very small linguistically defined group, the Venusians, whose interests, wishes, language, moral convictions, and religious beliefs are significantly different from those shared by most other members of Athenia. Given their minority status, it is unlikely that the Venusians will have succeeded in helping to elect a representative whose actions in the assembly adequately reflect their issues and concerns. Atticus is, we will suppose, a highly responsible representative, and so he can be counted on not to go out of his way to ignore the Venusians and their minority concerns. But this may not be enough to lead him to give those concerns adequate airing and support in legislative debates and votes. In fact, in any case in which Venusian views, wishes, or interests are significantly at odds with those of the majority, it is more likely than not that Atticus will find himself compelled to support the latter if a choice has to be made. His commitment will ultimately be to the majority, and this will incline him away from supporting minority interests and concerns. He will, in effect, be *the majority's* representative, elected by *them* to serve *their* interests and honour *their* expressed wishes. Were he to do otherwise, he would be severely criticized for reneging on his duties as a representative, for allowing the "tail to wag the dog."

As an aside, it is worth noting that even if Venusians had formed the majority in Athenia, their interests and wishes might still have lacked adequate represen-tation. One can assume that, under these alternative conditions, Atticus could be counted on to voice their views and support their interests and wishes. After all, to do otherwise would, again, be viewed as allowing the tail to wag the dog. Furthermore, his success in the election will presumably have been based on widespread support among the Venusians and he will be keen, especially if he desires reelection, not to disappoint his base. But that might not be enough to guarantee success for the Venusians. It will not be enough if, for example, their numbers are restricted to Athenia, or if they form only a tiny minority in each of the other constituencies of Demos. The representatives of these other con-stituencies will, like Atticus, be keen to advance the views, wishes, and interests of *their* constituents who together would, under the stated conditions, make up a very powerful overall majority in Demos and its representative assembly. More or less permanent disenfranchisement of Venusians, on many important matters, will be an almost inevitable consequence of this scenario too, even though Venusians form a large majority in Athenia and have a representative who fully supports their concerns in both word and deed.

So in either of the two social situations just described, the concerns of Venu-sians are not likely to be adequately reflected in legislative measures. Let's restrict our attention to the first scenario, wherein Venusians constitute a small minority in both Athenia and Demos. It's simpler and so we can more easily see and explore the issues that concern us. Suppose a measure is before the Assembly that has the effect of denying Venusians the widespread freedoms of expression hitherto enjoyed by all members of Demos. A proposed language law denies citizens the right to use the Venusian language – this despite the fact that the vast majority of Venusians are fluent in no other language. Why might such a measure be introduced? And how might Atticus approach his decision whether to vote in favour of this particular legislative measure? What will he see his role as being and to which arguments – and political forces – is he likely to be responsive? In answering these questions we will begin to see the emergence of the Standard Case.

H. The Language Law

Let's begin by examining some of the reasons why the citizens of Demos might wish to see the language law enacted – even though it clearly submits Venusians to significant disadvantage.

i. The Greatest Good of the Greatest Number

There may be nothing more sinister behind the community's desire to adopt the language law than a simple failure to appreciate – or care about – the extent to which it affects the interests of Venusians. It is no doubt easier for people to converse with one another when they share a language. They thereby avoid the many costs and inconveniences associated with exercises in translation. In light of this, Demosians might see considerable advantage in encouraging everyone to learn and use the majority language. And the best way to encourage that, they might think, is to make it illegal to speak Venusian. Any disadvantages incurred by the few Venusians who are neither bilingual nor willing or able to acquire the Demosian language will be more than offset by the overriding interest of the majority in avoiding translation costs. The greatest good of the greatest number warrants this conclusion. Furthermore, Demos professes to be a democracy, and a democracy is a system in which the people are supposed to rule. Yet how else can the people rule except by way of majority votes that reflect what most of them think and wish? It's too bad for the Venusians, but they can always accommodate.

ii. Simple Prejudice

So lack of concern for the interests and wishes of Venusians might be behind the majority's support for the language law. This can be due to a lack of knowledge – failure to grasp and appreciate fully what it means not to be able to communicate in one's own language, and how difficult and inconvenient it can be to overcome this burden – or sheer indifference. In the first case, the majority doesn't know; in the second, it doesn't much care. Yet another possible factor might be deep-seated prejudice. It is an undeniable fact of human life that some people just don't like other people who are different from them in some noticeable way. This is true whether the difference resides in skin colour, ethnic origin, religion or gender, or in the fact that the other person speaks a different language or enjoys a different culture. Such people are apt, either consciously or without awareness, to discriminate against those who are different. Acts of discrimination can range from simple social ostracism to the denial of fundamental rights and freedoms that are generally accepted as applying to everyone else. Such might be the case here. Members of the majority in Demos might be deeply prejudiced against Venusians and be prepared to deny them full rights to free expression, including the right to speak their mind in their own language. They might support this denial even when the costs of full recognition, including the costs associated with translation funded at the public's expense, are quite minimal as compared with the serious hardship and insult caused to one who is denied the right to use her own language. For such prejudiced people, a tiny burden of inconvenience is something they are not prepared to shoulder for the sake of the much greater good of the smaller number. In fact, Demosians might dislike – indeed hate – Venusians so much that they would be prepared themselves to shoulder significant personal costs in order to *undermine* the latter's aspirations and interests. Prejudice sometimes goes that deep.

iii. Fear of "the Other"

So prejudice grounded in a variety of attitudes, ranging from simple dislike to intense hatred of those who are different, can lie behind support for measures that have a negative impact on the interests and wishes of other people. This prejudice is based on little more than the fact that these others eat different food, listen to different music, follow cultural practices that seem foreign, and so on. At other times, however, prejudice becomes combined with fear. The result can be a lethal concoction. Fear of the unknown and of the different are powerful forces, leading to deep suspicion and oppressive measures. In times of crisis this fear can lead to measures that would not be tolerated in normal circumstances. Once again, the example of the internment of North Americans of Japanese descent during World War II comes readily to mind. In this century, one's thoughts turn naturally to various anti-terrorism measures adopted by many Western nations, measures that deny the fundamental rights of certain minorities and come perilously close to the imposition of martial law. In this particular case, fear of the unknown has been an extremely powerful force. It has led us to lump some persons of a particular religious persuasion and/or descent together with others within these broad categories whose views and commitments we rightly fear. We fail to understand the Muslim faith and the cultures of those who profess it. We fail to appreciate that not all Muslims, and not all Arabs, sanction acts of terrorism, any more than all Catholics believe in papal infallibility. Our lack of understanding, and the prejudice and stereotyping to which it gives rise, when combined with our justifiable fear of militant strands of Islam or of those who misuse the tenets of the Islamic faith to rationalize their barbarous acts, has led us and our governments to measures we would otherwise be ashamed to endorse. They have led us seriously to compromise the fundamental interests of all Muslims and all people of Arab descent – to deny them their full civil and moral rights.

Suppose that something along these same lines has taken place in Demos. Suppose, in particular, that a tiny number of Venusians have begun, both privately and in public, to promote terrorist activity as a necessary means of bringing about political change. In their view, the concerns of Venusians have been suppressed or ignored for far too long. Something needs to be done. The only effective means of persuasion available under the present circumstances is to threaten, and carry out if necessary, terrorist activities. Only in this way will Venusians be heard. One can well imagine the language law's being the majority's first – if wholly misguided – response to these mounting pressures. Fearful of the result if they fail to act, one can easily imagine their attraction to the following line of reasoning:

> We need to cut this movement off at the knees before it can begin to get a foothold. The best way to do that is to stop militant Venusians from promoting terrorism. The only effective way to stop them from doing that is to deny them the primary vehicle through which they can most effectively marshal support for their cause. That main vehicle is, of course, use of the Venusian language, which is shared by all Venusians and which most of us do not understand. How can we ever be sure that terrorism is not being promoted right before our very eyes without our even knowing it? The best way to stop the terrorist threat is to adopt a flat-out ban on use of the Venusian language. Only in this way do we have any hope of ever being secure in our own homes.

Of course, this line of argument is seriously flawed on a number of fronts. First, it assumes that all or most Venusians share these militant views, or that they will be persuaded by the rhetoric of a few extremists either to join the cause or to turn a blind eye to what is going on. Speech can be powerful, but its effect can be overcome by reason and common sense. Second, it seriously underplays the role that language plays in a culture and minimizes the effects of its suppression on the people whose primary mode of communication it is.[11] Some stories cannot be fully translated, and some rituals lose all meaning when a different language is used.

The importance of language rights is grounded in the essential role that language plays in human existence, development and dignity. It is through language that we are able to form concepts, to structure and order the world around us. Language bridges the gap between isolation and community, allowing humans to delineate the rights and duties they hold in respect of one another, and thus to live in society.[12]

---

11 See, for example, Les Green, "Are Language Rights Fundamental?" *Osgoode Hall Law Journal* 25 (1987), 649; Denise Reaume, "The Constitutional Protection of Language: Security versus Survival," in David Schneiderman, ed., *Language and the State: The Law and Politics of Identity* (Montreal: Yvon Blais, 1991), and "The Group Right to Linguistic Security," in Judith Baker, ed., *Group Rights* (Toronto: University of Toronto Press, 1994).

12 *Reference Re Language Rights under s. 23 of Manitoba Act, 1870 and s. 133 of Constitution Act, 1867 [1985]* 1 S.C.R 721.

Language is so intimately related to the form and content of expression that there cannot be true freedom of expression by means of language if one is prohibited from using the language of one's choice. Language is not merely a means or medium of expression; it colours the content and meaning of expression. It is a means by which a people may express its cultural identity.[13]

Third – and perhaps in this particular context most important – the argument fails to account for the fact that the measures contemplated are more likely than not to be counterproductive. They are more likely than not to add support to the movement they were intended to suppress. One can well imagine hitherto nonmilitant Venusians reasoning as follows:

Our interests, aspirations, and views have not always been adequately represented by Atticus and respected by the majorities in Athenia and Demos. The result has been that we do not always get what we need and deserve. But Atticus is our representative, and he often does make good-faith efforts to promote our concerns in the legislature. He has not, of course, always done so. His role, as he rightly sees it, is to represent the concerns of all his constituents, of which we form only a tiny minority. Even when he has actively promoted our interests or voiced our particular concerns and points of view, he has not always met with success. This has been due to factors like ignorance, indifference, dislike, hatred, and fear on the part of the majorities in Athenia and Demos. However, these failures do not occur all the time. Sometimes our voice is heard and accommodated to our satisfaction, especially when the issue concerns a matter of fundamental significance to us but is of marginal interest to the majority. Our faith that the majority of Athenians and Demosians will either see, or be led to see, the importance of accommodating our different interests and concerns has not always been misguided. And after all, democracy is a system of give and take. Although we perhaps give more than we take, we have never been so badly off as to be left with no other option but threat of force. *But now this has all changed.* Our faith in the majority and its sensitivity to our concerns has been shown to have been misplaced, if not foolish. One of the fundamental elements of our very identity as Venusians – our language – is now under threat with the adoption of the language law. We obviously no longer have the respect of the majority, else they would never contemplate such an insensitive, unnecessary measure. They are prepared to treat us as second-class citizens unworthy of one of the most fundamental rights of democratic citizenship – the right to speak one's mind using whatever means of expression one finds it necessary to employ. If we cannot speak, we cannot be heard. We cannot live as Venusians. The only remaining option is for our actions to speak for us. The only actions likely to be heard in the sorry state to which Demos has descended are acts of violence. Terrorism is our only option. We have nothing to lose at this point.

In ascribing this line of reasoning to hitherto moderate Venusians, my intention is to suggest neither that it is the line that would inevitably be taken in the conditions described, nor that the reasoning I have ascribed to them is sound.

---

13 *Ford v. Quebec* (A.G.) [1988] 2 S.C.R. 712, at 716.

But it will likely be viewed that way by many who will find it eminently persuasive. Fear will have led Demos to a situation in which its very existence as a democratic society has been threatened.

I. Atticus and the Language Law

Let's now turn to Atticus. How might he respond to all this? In particular, to what arguments might he be receptive – and to which forces will he be susceptible? Let's begin by making explicit a key assumption that has been at work throughout our discussions of his role. Atticus is a man of principle, as one might expect of a character named after that other famous man of principle who appears in Harper Lee's splendid novel *To Kill a Mockingbird*.[14] Atticus Finch felt morally compelled to protect his client's legal rights despite the many risks he and his family thereby assumed in their fight to overcome hatred and prejudice in the American South. Our Atticus feels no less compelled to protect the interests of his "clients," despite the many risks he thereby assumes. His clients are, of course, all the citizens of Athenia. But included in this group are the Venusians, whose fundamental interests are threatened by the language law. Suppose that this law is brought before the assembly and Atticus must decide how to cast his vote. On what grounds will he base his decision?

We can suppose that Atticus has thought long and hard about the various issues we raised earlier when we explored the concept of representation. He will know, for example, that his primary duty as a representative is to act on behalf of his constituents, and that normally this entails honouring their clearly expressed wishes. He knows that the expressed wish of the majority is that he vote in favour of the language law. Were he to follow Beverly Oda's lead, he would of course respect that wish and vote in favour of the measure. Recall Ms. Oda's assertion that "her vote will reflect the views of her constituents regardless of what she thinks."[15] But Atticus will see the folly of this view. He will acknowledge that he is a responsible moral agent who cannot so easily escape his moral duties by relinquishing all responsibility to his constituents. To be sure, he is a legislative representative; but he is also a moral agent just like them. Among the duties he shares with them is the duty to avoid contributing to acts that cause significant harm to others. Yet this is exactly what he will be doing if he votes in favour of the language law. That law will not only be deeply harmful to Venusians, it is likely to be very harmful to every Athenian – indeed, every member of the wider Demosian community. Atticus will appreciate the extent to which the language law is likely to be counterproductive, how it is likely, in fact, to serve only to engender and strengthen the calls to violence

14 Harper Lee, *To Kill a Mockingbird* (Philadelphia: J.B. Lippincott, 1960).
15 *Globe and Mail*, December 14, 2004, A4.

it seeks to suppress. Given all this, it seems quite reasonable to think that
Atticus will deny that his duty lies in following the expressed wishes of his
constituents. Only a naïve view of a representative's role would lead him to think
otherwise.

Suppose, however, that Atticus remains unconvinced by the preceding line
of argument. He might, for example, lack confidence in his assessment of the
likely effects of the language law. Perhaps the Venusians will accommodate and
eventually be happy to speak Demosian. Indeed, they may come to believe that
terrorist activities can never be justified even in the face of grave injustice, if
only because of the cycles of violence that terrorism helps to perpetuate, and
the levels of mistrust, hatred, and prejudice it serves only to strengthen. If all
this might well turn out to be true, then perhaps his duty does reside in heeding
the expressed wishes of the majority – even though he thinks they are dead
wrong. They may not have quite the right reasons for wishing the language
law enacted, but maybe, just maybe, their view is the better one. What other
factors might Atticus bring to bear on his decision? In particular, what other
factors might incline him towards voting against the language law despite these
reservations?

At this stage in his thinking, Atticus might turn to the notion of authenticity
and question the extent to which the expressed wishes of (the majority of) his
constituents are in fact genuine or authentic. Recall our discussion of the case
in which I demand my car keys after the long night in the pub. Our conclusion
was that my expressed wish is inauthentic and that my friends were correct to
deny my request. This is not only because my best interests argued strongly in
favour of their rejecting my wish. It was also because acceding to my demand
would introduce a significant degree of evaluative dissonance. My friends easily
determined that there was a deep conflict between my current demand and
what were clearly my fundamental beliefs, values, commitments, and settled
preferences. A drink-emboldened machismo was behind my pleadings. *It* was
doing the talking, not me. Atticus might see the citizens of Demos and Athenia in
much the same light. Instead of machismo we have dislike, prejudice, and hatred
fuelled by fear, together with a demand for action that introduces significant
evaluative dissonance. Demos, we may suppose, is a community that values
moral equality. In other words, among its basic commitments is the belief that
all persons are entitled, as full members of the moral community, to what
Ronald Dworkin calls "equal concern and respect."[16] This commitment, we
may suppose, is expressed verbally and in public by people in Demos. More
frequently, it is expressed nonverbally, on an ongoing basis, in the day-to-day
lives of Demosians and the myriad activities in which they engage. It is also,

---

16 See *Taking Rights Seriously*, 180–3, 272–8. In drawing upon Dworkin here, I do not mean
to endorse his particular understanding of equality and equal moral status. It is being used
only for purposes of illustration.

we may suppose, expressed in various laws adopted by the Demosian assembly and in the fundamental democratic nature of their constitutional arrangements. The language law, however, seriously compromises this commitment. If so, then there is nothing to prevent Atticus from determining that the majority's expressed wish that the language law be enacted, and that he, Atticus, vote to support it, is *inauthentic*. And if this is so, then Atticus will have yet another reason to question whether his duty ultimately resides in following the expressed wishes of (the majority of) his constituents. Any qualms he might have had about the degree to which he risks contributing to the production of significant harm by voting in favour of the language law will begin to diminish. They will begin to diminish once the authenticity of the current demands comes into serious question. If my friends do no wrong in keeping my keys, then perhaps Atticus does no wrong in voting against the language law. My friends are only honouring my *authentic* wish to be a responsible moral agent who lives up to his most fundamental moral commitments. Atticus would only be honouring the *authentic* wish of Demosians to live up to their fundamental commitment to equal concern and respect.

Let's suppose, however, that Atticus is a very cautious man who remains uneasy. Reflecting a bit more on his role as a legislative representative, he reasons as follows:

Yes, Demos is committed to equality. And equality clearly argues against supporting the language law. But Demos is also a democracy, and whatever else we might mean in calling a system democratic, we mean that it is a system where "the people" are the ones who ultimately rule. It is a system in which no divinely ordained kings or queens, or Platonic Guardians with pipelines to the truth, determine for us how we shall be governed. It is a system in which it is the people themselves who make these decisions, normally through the voice of their elected representatives who act on their behalf, but sometimes in other ways, as when Regina ruled on behalf of her community. Right or wrong, the people of Demos have chosen democracy. And right or wrong, Athenians have, by way of clear majority consensus, determined that their wish is to see a language law enacted. If I am to honour their – and my – commitment to democracy, I must balance this against all the reasons pulling in the opposite direction. Perhaps I must vote in favour of the language law after all.

Atticus's reasoning brings us back to the fundamental questions about the nature of democracy to which we alluded earlier in this chapter. There we determined that modern democracies come in a wide variety of forms. We further determined that democratic systems utilize a number of mechanisms by which law-determining decisions are distanced from the people on whose authority they are ultimately made. Modern democracies typically employ decision procedures premised on majority vote. Furthermore, they are all indirect in nature, which means that they make use of select individuals, not all of whom are elected representatives, to make law-determining decisions, often by way of majority voting procedures.[17] This combination of factors can, as we have seen, lead to a feeling of disenfranchisement on the part of entrenched minorities like the Venusians. One who finds himself, perhaps consistently, on the losing end of majority votes taken in an assembly of representatives may well question the extent to which he is part of a process of *self*-rule. For him, such a system of governance may be no more responsive to his needs, interests, points of view, and aspirations than rule by a king. Indeed, it may respect his right to self-determination no more than a system premised on the divine right of kings.

So modern democracies are indirect and based on majority-rule decision procedures. It is this combination of features that is largely responsible for Atticus's dilemma. In pondering his duty as an elected representative empowered to contribute to the making of law-determining decisions, Atticus is in effect asking how he is to manage the distance between his judgments and those of the people in whose name he acts. Does the fact that his judgments are those of a *democratically elected* representative mean that he must ultimately defer to the wishes of the community? More precisely, does it mean that he must defer to the expressed wishes of the *majority*, despite the various countervailing considerations explored above? Does democracy trump or override all other factors? Atticus's answer to this particular set of questions will ultimately depend on which of two competing conceptions of democracy he endorses. There are, in actual fact, many different conceptions of democracy.[18] But however a particular theory is fleshed out in detail, it is likely to fall under one of two very broad umbrellas. The first umbrella we will call the "procedural conception" of democracy. The second will be called the "constitutional conception."

J. Two Conceptions of Democracy

As one might expect, the procedural conception views democracy as fundamentally a matter of the procedures or processes by which law-determining decisions are made. Samuel Freedman nicely summarizes this conception as follows:

... [W]e might understand democracy in purely procedural terms. By a procedural conception I mean the identification of democracy with a form of government

---

17 Even direct democracies that utilize majority rule might be described as having adopted a distancing mechanism. In direct democracies employing a unanimity rule, it is fairly clear how each individual contributes to self-governance. He never sees rules imposed upon himself to which he does not assent. There is no distance between his decisions and the decisions that determine the laws by which he is to be governed. Rules unanimously endorsed by everyone are as close as one can get to true "rule by the people," the animating idea of democracy.

18 See Thomas Christiano, *Philosophy and Democracy: An Anthology* (New York: Oxford University Press, 2003).

decision-making where each is guaranteed equal rights of participation and influence in procedures that determine laws and social policies, and where decisions are reached in accordance with the principle of majority rule. A procedural conception of democracy involves no substantive restrictions on outcome reached by legislative determinations, other than those rights necessary to sustain legislative procedures themselves.[19]

We would have a procedural conception in mind were we to characterize Demos as democratic in nature because: (a) each Demosian, including each member of the Venusian minority, is equally entitled to vote in general elections intended to select representatives to the Assembly; (b) the results of these elections are determined by majority vote; (c) in each instance the choice is of a representative who is empowered to act on behalf of the members of the particular community that elects him; (d) the needs, interests, wishes, and convictions of these members are the main factors to which the relevant representative is responsive when law-determining decisions are made; (e) these decisions are themselves also (or at least typically) made in accordance with majority-voting procedures; (f) by voting in this way for a representative whose role is conceived in this way, each Demosian *participates*, on equal footing with all other members of Demos, in the process by which law-determining decisions are made; that is, (g) he participates, on equal footing, in a process of *self-governance*. Whatever law-determining decision is generated under these conditions comes with a full democratic pedigree – that is, it is the product of an exercise in self-government. This will be true (h) regardless of the content of the particular decisions – the outcomes – generated by these democratic procedures. It will be true even if the decision reached is to adopt a language law.[20]

One who adopts the constitutional conception of democracy sees things very differently. She views democracy as fundamentally not about which decision-making procedures are followed but about whether, and to what extent, the particular procedures chosen, and the particular decisions made using them, respect what Ronald Dworkin calls "the democratic conditions." In Dworkin's view, these conditions can be many and varied. They include, for instance, the "requirement that public offices must in principle be open to members of all races and groups on equal terms."[21] Further conditions are necessary for democracy, and these are all subject to reasonable disagreement. But whichever set of conditions is settled upon in a particular theory or community, the claim is that these conditions derive their value from their contribution to the realization of

---

19 Samuel Freeman, "Constitutional Democracy and the Legitimacy of Judicial Review," *Law and Philosophy* 9 (1990–1), 335. Freeman himself endorses the constitutional conception.
20 As we will see shortly, the procedural conception is actually a bit richer than this description suggests. But for now, we can accept that description as our working account of the procedural conception.
21 *Freedom's Law: The Moral Reading of the American Constitution* (Cambridge, Mass.: Harvard University Press, 1996), 17.

democracy's animating ideal: the principle of equal status. Dworkin's particular version of the constitutional conception

> ... denies that it is a defining goal of democracy that collective decisions always or normally be those that a majority or plurality of citizens would favor [even] if fully informed and rational. It takes the defining aim of democracy to be a different one: that collective decisions be made by political institutions whose structure, composition, and practices treat all members of the community, as individuals, with equal concern and respect.... Democracy means government subject to conditions – we might call these the "democratic conditions" – of equal status for all citizens.[22]

So on Dworkin's conception of democracy, democratic decision procedures and the results of their use are justified only to the extent that they contribute to a state of affairs in which all members of the community are accorded equal status, which, in Dworkin's view, means that they are all treated with equal concern and respect. Dworkin goes on to add that his conception demands much the same "structure of government" – in particular, the same "majoritarian procedures" – as does the procedural conception. But "the constitutional conception requires these majoritarian procedures out of a concern for the equal status of citizens, and not out of any commitment to the goals of majority rule."[23] It follows from this that full compliance with majoritarian procedures in no way guarantees or entails that the system, or the decisions generated by these procedures, will warrant the honorific "democratic." Majority vote can lead to undemocratic decision making, and to particular decisions that are properly condemned as undemocratic. In other words, satisfaction of the procedural conception is at best a necessary, not a sufficient, condition of democracy. I say "at best" because it is not at all clear that the constitutional conception of democracy actually does demand majoritarian procedures in all circumstances. It was something like the constitutional conception that was behind my earlier claim that it is possible to view Regina's regime as approaching a rudimentary form of democracy, even though decisions were not made in anything like a representative assembly governed by majority-voting procedures such as one finds in Demos and modern democracies. One might reasonably claim that what determines whether a system is democratic is whether, and to what extent, the interests, wishes, and convictions of citizens are reflected in whatever decision-making procedure is adopted, and whether the adoption of that procedure is something to which all can be viewed as in some sense as assenting or agreeing. In Regina's case, both conditions were met – at least initially. This is not to deny that, in the real world of everyday politics, that democratic conditions cannot be realized unless majoritarian procedures are used in electing an assembly of representatives who themselves make use of this procedure. But as Dworkin might say,

22 *Ibid.*
23 *Ibid.*

there is nothing magical about these procedures independent of their tendency, in the world of human politics, to generate decisions that respect the principle of equal concern and respect and the goal of self-governance. And there is no reason to think that the adoption of such procedures would exhaust our commitment to democracy. In other words, even if the adoption of majoritarian procedures is a necessary condition of democracy, it does not follow that it is a sufficient condition.

So an important implication of Dworkin's constitutional conception is that there is "no reason why some nonmajoritarian procedure should not be employed on special occasions when this would better protect or enhance the equal status that it declares to be the essence of democracy, and it does not accept that these exceptions are a cause of moral regret."[24] If my thoughts in the preceding paragraph on the democratic pedigree of Regina's regime are correct, then there is no good reason to restrict such procedures to "special occasions." But whichever way one decides this particular issue, the fact remains that, on the constitutional conception, democracy is more about values such as equal status and self-governance and less about the decision-making procedures through which these values are (sometimes) realized. And this, in turn, has important implications for our investigation of judicial review. Empowering unelected judges to strike down legislation on the ground that it violates a Charter is often condemned as anti-democratic. It is condemned because it is thought to rob the people of the right to determine, through the decisions of their elected representatives, the laws by which they are to be governed. But if democracy is not so much a matter of who makes decisions using which procedures but a matter of whether the system chosen respects the equal status of all members of the community, then it is far from clear that judicial review is necessarily undemocratic. It is quite conceivable that a system which includes this mode of decision making might well end up respecting these ideals better than one that incorporates only majoritarian decision-making procedures. It is, in short, quite conceivable that a system which includes judicial review might well be preferable *on democratic grounds* to one that does not. Judicial review may not, in the end, conflict with democracy; it might be part of a system that turns out to be the most viable mode of its very implementation.

K. Atticus Again

It is time to return to Atticus and the decision with which he is faced. Recall that Atticus was inclined to vote against the language law because of the various arguments considered in the preceding section – it will likely cause significant harm to the community, it is based on inauthentic wishes, and so on. But he

---

24 *Ibid.*

remained troubled by the apparently undemocratic nature of such a vote. Voting against the language law appears to violate Atticus's commitment to democracy, a commitment he presumably shares with all members of his community. So he was left with a dilemma: He must either vote against a measure that he believes should not be passed; or he must vote in its favour because this is what his constituents want him to do. We are now in a position to appreciate that the way out of this dilemma will depend crucially on which of our two competing conceptions of democracy Atticus ultimately finds acceptable. Let's begin by examining the answer provided by the constitutional conception and then go on to consider the procedural conception, which, surprisingly enough, provides Atticus with some fairly strong reasons to vote against the language law.

It is fairly clear how the constitutional conception of democracy – or at least Dworkin's version of it – can be used by Atticus to support a negative vote. Given that the language law is apt to cause significant harm to the Venusian minority, that it significantly curtails their ability to engage in a variety of important cultural practices central to the Venusian way of life, that it is based on prejudice against and possibly hatred for members of the Venusian minority, and so on, a case can easily be made that the language law denies Venusians equal concern and respect. It clearly denies them the equal status as full members of the moral and political community it is the very purpose of democratic institutions to guarantee. It therefore flouts the animating ideals of democracy. It is, in short, a profoundly undemocratic law. It follows that a decision to vote against the language law can hardly be condemned as undemocratic, even if that decision runs counter to the clearly expressed wishes of the majority – and despite the fact that Atticus's primary (though, it is important to note, not absolute) duty, under normal conditions, is to respect the majority's wishes. But these are far from normal conditions. The ideals of democracy cannot demand decisions that blatantly flout these very same ideals.

So it is fairly clear how the constitutional conception supports Atticus's wish to vote against the language law. But the same can in fact be said of the procedural conception. Initially at least, it would seem to offer Atticus very little support. If democracy is solely a matter of following the correct procedures, and if those procedures have indeed been followed, then it would seem that the decision made, however questionable it might be on other grounds, can hardly be condemned as undemocratic. In other words, if democracy is a means by which citizens ultimately determine the laws by which they are governed, then democracy seems to require that the people's wishes concerning which laws should be enacted must always be respected.[25] And because it is clear that the people of Athenia, by way of majority consensus, support the language law,

---

25 Hence Ms. Oda's view on her duty to vote against Canadian legislation recognizing the validity of same-sex marriages.

democracy, on the procedural conception, seems to require that Atticus vote in its favour. At least that's how things might appear initially. Further reflection casts doubt on this simple picture.

Recall our earlier reflections on representation, evaluative dissonance, and the authenticity of expressed wishes. It made sense for the daughter to declare "That's not my mother speaking." It made sense for my friends to say "You don't really want to drive home in that drunken state." And, perhaps most important, it made sense to say, in each of these cases, that respecting the agent's fundamental convictions, values, and settled preferences is (or at least might be) the right course of action – even though it is contrary to the agent's currently expressed wishes. The same can be true here. This becomes apparent once we consider that the procedural conception is actually quite like the constitutional conception in requiring adherence to democratic conditions. The conditions are very different, of course, but they are conditions nonetheless. And if there is a failure to meet them, then the decisions generated, and quite possibly the system by which they are generated, can be of questionable democratic pedigree. But what are these conditions, and how could they figure in an argument to justify voting against the language law?

Let's begin by returning briefly to the constitutional conception. On this conception, it will be recalled, democratic procedures are justified only to the extent that they respect appropriate democratic conditions. In Dworkin's view, these conditions all derive from the animating ideal of democracy: equal concern and respect. If a decision, or the procedure(s) by which it is generated, seriously runs afoul of this ideal, then it, or they, can be condemned as undemocratic. Now one can in fact say much the same kind of thing on the procedural conception, the difference being in the ideal posited and the nature of (at least some of) the democratic conditions it supports. And the reason is this: Even on the procedural conception there is more to be said for democratic procedures than that they incorporate equal participation and majority decision making. The latter are democratic conditions – and they are of this nature because and to the extent that *they contribute to the ideal of self-governance*. It is this particular ideal that explains and justifies the particular democratic conditions recognized by the procedural conception. If the ideal is self-governance, then fulfillment of these and other democratic conditions is necessary as a means of achieving it. Among the relevant conditions are, of course, (a) equal participation and (b) majority rule. But they also include the requirement (c) that decisions reflect not the temporary, inauthentic wishes of an electorate but their more stable, authentic wishes, those which reflect and are consistent with their fundamental convictions, values, and settled preferences. In other words, there is more to the procedural conception than the fact that majority vote and sentiment determine the decision made. The "inputs," so to speak, must be *authentic*. Otherwise the "outputs" – the laws actually passed – will not contribute to the realization of *self-rule*. We will be no closer, as a community, to achieving true self-governance than I would have been had my friends allowed me to drive myself home in a drunken state. Bearing all this in mind, Atticus might well conclude that the majority's wish to see the language law enacted is clearly inauthentic. It is radically at odds with the fundamental convictions, values, and settled preferences of the majority of Athenians and Demosians. It's the fear and hatred talking, not the people he has been chosen to represent. If so, then acceding to this particular wish by voting in favour of the language law may in fact *detract* from the ideal of self-governance, the animating ideal of democracy on the procedural conception.

A fourth democratic condition deriving from the procedural conception becomes evident once we return to our earlier analysis of the doctrine of informed consent. A number of conclusions emerged from that analysis, among them the following: (1) Not all acts of consent are valid; (2) consent is valid only if a number of conditions are met; (3) these include the condition (a) that the agent is *legally competent*, (b) that consent is *freely given or voluntary*, and (c) that it is *informed*. We later added a further (admittedly contentious) condition (d) that the wish expressed in an act of consent must be *authentic* or *genuine*; and, finally, (4) that conditions (a)–(d) are required by the ideal of autonomy or self-governance. It is of crucial value in our societies that individuals retain as much control over their own lives and bodies as possible, that they be self-governing. Allowing them to determine when and if they are to undergo medical treatment is one important way in which we attempt to secure this value. Given that the procedural conception of democracy shares the ideal of self-governance, it's not at all surprising that it shares analogous conditions for what we might call *valid democratic decision making*. We have seen one of these already at work in the suggestion that, even on the procedural conception, so-called democratic procedures, and the decisions made using them, are justified only if and to the extent that they meet certain conditions – (1) and (2) above – that are in turn explained and justified by their role in promoting the ideal of self-governance (4). Yet another is at work in the claim that a decision by Atticus to vote against the language law could not properly be condemned as undemocratic because the community's demand rests on an inauthentic wish: 3(d). We can see another analogous condition at work in the claim that it is the fear talking, not the people of Athenia, strongly suggesting that the majority's wish to see the language law enacted, together with their demand that Atticus vote in its favour, is less than fully voluntary (3b). This is not the demand of a free people exhibiting autonomy and control over their lives but of a community drunk with fear.

But what about 3(c)? Is there something analogous to it that could help Atticus justify the vote he desperately wishes to cast? Let's suppose it would be stretching things to suggest that the majority in Athenia are not fairly well informed about what they are doing in supporting the language law and demanding that Atticus do the same. Let's suppose, in other words, that they appreciate how profoundly affected the Venusians will be if they are denied use of their own language. They are also cognizant of the serious risk of violent backlash that such a denial is bound to create. Furthermore, they are fully aware of the deep evaluative dissonance introduced into Demos by the language law and of how morally compromised Atticus will feel if he is forced to vote in its favour. Finally, let's assume that the majority is perfectly happy to live with all of these consequences. There may yet be a way for Atticus to stand his ground – to vote against the language law in the name of democracy.

Condition 3(c) tells us that consent is valid only if it is fully informed by all pertinent information. The reasons for this condition are fairly straightforward. To provide consent is to exercise one's autonomy, but autonomous decision is possible and valuable only when it is guided by sound reasoning and adequate information. There are two reasons why this is so – one consequential, the other rooted in deontology. First, one who chooses in ignorance often causes significant harm to himself and others. Being informed in one's choices allows one the opportunity to avoid such harms. Second, one who chooses in the dark can hardly be said to be exercising self-control – to be engaged in an exercise of self-*governance*. He is not governing himself so much as directing his conduct in an arbitrary fashion. We can say much the same about democracy. A people's capacity to govern themselves is possible and valuable only if and to the extent that their choices are informed by sound reasoning and relevant information. Otherwise, they run the risk of causing great harm to themselves and to others. They also fail miserably to live up to the ideal of self-governance. As Steven Holmes says, "Not any 'will,' but only a will formed in vigorous and wide-open debate, should be given sovereign authority."[26] But we have been supposing that Athenians are aware of what they are doing when, in an exercise of self-governance, they lend their support to the language law and demand that Atticus do the same. But are they, in fact, *fully* aware of *all* the relevant information? They may know the effects of such a law on the Venusians. They may also know about the possibility of backlash. But they have ignored the wider effects of such a law *on the democratic process itself.* These effects provide Atticus with considerable ammunition with which to oppose the language law on grounds of democracy.

As we have repeatedly seen, democracy is more than a matter of simply tallying up votes and allowing the wishes of a majority to carry the day. Democracy is, at a minimum, a commitment to the ideal of self-governance. To that end, it demands informed decision making. It requires, for both consequentialist and deontological reasons, that the people and their representatives be fully informed of information relevant to whatever social decision needs to be made.

---

26 Holmes, "Precommitment and the Paradox of Democracy," in Jon Elster and Rune Slagstad, eds., *Constitutionalism and Democracy* (Cambridge: Cambridge University Press, 1988), 233.

Yet as Mill is famous for stressing, informed decisions are possible only when competing points of view are aired, when dissenting voices are heard.[27] It is for this reason that democracy demands not only equal participation in the political process but also a very strong right to free expression. This is a point repeatedly stressed by countless authors and courts. In *Keegstra*, for example, the Supreme Court of Canada faced the question of whether Canadian Criminal Code provisions prohibiting the expression of "hate speech" unjustifiably infringe section 2(b) of the Canadian *Charter*, ultimately ruling in favour of the provisions. In her dissenting judgment, Justice Beverley McLachlin, considering the crucial role of free expression in a "free and democratic society," outlined the following bases for her dissent, bases that an earlier Court had developed in *Irwin Toy*:

First, "seeking and attaining the truth is an inherently good activity." Second, "participation in social and political decision-making is to be fostered and encouraged." Third, "the diversity in forms of individual self-fulfillment and human flourishing ought to be cultivated in an essentially tolerant, indeed welcoming, environment not only for the sake of those who convey a meaning, but also for the sake of those to whom it is conveyed": *Irwin Toy*, at p. 976.[28]

As McLachlin's analysis suggests, eliminating or reducing the capacity of individuals, particularly those in the minority, to voice their views and concerns hinders the pursuit of truth, curtails the capacity for individual self-fulfillment, stifles democratic political processes, and creates a less-than-welcoming environment for those whose views differ from the majority's. It can lead to heightened prejudice and to situations in which entrenched minorities – like the Venusians – will find it necessary to employ less agreeable means of meeting their needs than full participation in the political process. It can, in short, lead to the undermining of democracy itself. So the right to free expression, a vital cog in the very procedures by which his society has chosen to govern itself, provides Atticus with a powerful reason for voting against the language law. It provides a powerful reason that is not at all in competition with his (and their) commitment to democracy but one that is founded on that very ideal.

Atticus has reached the end of his reflections. He is now in a position to decide. It seems clear, in light of the various arguments put forth above, what his decision must be: He must vote against the language law. It has the potential to cause great social and personal harm; it is based on inauthentic wishes on the part of the electorate; it introduces significant evaluative dissonance; and it threatens the very democracy Atticus is sworn to uphold. Despite all this, Atticus continues to worry. Why? Because he is a politician who desires reelection. He knows that his constituents are wrong. But he also knows that

---

27 See John Stuart Mill, *On Liberty*, Chapter 3, "Of the Liberty of thought and discussion" in Stefan Collini, ed., J. S. Mill, *On Liberty and Other Writings* (Cambridge: Cambridge University Press, 1989).
28 *R. v. Keegstra*, at 827–8. p. 175; *Irwin Toy Ltd. v. Quebec* (Attorney General), [1989] 1 S.C.R., 927, at 976.

they will hold him accountable if he does not respect their clearly expressed wishes. Their very security is, they honestly believe, in the balance – and any representative who is insensitive to this fact is unworthy of that role. If he votes against the measure, Atticus will almost certainly be relieved of office at the first opportunity. Morality tells Atticus that he must reject the language law, but personal interest, combined with the harsh demands of electoral politics, compels him to cast his vote in its favour. Can he really be expected to do otherwise? He is, after all, only human. But recall that our Atticus was named after Atticus Finch, the courageous lawyer who was willing to run grave risk to defend an innocent black man. Our Atticus is equally a man of principle and equally a man of courage and firm resolve. He is unwilling, despite the call of self-interest, to pursue a course of action that he firmly believes to be deeply wrong. Despite the personal risks involved, he follows the lead of Atticus Finch. He votes against the language law.

L. Lessons to Be Learned – The Standard Case

It is now time to take stock. Recall our motivation in exploring the worlds of Regas and Demos and the questions we hoped to answer by engaging in that exploration. Our aim was a clear, manageable statement of the Standard Case for Charters. We wanted to know why a democratic society would choose, from among the numerous possibilities open to it, a system of government in which the powers of government are limited by an entrenched, written Charter of Rights. We also wanted to know why it might then call upon one of the parties whose powers are created and regulated by constitutional law and convention – the judiciary – to apply this Charter in ways that could ultimately thwart the will of the legislature and, arguably, the people upon whose authority the legitimacy of the entire system rests. We wanted to know what could possibly justify taking such a monumental step. We are now in a position to provide answers to these questions and in so doing, provide an informative sketch of the Standard Case in favour of judicial review.

Let's begin with the first question. Why would a democratic society opt in favour of an entrenched Charter of Rights? The most important reason is, of course, protection of minority interests and rights. Our discussion of the Demosian language law and the dilemmas it posed for Atticus was designed to reveal the extent to which minorities are vulnerable to what Mill famously termed "tyranny of the majority."[29] As we have seen, majority wishes and interests are likely to drive decision making in representative assemblies governed by majority rule. Even when a majority's motivations are perfectly honourable, sheer numbers will work against those whose wishes and interests are different. Majority-voting procedures, coupled with the fairly widespread belief that

---

29 Mill, *On Liberty*, 8. The phrase "tyranny of the majority" was taken from Alexis de Tocqueville's *Democracy in America* (New York: Schocken Books, 1961).

a representative's role is simply to vote as her constituents wish her to vote, make it almost inevitable that minority interests will be given short shrift. In other words, even when they function *as they should*, with each representative merely reflecting the best interests and the fully informed, authentic wishes of her constituents, democratic procedures will often leave minorities holding the short end of the stick.

No matter how open the process, those with most of the votes are in a position to vote themselves advantages at the expense of the others, or otherwise to refuse to take their interests into account. "'One person, one vote,' under these circumstances, makes a travesty of the equality principle."...[O]f course...sometimes...minorities *can* protect themselves by striking deals and stressing the ties that bind the interests of other groups to their own. But sometimes it doesn't, as the single example of how [American] society has treated its black minority (even after that minority had gained every official attribute of access to the process) is more than sufficient to prove.[30]

Demos and its language law provide yet another, no less dramatic illustration of the tendency in question. Majority-voting procedures will tend to marginalize minority interests, even under the best of circumstances. Again, this tendency does not reveal a major *defect* in majoritarian decision making, one that necessitates its utter abandonment in favour of some other means of making law-determining decisions. But it is a feature which gives one reason to think that it might well be supplemented by other forms of law-determining decision making. Further support for this thought emerges when factors like ignorance, sheer indifference, prejudice, hatred, and fear are added to the mix. In light of these and other factors, it seems clear to many that an entrenched Charter of Rights is essential for minority protection. It serves to protect vulnerable minorities from the excesses and inherent deficiencies of unencumbered majoritarianism. Instead of hoping – often against hope – that majorities will see the folly in denials of minority rights, either because the long-range interests of majorities almost always require the accommodation of minorities (backlash, threat of violence, etc.) or because such denials undermine equal status, which is a bad thing independently of any bad consequences such denials might cause, the most effective way to guarantee minority protection is to adopt a constitutional Charter. And the only effective way to ensure that such a Charter can serve its vital purpose is to entrench it and add to the constitutional mix the power of judges to enforce this Charter in constitutional cases. Judicial review, in other words, is the only viable option. U.S. Supreme Court Justice Robert Jackson expressed this point of view forcefully when he said:

The very purpose of a Bill of Rights was to withdraw certain subjects from the vicissitudes of political controversy, to place them beyond the reach of majorities and officials and to

---

30 John Hart Ely, *Democracy and Distrust*, 135, quoting J. Pennock, *Democratic Political Theory* (Princeton, N.J.:, Princeton University Press, 1979).

establish them as legal principles to be applied by the courts. One's right to life, liberty, and property, to free speech, a free press, freedom of worship and assembly, and other fundamental rights may not be submitted to vote: they depend on the outcomes of no elections.[31]

So a perceived need to protect minorities from the perfectly normal vicissitudes of everyday politics, and from the unjustifiable demands and excesses of majorities, is a fundamental plank in the Standard Case. By removing certain matters from everyday politics, we are able to achieve a better level of minority protection. We are better able to ensure equal status for all by ensuring that certain matters of fundamental importance depend on the outcomes of no elections. The best – perhaps only – way to do this is to enshrine minority rights in an entrenched Charter that, owing to its entrenchment, enjoys immunity from ordinary processes of political change. The answer to the question "Why entrenchment?" is implicit in the words of Justice Jackson. According to the Standard Case, effective Charter protection demands that certain matters be removed from the vicissitudes of everyday political controversy. Were the protection of minority rights left to legislative representatives – that is, were the latter able, via a simple act of legislation, to eliminate a minority protection whenever they chose to do so – protection would, in reality, be a sham. There would be a standing temptation to eliminate the protection whenever it seemed convenient or desirable to do so. Majorities could, under conditions such as we found in Demos, easily demand this of their representatives, who would, in all likelihood, follow Ms. Oda's prescription and do what their constituents wanted them to do. They would do so regardless of what they themselves might have thought about the matter. After all, most real-world representatives, honourable as they all might be, lack the moral fibre and insight of Atticus. Self-interest, and possibly misguided views about the demands of the representative role, will lead them to accede to the demands of their constituents. They will be led in this direction, even when they believe that those demands are ill informed, inauthentic, or motivated by prejudice, hatred, or fear. Entrenching Charter rights helps to eliminate this possibility. At the very least, it puts a brake on it. In summarizing F. A. Hayek's view on the subject, Stephen Holmes characterizes the need for entrenchment in a way that expresses this point rather well and brings to mind our earlier discussions of Demos, the language law, and my evening in the pub:

A [Charter], in his view, is nothing but a device for limiting the power of government. Present-day citizens are myopic; they have little self-control, are sadly undisciplined and are always prone to sacrifice enduring principles to short-run pleasures and benefits. A [Charter] is the institutionalized cure for this chronic myopia: it disempowers temporary

---

31 *West Virginia State Board of Education v. Barnette*, 319 U.S. 624, at 638, as quoted by Stephen Holmes in "Precommitment and the Paradox of Democracy," at 196.

majorities in the name of binding norms. A [Charter] is Peter sober while the electorate is Peter drunk. Citizens need a [Charter], just as Ulysses needed to be bound to his mast. If voters were allowed to get what they wanted, they would inevitably shipwreck themselves. By binding themselves to rigid rules, they can avoid tripping over their own feet.[32]

Enshrinement in an entrenched Charter then, is a means by which a society ties itself to the mast of its fundamental beliefs, values, commitments, and settled preferences. It is a means of helping to ensure that the legislative process never falls victim to the *inauthentic* wishes of a majority. It provides a (limited) immunity from such occurrences.

Yet another kind of immunity is introduced when the main burden of enforcement rests on the shoulders of judges. Unelected judges enjoy immunity from the political pressures to which even the most honourable and courageous politician are subject. Atticus found it very difficult to displease his constituents and came close to allowing his wish for reelection to tip the balance in favour of a positive vote. It is far from clear that a less resilient and courageous legislator could bring himself to do the same. We might even question whether it's fair to put him in the position where he is forced to make such a choice. Perhaps it is better to adopt a constitutional structure in which legislators are, to some extent at least, relieved of Atticus's burden. They are relieved of this particular burden by the knowledge that there are unelected judges better placed to deny the majority what they erroneously want and demand – that is, who have a kind of immunity from the effect of those political forces. This latter point is an extremely important one, largely missed or ignored by many critics. The claim is not that the judges are smarter, more honourable, or more courageous than the typical legislator, that they are the guardians of principle while the politicians are preoccupied with the pork barrel. Rather, the point is that their role, and the expectations and forces that go hand in hand with it, is decidedly different. Judges are, by virtue of their station, far less vulnerable to the forces and expectations under which Atticus and every legislator are forced to labour. And for this reason, they might be better situated to be guardians of minority rights and interests.

In Chapter 6, where we take up and answer many of the critics' challenges, this last line of argument will be explored in greater detail. For now, consider the following (somewhat loose) analogy, which might give some initial credence to the suggestion that we should look favourably upon the division of labour herein being proposed. Physicians are normally expected to pursue the medical interests of their patients as vigorously as possible, with whatever resources are made available to them and within boundaries set by law and policy. They must do everything they can, within these parameters, to make us well or to

---

32 Holmes, "Precommitment and the Paradox of Democracy," 196.

manage our suffering. Now imagine how displeased you would be if things were different. Suppose a situation in which your doctor declines to provide appropriate and available treatment on the ground that it would be better spent on some promising new medical research study. Suppose further that existing laws and policies sanction your treatment, but it's also the case that the system in which the physician discharges his responsibilities, authorizes him to question an existing policy, and to act on what he thinks would be a better alternative. And in your case, he correctly reasons that the money is better spent on the study, because there is little chance of the sanctioned treatment's succeeding in your case. This would pretty clearly be an inferior system to the one within which physicians, for the most part, currently work. It is far better to have a system in which physicians do all they can to help their individual patients within general boundaries set by someone else – someone else who is, at least temporarily, removed from the forces at play at the bedside. It is better if such "detached" persons determine binding guidelines, unencumbered by, for example, the prospect of having to tell someone who could be helped that the money is better spent elsewhere. To have physicians make such calls is unfair *both to the physician and to the patient* – and would no doubt be an entirely inefficient way of managing scarce medical resources. So we opt for a division of labour: physicians pursue their patients' interests as vigorously as possible, while third parties (sometimes a group of physicians wearing a different cap for the time being) establish general rules and guidelines free from the pressures and concerns that drive them in individual cases.

A somewhat similar analysis can, I think, be applied, to the practice(s) of judicial review. Having legislative representatives make all the calls in favour of minority protection may well be unfair to *them*, not only to the minorities whose interests may not be adequately protected under such an arrangement. It might also be an entirely inefficient way of ensuring an adequate level of minority protection. As we shall see more fully in Chapters 5 and 6, judicial review removes such decisions from the effects of political forces inevitably at play in majority-rule decision making. And for this reason alone it could well be the better option. At the very least, this seems a likely possibility.

So far we have been focusing exclusively on minority protection. Of course, members of minority groups are not the only ones who can be in need of protection in democratic societies. This need often extends to individual persons as well, many of whom are not members of a minority group, or ones whose threatened interests are related to their minority status. As Justice Jackson states, the purpose of a Charter or Bill of Rights is to place some subjects beyond the reach of majorities *and officials*. A government official or agency that unjustifiably withdraws a broadcast licence from one who is overly critical of government policy, or a judge who imprisons a person without due process or fines a reporter who declines to reveal his confidential sources, can be as much a threat to rights and other fundamental interests as any law adopted by a majority. Several of the rights and freedoms figuring in typical Charters – for example, the rights to free expression; due process; and life, liberty, and security of the person – are as much concerned with protecting individual interests as they are with protecting minority groups.

So the protection of minority and individual interests from government and majority excesses is a central element of the Standard Case. We'll conclude the present chapter by briefly exploring three other, less central elements of that case. In calling them "less central" I do not mean to imply that they are any less important than minority and individual protection. Indeed, at least two of them – the claim that the adoption of a Charter typically raises the level of public debate about matters of fundamental moral importance and the claim that a Charter can contribute to the establishment of a nation's moral identity – are equally important in the case for judicial review. This despite the fact that they are underplayed in both popular and scholarly discourse. Part of my aim, in later chapters, will be to develop these points in fashioning a better conception of Charters than the one presupposed by both critics and advocates of judicial review.

M. Further Elements

Chapter 1 began with a number of colourful pronouncements by a group of Canadian politicians who were instrumental in orchestrating the Charter revolution in Canada. According to the principal architect of that constitutional revolution, Prime Minister Pierre Elliott Trudeau, it was time for Canadians to "establish the basic principles, the basic values and beliefs which hold [them] together as Canadians, so that beyond [their] regional loyalties there [would be] a way of life and a system of values which [made them] proud of the country that [had] given [them] such freedom and such immeasurable joy."[33] Trudeau's Minister of Justice Jean Chrétien, who himself went on later to become prime minister, added the following, less colourful, observations:

In a free and democratic society, it is important that citizens know exactly what their rights and freedoms are, and where to turn to for help and advice in the event that those freedoms are denied or rights infringed upon. In a country like Canada – vast and diverse, with 11 governments, two official languages and a variety of ethnic origins – the only way to provide equal protection to everyone is to enshrine those basic rights and freedoms in the Constitution.

Now, for the first time, we will have a Canadian Charter of Rights and Freedoms that recognizes certain rights for all of us, wherever we may live in Canada. . . . Now that our

---

33 The Right Honourable Pierre Elliott Trudeau, cited in *The Charter of Rights and Freedoms: A Guide for Canadians*, 1.

rights will be written into the Constitution, it will be a constant reminder to our political leaders that they must wield their authority with caution and wisdom.[34]

It is possible to discern, in the words of Trudeau and Chrétien, a number of further elements we can add to the Standard Case. Charters bring with them increased knowledge of rights. Instead of one's having to scour the law books and case reports for evidence of one's basic moral rights, Charters place them front and centre. Furthermore, they tell one what to do in the event that one's basic moral rights are denied or otherwise infringed. Charter rights enjoy, in other words, a place in public space that is often absent when other means of ensuring basic rights are relied upon. Not only are citizens well served in this regard. According to Chrétien, politicians too benefit from the enshrinement of basic moral rights in a Charter. When rights are written into the constitution, there "will be a constant reminder to our political leaders that they must wield their authority with caution and wisdom." Again, Charter rights enjoy a prominent place within public space and consciousness, a place that renders them less vulnerable to political and official abuse. Evil and other such negative forces tend to shun the light of public awareness.

So two further benefits of Charters, according to their advocates, are (a) increased knowledge and awareness of moral rights and (b) more effective enforcement of moral rights, owing to the prominent place held by Charter rights within public space. A closely related benefit, claimed by many advocates, is the raising of public debate concerning fundamental questions of political morality. According to Ronald Dworkin, among the foremost of advocates,

> When an issue is seen as constitutional . . . and as one that will ultimately be resolved by courts applying general constitutional principles, the quality of public argument is often improved, because the argument concentrates from the start on questions of political morality. . . . When a constitutional issue has been decided by the Supreme Court, and is important enough so that it can be expected to be elaborated, expanded, contracted, or even reversed by future decisions, a sustained national debate begins, in newspapers and other media, in law schools and classrooms, in public meetings and around dinner tables. That debate better matches [the] conception of republican government, in its emphasis on matters of principle, than almost anything the legislative process on its own is likely to produce.[35]

As we shall see in Chapter 4, this argument is vigorously opposed by Jeremy Waldron, our principal critic. But there is no denying that it represents, if sound, a powerful reason in favour of judicial review.

Two final elements in the Standard Case, not so prominent in public and scholarly discourse, are again evident in the words of Trudeau and Chrétien.

---

34 *Ibid.*, Preface, v.
35 *Freedom's Law*, at 345.

Charters, they claim, introduce a uniformity of rights that is often lacking in nations of diverse interests, ethnic communities, and cultures. A good deal of Saskatchewan law is different from Ontario law, which is in turn different, in a good many respects, from the law of Quebec. The cultural practices of those Canadians who embrace a fundamentalist strand of Islam are very different from the corresponding practices of those who embrace a fundamentalist strand of Christianity. Absent a Charter applying to all provinces, all territories, and all communities, what is condemned as discriminatory in one location might well be considered perfectly legitimate in another. The adoption of a national Charter is said to change all that. "Now, for the first time, we will have a Canadian Charter of Rights and Freedoms that recognizes certain rights for all of us, wherever we may live in Canada . . ." So uniformity of rights protection across a nation is one of the claimed benefits of a national Charter.

A closely related benefit is alluded to by Trudeau. Charters not only introduce uniformity across the nation. They also express a common commitment to a set of values and ideals that can help establish and enforce a kind of national moral identity – an identity of which all members of the nation can be rightly proud. A Charter has the capacity to "establish the basic principles, the basic values and beliefs which hold [a nation] together . . . so that beyond [their] regional loyalties there is a way of life and a system of values which make [them] proud of the country . . ." It helps to establish the nation's moral identity as one committed, publicly, to recognition of the rights its enshrines. It is, in short, a public declaration that it is a nation defined, in part, by its *taking rights seriously*.[36]

36 I am, of course, alluding here to the title of Dworkin's influential book.

4

The Critics' Case

A. The Road Ahead

We have now examined the Standard Case for judicial review. As we have seen, a number of different arguments figure in this case. For example, judicial review is often applauded for the protections it is said to afford minorities or individuals whose moral rights are threatened by government action or inaction, and for the help it provides in securing certain fundamental conditions of a thriving democracy. Sometimes these conditions are thought to derive from the constitutional conception of democracy. At other times they are said to follow from a less ambitious procedural conception. But judicial review is not without its detractors. Many public figures and scholars – whom we lumped together and dubbed "the Critics" – are equally adamant in condemning judicial review on a wide range of philosophical and practical grounds. Because the principal aim of this book is a plausible defence of Charters and the practices of judicial review to which they give rise, it is incumbent on me to explore and answer the Critics' most important objections. This I shall begin to do in the present chapter. In defending a practice, the best strategy is usually to address the arguments of its strongest critic, and it is for this reason that we will be focusing, though not exclusively, on the work of Jeremy Waldron, who, in two important books, *The Dignity of Legislation* and *Law and Disagreement*, argues strenuously against Charters and their enforcement by judges.[1]

Waldron's formidable critique represents the most serious challenge to the intelligibility and desirability of judicial review existing in the literature. In our engagement with his arguments and those of his fellow Critics, we will be addressing some of their vulnerable points. But, more important, we will be setting the stage for a more positive effort: the development of an alternative to the conception of Charters that underlies both the Critics' critique and the

---

1 Jeremy Waldron, *Law and Disagreement* (Oxford: Oxford University Press, 1999); Jeremy Waldron, *The Dignity of Legislation* (Cambridge: Cambridge University Press, 1999).

contrary views of the Advocates with their Standard Case. I will be particularly concerned to challenge what I think is their shared picture of the primary role(s) a Charter plays within the realms of law and politics. As we shall see, most authors view Charters as attempts to provide a (more or less) stable, fixed point of agreement on and pre-commitment to moral limits to government power – limits found, paradigmatically, in moral rights upon which valid government action is supposedly not to infringe. In other words, most authors view Charters as resting on what we earlier called "the fixed view" of constitutions. Typically the relevant government powers a Charter purports to limit via the fixed points it aims to establish are exercised in legislative actions, but as we saw earlier, they can be exercised in any number of other ways as well, for example in executive or judicial orders or in decisions by administrative bodies empowered by legislation to develop standards or render decisions within particular domains of competence. The Advocates argue that such fixed, stable limits to government powers are not only possible, despite some acknowledged measure of disagreement and controversy about their precise content, and despite the inevitable changes to them which are inadvertently brought about through constitutional amendments and landmark interpretations of a Charter's provisions; they also argue that this stable framework of limitations is, largely for the reasons outlined in the two preceding chapters, highly desirable, perhaps even essential, both morally and politically. Recall the claim of Prime Minister Jean Chrétien in Chapter 1 that "it is important that citizens know exactly what their rights and freedoms are, and where to turn to for help and advice in the event that those freedoms are denied or rights infringed upon." In Chrétien's view, the Canadian Charter provides this essential knowledge. According to the Critics, it can do no such thing, thus sowing the seeds of a very heated, largely intractable debate. Many Critics – and Waldron is no exception – challenge (a) the very *intelligibility* of the Advocates' conception of Charters; (b) the moral and political *desirability* of attempting to have them play the assigned role; and (c) the various *arguments* and *analogies* put forward in defense of (b). The agreement and pre-commitment presupposed by the Advocates' fixed view simply cannot exist within what Waldron aptly calls "the circumstances of politics." These circumstances consist in the "felt need among the members of a certain group for a common framework or decision or course of action on some matter, even in the face of disagreement about what that framework, decision or action should be."[2] They include not only the desire to act in concert politically and in ways that do not infringe the fundamental rights of individuals; they also include radical disagreement about how we should go about achieving these results – that is, deep disagreement about what our rights actually are and how they are to be understood and applied. These disagreements extend to questions

2 *Law and Disagreement*, 102.

concerning whether to adopt a Charter, what rights to include within it, and how these rights are to be applied in the concrete circumstances of everyday life and politics, and, perhaps most important for our purposes, in the Charter disputes that these inevitably bring to light. According to Waldron, "it looks as though it is disagreement all the way down, so far as constitutional choice is concerned."[3] Yet if members of a community cannot agree, at any particular moment in time, let alone across generations, on the nature and content of the moral rights enshrined in their Charter, they cannot intelligibly pre-commit to the stable, fixed point of constitutional limits within which government power is supposed to be exercised on their behalf. Instead of a relatively stable, fixed point of pre-commitment, imposed by the people themselves and enforced by judges on their behalf, they will, in adopting a Charter, have offered an ill-advised, open-ended invitation to judges to impose unprincipled and arbitrary constraints upon their right to self-determination; and whatever else might be said about them, such impositions cannot possibly be squared with the ideals of democracy. And even if, at some moment in time when the decision is taken to enshrine a set of Charter rights, we happen to have complete agreement on which rights to include and how these are to be interpreted and applied, the fact of the matter is that citizens in a few years' time will inevitably disagree with some or all of the previously agreed-upon answers. Why, then, should the people-*now* be bound by what the people-*then* agreed were appropriate constraints on the powers of government? How can this possibly be squared with the ideals of autonomy and ongoing self-government at the heart of our democratic commitments?

If this "Standard Conception" or "Standard Picture" of the role Charters are supposed to play is accepted, then there is no doubt that the Critics will eventually win the day. An Advocate might attempt to establish a temporally extended, perhaps even cross-generational, basis of rational, implicit, or hypothetical agreement upon which some notion of democratically legitimate pre-commitment could be based by offering a philosophical theory that, in his view, no reasonable person, then or now, could possibly dispute. But it is not clear that this strategy will, in the end, work. The main problem is one that Waldron highlights to great effect: No theory of political morality has ever stood the no-reasonable-disagreement test, and there is little hope that one ever will.[4] Rawlsian "burdens of judgment" apply to philosophers as much as to legislators, judges, and ordinary citizens, leading to the inevitable conclusion that we will all continue to disagree about moral rights so long as we remain human beings with an interest in politics, political theory, and the pursuit of what we

---

3 *Ibid.*, at 295.
4 This indictment extends to Waldron's own theory. The significance of this fact will be addressed in Chapter 6, section I.

judge to be the good life.[5] One might alternatively seek a basis for agreement in something less ambitious than sound moral philosophy. One might, for example, attempt to base it on an "overlapping consensus" of moral judgments held within the community over time, even if that overlapping consensus fails, in the view of some at least, to stand the test of philosophical scrutiny. Perhaps one could discover something like Rawls's "free standing" political conception of justice that could serve as the basis of a kind of shared "public reason" that naturally finds expression in Charters. But as many have pointed out, even here the prospects do not look very promising. Supposing that some such consensus could be found – and I think it often can – it is not clear that it could ever be stable over time. Whatever overlapping consensus about racial equality may have existed 200 years ago in Western democracies, it is pretty clear that it is significantly different from any consensus that might exist at the present time. In Canada, any overlapping consensus that might have existed as little as five years ago on the question of gay marriage would have been plainly against the practice. At present no such consensus exists, or, if it does, it has shifted in favour of the idea. But if this kind of shift occurs, as it appears to do on a fairly regular basis, then we are left wondering, once again, about the very intelligibility of the notion that Charters can, to any extent, be thought to represent stable, fixed points of agreement and pre-commitment that render them helpful not only in securing fundamental rights but also in ways that are consistent with democratic ideals, let alone an embodiment of them.

Much in the Critics' case commands our respect if not our agreement. If Charters are conceived in the way that the Standard Case presupposes – if, that is, we think of them as attempts to establish fixed points – then it is not at all an easy task to defend them. In fact, the task may be impossible to accomplish with even a modest degree of success. So if our instincts tell us that Charters *must be* good things to have in a constitutional democracy, we would do well to challenge the very conception of Charters that is being presupposed in these debates between the Advocates and the Critics. And this is exactly what we shall be doing in the remaining chapters. Instead of attempting to discover a basis upon which the notion of rational pre-commitment to a stable, fixed point of moral agreement could be based, we will explore an alternative account of Charters

---

5 In *Political Liberalism* (New York: Columbia University Press, 1996), Rawls writes that "the idea of reasonable disagreement involves an account of the sources, or causes, of disagreement between reasonable persons so defined. These sources I refer to as the burdens of judgment . . . [They are] the many hazards involved in the correct (and conscientious) exercise of our powers of reason and judgment in the ordinary course of political life" (55–6). The burdens of judgment include things like conflicting evidence, disagreements about the proper weighting of evidence, vague and indeterminate concepts and conceptions, differences in individual backgrounds that influence individual interpretation of evidence, and so on. These burdens can result in different judgments based on the same "evidence," differing judgments that are nevertheless "compatible with those judging being fully reasonable" (58).

and the roles they aspire to play. On this conception, Charters are far from aspiring to set fixed points, and, it is important to note, they do not presuppose the level of confidence in the rectitude of our moral judgment presupposed by most Advocates. I am going to suggest that we instead view Charters as representing a mixture of only very modest pre-commitment combined with a considerable measure of humility about the limits of our moral knowledge. The latter stems from recognition that we do *not* in fact have all the answers when it comes to moral rights, and that we should do all we can to ensure that our moral short-sightedness does not, in the circumstances of politics, lead to morally questionable government action. Far from being based on the (unwarranted) assumption that we have the right answers to the controversial issues of political morality arising under Charter challenges, the alternative conception stems from the exact opposite: from a recognition that we do *not* have all the answers, and that we are best off designing our political and legal institutions in ways that are sensitive to this feature of our predicament. *Contra* Waldron and his fellow Critics, Charters need not be seen as embodying a naïve confidence in our judgments about which rights count, how they are to be interpreted, and which political actions (including legislative acts) are consistent with fundamental rights. Charters can and should be viewed as representing a *concession* to our *inability* fully to understand both the nature of fundamental rights and how these might be infringed by government action – and this includes, paradigmatically, government actions premised on the relatively blunt instrument of binding general legislation. Once we see Charters in this very different light – once we, in effect, adopt a Copernican revolution in our understanding of Charters and judicial review – we can begin to see a bit more clearly not only why they might well be good things to have, but we can also see our way clear to answering the various arguments offered by Waldron and other Critics against their adoption. Or at least that is what I hope to show. But it is time to return to the task at hand, which is an initial exploration of the Critics' case.

We'll begin, in the following section, by analytically separating four questions concerning Charters. These questions are often run together – by both Advocates and Critics – in discussions of judicial review, leading, of course, to inevitable confusion and argument at cross-purposes. It will be important to try our best to prevent this from happening here. In the remainder of the chapter, I will sketch some of the more popular, standard objections to Charters on offer from the Critics, attempting, as I did with the Advocates' Standard Case, to outline their objections and arguments in as sympathetic and forceful a manner as possible. This is not to say that the presentation will be wholly uncritical. As noted very early on, the Critics' rhetoric often outstrips the soundness of their arguments. When appropriate, this will be noted. Ultimately, however, the aim is to set the stage for the development of my alternative conception of Charters. As we shall see, each of the objections considered crucially relies on the standard conception of Charters sketched above, that they aspire to establish fixed moral

made because the UK has long recognized constitutional limits on Parliament; some of these are statutory in origin, while others have emerged as part of the common law or are matters of constitutional convention. Yet another reason is that the UK has, for some time now, been engaged in a debate over the relative merits of adopting a constitutional Charter of Rights.[7] Closely connected to Question 1 is, of course, Question 2, which would have us ask why we would want a Charter that serves the role assigned to it by our answer to Question 1. Because the focus is, once again, on constitutional democracies, the answer we end up giving to Question 2 will be intimately tied to the nature of constitutions and constitutional democracies and our reasons for wanting some version of that form of government.

In answering Question (3) it is important to bear in mind that judicial review actually comes in a variety of different forms. It is often assumed, in discussions of the relative merits and deficiencies of judicial review, that the form in question is the very strong form adopted in American practice. On the received view of that particular form of the practice, a U.S. Supreme Court's determination that the actions of some other court or branch of government exceeds its constitutional authority under the Bill of Rights renders that action invalid – of no legal force and effect. It is not law. But this is far from being the only form of judicial review on offer: There are alternatives to this system of judicial supremacy. For example, in New Zealand courts rule on the constitutionality of legislation even though they are barred from striking it down. New Zealand's *Bill of Rights Act* 1990, section 4, states: "No court shall, in relation to any enactment (whether passed or made before or after the commencement of this Bill of Rights) – (a) [h]old any provision of the enactment to be impliedly repealed or revoked, or to be in any way invalid or ineffective; or (b) [d]ecline to apply any provision of the enactment – by reason only that the provision is inconsistent with any provision of this Bill of Rights." Furthermore, section 7 provides for the Attorney General to intervene in legislative debate to warn of a possible infringement of the Bill of Rights. "Where any Bill is introduced into the House of Representatives, the Attorney-General shall, (a) [i]n the case of a Government Bill, on the introduction of that Bill; or (b) [i]n any other case, as soon as practicable after the introduction of the Bill, bring to the attention of the House of Representatives any provision in the Bill that appears to be inconsistent with any of the rights and freedoms contained in this Bill of Rights."[8] In

---

7 Among those on the Advocates side of the UK debate is Ronald Dworkin, whose book *A Bill of Rights for Britain* (London: Chatto and Windrus, 1990) argues strenuously in favour of the idea. Among those on the corresponding Critics' side is, of course, Waldron, whose views are carefully outlined in *Law and Disagreement* and *The Dignity of Legislation*.

8 I owe these references to a paper, "Some Models of Dialogue between Judges and Legislators," delivered by Waldron at a conference at the University of Western Ontario in September 2003 and published later in *Constitutionalism in the Charter Era*, eds. G. Huscroft and I. Broadie (Markham, Ontario: Butterworths, 2004), 7–47.

Canada, the legislative override included in section 33 of *The Constitution Act* empowers Parliament or a provincial legislature to introduce, for a period of time and subject to renewal every five years, legislation that the legislative body acknowledges either infringes a right enshrined in the *Charter* or is inconsistent with a judicial ruling – in the view of the legislature, an incorrect ruling – on what that right means or entails for legal purposes. Although the Notwithstanding Clause, as section 33 has come to be known, is not frequently invoked, and despite the belief by some that something approaching a constitutional convention has arisen forbidding its use, the fact remains that section 33 is available to Parliament or a provincial legislature bent on escaping the effect of a Supreme Court decision. This is hardly the strong form of judicial review – arguably a form of judicial supremacy – that is in operation in the American constitutional system.[9]

Finally, we come to Question (4), which can – and should – be broken down into two further questions. First, there is the *normative* question, (4a), concerning the kinds of decisions judges *should be* making when they apply and enforce a Charter of Rights – that is, the kinds of factors to which they *should be* appealing in justifying their decisions.[10] But there is the equally important *empirical* question, (4b): whether they are in fact making such decisions and successfully appealing to such factors, or doing something else entirely. It is vital that Questions (4a) and (4b) be distinguished from each other and from Questions (1) and (2). In particular, it is crucial that the question of whether a Charter is a good thing to have be distinguished from the question of what the judges have in fact been doing with it – that is, (4b). As we saw in Chapter 1, judges are often roundly condemned for the decisions they make in Charter cases. They are sometimes said to be "too active" or "too political," to have usurped the role properly played by members of the legislature. Recall the words of Jeffrey Simpson, by no means one of the Canadian judiciary's harshest critics. Following the *Montfort* decision, Simpson wrote:

That decision was one of the most aggressive in asserting judicial supremacy over Parliament. It dismissed parliamentary debates on the issue as having offered "more fulmination than illumination." . . . So much for the vaunted but rather tattered notion of the Supreme Court and Parliament engaged in a "dialogue." It's more like diktat from the court.[11]

---

9 For discussion of the Notwithstanding Clause, see, for example, Jamie Cameron, "The Charter's Legislative Override: Feat or Figment of the Constitutional Imagination"; Janet Hiebert, "Is It Too Late to Rehabilitate Canada's Notwithstanding Clause?"; and Tsvi Kahana, "What Makes for a Good Use of the Notwithstanding Mechanism?" in *ibid*. Though not directly on the Canadian Notwithstanding Clause, but of equal interest and relevance, is Mark Tushnet's "Weak-Form Judicial Review: Its Implications for Legislatures," which can be found in the same volume.

10 We explored some of the standard answers to this question in Chapter 2.

11 "The Court of No Resort," *Globe and Mail*, Friday, November 22, 2002, A25.

It would be easy – but dead wrong – to infer from such indictments that Charters are bad things to have and that Canadians would be better off abandoning that instrument in favour of a form of parliamentary supremacy associated with Dicey. But this follows only if the judges are performing as they should be. Perhaps the answer to the problems detected is to insist that judges change their approach in dealing with the Charter, to display, for example, a greater degree of deference to the judgments of Parliament. Of course an argument can always be made that such judicial misbehaviour is an inevitable consequence of judicial review, regardless of the role officially assigned to the judiciary and despite any good-faith efforts on the part of judges to do better. Be that as it may, it remains true that an *argument* to that effect must be made. It is not enough to find fault with an isolated Charter decision, or even a string of such, and to infer from this that Charters are not good things to have. Were the argument only that simple.

So it is important that the preceding four questions be distinguished from one another. This is not to suggest, however, that the questions are completely unrelated. This is far from true. For instance, the answer one gives to Question (4a) will depend crucially on how one answers (2) and (3). The reasons why Charters are (or are not) good things to have, and the type of judicial review they licence, are all factors that are bound, in one way or another, to have a bearing on how they should be applied and interpreted. For instance, a court whose decisions do not have the effect of striking down a legislative act, or whose decision can, as in Canada, be overridden by a special legislative initiative (section 33), might feel much freer to interpret a Charter's moral provisions according to moral views not widely shared within the legislature or the general population than would be true were the court's decision to have the effect of rendering the law invalid or inoperable. In the former case, a kind of built-in safety valve can serve to relieve the burden of final judgment that is bound to be felt in the latter system. If no such safety valve is built into the process of judicial review because, for example, the court's decision has the effect of overruling the legislature's judgment and is binding, the judges may feel (perhaps justifiably) hesitant to intervene or to offer unorthodox interpretations, preferring instead to be far more deferential to the legislature's pronounced moral views and intentions or the views widely shared within the community. Their deferential attitude – which they might reasonably believe to be fully justified given the nature of the Charter and the considerable power it provides them – could well lead judges to seek refuge in factors like "legislative intent" or "plain meanings," factors that will appear to relieve them of the responsibility of expressing and enforcing their own substantive moral views.

In a similar vein, the ways in which one answers Questions (2) and (3) are going to depend on how one conceives the role served by a Charter – that is, on how one answers Question (1). As we have seen, the standard answer to (1) goes something like this: All constitutions, written or unwritten, include norms that create and structure the organs of government – that is, the fundamental executive, legislative, and judicial powers that together give shape to political and legal systems. But constitutions that include Charters go well beyond this; they entrench certain basic moral rights as fixed points that the organs of government created by the constitution are forbidden from infringing upon when they exercise their constitutionally licenced powers – at least until such time as a formal constitutional amendment is introduced, something that happens very rarely and requires levels of political will, commitment, and agreement that can be very difficult to marshal. Most other substantive issues of policy and principle are up for grabs in the everyday thrust and parry of political decision making, but Charters set fixed moral limits upon which (ideally at least) everyone is in agreement. They represent agreed-upon moral boundaries for the legally valid exercise of government power.

Many standard reasons are offered both in public discourse and in the philosophical literature for this kind of arrangement. These add up to the Standard Case. Charters are heralded as useful or essential vehicles for the protection of minorities from Mill's tyranny of the majority. They are viewed as embodying the rational pre-commitment of the community to observe certain fundamental rights essential to (a) enlightened democratic rule and (b) the free and equal exercise of individual autonomy. (a) is thought to require such things as the right to vote and freedom of the press, while (b) is thought to require artistic freedom, equality before and under the law, the right to privacy, to use of one's own language, and so on. These are all stressed, to varying degrees, by Advocates such as Rawls, Dworkin, and Samuel Freeman.[12] Although the factor is seriously underplayed in arguments surrounding their merits or drawbacks, Charters are also applauded for the symbolic value they are capable of embodying. They can help define and reinforce the character of the nation as one publicly committed, in its legal and moral practices, to the fundamental rights and values it includes. As such, they help establish the identity of the community and serve as the moral and conceptual backdrop within which public policy debates take place.

With these preliminaries now firmly in mind, it is time to turn to the Critics' case against Charters. Again, it is important to bear in mind that the case outlined represents an amalgam of different views voiced by a number of different individuals, with different complaints, and offered from different philosophical, moral, and political perspectives. As with my earlier rendition of the Standard Case in favour of Charters, it is hoped that the sketch of the Critics' case herein provided does not in any way distort or mislead. It is also hoped that it will serve to highlight both the good sense contained within many attacks on

---

12 See Rawls, *A Theory of Justice* and *Political Liberalism*; Dworkin, *Taking Rights Seriously, A Law's Empire, A Bill of Rights for Britain, Freedom's Law: The Moral Reading of the American Constitution*, and *A Matter of Principle* (Cambridge, Mass.: Harvard University Press, 1985); Freeman, "Constitutional Democracy and the Legitimacy of Judicial Review" (1990), *Law and Philosophy* at 9.

judicial review, as well as the excessive rhetoric sometimes contained within them. Finally, it is hoped that an exploration of the Critic's case will provide us with a profitable springboard from which to move on to the alternative common law conception of Charters, an alternative that allows us to answer the Critics' most serious objections by revealing a entirely different way of conceiving of judicial review.

C. The Case Against

i. The Denial of Self-Government

The most common and persistent objection to Charters is that they seriously compromise the ideals of democratic self-rule. This objection stems mainly from two of the key features of constitutional Charters explored in Chapters 2 and 3: entrenchment and judicial enforcement. Among the many lessons learned from the plight of Atticus is that the effectiveness of a Charter of Rights arguably requires its entrenchment against the actions of majorities who might, if they could do so easily through simple majority vote, be motivated to circumvent constitutionally recognized moral limits on their power. That is, they or their representatives might be inclined to circumvent these limits by eliminating them, or by interpreting them in a way that effectively allows them to achieve the same result. Their motivation in pursuing such a course of action could stem from any number of reasons. These include, as we have seen, sheer ignorance, simple dislike, and hatred or fear of the unknown. An entrenched Charter, with its inherent resistance to change, eliminates, or at the very least reduces, these possibilities. It is a mechanism by which the community is able to tie itself to the mast of ongoing moral commitments made to minorities and other threatened individuals. It helps the community ensure that it acts only on the basis of *authentic* wishes.

A second lesson arguably learned from Atticus's dilemma is the need for judicial enforcement. According to the Advocates' Standard Case, courts must be called on to play a central role in a Charter's enforcement, including its enforcement against otherwise valid legislative initiatives, if it is to achieve its essential purposes. Individual and minority rights, even if entrenched, are not likely to receive adequate protection if their enforcement lies in the hands of the very majorities (and their representatives) who will often be motivated to infringe upon them. When push comes to shove, the perceived demands of self-interest, especially when fuelled by factors like fear and prejudice, will inevitably trump any majority's concern for the moral rights of vulnerable individuals and minorities. And representatives who lack the moral fibre of Atticus, or his complex understanding of the multi-faceted role of a democratic representative – which includes, as we saw, the responsibility sometimes to act against a majority's (inauthentic) expressed wishes and one's own self-interest – will inevitably succumb to these demands. The only effective way to combat this particular feature of representative democracy is to place the power of judicial review in the hands of unelected judges, usually those enjoying life tenure, in whose care the protection of minority and individual rights is more secure. To do otherwise would be to leave the fox in charge of the henhouse.

As one might expect, Critics are deeply troubled by these two key features of constitutional Charters highlighted in the Standard Case. In their view, the constitutional arrangements described cannot possibly be reconciled with the ideals of self-government or self-rule that lie at the very heart of democratic forms of government. Despite everything that might be said in its favour, there is no escaping the fact that entrenchment is a mechanism that can *thwart* the will of the people. It can restrict the people and their representatives from doing things they might now wish to do, and from achieving results they now wish to realize. It restricts them by imposing conditions that have often been set by other individuals who lived generations ago. Say what you will about the moral shortcomings of unbridled democratic procedures, the fact remains that these are the only forms of political decision making in which a free people's ongoing right to choose is respected, in which their right to determine, on an ongoing basis, the laws by which they are to be governed is actually given concrete, meaningful expression. Entrenching a judicially enforced Charter either removes or seriously hampers that choice. It works against the possibilities of self-government.

Things get even worse when one adds judicial enforcement to the mix. Allowing (largely) unelected judges to overrule the considered views of responsible, representative legislators represents the complete abandonment of self-government. It represents an unflattering admission that we are better off allowing a small cadre of judicial elites to make our decisions of political morality for us than we are making those decisions ourselves, if only through the agency of our elected representatives. Why, it is asked, should we not feel slighted by this kind of admission? Have we not here conceded that we are incapable of self-government? Jeremy Waldron clearly thinks so.

. . . if A is . . . excluded from [a] decision (for example because the final decision has been assigned to an aristocratic elite), A will feel slighted: he will feel that his own sense of justice has been denigrated as inadequate to the task of deciding not only something important, but something important in which he, A, has a stake as well as others. To feel this insult does not require him to think that his vote – if he had it – would give him substantial and palpable power. He knows that if he [or his elected representative] has the right to participate, so do millions [or hundreds] of others. All he asks – so far as participation is concerned – is that he and all others be treated as equals in matters affecting their interests, their rights, and their duties.[13]

---

13 *Law and Disagreement*, 239.

To think that a constitutional immunity is called for is to think oneself justified in disabling legislators in this respect (and thus, indirectly, in disabling the citizens whom they represent). It is . . . worth pondering the attitudes that lie behind the enthusiasm for imposing such disabilities.[14]

So entrenchment and judicial enforcement are said to threaten the very principles of democratic self-government. But is this really so? Let's begin with the problem of entrenchment.

ii. Entrenchment and Self-Government

According to Critics, Charter pre-commitment permits the "dead hand of the past" to determine our choices today, a situation that undermines the very notion of self-government. Not so, say the Advocates. Self-government is respected, perhaps even enhanced, because in constitutional democracies it is the people themselves who have chosen, in a free act of self-government, to impose the relevant limits on themselves.[15] Recall the analogous case of my drunken night in the pub. In a free act of rational, moral self-commitment, I exercised my right of self-determination by handing my car keys to my friends, knowing full well that they would later reject my drunken demand that the keys be returned. My decision to tie my hands in this way in no way *denigrates* my right of self-determination. On the contrary, it is a particularly noble expression of it. Waluchow sober has put in place a rational means by which the predictable, *inauthentic* wishes of Waluchow drunk have been disabled. It is a means by which I am able to ensure that my *authentic* wishes remain effective. The same is true of a people and their decision to bind themselves through judicial review. In so doing, the community, in a free act of rational, moral self-commitment, exercises its right of self-determination by entrenching a Charter and placing its enforcement in the hands of judges. Just as I count on my friends not to accede to my later demand, the community counts on its judges not to succumb to powerful demands that conflict with its authentic wishes and moral commitments. They do so by giving their moral keys to these judges.

Enticing as this analogy might be, it is open to at least one very serious objection. It would appear that the people who have signed on to the entrenched commitments one finds in a Charter are seldom identical to the people whose options are being restricted. In other words, those who do the committing are more often than not different from those who are expected to live by those commitments. A crucial feature of the pub example is that the one bound and the one doing the binding – in both cases me – are one and the same person. It is *this* feature which explains why we are able to refer to my decision as an

---

14 *Ibid.*, 221.
15 Remember, we have restricted our analysis to indirect, constitutional democracies.

exercise in rational *self*-determination. We would not be able to say the same thing, however, if this feature were absent. Imagine the following variation on the example: Suppose that it is not I who hands the keys over to my friends, but my father. Now my father may be a wise man – indeed, his wisdom may surpass mine in countless ways. And so there may be very good reason to think, in any given case, that his practical decisions will be better than mine. There might, as a consequence, be every reason to think that, when it comes to pubs and the consumption of copious pints of Old Peculier, his decisions about how best to protect against the macho impulses that almost inevitably lead to drunk driving will be better than mine – they might be grounded in better reasons. And so everyone affected by my actions might be better off if he intervened and arranged for my friends to take my keys and if they agreed not to return them to me. All this may be true. But so is the following crucial point: My right to self-determination will still have been infringed upon. And if this is among the most important of my moral rights, then it is quite possible that the actions of my friends and my father are in no way justified.

According to the Critics, much the same is true when we turn to a judicially enforced Charter. It too represents a serious infringement upon the right to self-determination, an infringement that, in this particular case, cannot possibly be justified. The reason is quite simple. The moral limits enshrined in a judicially enforced, entrenched Charter are, as noted, often ones that were set years, perhaps generations, ago. This means that the individuals through whose actions the limits were imposed are usually not identical to the ones who are expected to abide by them. This leads to an inevitable question: Why should the people-now be restricted in their current choices by what the people-then might have decided were appropriate limits to entrench in a constitutional document – especially given the bias against change that constitutional amending formulae typically build right in to constitutions?[16] Regardless of what else might be said in its favour, such an arrangement compromises democratic ideals. It is flatly *inconsistent* with the notion of ongoing self-government that lies at the heart of such ideals. This follows in any situation where it's not one and the same community that imposes and is expected to live by the required limits. The people-then are not the people-now any more than I am my father.

True, I am not my father. But perhaps the people-then are indeed identical to the people-now. Is it obvious that the American people of 1906 are not the same as the American people of 2006? Jed Rubenfeld thinks not. In fact, in his view, they *must* be the same people if the ideal of self-government is to be realized.

Of all animals, only humans make history; only humans make themselves over time. Extended temporality is a constituent part of our being. To be a person takes time. A

16 There is a further, related question to which some attention will be given shortly: Not even everyone who might be living at the time of its adoption can reasonably be thought to have consented to its imposition.

person, we might say, does not exist at any given time. This means that freedom is possible only over time. To be free in the human sense, it is not sufficient to act on one's will at each successive moment. That is animal freedom. Human freedom requires a relationship of self-making to one's life as a whole. It requires individuals to give their temporally extended being a shape or purpose of their own determination. . . .

Similarly, to be a people takes time; it takes generations. To realize within a polity a new set of foundational principles may take a century – or two or more. To be self-governing, a people must attempt the kind of self-government that takes place over generations. It must attempt the reins of time.[17]

If Rubenfeld is right, then the people-then, who committed to the American Bill of Rights and its various amendments, may indeed be identical to the people-now, who continue to be bound by those commitments. Some might think that this way of looking at community identity is utter nonsense, or at best an exercise in poetic license. But consider what we are prepared to say in less contentious cases. Few deny that Tony Blair, Oxford undergraduate, is identical to Tony Blair, prime minister of the United Kingdom, despite the facts to which Locke long ago drew our attention: The bits of matter and thoughts and memories of undergraduate Tony are very different from those of the prime minister.[18] They are of course all related to one another, and to the matter, thoughts, and memories of Tony Blair as he existed at various points of time in the interim, but they are not the same. Despite all this, we continue to think of the Oxford undergraduate and the prime minister as one and the same person. Blair's case is of course one of *personal* identity: that is, identity through time concerns one and the same person. And so any analogy drawn between Blair's case and the case of a *community* like the United States that comprises many different people living at many different times is not as strict as one might like. So let's consider a case in which the analogy is a bit tighter. In one perfectly acceptable sense of the term "identical," Babe Ruth's Boston Red Sox team is identical to the team that won the World Series in 2004. The assumption of identity is reflected in claims like "The Red Sox hadn't won the World Series in over 80 years" or "The curse of the Bambino hung over the team for close to a century." Such claims apply to a team comprising many members but with

---

17 Jed Rubenfeld, "Legitimacy and Interpretation," in L. Alexander, ed., *Constitutionalism* (Cambridge: Cambridge University Press, 1998), 213–14. Cf. Harry Wellington, "The Nature of Judicial Review," *91 Yale L.J.* 486, especially 494, where Wellington writes: "[A] government structure that fails to unite a nation's present with its past necessarily fails to preserve values to which its citizens may attach considerable weight. It fails to make a contemporary effort to understand what we have been or have wished as a people to become, and thus it fails to give effect to what might be called the moral ideals of the community."

18 Locke's views on identity, including "personal identity," can be found in his book *An Essay Concerning Human Understanding*, but especially in Book II, Chapter XXVII, "Of Identity and Diversity." For a more recent, but already classic, discussion of personal identity, see Derek Parfit, *Reasons and Persons* (Oxford: Oxford University Press, 1984).

an identity of its own, an identity that extends over time and outlives that of its current and past members. We are prepared to view the Red Sox as a team that exists through the decades, despite the different individuals who, from time to time, serve as current members. Group identity is not, of course, restricted to teams. For example, this metaphysical status is assumed whenever a nation claims the accomplishments of its members as its own. Nations take pride not only when their athletes excel in international competition, viewing such acts of accomplishment as at least partly their own; they do so when one of their own writes an outstanding symphony or invents a device that revolutionizes the way we do things. Germans are rightly proud of Beethoven's Ninth, claiming it and their celebrated composer as one of *their own*. They are also rightly ashamed of the Holocaust, a stain not only on the record of the Nazis and those who facilitated their horrific reign but also on the moral record of the German people itself – a stain for which many modern Germans feel responsible and for which they continue to seek atonement.

So the notion of community identity is not entirely lacking in plausibility. A thorough examination of this complex issue requires, of course, a level of metaphysical analysis well beyond the scope of this book. But enough has been said, I hope, to make us at least pause in accepting uncritically the Critics' claim that entrenchment cannot possibly be reconciled with the ideals of self-government because the self that imposes entrenched Charter restraints is seldom the self that is expected to live by them.

The Critic has one further card up his sleeve in responding to the Advocate's case for entrenchment. Suppose we accept the idea of community identity over time. Suppose, in fact, that we accept Rubenfeld's claim that both personal and community self-determination *require* identity over time. It may also require commitments, to self and others, that extend well beyond the initial moments of commitment. That is, a community that changes its commitments to minorities and vulnerable individuals as people change their clothes is not a community engaged in practices of self-government. Fair enough. But now consider the following equally important point: Self-government, like self-determination, requires the capacity to *change one's mind*, to reevaluate and alter one's commitments in light of changing circumstances and increased knowledge. Self-government means *ongoing* self-government. One is hardly free if one is never able to change one's mind or alter one's course of conduct. But this ability is precisely what entrenchment all but eliminates. It denies a community the power to reevaluate and alter its commitments as new circumstances arise and new knowledge is acquired. By denying it the right to change its mind, entrenchment effectively denies self-government. It flies in the face of democratic ideals.

How might an Advocate respond to this particular point? No doubt his first move will be to suggest that the Critics' argument seriously overstates the extent to which entrenchment really does affect a community's ability to change its mind. This is a case in which the rhetoric clearly overwhelms the logic of the argument. After all, constitutional amending formulae are (almost) invariably included within Charters. They may be difficult to trigger, and amendments may sometimes be all but impossible to secure politically, but the fact of the matter is that the people have these devices within their control. And these do allow for change if there is enough consensus in their favour. If there is sufficient consensus in favour of fundamental change, and yet institutional mechanisms and political forces work together to ensure that it fails to find expression in constitutional change, then the people have one final resort at their disposal: alteration or abandonment of the constitution and its substitution with something better.[19] Perhaps a constitution with less restrictive amending formulae is the answer. And if a movement in this direction fails too, then there is always the option of revolution, a right to which a free people are ultimately entitled to resort.

A second response open to the Advocate gets a bit closer to the heart of the matter. One might ask whether, in mounting his case against entrenchment on democratic grounds, the Critic is implicitly relying on a particular conception of democracy. In suggesting that entrenchment is problematic because it hinders the people's ability to act on their current choices, one cannot help but wonder whether the Critic has thereby assumed the procedural conception of democracy. According to this conception, it will be recalled, democracy is fundamentally a matter of correct procedures. It is fundamentally about procedures through which the wishes of the majority can be rendered effective on an ongoing basis. Because entrenchment clearly puts roadblocks in a majority's way, it is easy to see why, on the procedural conception, it might be thought to compromise democracy. But as we have seen, democracy is arguably about something a bit more fundamental than an efficient way to render the current wishes of the majority effective. The constitutional conception, we noted, denies that it is a defining goal of democracy that collective decisions always or normally be those with which a majority of citizens are in agreement, or would be if fully informed and rational. It takes the defining aim of democracy to be quite different. On one prominent version of that conception, the goal of democracy is to ensure "that collective decisions [are] made by political institutions whose structure, composition, and practices treat all members of the community, as individuals, with equal concern and respect. . . ."[20] If so, then it is not at all obvious that entrenchment is necessarily undemocratic. If it is part of a complex set of

---

19 Bruce Ackerman argues that the U.S. Constitution has actually undergone a number of less formal amendments since its inception. In *We The People: Foundations* (Cambridge, Mass.: Harvard University Press, 1991) and *We The People: Transformations* (Cambridge, Mass.: Harvard University Press, 1998), Ackerman suggests a "dualist conception" of American democracy according to which the people have from time to time engaged in "higher lawmaking" that resulted in profound change to their constitution. These transformative occasions Ackerman terms "constitutional moments."

20 Dworkin, *Freedom's Law*, 17.

political institutions that helps secure conditions under which all members of the community, as individuals, are treated with equal concern and respect, then it may well be a valuable democratic tool.

This brings us to a third response open to the Advocate, one based on the views of Joseph Raz. In his penetrating analysis of the authority and interpretation of constitutions, Raz considers a number of different ways in which one might attempt to justify a constitutional regime, one that presumably includes features like entrenchment.[21] He begins with the possibility that justification derives from the authority of a constitution's authors or framers. This is the view of those who seek to justify the U.S. Constitution (or a particular method of interpreting it) by invoking the authority of framers like Jefferson and Madison. On this theory, the U.S. Constitution is justified because it was the creation of framers who possessed the authority to create and establish a constitutional regime. An immediate question that arises for any such analysis is: Why should we think that *these* individuals had that kind of authority? In other words, why should we suppose that *their* decisions and actions were, and continue to be, authoritative? The answer cannot, of course, be their legal authority, because legal authority exists only when there is a constitution in place to which one can ultimately trace that authority. Statutes have authority because they are enacted by Parliament or Congress, each of which in turn has the legal authority to create laws because of the constitution. It follows that any attempt to ascribe *legal* authority to the founders will be the product of circular reasoning.[22]

So the authority in question cannot be legal. Perhaps it's moral, the only other obvious possibility. What could possibly justify the claim that the authors of the U.S. Constitution possessed moral authority to create what they did? The only obvious answer would appear to be their superior moral and political knowledge or acumen. The frequency with which American politicians, judges, and scholars invoke "the wisdom of the framers" in justifying a constitutional claim strongly suggests that it is exactly this possibility which many of them have in mind. It is important to note, however, that this argument has little hope of establishing the legitimacy of the U.S. Constitution unless our interest is in its legitimacy at, or very near, the time of its adoption. It's not likely to justify authority today, if only because social conditions have changed and knowledge,

---

21 Raz, "On the Authority and Interpretation of Constitutions," in Alexander, ed., *Constitutionalism*.

22 As Raz notes, few constitutions actually originate, from scratch, in the actions of founders. Most "are made by legitimate authorities as part of a process of legal reform. Even constitutions that stand at the birth of a new independent country are often made in pursuance of legal authority conferred on their makers by the previous legal order in force in these countries, often a colonial regime. This is the way most of the countries of the British Commonwealth acquired their independence" (*Ibid.*, 158–9). This was certainly true of Canada's early emergence as an independent nation, and certainly true of Canada in respect of its adoption of its *Charter of Rights and Freedoms*.

including moral and political knowledge, has deepened and improved in ways the founders could not possibly have contemplated. This leads to the inevitable question: Why should the American people *continue* to be bound by authoritative acts that might well have long outlived their rationales? Why should the judgments of a group of white, racist, misogynist males, with possibly outdated views of human nature, morality, and the government structures necessary for a thriving democratic society, continue to have authority over a people whose beliefs, values, practices, and views are very different – and in many respects much better?

These concerns about supposing that the dead, misguided hand of the past continues to bind the present can lead a theorist in two different directions. Let's assume that, early in its history, the authority of the particular constitution in which we have an interest does rest on the authority of its creators. At the time of its creation, their knowledge was superior. At the very least, they were capable of setting up a manageable system that allowed their community to derive the ongoing benefits of coordinated political action made possible by the introduction of the political and legal structures of government they happened to settle upon. Let's further suppose that the constitution and the system it brought into existence were marred by no serious moral flaws – they did not, for example, establish slavery, or otherwise violate fundamental moral rights. Now as we have just seen, the authority of such a constitution cannot be based forever on the authority of its authors – unless they are Platonic Guardians with unimpeachable insight *and* foresight, which we can safely suppose will never be the case. Not even Jefferson and Madison were that enlightened and prescient. "[T]he authority of the law can be said to derive from that of its author[s] at least inasmuch as the laws determine the temporary, and socially sensitive, way in which moral principles are to be enshrined into law. But that does not help show that anyone can have lawmaking authority to make laws that last very long."[23] So if, under normal human conditions, the constitution *continues* to be justified in the long run, this cannot be due to the authority of its authors. We have to look for another reason.

One such reason might be the consent of the governed. The actions of the American framers may not have been based on Platonic insight and prescience. Indeed, they might not even have been based on the best of reasons available at the time to persons of wisdom. But they did put in place a constitutional regime, one since modified on a number of different occasions, to which the American people continue to consent. If one rejects the notion of community identity over time, one can restrict the claim by saying that it's only the people-now whose consent establishes the "legitimacy-now" of the U.S. Constitution. However one cashes things out metaphysically, however, the fact remains that it is the current

---

23 *Ibid.*, 167.

consent of the governed, not the superior wisdom and actions of the framers, that establishes the legitimacy-now of the Constitution.

Consent theories face a number of daunting challenges, many of which are canvassed by Raz. One problem is that "some people may refuse their consent by whim in a totally arbitrary or irrational manner."[24] If the legitimacy of a constitution rests on the consent of the individual(s) to whom it is applicable, then those who do refuse will presumably not be bound by the constitution and the laws it empowers political and legal authorities to make. They will therefore be free to "break the law with impunity." But, as Raz observes, it is highly implausible to suppose that one can so easily escape the authority of the state in this way. A second, more difficult problem is that many people have neither given nor refused consent to a constitution. "Many may have failed to consent to it simply because it never occurred to them that they should."[25] Once again, it is highly implausible to suppose that all these people are exempt from the authority of the constitution and the system it establishes. Those who continue to believe that the key to the authority of a constitution lies in consent will, at this point, inevitably turn to one of two possibilities. One option is to claim that (continued) residence in the community governed by a constitution constitutes tacit expression of consent, whether one knows it or not, and whether one intends ones conduct to be taken this way. This claim is open to a host of objections not least of which is that it presupposes an unrealistic picture of the freedom of individuals to leave. Consent, as we saw in Chapter 3, must be freely given if it is to be valid. One who has no real option but to stay in a community can hardly be said to have thereby validly consented to the existing constitutional regime. A second possible way around the problem of those who do not in fact seem to give consent is to invoke the notion of "hypothetical consent." What is of relevance in establishing the authority of a constitution is not whether persons actually do consent to it either tacitly or expressly but whether they *would* do so under ideal conditions of deliberation. The difficulties with hypothetical-consent theories are well known and numerous, and for our purposes these can be left unexplored. Suffice it to say, along with Raz, that

[t]here is some normative force to the fact that one gives one's free and informed consent to an arrangement affecting oneself, which hypothetical consent does not have. Consent, whether wise or foolish, expresses the will of the agent concerning the conduct of his own life. Whatever mess results from his consent is, in part at least, of his own making. Since his life is his own, it is relevant whether it is under his control or not, and [valid] consent shows that it is. So even if real consent is a source of authority, it is far from clear that hypothetical consent is. I know of no argument which shows that it is.[26]

These difficulties with consent theories would be a source of considerable difficulty were they the only available basis for the legitimacy-now of a constitution.

24 *Ibid.*, 162.
25 *Ibid.*
26 *Ibid.*, 162–3.

Even if everyone now alive were asked to provide explicit consent to a constitution, the fact of the matter is that many would not be willing to do so. And those who chose to decline would, it would seem, be immune to the law's demands. Fortunately these difficulties are of little consequence because, as Raz observes, it is neither necessary nor always possible to base the authority of a constitution solely on the consent of the governed. "An important aspect of consent, as of all human action, is that it is given for a reason – that is, a reason the agent regards as a good reason, in light of all the considerations, moral considerations included, that apply to the case."[27] The agent is not always correct, of course, in his assessment of the relevant reasons, and so his consent may not be well founded. If it is not, then it may well lack validity. And if it lacks validity, it cannot serve as a basis for acting on that consent.[28] Consent, in other words, is not sufficient to establish legitimacy. For example, one cannot, via an act of consent, transform an immoral course of conduct into a moral one: One cannot, for example, relieve someone of a murder charge by consenting to be killed. The same is true of consent to constitutions. "[I]t would be impossible to base authority [of a law or a constitution] on consent that is misguided and ill-founded...."[29] If, for example, a constitution establishes a slave regime, consenting to it neither legitimates the regime established nor warrants acting on the basis of its immoral demands. It is only when the reasons for consenting are valid that consent to a constitution can play any role in establishing its legitimacy and authority. But if so, then the "question arises whether these considerations are not enough to establish the authority of [the constitution] independently of the consent."[30] "If consent to authority is effective only when based on adequate reasons to recognize the authority, why are these reasons not enough in themselves to establish that authority?"[31] Indeed, "it seems reasonable to suppose that, regarding such matters, the only reasons which justify consent to [the] authority [of a constitution] also justify the authority without consent."[32]

So where does this leave us? If the legitimacy of a constitutional Charter in a democratic regime cannot (at least in the long run) rest with the authority of its makers, and if consent can play a role only if it is backed by reasons

---

27 *Ibid.*, 163. For extended analysis of this feature of acting on reasons, see Raz's *Engaging Reason: On the Theory of Value and Action* (Oxford: Oxford University Press, 1999). See also *The Morality of Freedom* (Oxford: Clarendon Press, 1986), especially Chapters 13 and 14.

28 As we saw in Chapter 3, there may be good reasons behind policies on which the validity of consent must be presumed in all but very special circumstances. In these cases, consent may be invalid, even though the relevant decision maker, for example a physician, is not entitled to suppose that it is.

29 Raz, "On the Authority and Interpretation of Constitutions," 163.

30 *Ibid.*

31 *Ibid.*, 164.

32 *Ibid.* I have provided only a thumbnail sketch of a very complex argument. For further detail, the reader is directed to the works by Raz cited in notes 27 and 29.

which warrant that consent (and possibly not even then), and if these reasons would on their own justify the constitution absent consent, then presumably we have to look for reasons why we should now have a constitutional Charter. And presumably they will be reasons like those explored in Chapters 2 and 3. One might argue that constitutionally entrenched Charters are justified insofar as they serve to provide a stable framework of fixed points for politics, offer agreed protections to minorities and individuals from the excesses and deficiencies of unbridled majoritarianism, and so on. We will ultimately reject this list of reasons if understood as the Standard Conception presupposes. But for now we can at least agree to the following: It is a mistake to look to consent, or to the dead, probably misguided hand of the past, as providing a sound basis for reconciling democracy with entrenchment. We should be looking at the reasons why, at present, we do well to subscribe to a system of government that includes this feature – reasons that would justify consenting now to such an arrangement were we ever asked to do so but that serve to establish its legitimacy even if the invitation were never extended.

So again, where does this leave us? It leaves us with the following conclusions: Entrenchment, though an arguably essential feature of constitutional Charters, is not without its difficulties. Despite the preceding arguments, the suspicion remains that entrenchment somehow stands in conflict with the ideal of self-government. Why, it might be asked, should a free and equal people wish to endorse this arrangement? Why should they handcuff themselves in this way? Why should they think of themselves as in any way analogous to a drunk in a bar from whom others need protection? Would this not be to suppose a terribly unflattering self-portrait? As we shall see more fully in Chapters 5 and 6, much of this uneasiness over entrenchment stems from the Standard Conception of Charters presupposed in both the Standard Case and the Critics' response to it. If we view Charters as attempting to establish fixed moral limits, then the cited difficulties will inevitably come to the fore and will be difficult to reconcile with our intuitions about self-government. But if the common law conception is substituted for the presupposed Standard Conception, many of these problems will be seen to fade away into minor concerns. But, again, we should not get too far ahead of ourselves. We need to return to the topic of judicial enforceability, the second of the two key features of Charters that lie behind the charge of inconsistency with democratic ideals.

iii. Charter Review and Self-Government

Relying on unelected, unaccountable judges for Charter enforcement is a travesty: it is to abandon democracy entirely. The will of the people has been replaced by the will of a small band of judges, usually with life tenure, who occasionally present themselves to the public decked out in robes and wigs to pronounce on the wisdom, or lack thereof, of the views and actions of others. How can this possibly be consistent with our democratic commitments? Does this not empower those who in no way represent the people to thwart the efforts of those who do? "Putting the bare phrase 'freedom of association' in a document administered by an unfettered judiciary not responsible to anyone is unimaginable in any society we would call democratic. . . . "[33] We do not have a democracy "if we are not allowed to make up our own minds about what freedom of association entails, but instead must hand the question over to a few of our betters to decide the matter for us under the pretext of interpretation. . . ."[34]

So goes one of the most rhetorically powerful and (to many) persuasive objections to Charters and judicial review. Is there a sound argument behind the rhetoric? If there is, it's of far less force than initially meets the eye. Consider the extent to which the objection, as it stands, fails to acknowledge a whole host of complicating factors. It fails, for example, to acknowledge that most of the time it isn't "the people" who make law-determining decisions. In indirect forms of democracy, statutory laws are made by a relatively small group of individuals who, in their capacity as legislators, are expected to represent their constituents in the various ways explored in Chapter 3. We saw there that representation is a very complex matter. We also saw that it is not always the task of a conscientious representative to accede to current demands of the electorate. Representing X is not always a matter of doing what X instructs one to do. It is certainly not a matter of doing what *everyone* whom one represents wishes one to do. Minority interests and wishes often go unfulfilled in representative democracies. This is a crucial point if only because much of the rhetorical force of the Critics' stems from the idea that in a democracy it is we – that is, *all of us* – who are making the law-determining decisions that affect us, not the judges. But that force is greatly reduced once it's acknowledged that "we" seldom make any such decisions; on the contrary, "we" have other people to do this on our behalf. In short, more often than not law-determining decisions that affect each one of us, often profoundly, are made by somebody else.

These thoughts on the distance between the people and the law-determining decisions made on their behalf lead to yet another point of considerable significance. The Critics' objection to judicial review by judges seriously underplays the significant degree to which law-determining decisions in our modern, indirect democracies are made by *unelected* individuals. Consider, once again, the vast array of administrative bodies, populated by persons appointed to their posts, whose job it is to develop legally binding rules and regulations, to flesh out laws consistent with the broad outlines of statute. This situation completely undermines the assumption that members of a democratic community, through their votes and the actions of their elected representatives, are always directly involved in law-determining decisions. At the very least, it undermines the suggestion that we consider a system in which law-determining decisions are

---

33 Michael Mandel, *The Charter of Rights and the Legalization of Politics*, 458.
34 *Ibid.*

sometimes made by unelected representatives unworthy of the title "democratic."

So democratic communities adopt a wide range of mechanisms that distance law-determining decisions from the people whose laws they eventually become. And often the mechanisms in question involve an active role for unelected officials. What reason is there to deny that one such distancing mechanism might involve judicial review of legislation on the basis of a Charter? It cannot be because judges are (often) unelected, because many other unelected officials in democracies make law-determining decisions. It also cannot be because they, unlike members of administrative agencies, are not appointed by representatives who have been elected by the people. It is tempting to think that with administrative officials we have a genuine democratic pedigree that is lacking in the case of judges. In the former case, if we trace the line of authority back far enough we eventually come to decisions made by the people themselves. The people elect government officials who are responsible for the appointment and supervision of the unelected bureaucrats who fulfill the various roles described. But this cannot help the Critics' case, and the reason is simple. Much the same thing is true of unelected judges. They too are appointed, and often vetted, by government representatives. Supreme Court justices in the United States, to cite but one example, are nominated by the (elected) American president. And each nomination must be confirmed by the Senate, often after long, bitter debates before the relevant committee, as was the case with Justice Clarence Thomas and Judge Robert Bork, the latter of whom failed to receive confirmation.

So judicial review, even when undertaken by unelected judges, shares much of the democratic pedigree we accord many other law-determining bodies. Yet another reason for questioning the Critics' objection is that much of its force derives from the false assumption that judicial review is necessarily the strong form one finds in the United States. As noted earlier, a U.S. Supreme Court's decision that some other branch of government has exceeded its constitutional authority under the Bill of Rights renders the impugned action invalid. It renders it of no legal force and effect. Yet as we saw, this system of judicial supremacy is far from being the only form of judicial review available to a community. New Zealand serves as an obvious example of an alternative. So too does Canada with its section 33 override, which, despite some reluctance on the part of politicians to use it, remains a potentially powerful tool for asserting Parliamentary authority. In addition, the idea of a shared partnership, involving a dialogue between Parliament and the courts, has begun to take hold in both public debate and judicial decisions in Canada. According to this particular reading of the constitutional landscape, the decisions of judges are seldom "final" in any objectionable sense of the term. As Peter Hogg and Allison Bushell have demonstrated, the actions of a Canadian court in enforcing the

Charter seldom result in an imposition that thwarts the democratic will but is one stage in the ongoing democratic process.[35] Hogg and Bushell demonstrate that Charter cases in which legislation is ruled unconstitutional are almost always followed by new legislation that accomplishes the very same objectives as the offending legislation but in ways that are no longer seen to violate Charter rights. The resulting effect is rarely to thwart the democratic will but to influence the design and implementation of legislation expressive of that will.[36]

One can imagine a critic of judicial review responding to all this talk of "dialogue" in the following manner: "Yes, the judges often talk as if they are in constant dialogue with Parliament, and yes, they do sometimes come to decisions that defer to Parliament's wishes."[37] But this is nothing but shallow rhetoric. Unlike an unelected government administrator who can always be disciplined or replaced if her performance displeases the public or the elected politicians under whose authority she serves, nothing prevents the Supreme Court from removing itself from the dialogue whenever it sees fit to do so. There is, for example, nothing to prevent it from insisting on *its* particular reading of a Charter provision over one for which Parliament has expressed its decided preference in legislating as it did. It is true that the courts sometimes defer to Parliament and declare themselves to be doing so out of respect for Parliament's democratic authority. But this is all window dressing. It ignores one glaring fact: The Supreme Court justices are accountable to no one but themselves. Should they choose to impose their will, there is no one in a position to stop them. Simpson is right: "So much for the vaunted but rather tattered notion of the Supreme Court and Parliament engaged in a 'dialogue.' It's more like diktat from the court."

In Chapter 2, we had occasion to draw an important distinction between two senses of the word "freedom." First, there is the *normative* sense according

---

35 Peter Hogg and Allison Bushell, "The Charter Dialogue Between Courts and Legislatures (Or Perhaps The Charter of Rights Isn't Such a Bad Thing After All)," 35 *Osgoode Hall Law Journal* (1997), 75–124.

36 The "dialogue" metaphor, despite its popularity and influence, has not been immune to popular and scholarly criticism. Recall Jeffrey Simpson's assessment, in the *Globe and Mail*, of the *Montford* decision. "That decision was one of the most aggressive in asserting judicial supremacy over Parliament. It dismissed parliamentary debates on the issue as having offered 'more fulmination than illumination' . . . So much for the vaunted but rather tattered notion of the Supreme Court and Parliament engaged in a 'dialogue.' It's more like diktat from the court." For scholarly criticism see, for example, G. Huscroft and I. Brodie, eds., *Constitutionalism in the Charter Era*, Part I.

37 According to one former Supreme Court justice, deference to Parliament has in fact gone too far. In a recent case involving the granting of bail, Justice Frank Iacobucci (as he then was) wrote the following: "In my respectful view, by upholding the impugned provision – at least in part – my colleague has transformed dialogue into abdication." *David Scott Hall v. Her Majesty the Queen and The Attorney General of Canada, The Attorney General of Quebec, The Criminal Lawyers' Association (Ontario) and The Association Des Advocats De La Defense de Montreal* [2002] 3 S.C.R., 64 at 127.

to which to be free of limitation is to enjoy a Hohfeldian privilege or immunity – that it, one is subject to no relevant duties or restrictions on one's normative liberties or powers. It is this meaning we had in mind when we said that Rex was free of constitutional limitation but Regina was not, because there were constitutional limits on her powers to legislate. The appropriate secondary rules did exist in her case and these did limit her powers. As we observed, this remained true of Regina even if she chose to ignore the incorporated limits. She was not, in the normative sense of the term, free to do so. Another important feature of Regina's situation was that the norms under which her powers were limited were not themselves under her Hohfeldian control. That is, it was not within her normative power to alter or eliminate the relevant constitutional limitations. This was because those limitations, and the powers they modified, were products of Hartian social rules whose existence was a function not only of Regina's actions and attitudes but those of other members of her community. All this meant that she was not normatively free to legislate in any manner she saw fit, nor was she normatively free to eliminate or alter her constitutional limitations at will. She remained normatively bound.

The same, I suggest, is true of Supreme Court justices and their normative powers. By both law and convention, judges are bound to apply the constitution. They are certainly not at liberty to ignore its requirements. Nor are they free to disregard what we earlier termed the "good-faith requirement," the requirement that individuals normatively bound by rules (or other types of normative standard) always attempt to interpret and apply them in good faith. This includes, we noted, the duty to come to one's best understanding of the rules by which one is bound. It is also important to note that the constitutional rules defining the role of Supreme Court justices are not entirely within the normative power of judges to change or eliminate. On the contrary, they are rules of the political system, and the justices play only one part – admittedly a very large part – in that system. As Hart's theory suggests, it is a system whose identity and effectiveness is a function of widespread acceptance by the general population, as well as by all the official actors who more directly play a role in establishing its identity and effectiveness. All this is evidenced by the following features of the Canadian political landscape. Decisions that seem to tread too heavily on Parliamentary authority are often roundly condemned by the public and by other official actors on the constitutional stage. They have led, for example, to Simpson's seething comments on the *Montfort* decision and to Morton and Knopff's condemnation of "Charter politics." Such reactions have, in turn, arguably led to decisions such as *David Scott Hall v. Her Majesty the Queen et al.*, wherein Justice Frank Iacobucci derided the Court for abdicating its responsibilities to Parliament. They might also be responsible, at least in part, for the Supreme Court's more recent *Reference* decision on same-sex marriage, in which the Court deliberately chose to defer to Parliament in settling the contentious issue of whether the common law definition of marriage violates the Canadian Charter.[38] The Court did this despite the government's explicit – some might say desperate – call on them to settle that issue for them. This is hardly a case of a judiciary drunk with power.

So it is not at all clear that Supreme Court justices always have the normative powers assumed in the Critics' objection to judicial review. But recall that there was a second sense of the term "free" – what we called *de facto* freedom. It was this sense of the term that was in play when we said that Regina remained free to legislate as she saw fit, despite the existence of constitutional rules limiting her powers. This second sense of the term is invoked when what is meant is that there is no one who can coerce, force, or otherwise motivate an individual to act against her will. One can well imagine a Critic replying as follows: "Regardless of any normative limits under which judges labour in interpreting and enforcing a Charter, the fact remains that they – particularly Supreme Court justices – are accountable to no one. Unlike elected representatives, whom we can always turn out at the next election should we disagree with their decisions, or unelected bureaucrats who may meet a similar fate should their decisions displease us or our representatives, judicial independence and life tenure (or something close to this) render Supreme Court justices untouchable. They are immune to the forces that compel politicians and bureaucrats to serve the expressed wishes and interest of the community. They have unbridled *de facto* freedom. Power in the hands of one who is unaccountable is power that cannot possibly be tolerated in a democratic community. It does violence to the ideals of self-government."

How could an Advocate respond to this worry? Is it not enough to reply that judges are reasonable people of good will and integrity upon whom we can usually count to fulfil their roles in accordance with the good-faith requirement? There may be no one who can force the judges to comply with their duty to apply the Charter in good faith. And there may be no one who can remove them from office if they should fail to do so on a regular basis. But if they are persons of integrity upon whom we are able to count to observe their good-faith requirement, should this not be enough? Do we really need extra protections? Is it simply naïve to think that we don't? I should hope that it is not hopelessly naïve to think this way, else our democratic systems of government, which rest to a very great extent on dutiful attempts by those in authority to honour the good-faith requirement, are destined to abject failure. Those who remain unconvinced that this is not enough, who believe that the Advocates have paid insufficient attention to Plato's question "Who is to guard the Guardians?" can perhaps be at least partly reassured by the following thoughts: As with Regina, we must bear in mind that the fundamental rules in terms of which we establish our political systems are *social* rules. They exist within, and only within, a

---

38 *See Reference re Same-Sex Marriage* [2004] 3 S.C.R. 698. As noted earlier, Parliament rose to the challenge and eventually passed *Bill C-38: The Civil Marriage Act.*

complex web of practices involving the behaviour and attitudes of a great many people serving in a great many roles. Individuals who ignore these rules threaten the very foundations of the system, a system that most of us find conducive to our interests and that we will normally take great pains to protect through a variety of social pressures. Judges who flout their constitutional duties will not be immune from these pressures. Indeed, the critical reactions – and judicial reactions to these critical reactions – cited above suggest that judges are quite sensitive to the various pressures emanating from the public, and from the wider political sphere in which they operate. Judges do not want to be seen as usurping someone else's role. They do not want to be seen as violating the fundamental rules of the constitutional system of which they form an integral part. If we cannot trust our judges to act with integrity in honouring their constitutional duties – including the ever-present good-faith requirement – in the face of such pressures, then what hope is there for constitutional democracy?

iv. Hobbesean Predators and Respect for Persons

Earlier, we drew attention to the unflattering picture of democratic society that some Critics claim is presupposed by the case for entrenchment. The picture is of a society modeled on the analogy of the drunken pub-crawler from whom the public requires protection. This particular line of argument is advanced most forcefully by Jeremy Waldron, who argues that such analogies reveal a deep inconsistency built right in to Charters. On the one hand, the Advocates present their standard picture of Charters as providing minorities and individuals with vital protections against mistaken, overzealous, prejudiced, perhaps even irrational majorities – protections that they believe, with utmost confidence, to be essential within constitutional democracies and therefore worthy of entrenchment. On the other hand, they presuppose the liberal democratic view of individual citizens as agents worthy of exercising, in a responsible manner, the fundamental rights enunciated in a Charter. This view underlies both democratic ideals and the view that we are creatures with dignity, deserving of the rights assigned to us in liberal democratic theory and the societies they applaud. The Standard Argument tries to put these two views together into one consistent package. But this cannot be done. To adopt judicial review is to combine

> . . . self assurance and mistrust: self assurance in the proponent's conviction that what he is putting forward really *is* a matter of fundamental right and that he has captured it adequately in the particular formulation he is propounding; and mistrust, implicit in his view that any alterative conception that might be conceived by elected legislators next year or in ten years' time is so likely to be wrong-headed or ill-motivated that *his own* formulation is to be elevated immediately beyond the reach of ordinary legislative revision.[39]

39 Waldron, *Law and Disagreement*, 221–2.

Yet constraining future majorities by putting constitutionally entrenched, judicially enforced roadblocks in their way

> does not sit particularly well with the aura of respect for their autonomy and responsibility that is conveyed by the substance of the rights which are being entrenched.... If the desire for entrenchment is motivated by a predatory view of human nature and of what people will do to one another when let loose in the arena of democratic politics, it will be difficult to explain how or why people are to be viewed as essentially bearers of rights.[40]

So there is a deep inconsistency in the very idea of judicial review, an inconsistency that renders it all but unintelligible. On the one hand, we say that people are autonomous moral agents worthy of the possession and informed, responsible exercise of the moral rights we (typically) enshrine in Charters. We view them as responsible moral agents fully capable of pursuing their own conceptions of the good life on an ongoing basis, and willing and able to contribute meaningfully and responsibly to collective efforts of self-government through participation in democratic politics. This status, this inherent human dignity, not only deems them worthy of rights and whatever protections are necessary for securing them (including the adoption of a Charter of Rights), it also deems them worthy of helping to determine, on an ongoing and continual basis, what those rights entail or amount to, and how public policy should be shaped so as not to infringe upon those rights so understood. This they do by participating in democratic politics, if only through the vehicle of electing responsible and accountable legislators, empowered to make decisions on their behalf. On the other hand, we also view them (and their agents in the legislature) as predators, unable to constrain themselves if "let loose in the arena of democratic politics." They cannot be trusted to exercise their rights responsibly without undermining the rights of others. Nor can they be trusted, in hard cases, to provide balanced views about the concrete implications of the rights they trumpet. They are lacking in both self-restraint and knowledge – areas in which, by comparison, judges and the authors of Charters are presumably thought to excel. Hence the need for Charter constraint of democratic power – and the saving grace of judges. Waldron is right: These two views of human agents cannot possibly be reconciled.

But is this the picture presupposed by the Standard Case? Not necessarily. Recall our earlier exploration of Demos and its language law, and of the various reasons for adopting judicial review it brought to our attention. Few of these presupposed predatory instincts on the part of Demosians. There may have been nothing more sinister behind the community's desire to adopt the language law than simple failure to appreciate or care about the extent to which it would affect the interests of Venusians. They might simply have failed to empathize with the Venusians, to grasp and appreciate fully what it means not to be able to

---

40 *Ibid.*, 222.

communicate in one's own language. They may also have underestimated the difficulty and inconvenience involved in overcoming this burden. We have here nothing remotely like a band of Hobbesean predators. Of course another possible factor at work might have been prejudice. It is an undeniable fact of human life, we observed, that some people just don't like other people who are different from them in some noticeable way, like skin colour, ethnic origin, religion, or gender. Or they might not like them because they speak a different language or enjoy a different culture. Such individuals are apt, either consciously or without awareness, to discriminate against those who are different. Prejudice grounded in a variety of attitudes, ranging from simple dislike to intense hatred of those who are different, can lie behind support for a measure that negatively affects the interests and wishes of other people. Sometimes this prejudice combines with fear, and the result, we noted, can be a lethal concoction. Fear of the unknown or the different is a powerful force, sometimes leading to deep suspicion and oppressive measures. In times of crisis this fear can produce measures that would not be tolerated in normal circumstances. In such situations, we approach a Hobbesean world, but one hopes that these occasions are rare and are eventually seen for what they are, as eventually happened following the internment of Japanese North Americans during World War II.

Only the latter reason for Charter protection comes close to embracing the Hobbesean picture. Yet in acknowledging this reason we in no way dishonour ourselves or threaten our belief in the inherent dignity of individuals presupposed by the liberal democratic conception of the human person. What we do is the following: We recognize that we are limited beings who are influenced, in both our everyday lives and in our political decisions, by a range of factors that often lead to less than desirable conduct. Furthermore, we recognize that our majoritarian procedures, though well designed to advance our collective interests in most cases, sometimes produce results to which we could not all agree in advance. They can lead to decisions that flout democratic conditions presupposed in either the procedural conceptions of democracy with its emphasis on self-determination or the much stronger constitutional conception and its more substantive ideals, such as the ideal of equal concern and respect. This, we recognize, can occur even when our majoritarian procedures are functioning *as designed* – that is, when no one is denied his right to participate on an equal footing with everyone else and decisions are not motivated by discreditable forces like fear and prejudice. In recognition of these limitations in ourselves and our procedures, we structure our constitution so as to overcome them. We opt for a constitutional arrangement involving judicial review. As I did before my night in the pub, we put in place mechanisms that we hope will, among other things, disable our inauthentic wishes. Taking these steps for these reasons is hardly a denial of our moral integrity and dignity. It is, I should think, a particularly noble exercise in rational, moral self-determination.

v. The Threat of Radical Dissensus: An Idiot's Search for Ulysses' Mast

In explaining the nature and appeal of judicial review, Advocates often cite the analogy of Ulysses' decision to have himself tied to the mast of his ship so as not to succumb to the tempting call of the Sirens.[41] Just as Ulysses knows, in advance, and in a moment of cool reflection, that he is justified in arranging now for a restriction on his freedom to choose and act later, we, as a people, can know, in advance, and in a moment of cool reflection (a moment of constitutional choice) that we are justified in tying ourselves to the mast of entrenched Charter rights and their enforcement, on our behalf, by the judiciary. Just as Ulysses knows that he will descend into madness when he hears the call of the Sirens, we can know that at some point we, like the Demosians, will inevitably succumb to the siren call of self-interest, prejudice, fear, hatred, or simple moral blindness and be led, in the course of everyday politics, to violate the rights of some of our fellow citizens. In Waldron's view, however, the Ulysses analogy is objectionable for at least two reasons.

Waldron's first objection rests on the unflattering manner in which the Ulysses analogy is said to portray democratic societies, as communities prone to madness. The appropriate response to this particular objection is essentially the same as our response to the Hobbesean predator argument: It's just an analogy. True, in the example cited, Ulysses does descend into madness. But this particular state, like the state of drunkenness in the pub analogy, is meant only to illustrate or represent a far broader range of structural and motivational factors that inevitably come into play in majoritarian decision making. If taken too strictly, the analogy will of course present an unflattering picture. But it will also underplay the full spectrum of forces at work in democratic society, forces that the analogy was never meant to obscure. It will also fail to do justice to our wisdom in correcting for them. The bottom line remains this: Recognizing one's limitations – not all of which are morally equivalent to madness or drunkenness – is by no means inconsistent with recognizing one's moral status as a being of dignity, worthy of concern and respect. Indeed, it may well be a precondition of recognizing the inherent dignity of persons who know fully well that they are all too human.

Waldron's second objection to the Ulysses analogy invokes the circumstances of modern politics. The radical dissensus inherent in the circumstances of modern politics is said to undercut the force of the analogy entirely. Leaving aside the nest of thorny questions introduced by the possibility of moral nihilism and skepticism about the "objectivity" of moral judgments to which we will soon turn, the fact of the matter is that we live in a pluralistic world of significant moral dissensus. People's moral and political views differ dramatically – and

---

41 The metaphor does much the same work as the pub analogy, but it's perhaps less vulnerable to the complaint that it paints an unflattering picture of democratic societies.

for all we can tell, reasonably – in ways that are not easily subject to mutual accommodation and efforts to achieve consensus. So even if there are right answers to questions about moral rights, we cannot agree on what these are or on what they entail for the questions of law, morality, and public policy with which Charters are supposed to deal. As Waldron insists, "even if there is an objectively right answer to the question of what rights we have, still people disagree implacably about what that right answer is."[42] Yet if we cannot agree on the rights we have, let alone what these entail for the complex questions of law and public policy that Charters bring to the fore, then it is sheer folly to believe that we – and this includes judges – could ever agree on what a Charter's provisions mean and on the limits they supposedly impose on government power. And if we cannot agree on the limits established by a Charter, we can hardly pre-commit to them in the manner of Ulysses. We cannot tie ourselves to the mast of entrenched moral rights if we cannot locate the mast, let alone agree on what it might look like. "My theme in all this is reasonable disagreement, but I cannot restrain myself from saying that anyone who thinks a narrative like this is appropriately modeled by the story of Ulysses and the sirens is an idiot."[43]

Radical dissensus poses the most serious threat to the Standard Case. If Waldron is correct in his reading of the political landscape, then it is indeed hopelessly naïve to suppose that Charters can possibly live up to the expectations presupposed by most Advocates. It is hopelessly naïve to think, along with Prime Minister Chrétien, that "in a free and democratic society, it is important that citizens know exactly what their rights and freedoms are, and where to turn to for help and advice in the event that those freedoms are denied or rights infringed upon." It can hardly be important that we have this knowledge, and the levels of protection and security supposedly based on it, if both are unattainable. If we cannot agree in advance what our rights and freedoms are, cannot know what these are and what it is we have committed ourselves to in adopting a system of judicial review that both embodies and protects them, then it cannot be important to have such a system. Nor can it be important to strive to achieve these lofty goals. It can only amount to sheer stupidity – or as Waldron might say, sheer idiocy.

Waldron's challenge to the Ulysses analogy is one to which we cannot respond fully at this stage. An effective answer requires philosophical resources that will become available to us only after we have developed our alternative to the fixed-view conception of Charters presupposed in the Standard Case. In short, a full and adequate response must await our development, in Chapters 5 and 6, of the common law conception.

---

42 *Law and Disagreement*, 244.
43 *Ibid.*, 268.

vi. The Threat of Moral Nihilism

A common objection to Charters[44] is that their appeal stems from discredited, naïve views of morality and rationality and the moral limits that Charters are meant to enshrine. More particularly, it stems from a naïve view concerning the possibility of "objectively right" answers to the moral and otherwise evaluative questions that typically arise in Charter cases. Unlike Waldron, who chooses to set aside meta-ethical questions in making his case against judicial review, many critics espouse utter skepticism about the "objectivity" of moral reasoning.[45] Morality, including the political morality at stake in most Charter disputes, is wholly "subjective" and/or "relative."

This utter skepticism about morality underlies many critiques of judicial review. Morton and Knopff, among the foremost critics of the practice in Canada, suggest that

[t]he Charter does not so much guarantee rights as give judges the power to make policy by choosing among competing interpretations of broadly worded provisions. . . . When judges disagree, each one indulges in the legal fiction that his understanding of the Charter is correct and that his colleagues are mistaken. In fact, there are usually several plausible interpretations and no obviously correct answer. The Charter, in short, is largely indeterminate with respect to the questions that arise under it. . . . No clear answer to these questions can be found in the broadly worded text of the Charter, and judges are thus free to choose.[46]

Morton and Knopff are not alone in their opinion of judicial review. Robert Martin, in analyzing the Canadian Supreme Court's record in dealing with free expression, pursues the same line of argument with a vengeance. He writes:

In *Edmonton Journal v. Alberta (A.G.)*, Justice Wilson invented what she was pleased to call the "contextual approach" to freedom of expression. The judge following this approach looks at the particular expression in order to determine whether he or she agrees with it. The judge then looks at the personal characteristics of the party claiming to rely on freedom of expression in order to determine whether he or she belongs to a social group the judge supports. Thus, if the judge likes me and agrees with what I am saying, my claim based on freedom of expression may succeed, otherwise it will not. The cumulative effect of these decisions is to make freedom of expression a decidedly hollow guarantee.

---

44 Few philosophers endorse this objection; Waldron certainly does not. It is, however, often encountered in popular discourse and in some philosophical circles.
45 According to Waldron, the objectivity of judgments of political morality – whether some are right and some are wrong – is irrelevant to Charter debates. What is of crucial importance is that we cannot agree in our judgments, even if we think that such judgments are objective and that our own answers are objectively correct – that we have "the right answers." Dissensus is all we need to discredit judicial review. See on this "The Irrelevance of Objectivity," Chapter 8 of *Law and Disagreement*.
46 T. Morton and R. Knopff, *The Charter Revolution and the Court Party*, 33–4.

The invention of the "contextual approach" to freedom of expression is another example of the judicial amendment of our Constitution. Section 2(b) of the Charter states that "everyone" has freedom of expression. The contextual approach amends that simple formulation so that it appears to read, "Anyone a judge likes and who is expressing ideas or analysis the judges agrees with may have freedom of expression." In sum, then, the Court has decided that the central consideration in freedom of expression cases is what it has been pleased to call "free expression values," although the Charter nowhere mentions "values" – which are, of course, totally subjective.[47]

According to Morton, Knopff, and Martin, the Canadian Charter imposes few substantive constraints on a judge's reasoning in Charter cases. Given this lack of constraint, judges cannot help but impose their own purely subjective moral understandings on the workings of the political process. The inevitable result, once again, is the total discrediting of Charters. The bulwark against arbitrary and otherwise unwarranted exercises of government power and oppression that Charters are meant to establish is nothing but a sham – and a seriously harmful one at that.

Once again, a full response to these objections must await development of the common law conception. But some preliminary comments are no doubt in order. Let's focus here on one question in particular: What could possibly lead Critics to claim that judicial review, at least as it is practiced by Canadian judges, is quite obviously "subjective"? What could possibly lead them to think it obvious that the Charter is "largely indeterminate with respect to the questions that arise under it" and that "judges are thus free to choose" in accordance with their subjective preferences? The answer would seem to be the following: "No *clear* answer to these questions can be found in the broadly worded text of the Charter." On the contrary, "there are usually several plausible interpretations and no *obviously correct* answer" (emphasis added in both cases). In other words, an absence of *clarity* and thus *agreement* on right answers, resulting, presumably, from the inability to demonstrate that one's moral conclusions are anything more than "plausible," means that the judges have unbridled discretion to follow their own subjective moral preferences. Buried beneath the Critics' moral skepticism, then, are two basic arguments: the "Argument from Disagreement" and the "Demonstrability Argument." Let's consider each in turn.[48]

A. THE ARGUMENT FROM DISAGREEMENT. Among the most commonly cited reasons in favour of moral skepticism is the undeniable fact of widespread differences of opinion on important moral questions. These differences exist

---

47 Robert I. Martin, *The Most Dangerous Branch*, 55–6.
48 Much of the following analysis derives from Waluchow, *The Dimensions of Ethics* (Peterborough, Ontario: Broadview Press, 2003), Chapter 3. This in turn owes much to Ronald Dworkin's *Taking Rights Seriously* and *Law's Empire, passim*. See also Dworkin's essay "Objectivity and Truth: You'd Better Believe It," *Philosophy and Public Affairs* 25, no. 2, Spring 1996.

both across and within societies. Some communities have considered slavery to be within the natural order of things, while others have condemned it as a moral abomination. Many individuals within contemporary Western societies view abortion as nothing short of murder, while others within these very same societies condemn attempts to prevent abortions as unacceptable violations of a woman's moral right to control her own reproductive processes. Issues surrounding same-sex marriage have split Western nations pretty much right down the middle, though a consensus in favour of recognition has begun to emerge in many of them. How, in the light of such vast differences of opinion, which can of course be endlessly multiplied, can it possibly be reasonable to believe in an objective moral truth for judges to discover and apply when they are engaged in judicial review? How reasonable can it be to believe that there are, in reality, objectively valid moral standards upon which well-informed, reasonable people – including judges – could be expected to agree? If there were such standards, would we not see a good deal more agreement on moral matters than is plainly the case? Would we not see more agreement on what Charters require – in particular, more unanimous judgments in Charter cases?

The Argument from Disagreement seems clearly behind the following observations by Morton and Knopff:

> How could it be that "we find ourselves arguing, so vehemently and so often, about the very core of what we have, as participants in a democratic polity, long since presumably agreed upon"? How can a society simultaneously agree upon and endlessly dispute its foundational norms? The answer is that our disagreements about the Charter – the questions we actually litigate – involve not the well established core but the indeterminate peripheral meaning of Charter rights. While the core meaning of a right may be widely agreed upon, its outer-limits are inherently contestable.[49]

According to the authors, moral standards have a "core," upon which there is some measure of agreement in liberal democracies. All agree, for example, that equality is important and that slavery is flatly inconsistent with it. But what is more important, moral standards have a substantial periphery or penumbra, with respect to which there is radical dissensus. Charter cases, which invariably involve this penumbra, raise issues upon which we cannot agree. This disagreement, in turn, entails "indeterminacy," " discretion," and the unbridled pursuit of judges' subjective moral preferences in Charter cases. "[L]egal indeterminacy and judicial discretion emerge not with respect to core values, about which consensus exists, but with respect to [penumbral] questions, about which dissensus prevails.... The text rarely settles such issues of reasonable disagreement: judges do."[50]

---

49 Morton and Knopff, *The Charter Revolution and the Court Party*, 35, quoting Sniderman, Fletcher, Russell, and Tetlock, *The Clash of Rights: Liberty, Equality and Legitimacy in Pluralist Democracy* (New Haven, Conn.: Yale University Press, 1996), 52.
50 *Ibid.*, 37.

B. THE DEMONSTRABILITY ARGUMENT. A second, closely related argument supporting moral skepticism seizes on the fact that it is seldom possible to demonstrate, to the satisfaction of all open-minded, reasonable individuals of good will and integrity, that one's morals judgments are correct. According to defenders of this second argument, the main reason there is little consensus in moral judgments is the absence of an agreed procedure or method of moral reasoning by which individuals can demonstrate to one another the correctness of their beliefs. Unlike, say, the natural sciences, where, it is said, there are such agreed procedures for demonstrating conclusions acceptable to the entire scientific community, moral reasoning affords no comparable methodology for demonstrating moral conclusions. In contrast with the sciences, one finds within the moral realm a plethora of moral codes, belief systems, and theories. These different theories not only include different moral standards but also prescribe different methods of moral assessment. Some theories are consequentialist; others are deontological. Some of the latter eschew appeal to consequences entirely; others believe only that more than consequences can be relevant. Some theories consider moral values to be central to moral life; others assert that values are secondary and dependent on judgments of obligation. In the light of such widespread disagreements, it would be foolish to believe that there is anything like a method of moral demonstration that comes even close to emulating the methods of the natural sciences. But absent the possibility of demonstration, moral views can be nothing more than matters of opinion or taste. And because Charter cases are inevitably dependent on answers to fundamental moral questions, they invariably involve indeterminacy, discretion, and subjective moral judgment on the part of judges. These are inevitable when the questions judges must ask are essentially moral ones like: What are the essential elements of a free and democratic society? What does equality mean and require within democratic societies? What is the fundamental moral basis of the right to freedom of conscience and expression? To what do we attribute the importance of freedom of expression? and so on.

C. INITIAL REPLIES. How might one inclined to defend judicial review respond to these skeptical objections?[51] To the Argument from Disagreement, one might begin by offering the following observations: *First*, from the fact that

---

51 Meta-ethical questions about the objectivity of morality and moral judgments are notoriously complex and deeply philosophical. Addressing them fully here would take us too far afield and so we must rest content with the few observations that follow. These observations should at the very least give one pause in accepting the Critics' assessment. For further discussion of these questions, see, for example, A. Marmor, *Positive Law and Objective Values* (Oxford: Clarendon Press, 2001), Chapter 6,"Three Concepts of Objectivity"; and Ronald Dworkin, "Objectivity and Truth: You'd Better Believe It," *Philosophy and Public Affairs* 25, no. 2, Spring 1996.

there is widespread disagreement on the right answer to a question, it fails to follow that there is no such answer. Uncertainty and disagreement are not identical to indeterminacy, where the latter connotes the absence of a right answer. Nor do the former entail the latter. Historians are often uncertain about and disagree profoundly on what occurred centuries ago. But few are willing to infer from this that there are no historical truths. Likewise, we may be uncertain about and disagree profoundly on questions concerning the future of our planet, or the state of the universe beyond our current powers of observation. But there are facts of the matter here and there are right answers to many of our questions, despite the fact that we currently have little epistemic access to them. *Second,* moral reasoning is very complex and difficult. Perhaps we have yet to reach the stage where we understand fully the complex dimensions of many moral issues, including those that arise in Charter cases. Maybe we are still trying to figure things out. But there is no denying that we have made progress over the years. Slavery was once believed to be a morally acceptable practice. It is now almost universally condemned as the moral abomination it surely is. Then there are the significant strides we have taken towards full recognition of the rights of gays and lesbians. It was not too long ago that private sexual acts between consenting gay adults were both morally condemned and subject to criminal penalty. This is no longer the case in most jurisdictions. And within Canada at least, we see an inexorable movement towards consensus on full social, moral, and legal recognition of gays and lesbians, which is likely to culminate soon in formal recognition of same-sex marriage. I take this all to be significant moral progress. Can we not hope for similar increases in moral enlightenment in the future? *Third,* many moral disputes actually rest on ignorance of relevant nonmoral facts. This may have been true in our imaginary case of Demos, where, I suggested, support for the language law could have rested on Demosians' failure to recognize or appreciate fully the interest all of us have in conversing in our own language. This deficiency in imagination was a deficiency in knowledge of relevant nonmoral facts. If brought to the attention of Demosians, they might well have withdrawn their support for the language law. Returning to a real-life example, acceptance of the institution of slavery rested largely on false factual beliefs about the intellectual and cognitive capacities of those deemed unworthy of full moral status. Science proved these beliefs to be groundless, thus giving force to movements in favour of abolition. Might not the same be true of disputes surrounding things like the use of human embryos for stem cell extraction, the effects of affirmative action programs, the existence of factory farms, or the social status of Aboriginal peoples who often fall victim to factually baseless stereotypes? Even if agreement on the relevant scientific facts does not always yield moral consensus, the fact remains that a good deal of moral disagreement is traceable to differences in factual beliefs. And there is no reason to deny that this might be true in many Charter cases as well.

The Demonstrability Argument is no more persuasive than the Argument from Disagreement. As noted above, the absence of agreed procedures for demonstrating moral conclusions is often taken to entail the absence of right answers. Morality, it is said, lacks the agreement on methods and procedures that one finds in the natural sciences – and perhaps other areas of law, like the rules of evidence for criminal trials. As a result, moral conclusions, including those that figure in instances of judicial review, cannot be demonstrated: They can be nothing more than matters of opinion. This popular argument is no better than the Argument for Disagreement. *First*, it rests on a highly dubious assumption: that the objectivity of judgment making requires agreed methods of demonstration that, when applied properly, always yield results upon which fully informed participants would be forced to agree (on pain of being deemed irrational). This assumption is, at best, questionable. Many social practices – for example, literary criticism, history, and philosophy – thrive in the absence of such agreed methods and results. Take historical explanation. There are few agreed standards of theory construction and evaluation upon which all historians agree. And for many historical events or trends, there are no historical explanations upon which all historians will ultimately agree. Yet virtually no one denies that there is (at least usually) a truth of the matter that historians seek to discover and explain. Historians believe that they are normally seeking the truth and are able, in perfectly disciplined and intelligent ways, to develop, evaluate, and criticize one another's historical explanations. All this despite the fact that they are seldom able to demonstrate their conclusions to the complete satisfaction of everyone. Why should the same not apply to one engaged in the kind of moral reasoning one finds on display in Charter cases? Unless we wish to condemn all of these practices as wholly misguided – as in no way based on intelligible, disciplined argumentation but only undisciplined opinion and taste – we must reject the Demonstrability Argument. It sets the standard of objectivity far too high. There is no reason, therefore, to conclude from the absence of agreement on clear-cut methods of demonstration that everything is up for grabs in judicial review, that there is no moral truth, and that judges are basing their decisions on nothing more disciplined than subjective preference and unbridled discretion.

A *second*, equally telling point against the Demonstrability Argument is that its comparison between morality and the natural sciences unjustifiably flatters the latter. The comparison between the supposed rigorous methodology of science with the relatively undisciplined methods of moral reasoning on display in judicial review rests upon an exaggerated contrast between the two.[52] The fact of the matter is that the history of science is replete with controversy about the

---

52 The same is true of the contrast sometimes drawn between judicial review, on the one hand, and legal reasoning in other areas of legal practice, such as the laws of tort, contract, and criminal procedure, on the other.

most fundamental of matters. There has been deep controversy about how to go about testing hypotheses, as well as disputes about substantive matters. Examples of the latter include widespread controversies about the nature of light (Is it composed of particles or waves?) and about whether space is a vacuum or is filled with a largely imperceptible ether. Then there are all the controversies about whether, and to the extent to which, science can be "value free." Scientists not only disagree about scientific facts and theories, they often disagree on what methods are to be employed in developing, defending, and evaluating their accounts, and whether these are in any sense of the term objective. For example, scientific differences can sometimes turn on disputes over the reliability of a certain apparatus – for example, a telescope or microscope – in establishing evidence. Other times, differences will hinge on the validity of certain mathematical models used in understanding natural phenomena. Science is not the absolutely rigorous machine many suppose it to be. Despite its many controversies, however, few people are willing to condemn science as wholly subjective and undisciplined. So why should we, on these very same grounds, condemn moral reasoning as a matter of mere opinion and subjective preference? And why should we then go on to conclude that judicial review, because it inevitably involves such reasoning, is subject to the same fate? The answer is obvious: We should not. It is simply fallacious to conclude, from the absence of agreed procedures of demonstration that always yield clear answers, that "judges are thus free to choose."[53]

As we will see in Chapter 6, there is much more to be said about the Argument from Disagreement and the Demonstrability Argument. When applied to judicial review, they both may rest on a questionable assumption: that the morality to which judges are to appeal in Charter cases is what we might term "true morality." By this is meant a morality that is universally applicable to any and all societies and that is "objectively" true or valid independent of our beliefs about it and independent of our variable social understandings and practices. If this is the morality to which judges are to appeal in rendering Charter decisions, then I suspect that the Critics' arguments will continue to be persuasive (though still unsound) even after the foregoing objections are brought to light. But it is not at all clear that this Platonic morality is the one to which Charters make reference. As we shall see, Charters are better thought of as embodying what we will call "the community's constitutional morality," a type of morality that contains considerable resources – some of it rooted in judicial review itself – upon which judges both can and do draw in deciding Charter cases. These resources often yield the right answers that appear so elusive if our focus is on a true morality upon which there is comparatively little agreement. But more on this in Chapter 6.

53 Morton and Knopff, *The Charter Revolution and the Court Party*, 34.

vii. Philosopher Kings and Queens

A fifth popular objection to judicial review picks up on our reference to the Platonic conception of morality.[54] One often hears the following kind of complaint: A very small group of judges sitting in chambers are no more competent than legislators, or the citizens they represent, to deal sensitively and effectively with the deeply controversial, complex issues of morality and public policy typically at stake in Charter cases. And yet this is precisely what Charters presuppose – else why have Charters and why assign their interpretation and enforcement to judges? But reality suggests a far different picture. Judges, though well schooled in the law, are in no sense of the term moral authorities who would ace their final exams in moral philosophy were they enrolled in Plato's Academy. Indeed, the notion of a moral expert or "moral authority" comes very close to contradiction.[55] Nor are they experts in the various fields of social policy with which government action typically deals. They most certainly do not exhibit levels of moral and public policy understanding superior to the levels enjoyed by the government authorities whose actions they are called on to sit in moral judgment of. They are thus no more able than these others to discern the content of the moral limits on government power contained within Charters. Why then should the people and their representatives bow to the no more authoritative moral decisions of this handful of judges on matters of common concern? Consider again the entirely plausible hypothesis, earlier dubbed "the multiple heads principle," that the greater the number of people of varying backgrounds, knowledge bases, perspectives, and so on that we have working on a complex social problem, the greater our chances of arriving at well-thought-out, reasonable solutions upon which agreement could be based. If the multiple heads principle is valid, then we should eschew a system under which a few weathered heads in chambers are allowed to substitute their judgments for those of a great many representative heads, elected by the people to serve their interests, honour their wishes, advance their perspectives, and be accountable to them on that score.

[It is] particularly insulting when [citizens and their elected representatives] discover that the judges disagree amongst themselves along exactly the same lines as the citizens and representatives do, and that the judges make their decisions, too, in the courtroom

---

54 The title of this section is the title of Chapter 3 of Martin's *The Most Dangerous Branch*.
55 I say "very close" because there are some, for example health care ethicists, who might be said to be moral authorities within their particular domains of special competence. This is because they have specialist knowledge of particular moral norms like those governing informed consent, or the conducting of research on human subjects. But their authority does not stem from special powers of moral insight; its stems from specialist knowledge of relevant nonmoral facts and from their having thought long and hard about the moral issues that arise within their special areas of activity. As will become clear in Chapters 5 and 6, something analogous is true of judges.

by majority voting. The citizens may well feel that if disagreements on these matters are to be settled by counting heads, then it is their heads or those of their accountable representatives that should be counted.[56]

There is good sense in Waldron's objection – but only if we accept two further assumptions: first, that the decisions we call on judges to make are the very same ones we ask our elected representatives to make; and second, that the context in which the two types of decisions are made are relevantly similar. As we shall see in Chapter 6, both assumptions are questionable. With respect to the first, we will see that Charter decisions often deal with questions about which our elected representatives were completely unaware. This is often for reasons that are perfectly understandable and predictable and that in no way reflect badly on the legislators. Judicial decisions in Charter cases are, in many cases, best viewed as supplementing, not replacing or trumping, decisions made by elected representatives. For this reason alone, they fail to threaten democratic ideals. As for the second assumption, we saw in Chapter 3 a variety of forces to which Atticus was susceptible in making his decision on the language law. These are forces to which virtually all elected representatives are vulnerable. Judges, because of their relative immunity from the effect of these forces, are sometimes able to make the hard decisions it would be unfair to expect of legislators, whose very careers often lie in the balance if they thwart the will of their constituents.

viii. Judges and the Elites of Society

A closely related objection goes beyond questioning the ability of judges to provide superior moral and public policy judgments. Many theorists, far more critical of legal practices than Waldron, point to the inevitable bias that is introduced into our political and legal cultures if judges are allowed to decide the kinds of questions raised by judicial review. Many critics point out that judges tend to originate from the social, political, and financial elites within society. "You don't get to be a judge by being a radical."[57] From this it is inferred that judges inevitably share the perspectives of these elites on the issues of morality and public policy around which Charter cases revolve. The consequence, it is said, is suppression of those – women, minority racial groups, the poor, and so on – whose interests are not adequately recognized or supported by the dominant, elite ideologies to which judges have an affinity. Instead of the curbing of unwarranted exercises of government power for which Charters are thought to stand, we have political suppression disguised in a cloak of false

---

56 *Law and Disagreement*, at 15. The sting of this insult was experienced by the many Americans who were utterly dismayed by the Supreme Court's decision in *George W. Bush, et al., Petitioners v. Albert Gore Jr. et al.* [2000] U.S. Supreme Court (00–949).

57 Michael Mandel, *The Charter of Rights and the Legalization of Politics in Canada*, 460.

constitutional legitimacy. Does this too not fly in the face of any sane conception of democracy?

Michael Mandel clearly thinks it does. Combining an apparent endorsement of the Argument from Disagreement with his concern about the social origins of Canadian judges, Mandel writes:

> [Charter] rights are what you make of them, and what you make of them depends upon your point of view. You do not have to read the thousands of pages of contradictory judicial opinions on their meaning to realize that the words of the Charter neither restrain nor guide the judges; you do not have to be a legal philosopher to realize that they were not intended to.
>
> As for the famous [Dworkinian] legal technique of finding the "right answer" in "hard cases," it may work in theory, but in practice it has a hard time being reconciled with the multitude of overruled decisions, split decisions, and decisions – almost all Charter decisions its seems – in which judges coming to the same conclusion do so for completely different reasons. . . .
>
> Once we admit the controversial nature of constitutional rights and the great differences of "interpretation" that can result from differing ideological points of view among judges, and between judges and the rest of us, the idea that judicial review is democratic, in the usual sense of enhancing popular power, evaporates into thin air.[58]

After noting "the inevitable class bias of the legal profession" from which judges are drawn, Mandel goes on to quote, with apparent approval, the views of Andrew Petter concerning the level of elitist thinking at play within the Canadian judiciary:

> There are few public institutions in this country whose composition more poorly reflects, and whose members have less direct exposure to, the interests of the economically and socially disadvantaged. . . . [I]f not of wealthy origin, most become wealthy or least achieved a degree of affluence before accepting their judicial appointments. The majority made their name in private practice where they held themselves out as business people and shared business concerns. . . . In short, there is nothing about the Canadian judiciary to suggest that they possess the experience, the training or the disposition to comprehend the social impact of claims made to them under the Charter, let alone to resolve those claims in ways that promote, or even protect, the interests of lower income Canadians.[59]

So the inevitable result of judicial review is not protection from tyranny of the majority, but exposure to the tyranny of a powerful minority elite. Judges, given their social backgrounds and political allegiances, are far from being an ideal choice for representing the interests of oppressed minorities and individuals. They may not be inclined to side with the majority – the "great unwashed." But their elite status means that they are no more likely to side with the oppressed. This will be so if only because of their lack of knowledge or appreciation of

---

58 *Ibid.*, 41–2.
59 *Ibid.*, 48, quoting Andrew Petter, "Immaculate Deception: The Charter's Hidden Agenda," *The Advocate* 45 (Pt. 6), 861.

what it's really like to be poor, or otherwise oppressed. In this respect, they're little better than the Demosians whose grasp of the plight of the Venusians under the language law was far from ideal.

How might one respond to this objection? First, we should note that legislatures are often, though not always, no more populated by members of society's elites than Courts are.[60] Huge sums of money are normally required for electoral success, leading to representative legislatures populated by financial elites – or by representatives closely tied to elites whose interests and wishes they will be motivated to serve. While it's true that elected representatives are expected to serve the wishes and interests of all their constituents, including their disadvantaged minorities, a variety of social and political forces will, as we have seen, often lead them to do otherwise. Judges, on the other hand, are not nearly as vulnerable to these particular factors. "Their relative insulation from the direct claims of special interest constituencies protects judges from the partisan views of other political actors."[61]

We should also insist, once again, on the importance of distinguishing between the merits and possibilities of judicial review on the one hand, and what current judges are doing (or might in fact be doing) under the form of judicial review currently in place on the other hand. In general, it is always important to distinguish between the empirical and the normative, and the current context provides no exception. Even if the ranks of the judiciary are largely filled by members of society's elites following ideologies associated with these privileged groups; even if "[i]n practice . . . the judges behave as if they possess unlimited power and are not subject to any legal constraints . . . [amending] the Constitution at will, rewriting it or inventing new principles, as if the Constitution were their private possession or plaything,"[62] it in no way follows that this is inevitable or as it should be. Perhaps our selection procedures need to be modified. Perhaps we should encourage the publication of more popular and scholarly articles critical of biased decision making in the courts. If the belief in judicial neutrality really is nothing more than a myth, then we are well past the point where a concern for its maintenance rules our public discussion and criticism of rulings from the bench. And finally, perhaps more effort should be made to ensure some kind of broad representation on the bench. It is no mere coincidence that four of the nine justices currently on the Canadian Supreme Court are female, and that at the head of this body sits a woman, Chief Justice Beverley McLachlin. A conscious effort has undoubtedly been

---

60 To a very great extent, the levels of elitism one finds in legislatures versus the judiciary depend greatly on social context. In the United Kingdom, for example, there are many more socialists and radicals in the House of Commons than one finds in the upper levels of the judiciary. The fact remains, however, that this need not be the case, especially if steps are taken to render the judiciary more "representative."
61 Wellington, "The Nature of Judicial Review," 493.
62 Martin, *The Most Dangerous Branch*, 7.

made to ensure that the interests of women are given adequate representation in judicial review. And one of the best ways – though not the only way – of ensuring this is to appoint more women.[63] There is also reason to believe that the Canadian Supreme Court may soon include representation of yet another historically disadvantaged group, Aboriginal peoples. A recent article from *The Globe and Mail* reports that Justice McLachlin "welcomes the possibility the court may soon have its first aboriginal judge – a goal [then] Justice Minister Irwin Cotler has expressed openly."[64]

Once again invoking the distinction between the empirical and the normative, we might add this reply to the claim that judicial review inevitably leads to judgments furthering the interests of elites. That one derives from, or is currently a member of, a particular social class does not, despite much rhetoric suggesting otherwise, mean that one will inevitably side with its interests and wishes. The role of a judge engaged in judicial review is, at least in part, to make a good-faith effort to ensure fair representation and consideration of the interests and authentic wishes of all individuals touched by government action. To be sure, they may more easily identify with those with whom they have a common background and with whom they therefore have more of an affinity. And they must be encouraged always to bear this fact in mind. But unless one accepts a very extreme form of skepticism that reduces all questions of political morality to the subjective preferences, tastes, and biases of those called upon to answer them, there is little reason to think that one who must make a Charter decision will inevitably – or even likely – be led to side with her "own kind." Rational, moral agents have the ability, with varying degrees of success, to distance themselves from the various forces inevitably at play in their thinking, forces that, if left completely unchecked, will inevitably introduce unacceptable bias into any decision made. This is as true in judging as it is true in marking student essays, drawing up a short list for job interviews, or evaluating the social value attached to various forms of public activity, for example hockey versus opera. No doubt judges should be conscious of the forces to which their backgrounds make them susceptible and that they cannot completely eliminate. But unless one accepts the radical skepticism just mentioned or believes that our powers of reasoning are a sham and that our actions and decisions are *entirely* the products of forces beyond our control, there is no reason to condemn judicial review as inexorably leading to suppression cloaked in the guise of fairness and objectivity. This *would* be to accept an unflattering picture of our status as

---

63 A variety of steps and devices are available for use in counteracting the forces of bias. For example, in law, we have well-established rules of evidence. In drawing up short lists for job candidates, we often employ the device of requiring that a certain number or percentage of applicants chosen for interview be from one or more designated group(s).

64 Kirk Makin, "Judicial Activism Debate on Decline, Top Judge Says," *Globe and Mail*, Saturday, January 8, 2005, A14.

moral beings. This *would* be to accept a picture that we must strenuously work to avoid.

Finally, we should once again reiterate that judicial review need not entail judicial supremacy. It certainly need not entail granting judges unlimited normative or *de facto* freedom to make binding decisions in whatever way they wish. A variety of mechanisms, for example an override mechanism like section 33 of the Canadian Charter, are always available should the judges for some reason choose to ignore their good-faith requirement and instead pursue the promptings of a dominant or elitist ideology. Furthermore, the fundamental rules defining and controlling the powers of judges are seldom, if ever, a function of their own choosing, or of their own attitudes and behaviour. They are a function of the activities, attitudes, decisions, and points of view of a broad range of official and non-official individuals all of whom share in the creation and maintenance of the fundamental social rules underlying their constitutional democracy. The judges no doubt have a very large say in the development of the rules by which they are bound, but they don't have the only say.

ix. The Futility of "Results Driven" Arguments

Recall Jeremy Waldron's claim that the circumstances of politics include radical dissensus about rights. This dissensus, he argues, undercuts the Ulysses analogy, thus undermining one of the more popular arguments figuring in the Standard Case. "I cannot restrain myself from saying that anyone who thinks [the Standard Case] is appropriately modeled by the story of Ulysses and the sirens is an idiot."[65] Radical dissensus has, Waldron thinks, further important implications for the Standard Case: (a) It rules out defences of judicial review premised on any kind of "results-driven" standard; (b) it reveals the deeply problematic nature of the constitutional conception of democracy; and (c) it drives us towards the rival procedural conception and its endorsement of majoritarian-decision procedures unbridled by substantive constraints.

Among the most common arguments advanced by Advocates is premised on the claim that Charters have a number of desirable effects, among the most important being stronger and more consistent rights enforcement. According to most Advocates, Charters are helpful, if not essential, devices for ensuring compliance with the democratic conditions prescribed by the constitutional conception. Ronald Dworkin, one of the foremost Advocates, asserts that "The United States is a more just society than it would have been had its constitutional rights been left to the conscience of majoritarian institutions."[66] That Charters are able to achieve these results serves not only to explain their nature and appeal, but it also serves to show why they are an essential component of thriving

---

65 *Law and Disagreement*, 268.
66 Dworkin, *Law's Empire*, 356.

democracies and fully justified for that reason alone. According to Dworkin, this kind of results-driven argument is the only one to which, ultimately, appeal can successfully be made in justifying judicial review.

> I see no alternative but to use a result-driven rather than a procedure-driven standard.... The best institutional structure is one best calculated to produce the best answers to the essentially moral question of what the democratic conditions actually are, and to secure stable compliance with those conditions.[67]

On this criterion, then, the adoption of judicial review is said to be clearly warranted because it secures better understanding and enforcement of important moral rights. It is an essential tool of democracy because it helps ensure compliance with the conditions inherent in the constitutional conception of democracy. Not surprisingly, Waldron disagrees. His response is to challenge both the truth of Dworkin's premises and the validity of *any* results-driven argument, of which Dworkin's is a prime example.

In rejecting Dworkin's premises, Waldron falls in line with other Critics who deny that judicial review has been shown to offer valuable protections to vulnerable individuals and minorities or deny that it leads generally to more effective rights enforcement. As Waldron rightly notes,

> Like any claim involving a counterfactual ("more just than it would have been if..."), [the claim that we get better rights protection with Charters than we do without them] is an extraordinarily difficult proposition to assess.... Verifying the counterfactual would involve not only an assessment of the impact of [cases like *Brown v. Board of Education of Topeka*[68] and *Roe v. Wade*[69]] but also a consideration of the way in which the struggle against segregation and similar injustices might have proceeded in the United States if there had been no Bill of Rights or no practice of judicial review. About the only evidence we have in this regard is the struggle against injustice in other societies which lacked these institutions.[70]

And what do we find when we look at these other societies? We find evidence to suggest that the level of rights protection is no worse, perhaps even better, than in Charter societies. Waldron is keen to contrast the so-called *Lochner* era, where a Charter – that is, the American Bill of Rights – existed but important rights were systematically thwarted by the courts, with the longstanding tradition of civil rights protection evident in other countries, for example the United Kingdom.[71] For years the UK did without a Charter and yet its courts consistently contributed to successful efforts to secure respect for fundamental rights. "Many such societies seem to be at least as free and as just as the

---

67 *Freedom's Law*, 34.
68 *Brown v. Board of Education of Topeka* [1954] 347 U.S. 483 (USSC).
69 *Roe v. Wade* [1973] 410 U.S. 113 (USSC).
70 Waldron, *Law and Disagreement*, 288.
71 *Lochner v. People of the State of New York* 198 U.S. 45 (1905).

United States, though it is of course arguable such comparisons underestimate the peculiarities of American politics and society."[72]

Yet another difficulty in drawing the comparisons upon which results-driven arguments are based is ensuring that one's characterizations of the societies being compared are accurate. Many Critics, Waldron included, are keen to point out that on this important criterion, Advocates' arguments fail miserably. They tend to focus selectively on landmark decisions like *Brown* and *Roe v. Wade* and on periods of American constitutional history in which the Courts were active in promoting civil rights. In so doing, they ignore other, equally noteworthy periods like the *Lochner* era where the courts are better viewed as having tried to consolidate an oppressive economic status quo that benefited no one save the nation's financial elites. But this kind of selective focus will not do. If we are going to look to results, we had better ensure that we look at all of them – or that our sample is a representative one. And on that score, Advocates' arguments are more often than not abysmal failures.

This indictment is one with which Michael Mandel is in full agreement. Upon noting the extent to which early Canadian Advocates drew upon the supposedly stellar record of rights protection under the American Bill of Rights in making their case for the Canadian Charter, Mandel offers the following observations:

> Naturally, the Canadian courts' performance *without a Charter* could not be relied upon; it was admittedly dismal. The Charter was intended to change all that. The sole source for the claim was the United States. But the US record was far from promising. Granted, when the Charter became a serious contender in Canada, the United States courts were behaving in a way that Canadian civil libertarians could applaud and indeed envy. But the twenty-year period bounded by the famous de-segregation decision in *Brown v. Board of Education of Topeka* and the equally liberal abortion de-criminalization decision in *Roe v. Wade* was the only such period in the US Supreme Court's entire two-hundred-year history. . . . [I]ts most active period other than that one was the period 1900–1937 [the *Lochner* era] when the Court found a vigorous rear-guard action on behalf of laissez-faire capitalism against the regulation of business, striking down such important social limits on profit-making as minimum wage laws and child labour prohibitions. . . . [F]or most of its history the Court has supported the legal status quo, no matter how contrary to contemporary civil libertarian conceptions. Famous examples include *Plessy v. Ferguson*[73] in which the Court upheld legislation requiring black people to ride in separate railway cars, the genesis of the "separate but equal" doctrine that stood for sixty years until *Brown*. Another is *Korematsu*[74] which sustained the wartime internment of Americans of Japanese descent without the necessity of any proof of anti-government activity.[75]

---

72 Waldron, *Law and Disagreement*, 288.
73 *Plessy v. Ferguson* [1896] 163 U.S. 537 (USSC).
74 *Korematsu v. United States* [1944] 323 U.S. 214 (USSC).
75 Michael Mandel, *The Charter of Rights and Freedoms and the Legalization of Politics in Canada*, 57.

If Mandel and Waldron are correct in their assessments, it is at the very least questionable whether we have enough evidence to support the premise of Dworkin's argument. American history certainly fails to provide unequivocal support, and comparisons between it and the companion history of the UK do nothing but flatter the latter.

So the truth of Dworkin's premise is highly questionable. But this is not all, according to Waldron. The radical dissensus inherent in the circumstances of politics renders the argument invalid as well. It also reveals the sheer folly of endorsing the constitutional conception of democracy.

> Even if they agree that democracy implicates certain rights, citizens will surely disagree what these rights are and what in detail they commit us to. But a citizenry who disagree about what would count as the right results are not in a position to construct their constitution on this basis.[76]

> We seem, then, to be in a bind. It looks as though it is disagreement all the way down, so far as constitutional choice is concerned.... [W]e cannot use a results-driven test, because we disagree about which results would count in favour of and which against a given decision-procedure.... [W]e cannot appeal to any procedural criterion either, since procedural questions are at the very nub of the disagreements we are talking about.[77]

So radical disagreement about rights invalidates any results-driven argument such as Dworkin's. If we cannot agree on the right results, then we cannot possibly compare systems based on their relative tendencies to generate these results. And if, despite (or because of) radical dissensus, we see a need to adopt mechanisms for making law-determining decisions, we will be forced to choose ones that allow us to rise above this disagreement. Such mechanisms are, of course, those recommended by the procedural conception of democracy. These are decision procedures that enable us to come to decisions that we can all accept as "our own" despite our serious differences of opinion on what those decisions should be. The futility of results-driven arguments leads us, then, towards unbridled majority rule and the rejection of judicial review.

A full defense of judicial review against Waldron's attempt to dismantle results-driven arguments must await development of the alternative common law conception of judicial review. Suffice it to say, at this stage, that we will need ways of assessing the results and promise of judicial review that do not depend on our denying the obvious: that there is considerable dissensus on political questions, including the nature of the democratic conditions that are part and parcel of the constitutional and, importantly, procedural conceptions of democracy; that arguments based on counterfactual comparisons are fraught

---

76 *Law and Disagreement*, at 294.
77 *Ibid.*, 295. Note Waldron's suggestion that radical dissensus extends to procedural questions. In Chapter 6, we will address the crucial implications of this admission for Waldron's case in favour of a procedural conception of democracy.

with serious philosophical difficulty; and that the record of judicial review in the United States and elsewhere is probably mixed at best. Our argument will also have to acknowledge the importance of differing social contexts in the kind of comparisons – either factual or counterfactual – upon which results-driven arguments rely. What might work in contemporary Canada or Mexico might not have worked in these countries in 1925; what might be necessary, at T1, in country X might not be necessary, or even helpful, at this very same time, T1, in a different country, Y, with a different culture of rights protection. Charters exist within broad social and political contexts, a fact that must never be overlooked when assessing their impact or potential.

x. Charters and the Level of Public Debate

As observed in the previous section, the Standard Case for judicial review often includes the claim that it is a valuable means for focusing and improving the level of public debate. Among its desirable consequences or results is a rise in the level and quality of democratic discourse. Dworkin again: "When an issue is seen as constitutional . . . and as one that will ultimately be resolved by courts applying general constitutional principles, the quality of public argument is often improved, because the argument concentrates from the start on questions of political morality."[78] Waldron's response? "I am afraid I do not agree with any of this."[79] *Contra* Dworkin and his fellow Advocates, transforming debates of political morality into constitutional disputes is as likely to reduce the level of public debate as improve it. In support of this indictment, Waldron cites two factors: history and the artificiality of constitutional debate under Charters.

My experience is that national debates about abortion are as robust and well informed in countries like the United Kingdom and New Zealand, where they are not consti-tutionalized, as they are in the United States – the more so perhaps because they are uncontaminated by quibbling about how to interpret the text of an eighteenth century document. It is sometimes liberating to be able to discuss issues like abortion directly, on the principles that ought to be engaged, rather than having to scramble around con-structing those principles out of scraps of some sacred text, in a tendentious exercise of constitutional calligraphy.[80]

Further points of comparison are also drawn by Waldron: debates about capi-tal punishment in countries free to focus on the general aims of penal policy, as compared with American debates centred on questions about the extent to which the practice is "cruel and unusual"; the lack of depth and sophistica-tion of the decision in *Bowers v. Hardwick*[81] as compared with debates about

---

78 *Freedom's Law*, at 345.
79 *Law and Disagreement*, at 290.
80 *Ibid.*
81 *Bowers v. Hardwick* [1986] 478 U.S. 186 (USSC).

homosexuality initiated in the UK by the Wolfenden Report and sustained in the comparatively sophisticated (and sensitive) exchange between H.L.A. Hart and Lord Patrick Devlin.[82] In summing up the judgment of history, Waldron writes: "If the debate that actually takes place in American society and American legislatures is as good as that in other countries, it is so *despite* the Supreme Court's framing of the issues, not because of it."[83]

This conclusion is one that would no doubt be applauded by many Canadian Critics. According to Robert Martin, the framing of social and moral debates in terms of Charter rights seriously threatens democratic discourse and our ability to discover mutually acceptable resolutions to the disputes that divide us.

The very process of turning political and social issues into legal battles over rights is by its nature anti-democratic. This process inhibits the kind of discourse essential to democracy. In the discourse of rights talk, a dispute between A and B can only go like this: A asserts, "I have a right to such and such." If B does not agree, her only reply can be, "No you don't." A is forced to respond, "Yes, I do." What results is a schoolyard fight, not the discourse among citizens which should exist in a democracy. The fact that abortion remains such a divisive and intractable social issue in Canada is probably the result of the attempt by the judiciary to resolve it. If politics really is the "art of the possible," notions of negotiations and give-and-take must inhere in any political process. But there is no negotiation, no give-and-take in the endless public shouting-match over abortion. . . . I suspect the main reason capital punishment is not a social issue in Canada today is that it was resolved by Parliament, not the courts.[84]

Morton and Knopff also see judicial review as a threat to democratic discourse. Following an extensive historical analysis of Canadian public policy on contentious issues like abortion and gay rights, they conclude with the following observations:

To transfer the resolution of reasonable disagreements from legislatures to courts inflates rhetoric to unwarranted levels and replaces negotiated, majoritarian compromise policies with the intensely held policy preferences of minorities. Rights-based judicial policy making also grants the policy preferences of courtroom victors an aura of coercive force and permanence that they do not deserve. Issues that should be subject to the ongoing flux of government by discussion are presented as beyond legitimate debate, with the partisans claiming the right to permanent victory. As the morality of rights displaces the morality of consent, the politics of coercion replaces the politics of persuasion. The result is to embitter politics and decrease the inclinations of political opponents to treat each other as fellow citizens – that is, as members of a sovereign people.[85]

---

82 Lord Patrick Devlin, *The Enforcement of Morals* (Oxford: Oxford University Press, 1959); H.L.A. Hart, *Law, Liberty and Morality* (Oxford: Oxford University Press, 1962).
83 *Law and Disagreement*, at 290.
84 Martin, *The Most Dangerous Branch*, 52–3.
85 Morton and Knopff, *The Charter Revolution and the Court Party*, 166. These authors follow Martin's lead in citing with approval Mary Ann Glendon's influential views as

According to these Critics, Charters transform complex issues of political morality, whose sensible resolution requires open discussion, the ability to see the other side's point of view, and ultimately compromise and mutual accommodation, into "them-against-us" battles. Instead of informed, respectful public discourse, we find an inflation of rhetoric, a selfish preoccupation with promoting one's own interests as matters of fundamental right, a hardening of positions, and, in some cases, a resort to coercion and violence.

Waldron adds yet another, somewhat different element, to this troubling picture. The comparatively low quality of political discourse one finds in Charter societies is partly explained, he thinks, by the "verbal rigidity" introduced by the choice to "constitutionalize" fundamental moral rights.

A legal right that finds protection in a Bill of Rights finds it under the auspices of some canonical form of words in which the provisions of the charter are enunciated. One lesson of American constitutional experience is that the words of each provision in the Bill of Rights tend to take on a life of their own, becoming the obsessive catchphrase for expressing everything one might want to say about the right in question. For example, First Amendment doctrine in America is obsessed to the point of scholasticism with the question of whether some problematic form of behaviour [e.g. flag burning, pornography, topless dancing] that the state has an interest in regulating is to be regarded as "speech" or not.[86]

Yet, Waldron adds, this is surely not the way to argue about fundamental rights. We can, he says, use phrases like "freedom of speech" to "pick out the sort of concerns we have in mind in invoking a particular right; but that is not the same as saying that the *word* 'speech' . . . is the key to our concerns in the area." [87] If instead we allow our evolving understandings of moral rights to be reflected in more flexible and less verbally constrained common law principles and precedents, "and easier still if rights take the form of 'conventional understandings' subscribed to the political community at large, as they have in Britain for many years," we will have a public discourse less constrained by verbal formulas and semantic obsessions and more able to ask the questions of moral substance that should really be our principal focus. What we need are institutional mechanisms for protecting rights which are "free from the obsessive verbalism of a particular written charter."[88]

If these Critics are correct, judicial review results in anything but an increase in the level of pubic discourse about important issues of political morality. How should we respond to this serious indictment? We should begin by questioning two key assumptions underlying the critique. First there is the assumption

---

expressed in her *Rights Talk* (New York: The Free Press, 1991). Glendon's views will be discussed below.

86 *Law and Disagreement*, 220.
87 *Ibid.*
88 *Ibid.*, 221.

(a) that framing social issues in terms of rights – which, of course a Charter of *Rights* is bound to do – inexorably leads to the undesirable consequences cited: inflated rhetoric, a selfish individualism that works against broader communal concerns better addressed in moral language more attuned to compromise and accommodation, and, ultimately, conflict and violence. Then there is the assumption (b) that Charters invariably introduce into issues of political morality a kind of rigidity owing to the fact that Charters are not only law, but written law. It's the fact that Charters transform political issues into legal ones, governed by written laws, which virtually guarantees that they will end up lowering, not raising, the level of public discourse and debate we would all like to see in a democratic society.

Let's begin with assumption (a). In suggesting that judicial review inexorably leads to heightened rhetoric, intransigence, and conflict, Critics are expressing an anti-rights sentiment common among many consequentialists, virtue ethicists, feminists, and communitarians. Among the most influential of these theorists is the legal scholar Mary Ann Glendon, whom Morton and Knopff cite with approval.[89] So too does Martin, who characterizes Glendon's work as having demonstrated the pernicious effects of "rights-talk." [90] The latter has, he believes, "been a major factor in creating the vicious and acrimonious atmosphere which surrounds the debate over abortion in North America. Conducted largely in the rhetoric of rights, public discourse about abortion has created a situation in which opponents regularly hurl abuse at each other, and sometimes murder each other." In Glendon's own words, America's framing of issues like abortion and divorce in terms of rights encourages "autonomy, separation, and isolation in the war of all against all." On the other hand, the more respectful, accommodating European approach, with its reduced reliance on rights-talk, has allowed for the realization of more communal values like "social solidarity."[91]

In responding to claims like these, we need to distinguish two questions. First, there is the causal question whether rights-talk does (or would) in actual fact lead to the undesirable consequences cited by the Critics. This is a very difficult empirical question to answer. It is not enough, of course, to point to differences between existing societies, some of which do and some of which do not engage in widespread rights-talk, unless one has reason to think that there is something in the nature of this rights-talk – or the rights it is about – that is causally responsible for the differences in effect. Otherwise there is no

---

89 See, for example, Morton and Knopff, *The Charter Revolution and the Court Party*, 156 and 163.
90 Martin, *The Most Dangerous Branch*, 228.
91 Glendon, *Abortion and Divorce in Western Law* (Cambridge, Mass.: Harvard University Press, 1987), 58.

reason to think that the differences could not be explained by mere coincidence, or other social and political factors left unexamined. A further difficulty is in verifying that there are indeed the differences in effect cited. In other words, in addition to knowing that the absence or prevalence of rights-talk is causally responsible for certain effects, we have to know that the effects attributed to these causes actually do exist in each case. With respect to Glendon's claims, we will want to know whether, in fact, the United States is properly characterized as, essentially, a nation of Hobbesean predators. Ronald Dworkin believes that the evidence for such a claim is questionable at best.

The United States' historical commitment to individual human rights has not proved isolating or Hobbesian, as [Glendon] and other critics have suggested. The United States is a nation of continental size, covering many very different and very large regions, and it is pluralist in almost every possible aspect: racial, ethnic, and cultural. In such a nation, individual rights, to the extent that they are recognized and actually enforced, offer the only possibility of genuine community in which all individuals participate as equals.[92]

Dworkin adds a further point of significance. Recall the Critics' claim that rights-talk leads to heightened rhetoric and to attempts to elevate what are better viewed as personal interests subject to compromise and accommodation in the give-and-take of democratic discourse and decision making, to the lofty status of intractable claims of fundamental rights. In response, Dworkin correctly observes:

It is true that many of the claims that different groups in America now make about what they are entitled to have by right are inflated and sometimes preposterous. But the possibility of abuse no more refutes the need for genuine individual rights than fascism or communism, each of which has claimed authority in the name of "solidarity," refutes Glendon's appeals for a greater sense of common goal and purpose.[93]

So there are good grounds to question the causal claim that rights-talk leads, or has led, to the undesirable consequences cited by the Critics – leading to the next obvious question. Is there something in the very nature of rights, and hence rights-talk, that might lead someone to *expect* these consequences despite the absence of adequate evidence that they do in fact exist? Many who share the anti-rights sentiment noted above believe so. They believe that rights, as individual "trumps" over the common good and the interests of other people, inevitably lead to the consequences cited by the Critics. In thinking of ourselves as bearers of rights, they claim, we are both presupposing and encouraging a picture of ourselves as socially isolated individuals, either indifferent or hostile

---

92 Ronald Dworkin, *Life's Dominion: An Argument About Abortion, Euthanasia, and Individual Freedom* (New York: Vintage Books, 1994), 61.
93 *Ibid.*

to one another, and in need of the hard-and-fast personal protections that rights are said to afford. This, the Critics argue, presents a warped picture of both ourselves and our moral universe. It mischaracterizes as Hobbesean what is in fact a moral universe in which features like caring, friendship, loyalty, and trust are central.[94]

How might an Advocate respond to this particular critique? There is much to be said about all this, a good deal of which can easily be found in the extensive literature responding to communitarian and feminist attempts to discredit rights-based theories. Here are some of the highlights. We might begin by questioning the assumption that all rights are necessarily individualist in nature or orientation. There is nothing in the very nature of rights which entails that they can be held only by individuals, or that their role must lie in the protection of interests that bear no relation to communal values. Survival rights, for example, are often ascribed to cultural groups and nations. Furthermore, these are conceived in ways that do not reduce, without remainder, to the rights and interests of individual members of these groups.[95] In addition, even individual rights are not always viewed as advancing only the freedoms and interests of individual rights holders. Many forms of utilitarianism link the possession of individual rights to gains in overall utility, while other non-utilitarian theories nevertheless tie the justification of individual liberal rights to the public good. A prime example of the latter is Joseph Raz, in whose view,

> rights such as freedom of expression, association and assembly, freedom of the press, and of religion, the right to privacy and the right against discrimination, rest on the importance of the interest of the right-holder which they serve. . . . [T]he importance we attribute to the protection of these interests results from their service to the promotion and protection of a certain public culture. That culture is in turn valued for its contribution to the well-being of members of the community generally, and not only to the right-holders. *The importance of liberal rights is in their service to the public good.* [96]

This is hardly a view premised on rampant individualism and Hobbesean psychology. It is a view in which community plays a key role in personal self-realization, and in which communal values serve to justify many of the rights ascribed to individuals in liberal democratic theory. It is, arguably, the kind of vision that is explicitly endorsed in section 27 of the Canadian Charter, which reads: "This Charter shall be interpreted in a manner consistent with the

---

94 Feminists are among the most prominent critics who pursue this line of argument. For further discussion of feminist critiques of "traditional" moral theories, including those that emphasize rights, see Waluchow, *The Dimensions of Ethics*, Chapter 10.

95 For discussion of "group rights" see Judith Baker, ed., *Group Rights*. Of particular relevance are Will Kymlicka, "Individual and Community Rights," 17–33; Leslie Green, "Internal Minorities and Their Rights," 100–17; and Denise Reaume, "The Group Rights to Linguistic Security: Whose Right, What Duties?" 118–41.

96 Joseph Raz, *The Morality of Freedom*, 256. Emphasis added.

preservation and enhancement of the multicultural heritage of Canadians." This clause clearly endorses the communal value of culture(s), suggesting that what might otherwise be construed as an instrument designed solely for the protection of individual rights and interests should not be considered in isolation of the cultural context(s) in which these rights function and from which they derive a good deal of their value and meaning.

A second response open to the Advocate is to question the Critics' assumption that rights are immune from compromise and accommodation. It is perhaps understandable that many Critics take this view: It is strongly suggested by the kind of language often used by rights advocates in discussing the role of rights in moral reasoning. Describing rights as "trumps" over arguments of utility and appeals to the common good strongly suggests the view that they are blunt instruments, immune from the kinds of balancing and compromise that are part and parcel of morality and politics.[97] But nothing in the logic of rights rules out their being weighed against other rights, or their being limited for reasons that bear directly on the wider context, including the wider cultural context. Again, one need only turn to the Canadian Charter to see this important conceptual point. As noted on several occasions above, section 1 specifies that the Charter "guarantees the rights and freedoms set out in it subject to such reasonable limits prescribed by law as can be demonstrably justified in a free and democratic society." The subsequent history of the Canadian courts in developing section 1 attests to their belief not only that Charter rights can be qualified by other Charter rights but also that individual rights must sometimes yield to the greater good. This is anything but the suggestion that rights are trumps. It is a message that rights are not absolute, that they are not blunt instruments with which to demand selfish advancement of one's own individual interests. It is also a message of which Canadians are well aware.

Yet another point to which we might draw attention is the important role in advancing social justice played by the rights-talk that the Critics so forcefully reject. Sometimes, in the face of fierce intransigence, motivated by factors like prejudice and fear, it is important that individuals and groups have rights in hand with which to press their demands. In some situations, more is needed than compromise, accommodation, and "social solidarity." Oftentimes, the social solidarity in play works forcefully against the vital interests of disadvantaged individuals and minorities. Social solidarity, in the hands of an entrenched majority, can lead to social injustice. One prime example is the plight of women and minorities in their ongoing struggles to achieve equality. In her controversial and influential defense of a legal right to pornography, Nadine Strossen, former president of the American Civil Liberties Union, takes

---

97 On rights as trumps, see Dworkin, "Rights as Trumps," in Jeremy Waldron, ed., *Theories of Rights* (Oxford: Oxford University Press, 1985).

on radical feminist critics of pornography who base their criticisms partly on their rejection of the culture of individual right that is said to underlie support for pornographers.[98] According to Strossen, feminists are like all who seek social change and equality; they are especially dependent on freedom of speech and its recognition via a strong right to free expression. Strong protections, in the form of individual rights to this freedom, have been essential, Strossen claims, to the struggles of all groups that have fought oppression within Western societies, including, paradigmatically, women and American blacks. The civil rights struggles of blacks during the 1950s and 1960s would, she argues, have been much more difficult had the speech of those involved been legally suppressed. The same is true of American women. They too have benefited greatly from the fact that no court or government can silence feminist authors because their views clearly run against the entrenched, traditional view of women. They have, in short, benefited greatly from rights.

And finally, we might stress, once again, that one can recognize the importance of rights without thinking that they exhaust the normative landscape. As Wayne Sumner correctly observes, rights are

specialized normative devices with a particular function, one to which they are very well adapted, but they cannot take the place of other equally important values such as loyalty, trust, and care. Nor are they a substitute for other means by which we judge personal character. . . . Anyone who believes that human interactions require nothing more than minimal regard for the rights of others would make a very unattractive friend or spouse or neighbour – or business associate for that matter. But it is no fault of rights that the indolent or small-minded might find it convenient to think that they exhaust the requirements of virtue, and is no solution to this problem to expel rights entirely from our moral thinking.[99]

Nothing, then, in the bare notion of rights would lead one to expect rights-talk to cause the many undesirable effects alluded to by the Critics. But recall Waldron's particular complaint. It wasn't that ascribing rights to individuals and minorities leads to a reduction in the level and quality of democratic discourse; it's their enshrinement in entrenched, written, legal form that has these disastrous results. Instead of being permitted to argue freely on principle, and in ways that are sensitive to ongoing social developments, increased knowledge, and improved understandings of issues of political morality, "we end up having to scramble around constructing . . . principles out of scraps of some sacred text, in a tendentious exercise of constitutional calligraphy."[100] There is a way of addressing Waldron's concern, but pursuing it requires that we return to basics. Waldron's indictment is one with which we cannot begin

---

98 See, generally, Nadine Strossen, *Defending Pornography*.
99 Wayne Sumner, "Rights," in Hugh LaFollette, ed., *The Blackwell Guide to Ethical Theory* (Oxford: Blackwell Publishers, 2000), 298.
100 *Law and Disagreement*, 290.

to deal, even in a preliminary way, without once again asking what we are doing – or trying to do – when we entrench rights in a Charter and require, for valid exercises of government power, that these rights be respected. It is now time to begin to develop an alternative to the Standard Conception of judicial review presupposed by both the Advocates and the Critics. With this alternative in hand, we will then be able to appreciate more clearly why some form of judicial review can in fact be a very good thing to have in a constitutional democracy.

5

A Mixed Blessing

A. A Fresh Start

The preceding chapter contains some of the strongest and most common objections to Charters one encounters in both public and academic discourse. The list is by no means exhaustive, and it no doubt fails fully to reflect the full spectrum of critical views. It does, however, provide what I believe to be a fair, representative picture of the kinds of objections on offer. In each instance there are immediate responses to be made, of course, some of which we have explored. Further responses exist in the vast literature dedicated to debates between Critics and Advocates. Of particular note are the many responses spawned by Waldron's penetrating critique of the Standard Case.[1] But instead of pursuing these debates further, I wish to take a different tack. Instead of answering the Critics in the terms presupposed by their debates with the Advocates, I will instead focus on two of the agreed, basic premises upon which much of that debate has been based. Consider again the various objections outlined. In each case we can see that the criticism is premised on one or both of two critical assumptions: (1) there are "objective" truths, concerning, for example, political morality, what the framers intended, or the Charter's plain or original meaning, which an impartial, morally neutral judiciary is capable of discerning and drawing upon in making Charter decisions; and (2) Charters aspire to entrench the rights these truths describe or establish, as fixed points of agreement on and precommitment to moral limits on government power. With these unstated assumptions in place, the Critic then goes on to argue that, for one reason or another, Charters so conceived either (a) fail to live up to this aspiration; or (b) would be unworthy of our allegiance in a democratic society even if they could do so.

---

1 See, for example, Joseph Raz, "Disagreement in Politics" (1998), 43 *American Journal of Jurisprudence* at 47; Thomas Christiano, "Waldron on *Law and Disagreement*" (2000) 19 *Law and Philosophy* at 513–43; David Estlund, "Waldron on *Law and Disagreement*" (2000) 99:1 *Philosophical Studies* at 111–28; and Aileen Kavanagh, "Participation and Judicial Review: A Reply to Waldron" (2003) 22 *Law and Philosophy*, at 451–86.

Factors like moral nihilism and skepticism about our capacity to grasp objective moral truths even if they do exist or about our ability to cobble together the intentions of the framers, when combined with claims revolving around additional factors like the elite status of the judiciary or their inability to agree on much of anything, are enough to undermine assumption (1) and establish conclusions (a) and (b). They show that judicial review is hardly the objective, morally neutral exercise Advocates (apparently) believe it to be. The supposed fact of radical dissensus, employed to such powerful effect by Waldron, undermines both assumption (1) and assumption (2), thereby lending further support to conclusion (a), that Charters simply cannot do the work their Advocates would have them do and cannot possibly be explained in the terms they suggest. The Ulysses metaphor, for instance, cannot sensibly serve to explain the nature and effect of Charters. It is a serious mistake to think that we can intelligibly pre-commit to limits upon which we cannot possibly agree in advance. At best we can pre-commit to an anti-democratic practice that licences other people – judges – to make our decisions for us on issues and questions upon which we ourselves cannot reach agreement and that we, as individuals whose self-image includes the honorific title "rights bearer," really should be making. If, despite acknowledged worries that disagreement just might go all the way down, we continue to hold on to the idea that Charters really can and do embody fixed points, then we will inevitably be led to serious concerns about their democratic pedigree, perhaps even to the unflattering picture of human beings (as Hobbesean predators) which that picture seems to suggest. We will be led to ask why the people-now should be hamstrung in their pursuit of sound, morally responsible public policy by decisions made earlier by the people-then and entrenched by *them*, not by *the people-now*, against efforts to change those decisions in light of the new and evolving understandings of a self-governing people characterized by its commitment to rights and the fundamental human dignity they presuppose. One might valiantly try, as Jed Rubenfeld does, to diminish the force of this objection by invoking the possibility of community identity across time, so that the people-then are really one and the same as the people-now.[2] But whether in the end this kind of strategy will work is highly questionable, and not only because of the deeply controversial metaphysical questions that invariably accompany theories of group identity and agency. However these latter questions are answered, we will be faced with a further, equally serious difficulty. Just as individuals often change their beliefs and commitments, sometimes in fundamental ways,[3] there is little reason to deny the very real possibility that one and the same people might, on many important issues, change their mind

---

2 See again, Jed Rubenfeld, "Legitimacy and Interpretation" in Larry Alexander, ed., *Constitutionalism*.

3 Think, for example, of a religious conversion, or how radical youths often turn out to be among the most committed middle-aged conservatives.

from one year to the next, let alone one generation to the next. If so, then the Critics' question remains valid: Why should the people's ability to change their mind about rights be denied or curtailed? Why should they be hamstrung in their ability to make those changes of mind effective in their everyday political decisions? True, there is always the process of constitutional amendment, but it would be difficult to overestimate the practical difficulties often associated with such a process. We must ask whether, in light of this fact, it is defensible to place such impediments in the people's way. Can they be made consistent with the picture we like to paint of ourselves – of a responsible, self-governing people who can be trusted, *on an ongoing basis*, with decisions about justice and rights? We do not, after all, really want to think of ourselves as drunken pub-crawlers.

So an Advocate who accepts the two key assumptions noted above is faced with an uphill battle. She seems left, then, with three options: (a) She can continue to seek the means to answer Waldron and his fellow Critics in the terms they have established[4]; (b) she can succumb to the force of their arguments and agree that Charters and their implementation via judicial review really are bad ideas after all; or (c) she can seek an alternative understanding of Charters, one that sees their aspirations as different. The remainder of this book is dedicated to an exploration of option (c). I shall be proposing an alternative understanding of a Charter according to which neither its coherence nor its legitimacy is undermined by the existence of Waldron's "circumstances of politics" – on the contrary, a Charter can be a quite sensible response to such circumstances. Its legitimacy can be explained by the role it plays in helping to overcome difficulties we inevitably encounter whenever we seek to govern ourselves by law, difficulties that are only exacerbated by the circumstances of politics. This alternative conception takes its inspiration from two sources. We will begin by drawing on the penetrating analysis of H.L.A. Hart, whose thoughts on the move from the pre-legal to the legal world, and the inherent limits and dangers of legal regulation, provide grounds for constructing a better understanding of Charters than the Standard Conception. Our second source will be an idea articulated long ago by Lord Sankey in *Edwards*,[5] that landmark Canadian constitutional case to which we made reference earlier, which was decided by the Privy Council of Britain in 1930 and is now commonly referred to as the *Persons* case. *Edwards* is notable for at least two reasons: (1) It established, for the first time in Canadian legal history, that women are indeed "persons" for purposes of appointment to the Senate; and (2) it introduced into Canadian constitutional law the living tree metaphor of constitutions to which we drew attention in dividing constitutional theories into two basic camps: fixed and living tree views. The living tree conception is one that, following *Edwards*,

---

4 We have already made (what I hope is) a very promising start in answering many of those objections in Chapter 4.
5 *Edwards v. A.-G. Canada* [1930] A.C. 124.

has been repeatedly endorsed by the Canadian courts in a string of important Charter cases.[6] On this conception, recall, constitutions, and hence those Charters that enjoy constitutional status, in no way represent attempts to establish fixed points of agreement and pre-commitment. By its nature, a Charter is "a living tree capable of growth and expansion within its natural limits."[7] It is an instrument that must, within limits inherent in its constitutional role, be allowed to grow and adapt to new contemporary circumstances and evolving normative beliefs, including those about justice. As we saw at the end of the previous chapter, Waldron claims that with Charters we lose "our ability to evolve a free and flexible discourse of politics," a discourse that is essential for ongoing democratic self-rule and that can easily evolve if, instead of introducing Charters, we rely for rights protection on "legal recognition in the form of common law principles and precedents" or "'conventional' understandings subscribed to in the political community at large." The living tree conception brings these two approaches together into a kind of common law understanding of Charters – one that seeks to combine both the relative fixity of entrenched, written law and the relative adaptability characteristic of the common law. If this option truly is open, then our choice is not simply between having a Charter or eschewing one altogether. We can also choose *how* our Charters are to function in constitutional democracies. My argument will be that, in choosing a living tree, common law conception, we are able to reap many of the benefits for which Charters are promoted by the Advocates, while avoiding most, if not all, of the difficulties cited by the Critics. In particular, we avoid the hubris, and the insult to democratic ideals and human dignity, that the fixed view and many of its underlying arguments seem to entail.

B. Hart and the Promise of Law

In H.L.A. Hart's view, every society needs some way of regulating behaviour if its members are to live together in close proximity. Even a society that somehow managed to do without formal political and legal structures would have to have *social rules* of the kind introduced in Chapter 2 to help govern various aspects of social behaviour. A social rule exists when there is a pattern of behaviour accompanied by the appropriate critical, reflective attitude – what Hart calls

---

6 See, for example, *A.-G. Que. V. Blaikie* [1979] 2 S.C.R. 1016, 1029 (language rights); *A.-G. B.C. v. Canada Trust Co.* [1980] 2 S.C.R. 466, 478 (powers of taxation); *Law Society of Upper Canada v. Shapinker* [1984] 1 S.C.R. 357, 365 (mobility rights). The idea of the constitution as a "living tree" is, of course, not unique to Canadian legal practice. Elsewhere the idea is expressed in theories that speak of a constitution as a "living thing" or as capable of "organic growth." For further exploration of the notion of a constitution as a living entity, see Aileen Kavanagh, "The Idea of a Living Constitution," (2003), XVI:1 *Canadian Journal of Law and Jurisprudence*, 55; Laurence Sager, "The Incorrigible Constitution" (1990), 65 *New York University Law Review*, 893; and William Rehnquist, "The Notion of a Living Constitution" (1976), 54 *Texas Law Review*, 693.

7 *Edwards*, 136.

"the internal point of view." Members of the group who observe a social rule not only engage in a fairly widespread and uniform pattern of behaviour, but they also take this internal point of view towards that pattern.

What is necessary is that there should be a critical reflective attitude to certain patterns of behaviour as a common standard, and that this should display itself in criticism (including self-criticism), demands for conformity, and in acknowledgements that such criticisms and demands are justified, all of which find their characteristic expression in the normative terminology of "ought," "must," and "should," "right," and "wrong."[8]

When these conditions are met, we can meaningfully say that the group has adopted the practice of observing a social rule. Included within a society's social rules will be some that are thought to impose obligations. These are the rules that the society's members generally view as important to social life or some crucial part of it and that they are, as a result, willing to back up with serious social pressure. These are also rules that they recognize as sometimes conflicting with self-interest. A rule prohibiting gratuitous infliction of harm would presumably count among a society's obligation rules; rules governing polite discourse presumably would not. Were a society governed exclusively by social rules, the "internal point of view" would of necessity have to be very widespread. The reason is a conceptual one: Without widespread acceptance of a rule, it could not exist as a social rule of the community. The appropriate practice(s) would not exist.

Notice that Hart's analysis is in no way intended to entail that rules identified as social rules be in any way justified, or give the individuals subject to them legitimate reasons for action. The analysis is undertaken from what Hart terms "the external point of view" – that is, from the point of view of an external observer concerned with developing a test by which one could determine when a society observes a social rule, as opposed to a mere pattern of behaviour.[9]

---

8 *The Concept of Law*, 57.
9 Hart actually mixes up two points of view when he refers to the "external point of view." First, there is the point of view of an external observer interested in identifying the rules observed by a group. Second, there is the point of view of a member of the group who does not accept the rule as providing legitimate reasons for action – that is, he does not take towards the rule the internal point of view that others share. If he complies with the rule, he likely does so only because he wishes to escape the criticism or social pressure that those who accept the rule are likely to subject him to. Such an individual is also said by Hart to take the external point of view. We could easily distinguish these two different points of view by calling the second the "external participant point of view," thus indicating that the individual in question is a member of the group whose practices give rise to the rule – he is, so to speak, an internal member of that group to which the rule applies, but he does not himself accept the rule as worthy of obedience. As for the first point of view, this might be called the "external theoretical point of view" to signal that it is someone who is not a member of the group concerned about whether the rule provides him with reasons for action but one who has an interest in understanding, describing, analyzing, or perhaps evaluating the rules and practices of the group.

He is concerned with the conditions under which we can correctly say that a social rule exists within a society, not the (normative) conditions under which such a rule might be justified or *ought* (in the moral sense of that term) to be followed. In saying that society S observes a social rule of obligation R – say, a rule requiring the return of escaped slaves to their owners – a theorist is in no way committed to saying, on Hart's analysis, that R really does impose an obligation. What he *is* committed to saying is that most members of S *believe* that R imposes the relevant obligation because (in their view) R really does protect an aspect of social life that is worthy of protection. But they could be wrong about that – and the belief that they are is one that the theorist might well share with those members of S who take the external participant point of view towards R.

Another important element of Hart's theory of the emergence of law is his distinction between primary and secondary rules. Primary rules are the ones most people usually have in mind when they think of legal rules. In referring to legal rules it is natural to think of laws that impose duties or obligations and that we can be said to obey or disobey. It is natural to think of law as a set of rules that require us to refrain from various kinds of harmful conduct whether we wish to or not and that we can be said to be under legal obligation to obey. An example of a primary rule is a rule prohibiting assaults, or one telling us to pay taxes or to provide the necessities of life to our children. But as we saw when we explored the imaginary worlds of Rex and Regina, there are other kinds of laws too, serving distinctive functions; and these are thought of as imposing duties only at the cost of great distortion. These other types of rules Hart calls "secondary rules" – rules about rules. The differences between primary and secondary rules are described by Hart as follows:

Under rules of the one type, which may well be considered the basic or primary type, human beings are required to do or abstain from certain actions whether they wish to or not. Rules of the other type are in a sense parasitic upon or secondary to the first; for they provide that human beings may by doing or saying certain things introduce new rules of the primary type, extinguish or modify old ones, or in various ways determine their incidence or control their operations. Rules of the first type impose duties; rules of the second type confer powers, public or private. Rules of the first type concern actions involving physical movement or changes; rules of the second type provide for operations which lead not merely to physical movement or change, but to the creation or variation of duties or obligations.[10]

Secondary rules do not impose duties; rather they typically facilitate our doing certain things. Some secondary rules are power-conferring – that is, they provide individuals with facilities and powers to create, by certain specified procedures and subject to enumerated conditions, structures of rights and duties within

10 *The Concept of Law*, 81.

the coercive framework of the law. As we saw in Chapter 2, they do this by defining, creating, granting, and regulating legal powers by which individuals are able to alter the legal status quo. They enable them to create new duties, rights, privileges, and so on. Some of the powers created by secondary rules are public, like those that governed Regina's power to legislate, while others, such as the rules governing the creation of legally binding wills, are private. In calling them private, we mean to say that they are rules that govern activities engaged in by citizens in their private capacities.

With these resources in hand, Hart asks a series of questions reminiscent of those addressed by early modern social contract theorists like Locke and Hobbes. Much as they did when they had us ponder our emergence from the state of nature, Hart has us consider life without law and how the introduction of a rudimentary legal system would help facilitate our overcoming a number of "defects" inherent in a hypothetical, pre-legal society.[11] In Hart's view, a legal system can emerge within a society only with the introduction of secondary rules and their "union" with the society's primary rules. The "key to the science of jurisprudence" lies, he thinks, in this "union of primary and secondary rules."[12] In order that we might better understand the nature and significance of this distinctly legal union, Hart has us imagine a hypothetical, pre-legal society governed exclusively by primary social rules.[13] Such a regime of primary rules could exist, Hart notes, only within "a small community closely knit by ties of kinship, common sentiment, and belief, and placed in a stable environment...."[14] In any other situation, including the ones in which we find ourselves in the circumstances of modern politics, serious difficulties would arise, and these would necessitate the introduction of secondary rules. According to Hart, there are three key "defects" that the introduction of secondary rules – and hence a legal system – works towards eliminating in these more familiar scenarios: *uncertainty*, the *static quality* of the rules, and *inefficiency* in their enforcement. Let's look briefly at each defect and how it can be remedied through the introduction of secondary rules.

---

11 I say "hypothetical" because Hart's argument in no way rests on the historical claim that pre-legal societies ever did exist. The notion of a pre-legal society serves as an analytical, explanatory device; it is not intended to describe a historical reality.

12 *The Concept of Law*, 99.

13 Although Hart seems to suggest that the union of primary and secondary rules is a distinctly legal phenomenon, it is not clear why we should accept this restriction. Social clubs, for example, can have formal structures that also depend on the union. For instance, the club might have secondary rules that empower a small committee to introduce, change, and modify club rules. This does not, I take it, transform the club into a legal system, even a rudimentary or subordinate one. His analysis also suggests that, before the emergence of law, all rules must be primary social rules. But it is difficult to see why this must be so. There seems no reason to deny that our social club, with its constituent secondary rules, might pre-exist the emergence of a legal system.

14 *The Concept of Law*, 92.

i. Uncertainty and the Rule of Recognition

A regime of primary rules is, as Hart notes, not a *system* of rules. It will "simply be a set of separate standards, without any identifying or common mark, except of course that they are the rules which a particular group of human beings accepts."[15] They will be, in other words, rather like the rules of etiquette, fashion, and colloquial expression. "Hence if doubts arise as to what the rules are or as to the precise scope of some given rule, there will be no procedure for settling this doubt either by reference to an authoritative text or to an official [e.g., Rex or Regina] whose declarations on this point are authoritative."[16] In other words, there may be uncertainty as to whether a rule is indeed a rule of the group and no means of settling this question, no test of what counts as a binding standard. The remedy for this defect is the introduction of a secondary, rule of recognition which . . . "will specify some feature or features possession of which by a suggested rule is taken as a conclusive affirmative indication that it is a rule of the group to be supported by the social pressure it exerts."[17] The rule of recognition can specify, as criteria for membership within the society's legal rules, any number of authoritative marks. These can range from inclusion of the rule within a sacred text to its enactment by a sovereign like Regina, perhaps even on a particular day of the week. Also important, it can include the rule's consistency with certain specified norms of political morality. This is what occurs in societies that choose to include a Charter within their foundational law. Hart is quite explicit about this possibility: "In some systems, as in the United States, the ultimate criteria of legal validity explicitly incorporate principles of justice or substantive moral values."[18] Rules that violate the specified moral

---

15 *Ibid.*, 92.
16 *Ibid.*
17 *Ibid.*
18 *Ibid.*, 204. Despite Hart's clear acceptance of moral criteria of validity, some legal philosophers deny that this is what he really meant to do, or that this acceptance by Hart is compatible with other elements of his legal philosophy. Those who agree that Hart accepted moral criteria, and that such criteria are indeed possible in the manner Hart describes, are now called "Inclusive Legal Positivists." Those who deny the possibility of moral criteria of validity are referred to as "Exclusive Legal Positivists." The literature spawned by debates between these two camps is quite extensive. For a sample, see Joseph Raz, *The Authority of Law: Ethics in the Public Domain*, rev. ed. (Oxford: Clarendon Press, 2001), especially Chapters 9–12 and 14; Leslie Green, "Legal Positivism," The Stanford Encyclopedia of Philosophy (Spring 2003 Edition), ed., N. Zalta, URL = http://plato.stanford.edu/archives/spr2003/legal-positivism/; Scott Shapiro, "On Hart's Way Out" (1998), 4 *Legal Theory*, 46; "Law, Morality, and the Guidance of Conduct" (2000), 6 *Legal Theory*, 127; Jules Coleman, "Negative and Positive Positivism," 11 *The Journal of Legal Studies* (1982), 139; *The Practice of Principle: In Defence of a Pragmatist Approach to Legal Theory* (Oxford: Oxford University Press, 2001), *Hart's Postscript: Essays on the Postscript to the Concept of Law* (ed.) (Oxford: Oxford University Press, 2001); Matthew Kramer, *In Defense of Legal Positivism: Law Without Trimmings* (Oxford: Oxford University Press, 1999), *Where Law and Morality Meet* (Oxford: Oxford University Press, 2004); Waluchow, *Inclusive Legal Positivism* (Oxford:

principles and values will not be valid rules of the system – on the contrary, they will be invalid and of no force or effect. On the other hand, rules that do fulfill these and all other relevant criteria will be *valid* rules existing within a *system* of rules – a legal system whose content is exhausted by the set of rules satisfying the various criteria included within the rule of recognition.

> By providing an authoritative mark [the rule of recognition] introduces, although in an embryonic form, the idea of a legal system: for the rules are now not just a discrete unconnected set but are, in a simple way, unified. Further, in the simple operation of identifying a given rule as possessing the required feature of being an item on an authoritative list of rules we have the germ of the idea of legal validity.[19]

So a legal system includes the rule of recognition together with all the rules valid under its terms. Through the introduction of this foundational secondary rule, societies are able to overcome the defect of uncertainty inherent in regimes of primary rules. They now have a means of identifying the rules by which they are all to be guided.

ii. Stasis and Rules of Change

A second defect characteristic of a regime of primary social rules is what Hart calls the "static" quality of its rules. Social rules can of course change, just as customs and habits change. But the "only mode of change in the rules known to such a society will be the slow process of growth . . . and the converse process of decay. . . ."[20] There will be, in other words, no means of *deliberately* adapting the rules to changing circumstances or beliefs. This is a point we considered in Chapter 2 when we discussed the belief, among some, that constitutional norms must be written rules if they are to serve their distinctive purposes. As we observed, informal social norms governing relations between the sexes, or between various racial or age groups, can often be more rigid and entrenched than written ones. This is because their elimination, alteration, or reinterpretation typically requires widespread changes in longstanding attitudes, beliefs, and behaviour on the part of a very large group of people. Many people are highly resistant to such changes. We observed that many otherwise liberal-minded people of the past few decades have been highly resistant to changes in social norms governing driving while under the influence of alcohol. Traditions like the customary after-work drink in the local pub were – and are – deeply entrenched in our social practices and work against changes that threaten them. Whether, in the end, informal drunk driving campaigns would have succeeded

Clarendon Press, 1994), "Legal Positivism: Inclusive versus Exclusive," in ed., E. Craig, *Routledge Encyclopedia of Philosophy* (London: Routledge, 2001), available online at http://www.rep.routledge.com.
19 *The Concept of Law*, 95.
20 *Ibid.*, 92.

on their own in modifying the relevant behavioural patterns in the desired ways, there is little doubt that whatever success has been achieved would likely have taken a considerably longer period of time if the matter had been left to informal social practice. Legislated changes to these very same practices – for example, those imposing much stiffer penalties for driving while under the influence, and the elimination, in some jurisdictions, of after-work "happy hours" – took effect very quickly and efficiently. This despite much grumbling and continued resistance, and despite the fact that the legislation's effectiveness was no doubt dependent upon concurrent underlying changes in social attitudes. This dependence should never be underestimated. Laws that work against highly entrenched social attitudes and practices often fail, as witnessed by the ultimately unsuccessful battle to implement legal prohibition of alcohol. Informal social rules have an inherently static quality about them.

In order to remedy this defect, societies introduce secondary rules of change that enable individuals – for example, Rex, Regina, or the UK Parliament – authoritatively to introduce new rules and eliminate old ones. As Hart notes, there will usually be a very close connection between secondary rules of change and the rule of recognition, because the latter will invariably make reference to acts of legislation as an identifying feature of valid rules. And many of these acts introduce changes to existing laws.

iii. Inefficiency and Rules of Adjudication

Another key defect of regimes of primary social rules rules is their "inefficiency." By this Hart means the

inefficiency of the diffuse social pressure by which the rules are maintained. Disputes as to whether an admitted rule has or has not been violated will always occur and will, in any but the smallest societies, continue interminably, if there is no agency specially empowered to ascertain finally, and authoritatively, the fact of violation.[21]

In order to overcome the inherent inefficiency of social rules, societies introduce a third kind of fundamental secondary rule that Hart calls "rules of adjudication." These are "secondary rules empowering individuals to make authoritative determinations of the question whether, on a particular occasion, a primary rule has been broken."[22] Rules of adjudication define and regulate the office of the *judiciary* and, like other secondary rules, "define a group of important legal concepts: in this case the concepts of judge or court, jurisdiction and judgment."[23]

So it is through the introduction of secondary rules of recognition, change, and adjudication that societies are able to overcome a number of key deficiencies

21 *Ibid.*, 93.
22 *Ibid.*, 96.
23 *Ibid.*, 97.

inherent in regimes of primary social rules. By introducing such secondary rules, these societies take the crucial step from the pre-legal to the legal world. They are now societies governed by a legal system. Success in overcoming the described deficiencies is by no means guaranteed, of course, but the potential is there – a potential that cannot be realized (except perhaps in all but the most unusual of circumstances) absent rules of recognition, change, and adjudication. That the introduction of secondary rules does not guarantee success is a point worth stressing. Consider the introduction of a rule of recognition. This step will not succeed in overcoming the defect of uncertainty if the rule's criteria are vague or ambiguous, or if they demand an unattainable level of consensus among courts or legislative bodies. This, as we shall see in section I, gives rise to an important argument against Charters. It might be suggested that, in the circumstances of politics, law would simply be incapable of serving its distinctive functions were legal validity taken to depend on conformity with enumerated rights of political morality. There can be no certainty about questions of legal validity if there is such deep-seated uncertainty and disagreement about the very criteria by which this is supposed to be determined. It follows that the benefits of law cannot be realized if Charters are accepted as establishing conditions for legal validity. But more on this argument in section I. The only point upon which we need to be clear at this stage is that law's success in achieving its potential requires rules of recognition, change, and adjudication and the social conditions in which they are able to operate effectively in eliminating – or at least reducing – the defects Hart highlights. In having us consider, in this way, the emergence of law from a pre-legal society, Hart hoped not only to illuminate the distinctive features of modern domestic legal systems, but to illustrate their social significance and their potential value. The union of primary rules with fundamental secondary rules of recognition, change, and adjudication not only transforms society, it does so in a way that creates the potential radically to improve the social condition. Our question will ultimately be: Do we lose all of this if we adopt Charters and judicial review? And our answer will be: not necessarily.

C. The Dangers of Law: The Descent into Hart's Hell

Despite its potential for good, Hart was all too aware that the promise of law is purchased at a potentially heavy cost. The very features of law by which it can achieve its potential for good also create the worrisome possibility that a community's law will war with its morality or with the demands of reason, (true) critical morality, or common sense.[24] Hart's reflections on the "pathology

---

24 One of the most thoughtful and illuminating discussions of this element of Hart's thinking is found in Waldron's "All We Like Sheep" (1999), XII: 1 *Canadian Journal of Law and Jurisprudence*, 169.

of a legal system" are a salutary reminder of the ever-present dangers inherent in the structures introduced by law.[25] Once accepted social rules – which cannot exist absent widespread acceptance among those to whom they apply – are replaced with rules satisfying a rule of recognition, the distinct possibility emerges of a complete divorce between validity and acceptance, between the rules that are to be applied because they are legally valid and those that are acceptable, morally or otherwise, to those whom they govern. This is because a rule of recognition typically does not require general acceptance of a rule that it validates: It can, for example, require nothing more than formal enactment by the appropriate person or bodies of persons. If so, then there is nothing to guarantee that the rules adopted as valid will be ones that citizens will find acceptable.

This divorce between validity and acceptance can take at least two forms. First, there is the rather distinct possibility that a particular law, or some other result of the exercise of government power – for example, an executive order or a ruling by a regulatory body like the Food and Drug Administration in the United States or the Canadian Radio-television and Telecommunications Commision in Canada – might be unacceptable to the community at large. This was plainly the case in many Western nations, for example Spain and the UK, whose governments decided to contribute to the 2003 American invasion of Iraq, despite widespread and well-documented popular disapproval. The decisions of these governments, though (arguably) legally valid, were anything but acceptable to those in whose name they were made. The result, in Spain, was likely the government's defeat in the subsequent election.[26] There are, of course, many other instances where legal validity has failed to track acceptability: Laws governing gambling, alcohol consumption, marijuana smoking, prostitution, capital punishment, and so on all attest to the dangers inherent in secondary rules that render legal validity independent of acceptability among the wider community. One of the desirable features of a regime of primary rules is that rules do not exist unless they are generally acceptable. Legal systems eliminate that guarantee.

Once the guarantee is removed, we encounter an even more worrisome possibility: that validity and acceptance might come apart to the point where no

---

25 See *The Concept of Law, passim*, but especially 117–23, and "Positivism and the Separation of Law and Morals," 71 *Harvard Law Review* (1957–8), 593, reprinted in Joel Feinberg and Jules Coleman, eds., *Philosophy of Law*, 6th edition (Belmont, Calif. Wadsworth, 2000). All page references are to this reprint.

26 There is no doubt that the terrorist attack on the Spanish rail system that occurred days before the March 2004 general election in which Jose Luis Zapatero was elected prime minister had its effect. Whether the previous government's decision in 2003 to support the U.S. effort in Iraq signaled its upcoming defeat in any case remains an open question. There is fairly strong evidence to suggest that it did not, however. See "Attacks Helped Socialists, Say Spaniards," published by Angus Reid Consultants on March 15, 2005, at http://wwwangus-reid.com/polls/index.cfm.

one accepts the system save those officials who exercise the various government powers made possible by its secondary rules. Though not nearly as likely as the state of affairs described above, where particular valid laws lack general acceptance, this scenario is one about which we should be no less vigilant. The relatively small chance of its occurrence is more than counterbalanced by the nightmare it represents. In a regime of primary rules,

> ... since there are no officials, the rules must be widely accepted as setting critical standards for the behaviour of the group. If, there, the internal point of view is not widely disseminated there could not logically be any rules. But where there is a union of primary and secondary rules ... the acceptance of the rules as common standards for the group may be split off from the relatively passive matter of the ordinary individual acquiescing in the rules by obeying them for his part alone. In an extreme case the internal point of view with its characteristic normative use of legal language ("This is a valid rule") might be confined to the official world. In this more complex system, only officials might accept and use the system's criteria of legal validity. The society in which this was so might be deplorably sheeplike; the sheep might end in the slaughterhouse. But there is little reason for thinking that it could not exist or for denying it the title of a legal system.[27]

So secondary rules, with their ability to "split off" validity and acceptance, bring with them significant dangers. There is nothing to guarantee that what is legally valid will be generally acceptable. Nor is there anything to guarantee that the rules will in any way serve the interests of justice, fairness, or utility. The importance of continually bearing this additional fact in mind is among the principal motivations of Hart and his fellow positivists in developing the theories they do.

What these thinkers were, in the main, concerned to promote was clarity and honesty in the formulation of the theoretical and moral issues raised by the existence of particular laws which were morally iniquitous but were enacted in proper form, clear in meaning, and satisfied all the acknowledged criteria of validity of a system. Their view [and Hart's] was that, in thinking about such laws, both the theorist and unfortunate official or private citizen who was called on to apply or obey them, could only be confused by an invitation to refuse the title "law" or "valid" to them. They thought that, to confront these problems, simpler, more candid resources were available, which would bring into focus far better, every relevant intellectual and moral consideration: we should say, "This is law; but it is too iniquitous to be applied or obeyed."[28]

There are, of course, many who think otherwise: who believe that the "separation of law and morals" recommended by positivists – a separation that divorces legal validity from conformity with moral principle – simply facilitates the descent into Hell. In response, Hart writes:

27 *The Concept of Law*, 117.
28 *Ibid.*, 207–8.

[This] criticism of the separation of law and morals . . . is less an intellectual argument against the [positivist's] distinction than a passionate appeal supported not by detailed reasoning but by reminders of a terrible experience. For it consists of the testimony of those who have descended into Hell, and, like Ulysses or Dante, brought back a message for human beings. Only in this case the Hell was not beneath or beyond earth, but on it; it was a Hell created on earth by men for other men.[29]

The Hell to which Hart refers is, of course, the Nazi regime. In response to Fuller's argument that there *must* be more to legal validity than satisfaction of a system's rule of recognition, that a legal system must satisfy an "inner morality of law" that demands of law qualities like impartiality, prospective application, and so on and whose recognition and observance work (Fuller claims) towards ensuring that the legally generated evils Hart highlights will not see the light of day, Hart adds:

. . . a legal system that satisfied [Fuller's] minimum requirements [to which Hart gives his qualified assent in his doctrine of "the minimum content of natural law"[30]] might apply, with the most pedantic impartiality as between the persons affected, laws which were hideously oppressive, and might deny to a vast rightless slave population the minimum benefits of protection from violence and theft. The stink of such societies is, after all, still in our nostrils and to argue that they have (or had) no legal system would only involve the repetition of the argument.[31]

So our emergence from a pre-legal society to one with law is, at best, a mixed blessing. The very features by which law is able to achieve its potential for good create the worrisome possibility – perhaps probability, should we for some reason not remain constantly vigilant – that our laws will war with our accepted moral norms, with common sense, and with the true or perceived demands of reason and morality. There are, of course, ways of protecting against these inherent dangers. Coupling law with democratic procedures is one of them. The deplorably sheeplike, morally bankrupt society Hart describes, wherein validity is all but divorced from general acceptance and the critical reflective attitude that is so essential in pre-legal society is replaced with unthinking passivity, is far less likely to emerge in a society in which legal validity is heavily dependent on the people's direct or indirect approval than in a society that tolerates too much distance between the people and law-determining decisions. What counts as "too much" is, of course, a contentious issue that we have been exploring and that we have yet to settle one way or the other. But however, in the end, we do settle it – whether, that is, we side with the Critics or with the Advocates – we should continue to bear in mind the lessons of earlier chapters: that sometimes our actions towards individuals and minorities are more "wolflike"

29 "Positivism and the Separation of Law and Morals," 68.
30 See *The Concept of Law*, 193–200.
31 "Positivism and the Separation of Law and Morals," 72.

than "sheeplike"; that sometimes our wishes are inauthentic; that sometimes these wishes war with our more settled beliefs, preferences, and convictions – that is, that they sometimes conflict with our true commitments, with what we, as a community, find *truly acceptable* – or *would* find acceptable if we were better informed about, or appreciative of, the nature or consequences of our proposed actions. If we can develop criteria of legal validity that are workable in the circumstances of politics, consistent with our democratic commitments, and sensitive to these lessons, then surely we would be well advised to consider them very seriously. To do otherwise would be to forgo, unnecessarily, further opportunities to decrease the likelihood of our descent into Hart's Hell.

D. The Limits of Law: Rule and Discretion

Another inherent hazard of legal regulation highlighted by Hart arises from the means by which law characteristically communicates its expectations: general rules. As countless legal theorists have observed over the centuries, law's effectiveness in guiding conduct requires the use of general rules, established in advance, either in practice (social rules) or in written form, and enforced (at least normally) when breached. But as these same theorists invariably go on to point out, general rules, no matter how well crafted or established, do not always live up to our expectations of them. Factors such as ignorance of fact, indeterminacy of aim, evolving technologies, changing social contexts, and so on, combine to create the ever-present possibility that perfectly acceptable general legal rules will lead, upon application to specific cases, to uncertain or otherwise unacceptable results. Let's call the circumstances that create this ever-present possibility "the circumstances of rule making." These circumstances are nicely illustrated by the oft-mentioned example of Hart's toy motor car.

A legal rule forbids you to take a vehicle into the public park. Plainly this forbids an automobile, but what about bicycles, roller skates, toy automobiles? What about airplanes? Are they, as we say, to be called "vehicles" for the purpose of the rule or not? If we are to communicate with each other at all, and if, as in the most elementary form of law, we are to express our intentions that a certain type of behaviour be regulated by rules, then the general words we use – like "vehicle" in the case I consider – must have some standard instances in which no doubts are felt about its application. There must be a core of settled meaning, but there will be, as well, a penumbra of debatable cases in which words are neither obviously applicable nor obviously ruled out. These cases will each have features in common with the standard case; they will lack others or be accompanied by features not present in the standard case. Human invention and natural processes continually throw up such variants on the familiar, and if we are to say that these ranges of facts do or do not fall under existing rules, then the classifier must make a decision which is not dictated to him, for the facts and phenomena to which we fit out words and apply our rules are as it were *dumb*. . . . Fact situations do not await us neatly labelled, creased, and folded, nor is their legal classification written on them to be simply read off by the judge. Instead, in applying legal rules, someone must take the responsibility of deciding that words do or do not cover some case in hand with all the practical consequences involved in this decision.[32]

Hart's example illustrates the empty promise of legal formalism: the belief that, the circumstances of rule making notwithstanding, we both can and ought to design rules, preferably written rules, in such a way as to (virtually) eliminate both the penumbra and the need to resort to judicial discretion as a means of dealing with it. But its real power, I suggest, lies in its highlighting the *moral* shortcomings of the formalist ideal. Written rules so tightly crafted that they leave, at point of application, no room for informed judgment and discretion represent a thoroughly unworthy ideal.

The vice known to legal theory as formalism or conceptualism consists in an attitude to verbally formulated rules which both seeks to disguise and to minimize the need for [further] choice once the general rule has been laid down. One way of doing this is to freeze the meaning of the rule so that its general terms must have the same meaning in every case where its application is in question. To secure this we may fasten on certain features present in the plain case and insist that these are both necessary and sufficient to bring anything which has them within the scope of the rule, whatever other features it may have or lack, and whatever may be the social consequences of applying the rule in this way. To do this is to secure a measure of certainty or predictability at the cost of blindly prejudging what is to be done in a range of future cases, about whose composition we are ignorant. We shall thus succeed in settling in advance, but also in the dark, issues which can only reasonably be settled when they arise and are identified. We shall be forced by this technique to include in the scope of a rule cases which we would wish to exclude in order to give effect to reasonable social aims, and which the open-textured terms of our language would have allowed us to exclude, had we left them less rigidly defined. The rigidity of our classifications will thus war with our aims in having or maintaining the rule.[33]

Fortunately, Hart suggests, we have many different ways of avoiding the pitfalls of formalism. For example, we can put to good use the "open texture" of natural language to which Hart draws our attention in the passage cited above. This feature permits some measure of the desired leeway. Sometimes it arises by accident, so to speak, as when a hard case just happens to fall within the "penumbra of uncertainty" and this fact is seized upon to avoid an absurd result, to decide on the merits of the case without (undue) concern about "the letter of the law." Take, for example, a judge's decision not to count as a vehicle for purpose of the rule a child's toy motor car in the event that some overzealous, anal-retentive enforcement officer lays charges against little Johnny and his mother. That such a mode of propulsion falls within the "penumbra of uncertainty" of "vehicle" permits the presiding judge to rule that the toy car does not,

32 "Positivism and the Separation of Law and Morals," 65.
33 *The Concept of Law*, 129–30.

for purposes of the rule, count as a vehicle. She will thus have exonerated this particular pair of "evil-doers," and, if the rules of adjudication under which she operates contemplate this possibility, she will have reduced the penumbra and expanded the "core of settled meaning" settling the issue whether toy motor cars are henceforth to be treated as vehicles. She will have settled the latter question by setting a precedent.

So open texture can sometimes inadvertently come to the rescue in dealing with the circumstances of rule making. What is perhaps more important, however, this particular feature of natural language, and related ones like vagueness and abstractness, can be put to use deliberately, and in advance, in a wide range of scenarios.[34] We can sometimes foresee that situations are very likely to arise in which blind pre-commitment to a particular legal result would have been foolish or morally problematic. We can know this *general* fact, even though we cannot foresee the particular unwanted results that are bound to arise. We can foresee that there are likely to be results that most everyone, including those who introduced the rules, would have wished to avoid had they foreseen them, even if we don't know what these will be. Some of these scenarios will be the product of rapidly changing technologies like those associated with the Internet. Others will be ones where significant, individuating factors are likely to be present in most every case arising under a rule, for example situations involving discrimination or the use of force in warding off perceived threats to person and property. Still others will arise from the fact that we sometimes change our minds or discover things we didn't know before. In such scenarios, Hart counsels, if legislation is to be the method of choice, legislators are wise deliberately to frame open-textured rules incorporating terms like "reasonable" and "fair" that require appeal to the prescribed normative standards by those charged with the responsibility of following the rules or applying them to others.[35] Instead of being instructed to pay workers no less than five dollars an hour, the rule might

---

34 The differences are not, for our purposes, important, but vagueness and open texture are different properties. By "open texture" Hart – and Waismann, from whom he borrowed the term – means the permanent possibility of vagueness. A term that, for all present purposes, is perfectly precise nevertheless has some degree of open texture because it is always logically possible that a completely novel case should arise about which we will not know what to do. A vague term, presumably, is one in which we are currently uncertain how it applies in an actual case with which we must currently deal. Vagueness also comes in degrees, and presumably one of the factors at play in determining the degree to which a term is vague is the number of cases in which application can be seriously questioned. In any case, unless there is reason within a particular context not to do so, I will use the term "open texture" and its cognates as referring not only to open texture but also to related properties like vagueness and abstractness. Waismann's theory of "open texture" can be found in "Verifiability," in A. Flew, ed., *Logic and Language* (Oxford: Blackwell, 1968).

35 By "legislators" I mean anyone charged with the responsibility of creating or developing a legal norm. This can include members of legislative assemblies, administrative bodies, or a court called upon to decide a case whose precedent-setting *ratio decidendi* might function as a legal norm.

require payment at a level that is "reasonable" for the type of work that is to be performed. Such a rule provides some level of antecedent guidance while allowing both citizen and judge to address, at point of application, normative questions that could not reasonably have been anticipated and settled in advance by the legislator(s).

So the use by legislators of open-textured terms is one way of dealing with the circumstances of rule making. Yet another is to leave rule development to the courts – that is, to adopt common law methodology. Let's pause briefly and consider the nature of this intriguing methodology, and how it has the potential to cater successfully to both of Hart's fundamental needs.

E. Common Law Method

"For all its ubiquity, the common law remains uncommonly puzzling. We are perplexed by the common law in a way that we are not, for example, by statutory interpretation, because the central features of common law method appear inconsistent with some of the primary assumptions of a traditional view of the rule of law."[36,37] Thus begins Fred Schauer's review of *The Nature of the Common Law* by Melvin Eisenberg. The features that prove so puzzling are nicely summarized by Schauer as follows:

First, the rules of the common law are nowhere canonically formulated. Indeed the absence of a single authoritative formulation is what distinguishes common law rules from legislative rules. Second, common law rules are not made by legislatures; they are created by courts simultaneously with the application of those rules to concrete cases. Third, not only are common law rules created in the very process of application, but also they are applied in – and to – the very case that prompted the rulemaking. Thus, common law rules are applied retroactively to facts arising prior to the establishment of the rule. Finally, and most importantly, common law rulemaking does not merely make new law where there is no existing law. Instead, the lawmaking power of common law courts is more than interstitial, and extends to modifying or replacing what had previously been thought to be the governing rule when applying that rule would generate a malignant result in the case at hand.[38]

---

36 Fred Schauer, "Is the Common Law Law?" (book review of Melvin Eisenberger, *The Nature of the Common Law* [Cambridge, Mass.: Harvard University Press, 1988]), 77 California L.R. 455.
37 For our purposes here, I shall attempt to provide a more or less standard or traditional account of the common law that remains neutral with respect to ongoing theoretical debates about its fundamental nature and its consistency with legal theories like legal positivism. For an excellent discussion of the common law tradition and Bentham's hostility towards it, see Gerald Postema, *Bentham and the Common Law* (Oxford: Clarendon Press, 1986). See also Postema's "Philosophy of the Common Law" in Jules Coleman and Scott Shapiro, eds., *The Oxford Handbook of Jurisprudence and Philosophy of Law* (Oxford: Oxford University Press, 2002), 588–622.
38 Fred Schauer, "Is the Common Law Law?" at 455.

It is easy to see why these features of common law methodology introduce puzzlement: To put it simply, we seem to have the rule of law without the rules. We seem to have a process whereby rules are either absent or made up as we go along and applied retroactively, only to be changed later when the next case comes along. Indeed, if we continue to bear in mind Hart's thoughts on the (hypothetical) emergence from pre-legal society, it would appear that, with common law, we are pretty much back where we started – without the certainty and predictability that the introduction of a legal system was supposed to have provided. We also seem to have a noticeable blending of the judicial and legislative functions that appears (to the Critics at least) to be profoundly undemocratic. We have unelected, unaccountable judges apparently creating new laws in the course of adjudicating cases, not applying laws previously created by democratic representatives. How could anyone in his right mind seriously advocate such a system? And how could he think that it represents anything remotely like the rule of law?

These latter questions are, of course, among those famously asked by Jeremy Bentham, whose critique of the English common law has approached legendary status.[39] But we must be cautious. Bentham's critique notwithstanding, common law methodology is not the undisciplined practice of making rules up as we go along that the above caricature seems to suggest. On the contrary, it is a highly disciplined system of practical reasoning that, if not as fully rule-like in nature as statutory regimes aspire to be, constrains judicial reasoning in significant ways. Schauer again:

common law judges made decisions by applying legal principles contained in generations of previous judicial opinions, with each of those previous opinions being the written justification and explanation of the decision in a particular lawsuit. As the stock of such opinions increases, certain justifications recur, and certain principles become ossified. The result is the eventual development of an array of general prescriptions, such as "Contracts must be based on consideration" and "Those whose wild animals injure others are liable in damages for the injuries caused regardless of fault." These general prescriptions appear as rules, and in any well-developed common law domain lawyers will have the ability to refer to rules, opinions will cite rules, and treatises will collect rules, even though one could not pick up an authoritative and canonical set of the rules of contract in a way that one could pick up the tax code or the rules of chess. Over time, therefore, there appear to be "rules" of tort, of contract, of property, and so on, even though the set of such rules nowhere exists in codified canonical form. . . . They are thought to be prescriptive, and common-law judges are thought to be constrained by them.[40]

Schauer's picture of the common law is one with which Hart was in full agreement.

---

39 Again, see Postema's *Bentham and the Common Law*.
40 Schauer, *Playing by the Rules*, 175.

Notwithstanding [the ability of courts to avoid precedents, in a variety of ways to be explored below] the result of the English [common law] system of precedent has been to produce, by its use, a body of rules of which a vast number, of both major and minor importance, are as determinate as any statutory rule. They can now only be altered where the "merits" seem to run counter to the requirements of the established precedents.[41]

So the common law does not do away with rules entirely – it is not the attempt to have the rule of law without any rules. Nevertheless, there is a reason why Schauer uses scare quotes in the above passage when talking about "the 'rules' of tort." The reason is simple: Common law rules are inherently revisable at point of application. New cases, exhibiting hitherto unappreciated features, can always prompt revisiting of the rule. As Hart notes, if the "merits" seem to run counter to the existing rule, then the rule can be modified. There are many different theories on the ability of common law courts to modify or otherwise escape the force of common law rules and rulings. Part of the difficulty is that the powers of distinguishing and overruling through which this is mainly done seem to vary from court to court and from one system to the next, making it very difficult to provide anything approaching a universal theory of common law reasoning. Despite these acknowledged limitations, Joseph Raz develops an enlightening account of the basic logic underlying the (variable) powers of English courts to deal with common law rules and precedents. Because we will be employing a similar account in defending the common law conception of Charters, we would perhaps do well to pause briefly to consider Raz's analysis.

F. Raz and the Powers of Common Law Courts

According to Raz, "The English doctrine of precedent is that a precedent must either be followed or distinguished (though some courts also have the power to overrule their own or other courts' decisions)."[42] As Raz goes on to note, "since 'distinguishing' means changing the rule which is being distinguished, the power to distinguish is a power to develop the law even when deciding regulated cases and even by courts which have no power to overrule."[43] On this picture, an earlier precedent-setting case establishes a rule, the *ratio decidendi*, that is open to modification by later courts. The existence and identity of *rationes* is a matter of considerable controversy, some skeptics claiming it to be whatever the later judge takes it to be, thus eliminating all meaningful constraint and putting paid to the idea of *rules* of the common *law*. But even those who are not so skeptical as to deny the existence of binding *rationes* altogether differ on how these are to be identified. They will differ on how to differentiate the *ratio* contained within a reported opinion from mere *obiter dicta*, where the former

---

41 *The Concept of Law*, 135.
42 Joseph Raz, *The Authority of Law*, 185.
43 *Ibid*.

is presumed to be binding on later courts while the latter is not. In Raz's view, "[e]ssentially the *ratio* is the reason(s) by which the court justifies its decision. Establishing the *ratio* is partly a matter of interpretation of a document [the case report]: What is the reason on which a judge relied in reaching his decision as conveyed by his judgment."[44] Often there is but one reasonable interpretation of the judge's reasons for judgment, and so there is little dispute over the identity of the binding *ratio*. When a *ratio* is thus identified, it is expressible as a rule that sets out sufficient conditions for the result reached in the case at hand, C1. It will be of the form: "R1: Whenever A, B, and C, then X" where "X" designates a legal result like "The defendant is liable in negligence" and A, B, and C are conditions deemed sufficient for this result – for example, that there is harm, that it was foreseeable, and the defendant's conduct was its proximate cause. In any later case, C2, in which A, B, and C are present, the court, if it is bound by rulings issuing from the originating court, will be required to hold the defendant liable in negligence as well. The court will be bound by the precedent established in C1 – unless, that is, it can distinguish the two cases. It does so by establishing a further, new condition for the application of R that allows it to avoid result X in C2. The court cites a fourth condition, D, whose presence in C1 and absence in C2 marks a significant difference between the two cases, a difference that the judge in C1 presumably failed to notice or foresee as relevant. The new rule, R2, will be of the form: "Whenever A, B, C, and D, then X." As Raz notes, distinguishing is a very restricted form of law creation. It is subject to at least two crucial conditions:

1. The modified rule must be the rule laid down in the precedent restricted by the addition of a further condition for its application.
2. The modified rule must be such as to justify the order made in the precedent.[45]

These conditions entail that distinguishing is a very limited power. Courts that distinguish do not substitute wholly new rules, nor do they expand those that already exist. On the contrary, the power to distinguish is essentially the power to narrow the effect of the prior ruling by refining it to exclude application to a new, unanticipated case or type of case. In distinguishing rules, courts can be seen as engaged not in wholesale revision of the law but in its incremental development. The court retains one foot firmly in the past and one foot tentatively in the future. There are, of course, often other conditions at work in distinguishing. For instance, the difference cited between two cases must be a "relevant" one, and it must be one that can reasonably be viewed as "significantly" improving the rule. Judging relevance or degree of improvement can

---

44 *Ibid.*, 184. Raz notes that his account follows the general lines of the view defended by Sir Rupert Cross in his classic text *Precedent in English Law, 2nd ed.* (Oxford: Oxford University Press, 1968).
45 *Ibid.*, 186.

be notoriously difficult, of course, and reasonable people will often disagree in their assessments. Is it relevant that the losses incurred by the victim were, in the instant case, largely a product of his own unstable emotional state? Or should this be of no consequence when assessing damages in tort? Reasonable people will differ on this question. In light of such disagreements, it might be argued that the relevance and significant-improvement conditions are nothing but sham restraints, revealing, once again, that common law "reasoning" is, at bottom, wholly undisciplined. If reasonable people disagree about whether citing difference D is relevant or constitutes an improvement in the law, then a judge is pretty much free to ignore it if this is his inclination. Alternatively, he can choose to include it in R2 if this is the option he prefers. Nothing in law prevents him from doing one or the other.

Here, once again, we encounter a now-familiar form of argument that inevitably surfaces whenever normative constraints are subject to reasonable disagreement. Recall our discussion in Chapter 2 in which we explored the requirements under which Regina laboured in creating laws in Regas. We determined there that meaningful constraint is indeed possible in such an instance even when reasonable people disagree about whether Sunday closing laws deal with a "religious matter." The same is true when judges are required to cite only relevant differences and ones that will result in significant improvement in the law. At the very least, they are bound by the good-faith requirement. Of equal relevance is the fact that the rules of adjudication under which common law judges labour are not mere playthings in their hands, let alone the hands of any individual judge in a specific case who might be tempted to cite an irrelevant difference in order to escape the force of a binding precedent. The prospect of sustained criticism from his fellow judges, other officials, and indeed members of the general population, together with concerns about being overruled by a higher court, will incline a judge away from any such action, even if the good-faith requirement fails to move him – which it alone should be (and normally is) capable of doing.

Returning to Raz, all courts – at the very least all English courts – are able to distinguish, and they frequently engage this power in deciding cases. Only some, however, have the much greater power to overrule a prior decision and the *ratio* it establishes. In overruling R1, a court is not restricted by the two conditions of distinguishing cited above. Instead of adding a new condition to R1, a court engaged in overruling is free to substitute an entirely new set of conditions. That is, the court is free to substitute for R1 a new rule of the form "R3: Whenever, P, Q, and R, then X." Furthermore, there is no requirement that R3, were it to have been applied to C1, would have yielded the decision actually made in that case. R3, had it been applied to C1, might have led to the result that the defendant was not in fact liable. Typically, the power of overruling is restricted to courts higher in the judicial hierarchy than the originating court. For example, an Ontario Appeal Court cannot overrule a judgment of the Supreme

Court of Canada, but the reverse is entirely possible. So courts that enjoy the power of overruling labour under far fewer constraints. This is not to say, however, that their power is unlimited. Judges who overrule are subject to the good-faith requirement, the relevance requirement, and the condition that the changes introduced by their decision are justified by reasons of very great significance. Overruling has the potential to introduce far greater disruption than distinguishing. The law is not merely being developed in the incremental way made possible by distinguishing; it is being changed, often in a wholesale manner. This fact is a crucial one that courts will often cite as inclining them away from overruling precedent, even when justice seems to call in its favour. Overruling can cause confusion; can unsettle expectations founded on the belief that normally, changes in the common law are incremental only; and can lead to complaints of unfairness on the part of those whose treatment under the old rules might have been different had the new ones been applied to their cases. But once all these factors are put into the balance, countervailing reasons of justice might still compel a decision to overrule a lower court's decision. It might even lead the higher court to overrule its own previous decisions. Consider the famous *Practice Statement* of 1966, in which the British House of Lords announced its intention to change its practice of considering itself absolutely bound by its own previous decisions. On June 26 of that year, Lord Gerald Gardiner announced the following:

Their Lordships regard the use of precedent as an indispensable foundation upon which to decide what is the law and its application to individual cases. It provides at least some degree of certainty upon which individuals can rely in the conduct of their affairs, as well as a basis for the orderly development of legal rules.

Their Lordships nevertheless recognize that too rigid adherence to precedent may lead to injustice in particular cases and unduly restrict the proper development of the law. They propose, therefore, to modify their present practice and, while treating former decisions of this House as normally binding, to depart from a previous decision when it appears right to do so.

In this connection, they will bear in mind the danger of disturbing retrospectively the basis on which contracts, settlements of property and fiscal arrangements have been entered into and also the especial need for certainty as to the criminal law. This announcement is not intended to affect the use of precedent elsewhere than in this House.[46]

So the Lords freed themselves from the binding effect of their own *rationes*. Nevertheless, the Lords did not consider this newly established power to overrule completely without limit. In the years following the *Practice Statement*, it became clear that they were prepared to overrule themselves only under very special circumstances. In, for example, *Fitzleet Estates v. Cherry*, Viscount Dilhorne said: "If the decision in the *Chancery Lane Case* was wrong, it

---

46 Cited in Cross, *Precedent in English Law*, 109.

certainly was not so clearly wrong and productive of injustice as to make it right for the House to depart from it."[47] Once again, we see recognition of a significant but controlled and disciplined power to change or depart from existing precedents and common law rules.

G. A Common Law Charter?

So the common law method of legal regulation strives to strike a balance between Hart's two fundamental needs: the need for clear, antecedent guidance by relatively fixed rules, and the need to leave open, for later settlement by an informed official choice, issues that can be properly appreciated and settled only when they arise in a concrete case. As Schauer puts it,

> ... not only does the common law as it actually exists appear willing to sacrifice some of the goals of predictability and efficiency on the altar of perfectability, but it seems also, much to Bentham's disgust, to be willing to entrust considerable decision-making to the judiciary ... By ameliorating rule-based decision-making, the common law allocates power to its judges, treating the risks consequent to that empowerment as less dangerous than those flowing from the application of crude canonical rules to circumstances their makers might not have imagined and producing results the society might not be willing to tolerate.[48]

Despite this well-known adaptability, which is either celebrated or condemned depending on the theorist's jurisprudential leanings, it is important not to underestimate the capacity of the common law to cater to the first of Hart's two fundamental needs: the need for antecedent guidance by settled rules requiring no further appeal to normative issues the settling of which (in all probability) prompted the rule's creation. The degree of fixity Hart ascribes to the English common law system in the passage cited above[49] has been challenged, most notably by Brian Simpson.[50] And even were Hart's characterization of (the then-current) state of English law correct, it remains true that a common law system can cater to the element of adaptability to a far greater extent than envisaged by Hart. Indeed, it might do so to the point where it would be perfectly reasonable to question whether that system had provided its judges with so much discretion to decide each case on its own individual merits that it had effectively abandoned the rule of law entirely. But somewhere between this scenario and the one Hart describes are other options in which more liberal

---

47 All ER 996, at 1000.
48 Schauer, *supra* note 40, 179.
49 Text accompanying note 41, pp. 332–3.
50 See A.W.B. Simpson, "The Common Law and Legal Theory" in A.W.B. Simpson, ed., *Oxford Essays in Jurisprudence* (2nd series) (Oxford: Clarendon Press, 1973), at 77. Simpson's major criticism is that it is wrong to view the common law as comprising highly adaptable rules, a view to which, he thinks, Hart is led owing to his commitment to positivist legal theory and "the model of rules."

powers of overruling and distinguishing precedents are possible, and these do not threaten the rule of law. Which of these options actually obtains in a particular system will depend on the demands placed on judges by the norms of adjudication circumscribing their powers of decision. But whatever blend the system embodies, the point remains that the common law has a long, established history, with which lawyers are familiar, of successfully combining (in various ways) fixity with adaptability. If so, then we might profitably look to the common law as a model for understanding Charters and the roles they are capable of playing. Why should we not view Charters as setting the stage for a kind of common law jurisprudence of the moral rights cited in the Charter?[51] This would be a jurisprudence according to which the abstract moral terms found within Charters make reference to concepts, like "equality before and under the law," whose understanding and development are analogous to the development of concepts like "negligent," "reasonable," and "foreseeable" in tort law. There will be differences, to be sure: After all, the constitutional status of a written Charter distinguishes it from the law of negligence. But these differences aside, one can easily envision mapping common law methodology onto the understanding and development of the moral concepts, principles, and values enshrined in Charters. As we will see in Chapter 6, one of the distinct advantages of doing so is that we are able to answer most, if not all, of the Critics' objections to judicial review – something that those who continue to believe that Charters *must* be good things to have will find of considerable value in making their case. But before we get to all that, it might be helpful to pause briefly to consider another area of law – Canadian discrimination law – in which the disastrous consequences of trying to establish (sensible) fixed points when no such points are to be found could have been avoided if common law methodology had been employed instead. The difficulties encountered in the area of Canadian discrimination law signal related ones that are bound to ensue if the common law approach to judicial review is rejected and we instead continue to seek those elusive fixed points of agreement and pre-commitment upon which the Standard Case rests and that serve to fuel the arguments of Waldron and his fellow Critics.

H. "Top-Down" and "Bottom-Up" Methodology

In her recent critique of human rights legislation in Canada, Denise Reaume nicely summarizes and illustrates the advantages that could have been (and

---

51 I have neither the space nor the legal competence to argue this point, but it would appear as though Charter adjudication in the United States and Canada is, in actual fact, modeled to a great extent on the common law. As Schauer notes in his review essay of Eisenberg's book, "I sneak in a constitutional example only to remind the reader that American constitutional adjudication in the Supreme Court seems a central case of common law methodology." See Schauer, "Is the Common Law Law?" 455.

perhaps still might be) realized were the common law approach that has been used to such good effect in negligence law been employed to develop the law of discrimination. According to Reaume, the state of Canadian discrimination law is in desperate need of change.[52] If injustice is to be dealt with effectively, an entirely new approach must be taken.

> With more than fifty years of experience in dealing with discrimination, we have ... outgrown the method of law-making that consists of using the legislative machinery to enact successive new pigeonholes each time a new kind of fact situation arises that deserves protection. It is time for a change. The phenomenon of discrimination – of those in relative positions of power denying full human status and opportunity to those in relative positions of disadvantage – is not capable of being codified in precise terms of the sort that have characterized past legislative efforts.[53]

In Reaume's view, this sorry state is the result of a failure to appreciate the inappropriateness, in the field of discrimination law, of what she calls the "top-down model" of legal regulation. This is a highly idealized model, most vigorously defended by Bentham and lying at one end of a spectrum of views on how best to pursue the rule of law. It is, in short, the formalist ideal. "In its ideal form, the top-down model conceptualizes the law-making enterprise as the task of stating a comprehensive system of detailed, precise rules grounded in a sound moral theory and designed to cover every situation to be regulated."[54] It is the formalist ideal of precise rules, announced in advance, and applied with no further need of law-creating activity, on the part of adjudicators. Of course, as Hart might have urged, few legislators have a fully worked-out moral theory in mind. And even when an individual legislator does have such a theory at hand, chances are, given the circumstances of politics and the equally important circumstances of rule making, that his theory will be significantly different from theories held by some of his fellow legislators – including those who join him in supporting the rules in question. Furthermore, few legislators would be prepared to say that their statutory rules are so airtight that they cover every conceivable case, or even every case that is likely to arise in future. Nevertheless, legislators who pursue the top-down model will have tried to come to their best understanding of the relevant moral issues and attempted to craft rules that deal with as many probable cases as possible. With respect to the unanticipated cases that will no doubt emerge, their belief is that these will be minimal, and that they can be dealt with either through legislative amendment, or (perhaps begrudgingly) through the decision of a judge in whatever rare penumbral case happens to come to the fore.

---

52 Denise Reaume, "Of Pigeonholes and Principles: A Reconsideration of Discrimination Law" 40 *Osgoode Hall L.J.* (2002), 113–44.
53 *Ibid.*, 143.
54 *Ibid.*, 116.

In the spirit of Hart's analysis and its recognition of the circumstances of rule making, Reaume notes that the top-down model can lead to successful legal regulation in the area of discrimination law only if at least two conditions are met. First, as should be obvious from the point made above, legislators must have at least some idea of an appropriate general moral theory underlying their enacted rules. This theory will be seen by them to justify and unify the rules enacted and establish them as a part of a coherent project of realizing concretely the more abstract commitments of their moral theory. Second, the fact situations covered by the rules must not be so variable and unpredictable that Hart's penumbra will come into play in too many cases, regardless of the legislators' best efforts to draft precise rules that eliminate it as much as is humanly possible. If these two conditions are not met, then "the resulting statutory rules will have something of the quality of arbitrary pigeonholes into which complainants must fit their situations or fail."[55] If there is little understanding of why the pigeonholes are as they are, then not only will the law lack coherence, judges will have difficulty knowing what to do in the unanticipated cases that are bound to arise. There will be little basis upon which to draw in extending the extant categories and rules in ways that are sensitive to their underlying rationale. Furthermore, the "precision of the rules" will also create "little incentive for adjudicators to search for a theory capable of explaining the rationale for the rules and guiding their intelligent development over time." Not only that, but "the more precise the rules, the more likely that adjudicative attempts to fill in gaps and develop norms will be met with the criticism that adjudicators have no authority to amend the rules laid down by Parliament."[56] In other words, adjudicators will find themselves forced to address a variation on the argument from democracy so often used by Charter Critics against the activities of judges in judicial review. The result will often be, in the case of discrimination law, that worthy candidates for remedy are denied. Reaume cites the case of the obese, whose struggles are often exacerbated by the fact that discrimination against them does not fit into the existing categories of discrimination.[57] Their case fails to fall within an existing pigeonhole. Should the legislature take notice of this unfortunate result, it can, of course intervene and change the law. But this is not always to be expected. And even when the legislature acts, the result will be of little solace to the aggrieved parties whose plight led to change in the law. Furthermore, without an understanding of what it is about the new and existing categories that justifies linking them in legislation, the result is likely to be a further pigeon hole and further cases of the very same phenomenon.

In contrast with the top-down model, Reaume outlines the "bottom-up model" of legal regulation, which lies at the other end of the spectrum of

---

55 *Ibid.*, 115.
56 *Ibid.*, 123.
57 See, for example, pp. 128–9.

possibilities for legal regulation. This is the model condemned by Bentham and celebrated by Blackstone and other proponents of the common law approach to legal regulation. In Reaume's understanding of it,

[t]he model holds that although we may agree on and be deeply committed to certain abstract values or principles, we cannot anticipate all the fact situations in which they may be implicated, nor can we fully map out a comprehensive view of the concrete consequences implicated by those values. We want our legal system to be informed by principles of justice, liberty and equality, but these are multi-faceted concepts whose full meaning is contested. In such situations, it is wise not to attempt a comprehensive theory issuing a precise network of rules at the outset, but rather to let the implications of the abstract principles be revealed incrementally through confronting fact situations on a case-by-case basis.[58]

Reaume argues that the bottom-up model is far more promising than the top-down model as a way of developing discrimination law. In making her case, she draws on a very telling analogy: development of the law of negligence. The top-down model is no more appropriate in the area of discrimination law than it would have been had the law of negligence been largely developed in its terms.

In retrospect, this law-making strategy has been as ill-conceived as if legislatures had pre-empted initial judicial reluctance to develop the action for trespass on the case by legislating negligence law. Just imagine what the law of negligence would have looked like: first a statute imposing liability on the drivers of horse-drawn coaches (later updated for automobiles), then another for manufacturers of household products, then another for landlords, followed by one for construction companies, after which one for accountants – each specifying what counts as negligence as understood at the time, and therefore having to be constantly updated to include new forms of negligence in the context. Given the boundless ingenuity of the human species in finding new ways to harm one another, this approach to negligence would have been madness.[59]

Fortunately, the law of negligence was developed – and continues to be developed – in the spirit of the bottom-up model, in full recognition of Lord Macmillan's observation that "The categories of negligence are never closed."[60] "Entrusted with working out general principles that keep the law relevant to the [ever-changing] social conditions with which it must deal, the adjudicators charged with the task in the common law courts have shown themselves more or less up to the challenge."[61] It is well past time, Reaume argues, for the courts to be allowed the same opportunity to develop the law of discrimination in the

---

58 *Ibid.*, 117. Reaume acknowledges that her depiction of the bottom-up model resembles Sunstein's theory of "incompletely theorized agreements." See Cass R. Sunstein, *Legal Reasoning and Political Conflict* (New York: Oxford University Press, 1996), especially Chapter 2.
59 *Ibid.*, 143–4.
60 *Donaghue v. Stevenson* [1932] A.C. 562, cited by Reaume at 144.
61 Reaume, "Of Pigeonholes and Principles: A Reconsideration of Discrimination Law," 144.

same sensitive and sensible manner. It is time to do away with pigeonholes and "recognize that discrimination law is an extension of the enterprise of figuring out how much care we each ought to take for the well-being of others."[62] To this we might add: It is time to do away with the notion that a Charter can, in the circumstances of politics and the equally crucial circumstances of rule making, establish pigeonholes serving as fixed points of agreement and pre-commitment to moral limits on government power. It is well past time to recognize that in this area too, "The categories. . . . are never closed." They demand the case-by-case, incremental changes and improvements that common law methodology makes possible.

I. Lessons to Be Learned

So what have we learned from the preceding few sections? First, there is the important moral lesson to be drawn from Hart's thoughts on the emergence and characteristic features of law: Despite its undeniable potential for good, law can not only be an unwieldy instrument, it can sometimes develop into a dangerous social tool. By its very nature, it has the potential to separate the validity of a norm both from its moral and rational merit, and, importantly, from its general acceptance among the society over which it governs. Legal structures created by the union of primary and secondary rules create these possibilities about which we should be ever vigilant. We should attempt to fashion our legal structures, within the boundaries identified in Hart's analysis, so as to minimize the chances of our descent into Hart's Hell. One way in which we might attempt to do this is to adopt judicial review that explicitly places moral conditions on the valid exercise of government powers.

A second important lesson we have learned is that there are different modes of legal regulation – in particular, different methods of attempting to deal with the circumstances of rule making. Whichever mode, or combination of modes, is employed, however, two facts remain indisputable: (a) We cannot always foresee the results to which general rules will lead; and (b) it would be foolish to ignore this point in thinking about how best to design our legal institutions. Given that legal norms are of practical necessity (typically) general in nature – that is, they deal with general classes of individuals, actions, situations, and so on – laws always have the potential to be what Fred Schauer nicely terms "over- or under-inclusive" and to lead to unforeseen, troublesome results in concrete cases of application.[63] If so, then we had better bear these features of legal regulation in mind if our efforts to secure the benefits of life under law are to meet with any degree of success – if our efforts to emerge from a pre-legal

---

62 *Ibid.*
63 The most developed and insightful analysis of this particular feature of general rules is Fred Schauer's *Playing by the Rules*.

state is to be at all worth the bother. These are all points well understood, if not always fully appreciated and implemented, within many realms of ordinary law. For instance, if Reaume is correct in her analysis, Canada has not fully appreciated the benefits of pursuing a common law of discrimination that, like the law of negligence, would be based on the bottom-up model of rule creation, which has worked so well in tort law. Yet these same points ((a) and (b)) seem largely to have been ignored in the debates between Advocates and Critics. My aim in the remainder of this book is to rectify this problem by feeding the insights of Hart, Reaume, and Schauer into the mix and seeing what results. The result is our alternative model of Charters and their legitimacy, the common law conception, which is in no way undermined by the circumstances of politics. On the contrary, Charters, conceived in this way, can be seen to be a quite sensible response to those circumstances and to the equally important circumstances of rule making.

So Hart's analysis reveals that law can be both an unwieldy and morally dangerous means of social regulation – and that we must always bear these facts in mind when considering how best to structure our legal systems. Yet it is equally important that we not lose sight of Hart's other insights into the more positive role that law is capable of playing, in particular its ability to facilitate our emergence from a pre-legal society with all its attendant defects. We must not underplay the important fact that law is able to accomplish much of its task(s) only through its ability to separate the validity and application of legal norms from contestable questions of reason, morality, and common sense and by its ability to let us know what will be expected of us. Only by some such separation and foreknowledge is law able to reduce the level of uncertainty that the introduction of a rule of recognition is supposed to help overcome. How can we be certain where we stand under legal rules if the validity of legal rules depends on conformity with contestable moral norms, or if they are developed in courts as the bottom-up model supposes? Have we not merely reintroduced the very defects we were attempting to overcome? True, governance by legal rules created as the top-down model supposes and validated by a rule of recognition has its limitations. But are these not limitations with which we simply must live if we are to pursue the benefits of law? Not necessarily. Our choices are not quite as limited as the objection seems to suppose. It is possible to combine moral conditions with an effective rule of recognition; it is possible to maintain an acceptable level of antecedent guidance while pursuing some version of the bottom-up model. Our choices are not between the rule-fetishism represented by the formalist ideal and a virtual return to pre-legal society. There are other options between these two extremes, and legal systems are able to choose among them.[64] Again, this is a point stressed not only by Hart but also by Schauer,

---

64 Remember that Reaume's two models are "idealized" versions of positions lying on a spectrum.

who is concerned to stress the wide variety of ways in which the rule of law can be achieved. According to Schauer, the top-down model, which embodies what Schauer calls "rule-based decision-making," is not the only option available:

[T]o the extent that legal systems embrace rule-based decision-making, they embrace as well those values of intertemporal consistency . . . stability for stability's sake, unwillingness to trust decision-makers to depart too dramatically from the past, and a conservatism committed to the view that changes from the past as more likely to be for the worse than for the better. . . . [N]othing inherent in the idea of a legal system mandates that it serves these values.[65]

This, of course, is a sentiment shared by Hart:

[A]ll systems, in different ways, compromise between two social needs: the need for certain rules which can, over great areas of conduct, safely be applied by private individuals to themselves without fresh official guidance or weighing up of social interests, and the need to leave open, for later settlement by an informed official choice, issues which can only be properly appreciated and settled when they arise in a concrete case. [W]e need to remind ourselves that human inability to anticipate the future, which is at the root of this indeterminacy, varies in degree in different fields of conduct, and that legal systems cater for this inability by a corresponding variety of techniques.[66]

That law should serve what Scott Shapiro calls its "essential guidance function" is undeniably true.[67] And this function may demand rules whose validity does not, for the most part, depend on contestable moral questions such as those dealt with in judicial review. Furthermore, it may also demand rules whose content is known in advance: We can hardly be guided by norms whose identity we learn only after they are created in a court in which our case is being decided. But as Hart correctly notes, there are always competing considerations at play, and ignoring these may leave us vulnerable to the temptations of formalism and to a system in which we strive to ensure that our binding legal rules are identified, interpreted, and fixed exclusively, decisively, and in advance, possibly by source-based considerations alone.[68] A society might in

---

65 Shauer, *Playing by the Rules*, 174. According to Schauer, all we need for a legal system to exist are "jurisdictional rules," which empower authoritative decision making by individuals who may or may not be bound (completely or to some degree) to decide according to pre-established legal rules. Weber's "qadi legal system" is a conceptual possibility. Cf., Raz's related suggestion that only norm-applying institutions are necessary for law. "[T]he existence of norm-creating institutions though characteristic of modern legal systems is not a necessary feature of all legal systems, but. . . . the existence of certain types of norm-applying institutions is." *The Authority of Law*, 105.

66 *The Concept of Law*, 130–1.

67 See "On Hart's Way Out," 46, and "Law, Morality, and the Guidance of Conduct," 127.

68 A source-based consideration is one that is concerned with the source of a norm – for example, its formal enactment – not its merit. According to Exclusive Legal Positivists, tests of legal validity are necessarily source-based only. According to Inclusive Positivists, on the other hand, more than the source of a norm can be relevant in determining its validity – its

some situations have ample reason to pursue this line of action vigorously. One needn't contemplate a Hobbesean state of nature to recognize the wisdom, in some social settings, of employing pre-existing, relatively hard and fast rules whose validity and concrete requirements leave little room for judgment (moral or otherwise) at the point of application. The wisdom of such a move is evident in far less brutish but narrowly circumscribed, stable, and well-understood situations. One thinks, for example, of situations defining offer and acceptance in contract law, our obligations to pay taxes, or the familiar signing of wills and the two-witnesses requirement. In each of these cases, the need for and possibility of relative certainty about the identity, requirements, and satisfaction of the relevant legal rules may be at a premium. In such situations, an appropriate level of the kind of antecedent guidance highlighted by Hart and invoked by Shapiro may be well-nigh impossible should controversial factors, particularly contestable moral norms, play a *prominent* role in determining the validity and application of the relevant rules, or if the (idealized, extreme version of the) bottom-up method were pursued. We would, in such an instance, come nowhere near dealing with the threat of uncertainty underlying the need for Hart's rule of recognition. But two further points, crucial to our understanding of judicial review, must be stressed at this stage: (1) that moral factors should not play too great a role in such situations in no way entails that they should play no role whatsoever, as they arguably did, for example, in *Riggs v. Palmer*, and countless other cases far too numerous and familiar to mention.[69] Nor does it entail (2) that situations cannot arise in which the acknowledged value of antecedent guidance by relatively fixed rules is trumped by our concern that those rules do not infringe, in cases that could not have been anticipated and in ways that could not have been foreseen or appreciated, important norms of morality or practical rationality.[70] As we saw when we examined the circumstances of rule making, we might not have foreseen some such conflict for any number of reasons. For example, unforeseeable developments in our ability to communicate electronically might well render rules that were, in the age of the telegraph, well designed and morally unproblematic, highly problematic in the age of the Internet with its potential threat to our privacy. In this kind of case, we might have been, and continue to be, in agreement about how to understand the moral value(s) at stake. What we have not been able to foresee, however, is how the rules in question would later affect the agreed value(s). On some other occasion, the problematic case might arise, not because of evolving

conformity with, for example, a moral norm enshrined in a Charter might also be necessary, and this cannot be determined without exploring more than its source.

69 *Riggs v. Palmer* 115 N.Y. 506, 22 N.E. 188 (1889). For detailed discussion of a Canadian case, *Andrews v. Law Society of BC*, 4 W.W.R 242 (BCCA), in which moral norms figured prominently, see Waluchow, *Inclusive Legal Positivism*, 149–55.

70 Again, think of Riggs, as well as the vast array of legal norms that make use of terms like "reasonable," "fair," and so on.

social circumstances in a context of relatively stable moral values and principles but because the relevant norms, or our understanding of them, have for some reason changed.[71] Our understanding of moral equality, for instance, has clearly changed in such a way that the "separate but equal" treatment, which was at one time in the racial history of the United States thought perfectly consistent with that value, is now generally agreed not to be so. I suspect that a time will soon come when it is generally realized that the option of disallowing gay marriage but providing for "civil unions" with legal rights more or less equivalent to those associated with the former institution is just another form of separate but equal treatment and equally condemned, on that account, by the norms of moral equality. In any case, it is with these factors in mind that we shall, in the next chapter, consider the possibilities open to us when the decision is taken to contemplate the adoption of a Charter.

One possibility that remains, of course, one that we must continue to bear in mind, is to avoid Charters altogether: This, of course, is the option urged by Waldron and other Critics. Recall Waldron's objection that Charters artificially constrain our ability to respond to changing views about rights – and that because of this they threaten the ideals of democracy by artificially constraining the abilities of the people-now to engage in continued, meaningful self-government by entrenching decisions taken by the people-then. Such responses will be easier, we are told, if, instead of adopting a Charter, we allow our evolving understandings of moral rights to be reflected in more flexible and less verbally constrained common law principles and precedents, "and easier still if rights take the form of 'conventional understandings' subscribed to the political community at large. . . ." Rejecting the call to adopt a Charter, we are told, will create (or maintain) the possibility of a public discourse less constrained by verbal formulae and semantic obsessions and more able to ask the questions of moral substance upon which we really should be focusing. What we need, in Waldron's view, are institutional mechanisms for protecting rights that are "free from the obsessive verbalism of a particular written charter." But this, I shall argue, is a case of throwing the baby out with the bathwater. One can agree with the need for institutional mechanisms that are free from "obsessive verbalism" and, importantly, from obsession with finding fixed points of agreement and pre-commitment that original meanings, original understandings, and the intentions of the framers are sometimes said to express without thereby rejecting written Charters altogether. One will be led to reject the latter for the sake of the former only if one views Charters as the choice of a society obsessed, for misguided normative or conceptual reasons, with the first of Hart's two needs:

---

71 A widespread change in the understanding of a moral value can be described as a change in social circumstances. By the latter phrase I mean to exclude that kind of change. I have in mind factors like technological development, changes in the basic structure of the work place or the family unit, and so on.

"the need for certain rules which can, over great areas of conduct, safely be applied by private individuals to themselves without fresh official guidance or weighing up of social interests" and unable to see the force of Hart's second need: "to leave open, for later settlement by an informed official choice, issues which can only be properly appreciated and settled when they arise in a concrete case." But nothing in the nature of law, or a Charter, prevents us from bearing this second need firmly in mind. In particular, nothing forces us to ignore the human inability to anticipate the future, to possess certain knowledge of moral truth both in the abstract and in the concrete circumstances of life and politics. Also, nothing forces us to deny the important insight that all "legal systems cater for [these] inabilit[ies] by a corresponding variety of techniques." One of the available techniques is the adoption of a Charter understood and applied as the living tree metaphor suggests. As we shall see, Charters both can and should be seen to represent a mixture of only very modest pre-commitment and confidence, combined with a considerable measure of humility. The latter stems from the recognition that we – and this includes our representative legislators and all others charged with the task of rendering law-determining decisions on our behalf – do *not* in fact have all the answers when it comes to moral rights and the impact of our actions on them, and that we should do all we can to ensure that our moral short-sightedness and other limitations do not, in the circumstances of politics and rule making, lead us to morally unworthy government action, understood, once again, as encompassing legislative, executive, and judicial acts.

Far from being based on the unwarranted assumption that we can have, in advance, all the right answers to the controversial issues of political morality that might arise under Charter challenges to government action, and that we are warranted in imposing these answers on those by whom we are succeeded, the common law conception stems – and it is this which leads me to claim that it represents a kind of Copernican revolution in our thinking – from the *exact opposite* sentiment: from a recognition that we do not have all the answers, and that we are well advised to design our political and legal institutions deliberately in ways that are sensitive to this feature of our predicament. *Contra* Waldron and many other Critics, Charters do not, of necessity, embody a naïve over-confidence in our judgments of political morality and an attendant belief that in this area of fundamental law the top-down model can safely be pursued. On the contrary, a Charter can be seen as embodying a *concession* to our inability fully to understand the nature of fundamental rights and how these might be infringed by government action. If a Charter is seen in this different light – as (among other things) a set of protections against the unforeseen impact of government action on moral rights and values – we can not only begin to see why it might be a good thing to have, we can see our way clear to answering the various arguments offered by Waldron and other Critics against its adoption.

Before turning to the various advantages – and potential drawbacks – of adopting such an approach to judicial review, I should perhaps quickly dispose of one obvious objection. One can easily imagine a Critic of my proposal offering the following objection.

Charters are the (typically) entrenched, written products of special acts of legislation, not judicial decision. Furthermore, their terms cannot, as common law rules can, be changed at point of application by judges. A judge cannot, for example, decide to eliminate section 15 from the Canadian Charter of Rights and Freedoms, or add a new clause which restricts its ambit. In other words, Charters are completely immune from the judicial powers of distinguishing and overruling so characteristic of common law rules and precedents. If a Charter is to be changed, this must take place via a special process of constitutional amendment in which judges typically play no part. The role of a judge is restricted to interpreting and applying the constitution, not changing or developing it. It follows that judicial review should be placed at the top-down end of Reaume's spectrum, not the bottom-up end where one finds the common law. It further follows that we should be looking to statutory law, not the common law, for a means of understanding the nature and role of Charters within constitutional democracies. It is simply silly to try to map common law methodology onto the practice of judicial review.

Though seemingly troublesome, this objection is easily answered. We can agree with the obvious fact that Charters take written, canonical form and that their terms are immune from being changed by the acts of judges whose responsibility it is to apply them in courts of law. In these respects, it must be agreed, Charters are more like statutory rules than common law rules and precedents. It is therefore tempting to try to find a place for them at or near the top-down end of Reaume's spectrum. But another, equally obvious fact about Charters, one that is in fact responsible for many of the Critics' most forceful objections, is one to which we have repeatedly drawn attention: that the most influential and contentious of a Charter's provisions are expressed using very abstract terminology whose understanding and application require appeal to contentious norms of political morality. Typical examples of such terminology include "equality," "fundamental justice," "due process," "free and democratic," and "the rule of law." This is a fact that would complicate matters considerably were we for some reason keen to insist on an understanding of Charters that places them at the top-down end where, as Reaume suggests, success can be achieved only if we can establish relatively precise, concrete rules both justified and unified by an agreed moral theory. But this is not even close to being true of Charters – unless there is an approach to understanding their terms that is more like the approach used in understanding a detailed tax code and less like the approach used in developing common law concepts like "negligent" and "foreseeable." The only available options would appear to be theories that attempt to tie the content of Charter provisions to factors like framers' intentions, original meaning, and the like. Yet as we saw in earlier chapters, such theories are not only fraught with serious theoretical difficulties, they are also, for now-familiar reasons, capable of producing highly undesirable effects if applied to Charters in the circumstances of politics and rule making. So we can agree that Charters take written form and their terms are not within the purview of judges to change, but there is every reason to believe that the development of our understanding of those terms can nevertheless be modeled on the common law.

6

Common Law Constitutionalism

A. Anteing Up

Among the standard arguments in the Standard Case for judicial review, the most compelling is that Charters serve as vehicles for the protection of entrenched or transitory minorities against the majoritarian biases, excesses, mistakes, inauthentic wishes, and insensitivities of democratic politics. They are applauded by their Advocates as embodying the rational pre-commitment of the community to work against these elements by tying itself to the mast of a chosen set of fundamental rights. Paradigmatically, these are rights thought essential to enlightened democratic rule, and to the free and equal exercise of individual autonomy. These are all stressed, to varying degrees, in public discourse and by philosophers such as Rawls, Dworkin, and Freeman. We have acknowledged that there are serious problems with this picture and with the Standard Case resting on it. Though many of the objections go too far, or rest on dubious premises, there is considerable merit in many of the Critics' complaints, particularly those raised by Waldron. For instance, although the Standard Case does not have to assume that we are all Hobbesean predators who cannot be trusted if let loose in the arena of democratic politics, it does seem to presuppose a level of pre-commitment that seems impossible in the circumstances of politics. There is just too much disagreement among us. The Standard Case also seems at war with our commitment to self-government, the animating ideal of democracy. This seems true whether that ideal is understood in terms of the constitutional conception defended by Dworkin or the procedural conception preferred by Waldron and Ely. Even if we could somehow make sense of the idea (defended by Rubenfeld) that the people-then and the people-now are in actual fact one and the same people, thereby avoiding a system of government in which one party (the people-then) sets terms under which another party (the people-now) is bound, the fact remains that true self-government seems to require an ability, on an ongoing basis, to change one's mind. At the very least, it requires an ability to alter one's commitments in light of new beliefs, changing circumstances, and unforeseen occurrences. But these abilities are severely hampered, if not eliminated entirely, by an entrenched Charter that embodies the fixed points presupposed in the Standard Case. The Standard Case also faces the difficulty of explaining why, given the degree of dissensus one finds in modern, pluralistic democracies, we could possibly justify the practice of having judges apply highly contestable moral norms masquerading as fixed limits on government power. If we cannot agree in advance what these norms mean, then it will be left to the judiciary to assign meanings for us. Does this not leave us prey to elitist judges and their subjective prejudices and agendas? Would we not, in agreeing to such an arrangement, have surrendered our autonomy? Would we not have reneged on our responsibility to decide, as a people, how we shall be governed? None of this, we agreed, could possibly be reconciled with the ideals of democracy and the image we like to paint of ourselves as a self-governing people.

So we acknowledged that the Standard Case for judicial review is in serious need of revision. Nevertheless, I suggested that there is little reason to think that many of its essential details cannot remain. It is now time to ante up and make good on this claim. I shall attempt to do so by invoking the common law conception and showing how it enables us to answer the Critics' remaining objections – that is, those the answering of which, as I acknowledged in Chapter 3, requires the resources of that conception. As before, the focus will be on Waldron, whose case against judicial review remains the strongest and most philosophically sophisticated on record. If we can succeed in answering the Critics' remaining objections, then we will have come a long way towards justifying judicial review and showing that it is not the threat to democratic self-government and practical rationality that Waldron and many others claim it to be. As we shall see, it is possible to retain the notion of pre-commitment in defending judicial review, so long as we are careful to acknowledge the inherent limitations of the notion when it is applied to the circumstances of politics and rule making. If we are careful in this way, then the practice, so understood, can withstand the objection that it presupposes a degree of moral knowledge and consensus of which we are simply incapable. Bearing in mind the insights of Hart, Schauer, Reaume, and others, we will be able to see that Charters do not, in fact, need to presuppose that we all agree on right answers to questions about the meaning and implications of fundamental moral rights. Indeed, they can be seen to represent an acknowledgement of the exact opposite: that our moral knowledge is limited – and that judicial review is a quite sensible institutional mechanism for dealing with this particular feature of the circumstances of politics – and with the equally important circumstances of rule making.

B. Other Options?

Let's begin with the following concern about the argument thus far, which we can suppose a Critic will be only too pleased to offer at this stage of the argument. Suppose that it's true, she says, that one can graft common law methodology onto a Charter in the ways defended in the previous chapter. Suppose further that this possibility reveals an important fact about current disputes between Advocates and their fellow Critics – much of it is suspect because the participants on both sides of the debate assume the thesis that Charters aspire to establish fixed points of agreement and commitment. And on that basis Charters are either celebrated or condemned, depending on the particular theorist's views concerning the possibility and desirability (morally and politically) of harnessing government power by reference to such fixed points. This we have now seen to be an unwarranted assumption because the common law conception is a live option.[1] Nevertheless, the Critic will go on to add, it in no way follows from this that we should opt for Charters, understood now in the manner proposed by the common law conception. In other words, it does not follow from the fact that the common law conception is an available option that it is the one we should actually pursue. And this is because we have yet to rule out another, equally live option: the rejection of judicial review altogether and the putting in place of something more like the means of harnessing government power recommended by Waldron. That is, perhaps we should adopt institutional mechanisms for protecting rights that are "free from the obsessive verbalism of a particular written charter."[2] What could possibly be gained if, instead of pursuing this non-Charter option, we opted for a written Charter whose role it is to set the stage for the development of a common law jurisprudence of moral rights? Much would depend, of course, on what these other "institutional mechanisms" would look like. If, with Waldron, we "are talking about legal recognition in the form of common law principles and precedents," then presumably we will still be talking about judicial review and the supposed insult to democracy and moral agency that Waldron envisages.[3] If we are talking about common law rights' taking "the form of 'conventional' understandings subscribed to in the political community at large," then at least two important questions arise. First, we might reasonably ask how Waldron could appeal to such understandings if the circumstances of politics truly are as he envisages.

---

1 This is not to say, of course, that there are not other options within the "living tree" family of theories. Indeed, Dworkin's constitutional theory might well be a variation of the common law conception coupled with a particular view about the kind of interpretive reasoning to be employed in Charter cases. It most certainly has more affinity with the common law conception than with any of the fixed views considered in Chapter 2. This may also be true of Bruce Ackerman's theory according to which the U.S. Constitution has been revised on a number of occasions described by Ackerman as "constitutional moments."

2 *Law and Disagreement*, 221.

3 *Ibid.*

"Conventional understandings" are unlikely to exist if, in fact, *disagreement goes all the way down.*[4] Second, we might ask what there is in the common law conception that could be thought to rule out conventional understandings as a possible source of guidance for the courts. Is this not in fact precisely what one would expect? We are, after all, taking about a form of law that, on most traditional understandings of its nature and purpose, is anchored, at least in part, in common beliefs and practices within the community. This brings us to an important third question that has, to this point in our discussion, been largely bracketed. To what kind of standards does (or can) a Charter refer when, for example, it reaches the conclusion that a statute is constitutionally invalid and of no force and effect because it denies "due process" or "equality before and under the law," or because it infringes unjustifiably on "the right to life, liberty and security of the person" in a manner that fails to comport with "the principles of fundamental justice"? Debates between Advocates and Critics – as well as debates among philosophers concerning the various relations that exist between law and morality – have been curiously silent on this important question. It is well past time to draw attention to it. As we shall see, the answer one provides will seriously affect one's assessment of judicial review.

So, to what kind of norm does a Charter appeal when it speaks of due process, equality, fundamental justice, and the like? In approaching this particular question, it will be useful to return to a particular complaint one often hears from Critics. Judicial review, it is said, allows judges to impose their own subjective moral views in ways that are both unfair to citizens (often those in the majority) whose views are different and a violation of democratic principle.[5] This objection, which we'll call "the popular complaint," often relies on a specific caricature of judges' activities when they are engaged in judicial review. Drawing on arguments advanced earlier, I will outline an alternative picture that yields the following results: (a) that the rights to which a Charter refers are best viewed as rights of political morality established within what we'll call the "community's constitutional morality"; (b) that the community can be wrong about what its own constitutional morality requires; (c) that a judge's views about what that morality requires in a particular case might, on the other hand, be correct, or at least better; (d) that when this is so, judges can be required by the Charter – by law – to enforce their own views of the community's constitutional morality against the erroneous beliefs of the community and its legislative representatives; (e) that when judges fulfill this duty, it is almost always misleading to view them as imposing *their own* subjective moral views;

---

4 Many positivists, particularly Jules Coleman, have spent considerable time and effort attempting to determine how much disagreement is compatible with the existence of conventional rules or understandings. But wherever the limit is set, it's pretty clear that a disagreement "which goes all the way down" goes well beyond it. See Coleman's *The Practice of Principle*, especially Lectures 7 and 8.

5 For examples of this complaint, see Chapters 1 and 2.

and finally, (f) that in enforcing their views about the rights of their community's constitutional morality recognized in a Charter, judges are in fact respecting, not violating, democratic principle. This is so, I shall argue, even in highly controversial and unpopular cases in which both public opinion and the language of the relevant black-letter law are reasonably (though erroneously) viewed by some as inconsistent with what the judges believe they are legally bound to decide.

C. Morality and the Charter

The popular complaint, recall, is that judges engaged in judicial review are being allowed, unjustifiably, to substitute their own subjective moral views for those of the community and its democratic representatives. The objection so stated seems to pose a choice between two conceptions of morality. First, there is the judges' own personal morality. This is what is usually meant when reference is made to the judge's "subjective moral views." These are moral views to which a judge, as an autonomous moral agent, is personally committed and that she might wish to see endorsed by her community and her legal system, even when they are not. She might wish to see this morality endorsed even if it flatly contradicts existing law. So construed, it is obvious that a judge's personal moral views can, at least in theory, diverge dramatically from popular opinion. They can also diverge from moral views endorsed by the law in legislation and precedent. Suppose, for example, that the judge is a closet racist who believes that East Indians and Aboriginals are less worthy than white, Anglo-Saxon Protestants and do not deserve protection against discrimination in employment. Her personal morality would in this instance conflict both with Canadian law and with the opinions, principles, and values of most of her fellow citizens. Or suppose the judge believes that a woman who shows up for a job interview wearing shorts and a halter top is just asking for trouble, and that the male interviewer who sexually harasses her is less at fault than if the woman had shown up wearing "a bonnet and crinolines."[6] In this instance – an actual case – the judge's personal morality was clearly at odds with the law, but it is not so clear that it conflicted with the moral opinions of many Canadians.[7]

Against personal morality so construed is pitted the community's morality, viewed not as the morality of any particular person or group of persons but of the community as a whole. How one identifies the relevant community is of

---

6 See *R. v. Ewanchuk [1999] 1 S.C.R.*, par. 88, where the Canadian Supreme Court condemned the following comments of Alberta Court of Appeal Justice John McClung: "... it must be pointed out that the complainant did not present herself to Ewanchuk or enter his trailer in a bonnet and crinolines."

7 Whether Justice McClung's opinion also conflicted with the community's constitutional morality, properly construed, is, as we shall see, not so clear. It depends on whether that morality, properly characterized, is consistent with McClung's moral opinion.

course a notoriously difficult and often crucial question in a wide range of cases. For example, criminal-code provisions governing indecency and obscenity are often interpreted in light of community standards of tolerance, but these can vary depending on how one identifies the relevant community.[8] The difficulty is particularly acute within multicultural, pluralistic societies like those of the United States, France, and Canada. If community standards are dependent on culture, and such societies include a plurality of different cultures, then it may well be foolish to assume that we could discover a single community with a single set of moral norms about indecency and obscenity that could be said to be recognized or reflected in obscenity law. If so, then what reason is there to think that things will be any different when one turns to Charter norms? The foolishness of the assumption that there are common norms to be discovered will depend, largely, on whether there is a sufficiently rich overlap in the relevant principles and judgments widely accepted within the various communities. It may well be that on at least some of the moral issues addressed in Charter challenges there is, in the relevant community moralities, something like a Rawlsian "overlapping consensus."[9] Rawls explains what he means by this phrase in the following passage:

There can, in fact, be considerable differences in citizens' conceptions of justice provided that these conceptions lead to similar political judgments. And this is possible, since different premises can yield the same conclusion. In this case there exists what we may refer to as overlapping consensus. Of course, this overlapping need not be perfect; it is enough that a condition of reciprocity is satisfied. Both sides must believe that however much their conceptions of justice differ, their views support the same judgment in the situation at hand, and would do so even should their respective positions be interchanged.[10]

Rawls seems to envision a situation in which we agree on particular conclusions but disagree about the general premises needed to yield them. In this respect, the state of overlapping consensus is like the situation in which an appeals court is unanimous in its judgment – for example, the defendant does

---

8 See, for example, *R. v. Butler* and *R. v. Jacob (1996) 31 O.R. (3d) 350.*
9 I say "something like" because Rawls's particular notion has been subject to much discussion and some dispute – and because I do not wish to become embroiled in the intricacies of Rawlsian exegesis.
10 *A Theory of Justice*, 387–8. It is not clear that this is the same notion of overlapping consensus as one finds in Rawls's more recent book *Political Liberalism*, revised edition (New York: Columbia University Press, 1996). There the object of the overlapping consensus appears to be a political conception of justice upon which all reasonable people, regardless of their acutely differing comprehensive doctrines, can be expected to agree. See *Political Liberalism*, 14–15. See especially note 17, where Rawls writes: "The idea of an overlapping consensus, or perhaps better the term, was introduced in *Theory*, pp. 387f., as a way to weaken the conditions for the reasonableness of civil disobedience in a nearly just democratic society. Here and later in these lectures I use it in a different sense and in a far wider context."

not have the right to compensation that he claims – but the judges disagree on their reasons for judgment. In other words, the judges agree on a result, but their concurring opinions reveal that they disagree on how that result is to be reached and justified. Whether this is an accurate reading of Rawls need not concern us. The important point to recognize is that there is no reason to restrict overlapping consensus in the way the passage appears to suggest. The consensus can indeed be on particular judgments, with differing premises yielding a shared conclusion. But it can also be on the premises, with differences of opinion emerging as to what these shared premises require in the way of particular judgments or rules. As Waldron points out, we often agree on abstract principles of justice, equality, and the like but disagree on the implications of these principles – more particular rules, policies, and decisions – for the concrete circumstances of democratic politics. Everyone agrees that we should pursue equality, but there is considerable disagreement about whether this justifies affirmative action programs.

In any event, I suggest that on many questions of political morality that arise in Charter challenges there is some measure of overlapping consensus within the relevant community on norms and/or judgments concerning justice, equality, and liberty that would emerge upon careful reflection. Lest I lose the reader instantly, I wish to stress the importance of the phrase "upon careful reflection," about which something will be said in a moment. There is no doubting the fact that, on many, many issues, we differ in ways stressed by Waldron. But often these disagreements are not as deep as can appear at first blush. A society that differs in many of its surface moral opinions is often one in which there is considerably more agreement than initially meets the eye – even if these are agreements that are "incompletely theorized," and even if they emerge only after an attempt has been made to eliminate signs of evaluative dissonance.[11] I also suggest that on many occasions we can in some way identify the relevant community, or perhaps set of communities, whose moralities enjoy a significant, if imperfect, overlap and can, by virtue of this fact, be said to constitute a kind of "community of communities." When I speak of "the community's constitutional morality," I mean my comments to apply to either possibility.

So how one identifies the relevant community is an important question. Equally crucial, however, is the question of how one conceives of the relevant standards of the community once it has been identified. It is here, I believe, where things get very murky indeed. And it is this murkiness that feeds the popular complaint, as well as many other associated objections put forward by Charter Critics.

11 The term "incompletely theorized agreements" derives from the work of Cass Sunstein. See his *Legal Reasoning and Political Conflict* (New York: Oxford University Press, 1996), especially Chapter 2.

D. Types of Morality

Whether we attribute it to a person, a community, or an institution such as an organized religion, a morality typically includes a range of different elements. It will usually include (a) a number of very general principles, values, and ideals; (b) more specific rules and maxims; and (c) opinions and judgments about particular cases and types of cases. Examples from the first category include Mill's Harm Principle, the value of autonomy, and the ideals of democracy; the second category might include the rule that someone other than the attending physician should seek consent to the patient's participation in a clinical trial, or the rule that one may keep the truth from one's small children in order to spare them nightmares; and the third category might include the belief that same-sex unions are immoral, that gays should not be allowed to adopt, that Bill Clinton was wrong in having sex with "that woman," or that a woman's provocative clothing serves as a mitigating factor in sexual harassment cases. It is a commonplace in moral philosophy that an individual's personal morality, so understood, can be internally inconsistent, based on false beliefs and prejudices, and otherwise subject to rational critique. It is also a commonplace that it is an ongoing task of moral life to explore and adjust one's personal morality so as to avoid such deficiencies, the source of what we earlier termed "evaluative dissonance." This is so whether one is a utilitarian or a Kantian, a social contract theorist, a feminist, or one who believes that moral judgments express universalizable prescriptions. It is even true of one who thinks that his moral judgments are in some fundamental way "subjective." Even he will recognize the need to ensure that his subjective moral beliefs are based on true nonmoral propositions, that they are relatively consistent with one another, and that they therefore do not embody deep evaluative dissonance. Whatever one's moral stripe, fresh cases, or old cases considered in a new light, lead us to explore the elements of our morality and to adjust them accordingly. We typically strive, in so doing, to achieve something like what Rawls calls a "reflective equilibrium," wherein our principles, rules, values, and maxims are internally consistent with one another, based on true beliefs and valid inferences, and in harmony with our "considered judgments" about particular cases and types of cases.[12] Reflective equilibrium is the state for which most of us aim, and moral justification rests, in part at least, upon how the set of general moral norms to which we subscribe "fits in with and organizes our considered judgments in reflective equilibrium...."[13]

In what follows, we will distinguish between mere *moral opinions*, on the one hand, and our *true moral commitments*, on the other. The former phrase

---

12 Again, I say "something like" because I do not wish to become embroiled in the intricacies of Rawlsian exegesis.

13 *A Theory of Justice*, 579.

describes moral views that have not been critically examined so as to achieve reflective equilibrium, and the latter those that have. In calling the latter "true" I do not mean to suggest that they are "correct" propositions or beliefs, only that they are ones to which we are truly committed. It's the commitments, not the beliefs, that are said to be true – although those who believe that moral sentences express propositions to which truth values can be assigned will hope that their beliefs share this property as well. Following Rawls, we can say that our moral opinions sometimes conflict with our true moral commitments. The moral views of many people on some contentious issue are mere opinions so construed – that is, their moral opinions do not reflect their true moral commitments. A person might, for example, believe that it is permissible to base a hiring decision on gender grounds only to discover, on reflection, that this particular opinion is deeply inconsistent with general principles she is not prepared to relinquish. Perhaps more important, people can differ in their moral opinions while sharing the same moral commitments, a source of common ground that often emerges as the product of vigorous, open-minded debate. They discover that they agree on much more than they thought they did – and that they know more than they thought they knew. This, we shall see, has crucial implications for our defence of judicial review.

E. Identifying a Community's Constitutional Morality

Most of the observations made in the preceding section are relatively straightforward and uncontroversial when applied to personal morality – except, perhaps, among philosophers, who will disagree about virtually anything! Aside from moral nihilists and those who believe that basic moral principles can be infallibly ascertained through pure reason, moral intuition, or the pronouncements of religious authorities, most individuals approach personal moral questions in the manner described.[14] What is surprising, however, is that these commonplace observations are almost completely ignored when the questions in play involve judges and judicial review. When Court decisions are criticized for being out of sync with the moral views of citizens, the focus is almost always on some widespread moral *opinion* that is at odds with the court's ruling. The focus is almost never on the general principles and values to which most citizens are actually committed – that is, their true commitments – or on moral judgments about the issue in question that could survive the test of reflective equilibrium. When judicial recognition of same-sex unions is criticised for being against the moral beliefs of Canadians, the reference is almost always to moral opinions. These are moral opinions that, upon reflection, flatly contradict fundamental beliefs, principles, values, and considered judgments that enjoy widespread, if

---

14 For further discussion of the many ways in which our judgments can be inconsistent with our fundamental beliefs, values, commitments, and authentic wishes, see Chapter 3.

not universal, currency within the community, and they introduce significant evaluative dissonance. They are also opinions that are inconsistent with any reasonable interpretation of the Charter and the many judicial decisions made in its name – and in the name of the people whose fundamental commitments all this represents. For example, the principles and considered judgments upon which most reasonable Canadians, of whatever political and moral stripe, are keen to condemn racial bigotry and sexism and that virtually all would agree are embodied in the Charter and the jurisprudence surrounding its interpretation equally condemn prejudice against same-sex marriage.[15] This despite the fact that many do not (yet, I hope) see this connection and will perhaps not do so unless it is pointed out to them by some other party, perhaps the Supreme Court in a landmark ruling.[16] Discovering, or being made to acknowledge, one's *true* commitments in reflective equilibrium is, I suggest, no less possible when it comes to a community's morality than it is when the morality in question is personal. But this vital point is almost never acknowledged. It is simply assumed that the commitments of a community's morality on some issue are whatever widespread opinion says they are. But once we acknowledge that this assumption is false, that a community's true moral commitments can be very different from what members of the community believe them to be, a crucial question comes to the fore: Why should judges in deciding moral questions under a system of judicial review be required, for reasons of democracy, fairness, and the like, to respect the community's moral opinions on the matter – as opposed to the

15 Many Canadian courts held that the opposite-sex requirement for civil marriage violates the equality guarantee enshrined in s. 15(1) of the Charter. As a result, same-sex marriages have generally come to be viewed as legal and have been regularly taking place in British Columbia, Ontario, Quebec, the Yukon, Manitoba, Nova Scotia, and Saskatchewan. See *EGALE Canada Inc. v. Canada (Attorney General)* (2003), *225 D.L.R. (4th) 472, 2003 BCCA 251*; *Halpern v. Canada (Attorney General) (2003)*, 65 O.R. (3d) 161 (C.A.); and *Hendricks v. Québec (Procureur général)*, [2002] R.J.Q. 2506 (Sup. Ct.); *Dunbar v. Yukon*, [2004] Y.J. No. 61 (QL), 2004 YKSC 54, *Vogel v. Canada (Attorney General)*, [2004] M.J. No. 418 (QL) (Q.B.), *Boutilier v. Nova Scotia (Attorney General)*, [2004] N.S.J. No. 357 (QL) (S.C.), and *N.W. v. Canada (Attorney General)*, [2004] S.J. No. 669 (QL), 2004 SKQB 434. In each of those instances, the Attorney General of Canada conceded that the common law definition of marriage was inconsistent with s. 15(1) of the Charter and was not justifiable under s. 1, and publicly adopted the position that the opposite-sex requirement for marriage was unconstitutional. In its recent Reference on Same Sex Marriage, the Supreme Court of Canada declined to rule on the constitutionality of the opposite-sex requirement, ruling that the burden of establishing the requirements of marriage in Canada lies, at present, on the shoulders of Parliament – subject, of course, to judicial review should a test case later be brought to the Court for decision. See *Reference re Same-Sex Marriage* (2004) SCC 79.

16 The Canadian Supreme Court never did rule on whether the common law definition of marriage, on which only members of the opposite sex can marry each other, is actually inconsistent with the Charter. In its *Same Sex Marriage* reference, the Court declined to take up the government's invitation to rule on this question, leaving it to Parliament to act on it – which it did, of course, when it enacted *Bill C-38*. The latter is, of course, still subject to future instances of judicial review. See *Reference re Same-Sex Marriage*, 79.

community's *true* moral commitments in reflective equilibrium? Why should they bend to the community's *inauthentic* wishes, not its *authentic* ones? As acknowledged in Chapter 4, judges are not philosopher-kings with a pipeline to moral truth. But they may well be in a very good position to determine the requirements of a community's true moral commitments and authentic wishes in particular cases. If this is so – and in sections E and F I shall argue that it is – then there is nothing amiss in asking judges to enforce *these* commitments and wishes against the mere opinions and inauthentic wishes of a possibly misguided public gripped by evaluative dissonance. This is no more problematic than acknowledging the duty of responsible legislators, like our Atticus, to do the same.

So in evaluating the popular complaint, it is important to distinguish between true moral commitments and moral opinions, and between an individual's personal morality and the morality ascribed to a community, or a community of communities, of which he is a member.[17] It is also useful, within the context of discussing judicial review, to distinguish a third category: what we will henceforth call "the community's constitutional morality." I should like to propose the possibility that the moral norms to which a Charter makes reference are not those of personal morality, true morality, or even community

---

17 Other theorists who invoke a similar notion of community morality in explaining the processes of judicial review include Harry Wellington in "The Nature of Judicial Review" and Christopher Eisgruber in *Constitutional Self Government* (Cambridge, Mass.: Harvard University Press, 2001). In Chapter 4, entitled "Text and History in Hard Cases," Eisgruber refers to the judges' task of discovering "The American people's conception of justice" in constitutional cases. Constructing this conception "is not the same thing as expressing one's own conception of justice or as expressing the best conception of justice, whatever that may mean. In a democratic political system, judges engaged in judicial review cannot simply act on the basis of their own best judgment about justice; they must instead act on the basis of a conception of justice with which Americans in general could plausibly identify themselves. If judges make judgments about justice in order to apply abstract constitutional provisions like the Equal Protection Clause or the Executive Power Clause, they will have to show that those judgments are plausibly attributable to the American people as a whole. To do that, judges will have to produce an interpretation of American politics consistent with the values the judge seeks to enforce on the people's behalf" (126). Later, Eisgruber notes "the distinction between a judge's own judgment about justice and that judge's judgment about the American people's judgment about justice" (131). Another theorist who invokes a similar notion of a community's morality is Melvin Eisenberg, who, in *The Nature of the Common Law* (Cambridge, Mass.: Harvard University Press, 1988), argues in favour of something rather like the common law conception of judicial review. "The question then arises, what criteria should a moral norm satisfy if it is to figure in common law reasoning? The answer is that when moral norms are relevant to establishing, applying, or changing common law rules, the courts should employ social morality, by which I mean moral standards that claim to be rooted in aspirations for the community as a whole, and that, on the basis of an appropriate methodology, can fairly be said to have substantial support in the community, can be derived from norms that have such support, or appear as if they have such support" (15). For a critique of the suggestion that community morality – or "conventional morality" – be invoked in interpreting a Charter, see A. Marmor, *Interpretation and Legal Theory*, revised second edition (Oxford: Hart Publishing, 2005), 160–2.

morality broadly construed but only those of the community's *constitutional* morality. By this latter phrase I mean the set of moral norms and considered judgments properly attributable to the community as a whole as representing its true commitments, but with the following additional property: They are in some way tied to its constitutional law and practices. Following Dworkin, we might say it is "the political morality presupposed by the laws and institutions of the community."[18] In drawing upon Dworkin, my intention is not to signal acceptance of the particular theory of interpretation he recommends for ascertaining the morality presupposed by or embedded in the law. For reasons that lie well beyond the scope of this investigation, I do not believe that an interpretation of a body of law must, as Dworkin claims, be a moral theory of that object to which the theorist personally subscribes. It can, instead, be what Julie Dickson aptly terms an "indirectly evaluative" theory of the sort outlined and defended by Jules Coleman.[19] It is a theory that invokes moral norms, not to justify the law but to explain why it is the way it is, to show its relationships with other areas of the law, and so on. One could, with this understanding in mind, explain – that is, interpret – much of early-twentieth-century South African law as presupposing racist moral norms and beliefs. Such norms and beliefs were part of that community's (deplorable) "constitutional morality."[20]

It is important to stress, once again, that a community's constitutional morality is not the personal morality of any particular person or institution. Nor is it the morality decreed by God, inherent in the fabric of the universe, or discernible via the exercise of pure practical reason. Rather it consists of the moral norms and convictions to which the community, via its various social forms and practices, has committed itself and that have in some way or other been drawn into the law via the rule of recognition and the law it validates. It is the morality actually embedded in social and legal practices in the way in which principles of corrective justice are embedded in our tort law. So construed, a community's constitutional morality is a subset of the wider community morality that includes norms and convictions which lack legal recognition. Even if there are norms governing friendship, gratitude, marital fidelity, and charitable giving within the community moralities of contemporary Western societies, these are not, in the main, part of the constitutional moralities of those societies because they lack legal recognition. Distinct (and different) principles of equality and fundamental justice are, on the other hand, characteristic elements of the constitutional moralities of Western societies. In the case of Canada and

---

18 *Taking Rights Seriously*, 126.
19 See Julie Dickson, *Evaluation and Legal Theory* (Oxford: Hart Publishing, 2001), and Jules Coleman, *The Practice of Principle*.
20 For further critique of Dworkin's theory of interpretation, see my *Inclusive Legal Positivism*.

the United States, legal recognition of such principles includes enshrinement in the Canadian Charter and the American Bill of Rights.

It might be thought, once again, that talk of a community's constitutional morality as a source of moral norms for determining legal validity is a complete nonstarter in light of the obvious fact that Western liberal societies are multicultural and pluralistic in nature. One can well imagine a Critic intervening to say that it is simply foolish and naïve to assume that we could find, within any particular pluralistic society, a single constitutional morality whose norms could function in the manner contemplated. But is this really a pipe dream? Once again, much will depend on whether there is a sufficiently rich overlap in the relevant norms, convictions, and judgments about particular cases, widely accepted informally within the community and/or formally within their legal judgments in constitutional cases. I hazard to suggest, once again, that on at least some of the fundamental issues addressed by Charters, there is some measure of overlapping consensus of particular judgments and general norms. If so, then it is possible that we can, in the area occupied by this overlap, identify a common constitutional morality sensibly attributable to the community as a whole that would emerge upon careful reflection. "Upon careful reflection" remains a critical phrase in this context because it is more than obvious that widespread moral differences of opinion do exist within modern pluralistic societies even on questions of constitutional morality. But such disagreement does not, for the reasons offered above, entail the absence of an overlapping consensus of true commitments. Common ground can exist in the absence of an *articulated consensus* and in the presence of radical disagreement about all sorts of questions, both particular and abstract.

I have herein provided little more than an admittedly sketchy account of a community's constitutional morality. I have also done little beyond establishing the live possibility that, the Critics' skepticism notwithstanding, an overlapping consensus of true commitments might indeed be there to be discovered. But enough has been said, I hope, to warrant the following tentative conclusions. First, it is far from clear that moral conditions of validity that invoke a community's constitutional morality are a complete nonstarter because they cannot work in the circumstances of politics. Individuals in pluralistic societies no doubt differ dramatically in their personal moral beliefs and convictions, a fact seized upon by Waldron and other Critics of judicial review. Yet there is reason to believe that the constitutional morality embedded in our shared social forms and practices – including our shared legal forms and practices with their wealth of rules, principles, and precedents – can include an overlapping consensus of true commitments on many issues, a consensus that may be "incompletely theorized" but that can emerge notwithstanding this fact into explicit agreement once an attempt is made to achieve reflective equilibrium. Of course it is almost certainly true that such an agreement will not always emerge. Indeed, on some highly contestable questions, for example questions concerning the morality of abortion, there may be no overlapping consensus, implicit or otherwise. If so, then the community's constitutional morality will fail to provide determinate answers in Charter cases, and judges will have to draw upon other resources, about which we will have to say something below. But there is little reason to think that this will *always* be so. Yet if the community's constitutional morality can sometimes provide the answers we seek, then it can supply norms against which legal validity can sensibly be measured.

A second important conclusion brings us back to Hart's thoughts on the dangers inherent in the union of primary and secondary rules. One such danger, we saw, is the possibility of a gap between validity and acceptance. Conceiving moral conditions on legal validity as invoking the community's constitutional morality has the potential to narrow this threatened gap without totally compromising the law's capacity to provide determinate antecedent guidance. With some rules of recognition we can, as we saw, achieve a high degree of guidance, but only at the cost of increasing the chances that our rules will be ones with which most of us cannot agree morally. If the law is whatever Rex decrees, then Rex's decrees will be valid regardless of the community's moral views of their content and their applications. One way to address this danger is, of course, to replace Rex with a democratically elected legislature whose decisions can usually, though not always, be counted on to reflect widespread views regarding the demands of morality and rationality. This is no doubt a step in the right direction, one that liberal societies have all chosen to take. Yet as Hart was at pains to stress, no legislature, not even a democratically chosen one fully informed of all the relevant facts and competing considerations, can anticipate all the undesirable results to which their general rules will inevitably lead. I want to stress that some of these unanticipated results will be the violation, in particular unforeseen cases, of the community's own moral commitments. Such conflicts, of which we become aware only at the point of application, are as inevitable as they are unforeseeable. They are unforeseeable in the sense that we cannot predict exactly when and in what particular contexts they will arise, and what they will look like when they are brought to our attention. What we can confidently foresee, however, is that many such cases will in fact arise, despite any and all efforts we might make to avoid them. If this is true, then an important question comes to the fore, one that will occupy us in the remainder of this book: Why should we not include conformity with the true commitments of our community's constitutional morality among our conditions of legal validity? Why should we not, at this crucial point in our attempt to achieve the benefits of life under law, continue to bear in mind Hart's insight concerning "the need to leave open, for later settlement by an informed official choice, issues which can only be properly appreciated and settled when they arise in a concrete case"? If we do bear this insight in mind, we will see good reason to choose conditions of validity that make reference to the community's constitutional morality, and to entrust our judges with the task of deciding whether and when the relevant norms of this morality have been compromised by general legislative rules. This is what they often do, I suggest, when they engage in judicial review.

F. Further Replies to the Critics

If the foregoing construal of a Charter's moral provisions, as a potentially valuable safeguard against unanticipated moral consequences, is at all plausible – and I fully acknowledge that I have yet to offer reasons to accept it that are anything but conclusive – then we have at our disposal a potentially powerful reply to the popular complaint and to many other related objections to judicial review. In ruling against a government action (e.g., a statute or judicial ruling) that has the support of popular moral opinion, judges might actually be *enforcing*, not *thwarting*, the community's very own political morality! Just as a person might come to discover, when she applies the test of reflective equilibrium, that some of her moral opinions conflict with general moral principles to which she is otherwise committed and that she is unwilling to relinquish, judges might be led to discover that the community's or the legislature's moral opinion on some issue – for example, same-sex unions or the rights of inmates to vote in elections – conflicts with its very own principles of political morality, and by implication other judgments of the community in analogous cases, for example those involving racial discrimination. The judges might, that is, discover that the relevant moral opinion is not a considered judgment that can remain in reflective equilibrium with these other elements of the community's own political morality. Add to this the fact that the relevant principles, values, and judgments are more often than not ones that the law explicitly recognizes in the constitution, subordinate legislation, and legal precedents – as it has in cases involving discrimination against women and racial minorities – and a court, in upholding these elements of the community's constitutional morality, will not only be respecting the community's *authentic* wishes and commitments, it will in fact be *upholding the law* – something, of course, we *want* our judges to be doing whenever they decide legal cases. If this is what judicial review is really all about, then the practice is anything but unfair and undemocratic.

Of course the Critic cannot be so easily defeated. The account to this point ignores many of the Critics' remaining objections to judicial review, as well as others that might be raised at this point. To these we must now turn. In answering these objections we will not only find further reason to reject the Critics' case against judicial review, we will also come to a deeper understanding of the common law conception and how it can be combined with the conception of the community's constitutional morality sketched above, to provide an attractive alternative to the Standard Case. So let's turn to some objections. We'll begin with some that have not yet been raised and end with those – principally

Waldron's – that were sketched in earlier chapters and that we have yet to address fully.

i. Personal Morality Still Being Imposed

One obvious objection to our proposal is this: Even if judges tried to invoke the community's constitutional morality in Charter cases, they would *still*, of necessity, end up imposing their own subjective moral preferences. If, as most everyone agrees, questions raised by a Charter's abstract clauses are (partly) moral in nature, if these moral questions are ones about which there is deep disagreement and controversy and if it is the judges to whom we turn to provide answers to these difficult questions, then they cannot help but impose their own subjective moral preferences. A judge simply cannot avoid interpreting the Charter in light of her own personal morality, despite any efforts and rhetoric to the contrary. And this is unfair, undemocratic, and so on.

For reasons that should now be clear, this very popular objection is seriously misguided. It is one thing to say that our legal fate hinges on the judge's own personal morality and quite another to say that it hinges on her own personal views about what the community's constitutional morality requires. The latter option describes a judgment about the true commitments of *the community's* morality – and this is not a judgment about which standards are best according to the judge's preferred moral theory. While it is true that we must rely on the personal views of judges, and while it is equally true that these views may be highly controversial, not amenable to conclusive demonstration, inconsistent with widespread moral opinion, and possibly biased, the fact remains that it is a personal, good-faith judgment about what the community's constitutional morality actually requires. It is no more disturbing to acknowledge the need for personal judgment on such a question than it is to acknowledge that the integrity of science depends on the personal judgments of scientists about what the evidence establishes. It is also important to bear in mind that virtually every issue, moral or otherwise, which comes before an appeals court for decision is controversial and not amenable to conclusive demonstration – and yet we rely on judges' personal judgments about such matters all the time. Think of a case turning on whether a person or corporation took reasonable steps to ensure the safety of others, or on whether the defendant's actions violated community standards of decency. We have to rely on *somebody's* controversial judgment about such matters, just as we must rely on *somebody's* judgment about the community's true moral commitments. Why shouldn't that somebody be a judge? Indeed, I hazard to suggest that a judge's training makes her in many ways an eminently suitable candidate for the job: the test of reflective equilibrium is not far removed from the more traditional task of common law decision making in, for example, tort and contract cases, where precedents and general principles must be reconciled with one another and where processes like drawing analogies, marking distinctions so as to distinguish cases, and so on is commonplace.[21] Considered judgments are rather like precedents; general principles are rather like prior rulings. We will return in section F(iv) to the question of whether judges are suitably placed to decide such questions of constitutional morality in Charter cases.

ii. A Community's Constitutional Morality and Legal Precedent

A second possible objection to my proposal that we view Charter provisions as invoking standards of the community's constitutional morality is that it seriously underplays the fact that Charter cases are *legal* cases. Notwithstanding the fact that reference has been made to the common law in describing the proposed alternative to the Standard Conception of Charters, the fact remains, it might be said, that the alternative seriously underplays the fact that Charter rights are *legal* rights. Charters are, after all, part of constitutional *law*, not morality. When the Supreme Court addresses a Charter issue, it draws support for its judgment from prior legal decisions and from legal doctrines and traditions. And when it settles an issue raised, for example, by a Charter's equality or due process provisions, a lower court is bound by the precedent set, even when that lower court thinks that the decision is incorrect in law, or is inconsistent with views generally held within the wider community. In such a case, the lower court is not free to interpret the relevant provision in accordance with its own views, or its views about the true commitments of the community's constitutional morality. The inevitable result is this: Over time, judicial decision, not the community's political morality, sets the appropriate standards for decisions in Charter cases. And if this is so, then Charter adjudication remains unfair, undemocratic, and so on. The judiciary – not individually perhaps, but as a multi-member body stretching over time – is actually the force behind the creation of the norms employed in deciding Charter cases. The result is that the *community's* own morality fails to play the role assigned to it in the common law conception being defended. It is no longer the community's constitutional morality that is being enforced by common law reasoning in Charter cases; it is the constitutional morality of the judiciary, particularly those members of the legal profession who happen to occupy the nation's Supreme Court.

In addressing this important objection, we should begin by stressing that precedent-setting judgments under the Charter's moral provisions are still, on the account herein defended, judgments about what the community's constitutional morality requires. And so it is not as if the relevant precedents are judgments stemming from the personal moralities of the judges who set them. Precedent undoubtedly plays a key role in adjudication under a Charter's moral

---

21 See, again, the discussion of common law reasoning in Chapter 5.

provisions; this I in no way wish to deny. But its role is to regulate judgments about what the community's constitutional morality requires, not what the judges would themselves prefer to see done.

A second, and possibly more interesting, reply is that the objection seems to rely on a misleading picture of the community's constitutional morality, as something wholly autonomous from the law and the decisions of judges. It is a commonplace among philosophers, as well as among other legal, political, and sociological scholars, that a community's political morality influences and shapes its law in many ways. We have the criminal law that we do, for example, largely because of our community's moral sense of right and wrong. Our notions of moral responsibility explain, for example, why there is more than one category of murder, and why some homicides are treated not as murders but as instances of manslaughter, a category reserved for cases in which responsibility is for some reason diminished. Tort law is based on moral notions of corrective justice, and so on. But the extent to which the community's political morality is in turn shaped by law is seriously underappreciated. Yet as Joseph Raz and Tony Honore have stressed, this is a serious mistake. The influence of law on morality is multi-faceted and significant. In his "Hart Memorial Lecture," Honore reminds us that the law serves several crucial functions "in regard to gaps in morality and to moral conflicts."[22] Much as Aquinas did when he outlined the need for a human sovereign one of whose tasks is the "determination of the common notions" set by the natural law, Honore notes that

... over a wide range of cases there can be no way of determining the right course of action without a legal component. Even a society of well-disposed angels, uniformly anxious to do right, needs a system of laws in order to know the right thing to do ... law is part of the morality of any complex society.... The picture of morality as a blueprint and law as a structure put up according to or in disregard of it is ... misleading. Morality is more like an outline from which details are missing. Laws, along with conventions, fill many of these in.[23]

Honore's insightful observations provide the basis for a second, more forceful reply to the objection under consideration. If the community's constitutional morality is partly determined, in complex societies like ours, by landmark political and legal decisions, then the possibility emerges that the judges, in deciding cases under the Charter's moral provisions, are in fact helping to shape and render more determinate the very content of political morality. Legal judgments under the Charter's moral provisions are not to be starkly contrasted with

---

22 A. M. Honore, "The Dependence of Morality on Law," 13 *Oxford Journal of Legal Studies* (1993), 3. For Hart's comments on the role of law in shaping morality, see *The Concept of Law*, 200.
23 *Ibid*. A thorough exploration of this view of morality would take us too far afield. Instead, I simply refer the reader to Raz's powerful defence in, among other places, *Engaging Reason*.

judgments of the community's constitutional morality. On the contrary, they are an important element within that morality, just as they are in Aquinas' natural law theory. As such, precedent-setting legal judgments must be accorded significant weight in attempts to reach reflective equilibrium within a community's political morality. The weight to be given these judgments can vary, of course, depending, among other things, on the fundamental secondary rules of adjudication practiced within the legal system, and on the degree of moral authority we are prepared to accord our judges in deciding questions of constitutional morality on our behalf. But the fact remains that if the content of the community's constitutional morality is partly determined by important judicial decisions about its content, then in saying that judges should interpret Charter rights in terms of the community's constitutional morality one does not thereby imply that judges are free to ignore legal precedent.

The fact that judicial decisions help shape and determine a community's constitutional morality has a third important consequence for debates about judicial review. As observed on numerous occasions above, many individuals are troubled by the idea of a system of government in which judges are either asked or permitted to decide contentious moral issues when engaged in judicial review. As Waldron stresses, this seems at the very least to compromise our commitment to self-government. We seem to have abandoned our allegiance to democracy if we don't settle these matters among ourselves, or through the efforts of legislators who are chosen *by us* to do this *for us*. Assigning the task to judges instead would be bad enough had we reason to believe that there is always a moral truth of the matter in a Charter case, and that judges are likely to discover and apply that truth when they interpret their Charter's moral norms. But if Honore and Raz – and, indeed, even Aquinas – are correct in their belief that morality provides only a partial blueprint with many details missing, and that legal judgments are required to fill these in, then things become far, far worse for the defender of judicial review. If someone has to fill in these details, should it not be the people themselves – or individuals elected by and responsible to the people for the choices they make? In representative democracies, should it not be elected legislators who fill in the blanks that our moral blueprint leaves open?

Not necessarily. Recall that legislatures cannot, for reasons of sheer practicality, enact legislation specific to each and every individual case that might arise in a particular social context. They must, of necessity, work with general categories covering a range of somewhat different individual cases. They must, that is, deal with types, not tokens. Now apply this to contexts in which moral norms of the kind recognized in Charters are likely to become relevant – that is, contexts in which the enacted legislation appears to have an unforeseen impact on the kinds of moral norms included within Charters, norms like "equality" and "due process." For reasons explored by Hart, Reaume, and other defenders of common law methodology, crafting workable general legislation to cover such cases in advance requires abilities well beyond the best of legislative bodies, leaving us with one of three options: (a) We can ignore the problem and run the risk of compromising important moral norms; (b) we can ask legislatures to deal with the difficulties and gaps in the blueprint as they arise; or (c) we can ask judges to employ common law reasoning to do so, on an ongoing basis, when they decide Charter cases. Presumably we would like to avoid option (a). As for (b), we will soon see that it is not much of an option either, leaving us with (c), the option recommended by the common law conception of judicial review. As we shall more fully below in section K, cases calling for decisions about the impact of government action on norms of constitutional morality are better dealt with by judges who are in a better position to appreciate the particular issues raised in the cases in which these impacts are felt and who will be able, through use of common law methodology, to deal with those issues in an intelligent, sensitive case-by-case manner. The judges will have to bear in mind, of course, that their decisions and rulings will usually set precedents for others. But common law methodology allows them the freedom to make their rulings with the knowledge that these can always be adjusted by later courts that will undoubtedly see further issues of relevance and further reasons to distinguish their cases from the one(s) decided before. Through the use of bottom-up, common law modes of reasoning, judges will be able to decide the unforeseeable issues of constitutional morality that are certain to arise in ways that allow for incremental changes and improvements in the moral blueprint. More on this in section K.

Another reason for thinking it a good idea to have judges, not legislators, fill in the details of the blueprint is that doing so is more likely to result in decisions to which most of us will be willing to subscribe. Those directly embroiled in conflict are not always able or willing to accept a decision made if the choice was determined by majority sentiment or by a vote among the disputants. But this is exactly what would occur were contentious issues of political morality settled, for example, by referendum or through the choices of legislators responsive to majority sentiment. On the other hand, people are often more able and willing to acknowledge and abide by a decision if it is made by someone other than the parties directly in dispute – that is, by a "neutral third party." And this will be so even when – perhaps *especially* when – the decision is recognized as being one that is underdetermined by the relevant factors and that therefore demands a kind of "free choice among available options." Under these conditions, the one who ends up making the decision will not be among those who profit by it. He will be an adjudicator, not an advocate. Of course it would be foolish not to acknowledge that judges are always part of the community whose members are in dispute, and so their views and interests will render them less than absolutely neutral in many Charter cases. But despite their vested interests, it is nevertheless reasonable to hope and expect that they will be able, in deciding contentious moral issues, to bracket those interests when they make their decisions – that is, that they will be able to display the same judicial virtues of objectivity, impartiality, and neutrality that they are generally thought to display in deciding most other types of cases. In other words, we can hope that they will be able, so far as it is possible for a human being to do so, to leave their biases and allegiances at the door and give due weight to the interests, settled preferences, and values of parties on all sides of the debate. We can also hope that, in insulating them from the forces that plagued Atticus by granting them some measure of judicial independence, we minimize the likelihood that our hopes are nothing short of naïve. If this is correct, then we should not be so quick to reject outright the suggestion that judges are perhaps in a better position than legislators to fill in many of the gaps that our constitutional morality leaves open.

iii. A Community's Constitutional Morality and the Protection of Minorities

A third rather serious concern that might be expressed over the invitation to view Charters as invoking the community's constitutional morality relates to the goal of minority protection. If one of the fundamental roles of judicial review is the protection of minorities, and yet a Charter's moral provisions are to be interpreted as they would be by the *community*, a body whose voice will in all likelihood be the voice of the majority of its members, have we not thereby abandoned one of its underlying purposes? Won't Mill's tyranny of the majority remain every bit as likely as it would be had we no Charter at all? Indeed, if the most radical of the Critics are correct, the oppressive forces of patriarchy, racism, and the like will continue to dominate both our law and our constitutional practices if a Charter is conceived in this way. If so, then the common law conception, so understood, will be unable to serve as the bulwark against oppression it was intended to be. The only way to pursue minority protection is to interpret the Charter's moral provisions not in terms of the community's possibly biased and oppressive morality but in terms of something else like "true" or "ideal" morality. Judges should seek moral truth in deciding Charter cases, not the morality of a possibly misguided citizenry against whom the Charter is supposed to serve as protection.[24]

We are, I hope, now in a position to see why this objection fails as well. First, it presupposes that a community's constitutional morality is identical to

---

24 A version of this argument is put forward by Marmor in *Interpretation and Legal Theory*, second edition, 161–2. Marmor underplays the importance of distinguishing between, on the one hand, the fundamental commitments of a community as expressed in its constitutional morality and, on the other hand, the community's particular opinions on some issue or other. As we have seen, the latter are often, for a variety of reasons, ill founded and inconsistent with the former. And it is the former that the common law conception requires judges to uphold.

the moral opinions widely shared within the community. But to repeat, the role of judges is not to bow to the inauthentic wishes of the majority and enforce their misguided moral opinions and evaluative dissonance, any more than it was Atticus's job to bow to the misguided wishes of his constituents. Their job is to respect and enforce the true commitments of the community's constitutional morality in reflective equilibrium. And this morality – at least as it exists within all the contemporary constitutional democracies with which we are concerned in this study – thoroughly rejects any opinion that oppresses a minority group, harbours the prejudices of patriarchy, and so on.[25] Judges within such systems who decide on the true commitments of their community's constitutional morality in reflective equilibrium, all of which represent the community's authentic wishes, will inevitably be led, as Atticus was, to protect minorities from the tyranny feared by Mill and condemned by radical Critics. They may not always succeed in making the right decisions, and we have yet to address the Critics' remaining objections to the practice of allowing judges to serve this role. But to the extent that they succeed in making the right decisions, minority protection will be the inevitable result. Furthermore, we must also remember that the community's constitutional morality in reflective equilibrium includes the judgments of courts in influential legal cases. In other words, we must not forget the role of legal judgments in shaping the principles of the community's constitutional morality. Both our communities' constitutional moralities and the more specific laws created to express and enforce these moralities condemn the oppression of women and minorities.

So a community's constitutional morality, properly understood, interpreted, and enforced by judges, has the potential, within the societies with which we are concerned, to provide significant protection against Mill's tyranny of the majority. Indeed, I submit that it is likely to provide a better guarantee than if judges were asked to decide in accordance with their own conceptions of

---

25 It must be acknowledged that the true commitments of a community's constitutional morality can sometimes be hostile to minority interests – far from the kind of morality presupposed in the Western democracies with which we are here concerned. The morality of apartheid South Africa leaps readily to mind. This fact, and the fact that, in some social contexts, judicial review could help entrench such an unworthy morality, might seem to undermine the position herein being defended. But against these unfortunate possibilities must be weighed all the advantages discussed in the text. It is also important to remember, as positivists have long insisted, that questions concerning legality – even those requiring appeal to a community's moral standards – must never be confused with, or supplant in our thinking, our ability to challenge accepted norms from the moral point of view. If radical change in a community's morality is called for, there is nothing to prevent reformers and critics from publicly pressing their case for change. There is, in other words, nothing to prevent them from saying; "The existence of law – including the law represented by our community's constitutional morality – is one thing, its merit or demerit quite another thing entirely." Judicial review, understood and practiced as the common law conception suggests, can be a powerful vehicle for moral good. But it would be a serious mistake to overestimate its power, or to suppose that it is the only vehicle at our disposal.

ideal or true morality. This suggestion might seem ludicrous at first glance. Surely moral truth offers far better protection to minorities than a community's constitutional morality, even when the latter has been sanitized by the test of reflective equilibrium. Perhaps, but there is reason to be very cautious in pursuing this line. As noted earlier, and as Critics are fond of pointing out, judges are not philosopher-kings with a pipeline to moral truth. They can easily get things wrong. Indeed, there is little reason to believe that a judge's personal morality is likely to be better than the community's constitutional morality, *properly understood*. A community's constitutional morality is, after all, the product of much moral and legal experience, longstanding traditions, and social consensus. In other words, it is the product of sustained efforts on the part of a great many people, each pursuing a form of largely bottom-up, case-by-case reasoning about issues of political morality for which the common law is applauded. Given the multiple heads principle, there is every reason to believe that a community's constitutional morality will be closer to the ideal for that community and the circumstances in which its members live their lives than the personal morality of any given judge. It may also be true that judges will be more likely to converge in their constitutional views if their judgments are the product of attempts to discern the requirements of the community's constitutional morality. If this last conjecture is correct, then we have yet further reason to pursue an understanding of Charters on which they embody norms of the community's constitutional morality. Convergence in belief and in decision may not be the most important values to be pursued by law, but they are certainly among the most important ones. Law is, after all, a social institution, based in large measure on basic conventions and shared understandings of the sort highlighted by legal theorists of all stripes.[26] As Hart and others have amply demonstrated, these are not only required for law's ability to offer guidance, including its guidance in filling out Honore's moral blueprint, but they are essential to law's very existence. If, in pursuing the community morality option – again properly conceived – judges are more likely to converge in their judgments regarding the fundamental issues raised by the Charter than if they pursue ideal moral theory, we have further reason to insist that this is in fact what they should be doing. If there is a further convergence between the judges' beliefs and those ascribable to the community at large, then we have even more reason to pursue this option. Little is lost, but much is gained.

iv. *Judicial Determination of Charter Rights Still Undemocratic*

We now come to what is perhaps the most troublesome objection to our proposal – one that returns us to Waldron and his forceful case against judicial

---

26 The exception may be some radical Critical theorists who see law as a complete sham – and a very dangerous one at that, because it is said to be a means by which the powerful within a society are able to exert power over the weak.

review. To be sure, minority oppression is a standing threat in any democratic society. And it may be that something like a written Charter of Rights, interpreted in light of the community's constitutional morality in reflective equilibrium, can, theoretically, be a useful tool for working against it. It still fails to follow that citizens of constitutional democracies, faced with the many difficulties encountered in the concrete circumstances of modern politics, should pursue any such option. It most certainly fails to follow that they should entrust the interpretation and enforcement of Charter protections, even when a Charter is understood in this way, *to judges.* We continue to dishonour a community's democratic representatives and the citizens they represent if we suppose that *their* current judgments concerning the protections afforded by the community's constitutional morality in reflective equilibrium should not be the ones that hold sway in democratic politics. It dishonours the community if we are so concerned about what they might do if the interpretation of their very own Charter is left in their hands or the hands of their representatives that we rely instead on the pronouncements of judges. Why should we think that judicial pronouncements on the content of a Charter's provisions are likely to be better or more trustworthy than the community's own judgments on these matters, as expressed through the voice of their democratically elected representatives? Why should we think that the latter are less likely to be correct, or as good, as the former? We have, Waldron will continue to insist, no good reason to think this at all. Indeed, we have still seen nothing approaching an adequate case against the charge that judicial review inevitably puts the community and its representatives in a bad moral light. If, despite everything that has been said against them, we continue to insist on having Charters, then we really should agree that their interpretation and enforcement should not be left to judges. Their interpretation and enforcement should be left to individuals who speak directly on behalf of the community – that is, their elected representatives. As we noted early on, there are many different forms of judicial review, only some of which invest judges with the powers of interpretation and enforcement one finds in nations like the United States and, to a lesser extent, Canada. It is possible for judges to enjoy nothing more threatening (to democracy) than an advisory role, as is true of those in New Zealand. But why should we go even this far? Why not simply do away with a Charter altogether, even one interpreted as the common law conception proposes? Why not adopt institutional mechanisms for protecting rights that are "free from the obsessive verbalism of a particular written charter"?[27] That is, why not rely on the good-faith efforts of legislators, unencumbered by the excess baggage of a written Charter, to offer the protections that defenders of Charters believe to be so important? This brings us around, once again, to Waldron's powerful case against judicial review. Answering this case, with the

27 *Law and Disagreement,* 221.

philosophical resources now available to us, will be the focus of our remaining efforts.

G. A Return to Waldron

According to Advocates, judicial review is an important vehicle for the protection of entrenched or transitory minorities against majoritarian biases, excesses, and so on. It is seen to embody the rational pre-commitment of the community to work against these factors by tying itself to the mast of a chosen set of fundamental rights. Paradigmatically, these are rights thought essential to enlightened democratic rule, and to the free and equal exercise of individual autonomy. We saw that there were serious problems with the standard picture and so we set out to modify it. We are now in a position to see, however, that some of the essential details can be retained. We can, for example, retain the notion of pre-commitment, so long as we're careful not to go too far. Recall, for example, the complaint that Charter pre-commitment allows the dead hand of the past to determine our choices today, a situation that is thought to undermine the very notion of ongoing self-government. A modicum of truth remains in this complaint because Charters do entrench prior decisions about which rights deserve constitutional protection. And if common law reasoning regarding the requirements of the community's constitutional morality is brought to bear on how, for purposes of constitutional practices, these rights are to be understood and applied, then the force of precedent (whatever that force happens to be in the particular jurisdiction in question) will always be a factor with which we will have to reckon. The dead hand of precedent has as much potential to constrain as the dead hand of the framers. But a number of countervailing considerations must now be added to the mix.

First, we should continue to bear in mind the ever-present possibility of constitutional amendment, difficult as it might be to marshal the political will and consensus required to exercise this power. Second, though there is often deep disagreement about the content of the rights enshrined in Charters, there is seldom serious disagreement over the legitimacy of the rights actually chosen. Most everyone, including those who preceded us decades or generations ago, would agree that rights to "equality before and under the law," "freedom of expression (or speech)," "due process," or "fundamental justice" are worthy of inclusion in a Charter. Reasonable people might wish, if we could start with a clean slate, for a slightly different collection of rights from those settled upon, but few would deny the legitimacy of the choice made.[28] There is almost

---

28 For instance, some in Canada believe that a right to property should have been included in the Canadian Charter – as it now is, somewhat paradoxically, in the constitution of the still–officially communist People's Republic of China. Few, if any, believe that the Canadian Charter is, for this reason, illegitimate.

always a range of morally acceptable Charters for any given society, just as there is almost always a range of morally acceptable institutional designs each of which is consonant with that community's particular needs and with the ideals of democracy. Each will be fully deserving of respect and allegiance if adopted by the relevant community. Recall Joseph Raz's observation that "Constitutions, at least old ones, do not derive their authority from the authority of their authors." On the contrary, they "are self-validating. They are valid just because they are there, enshrined in the practices of their countries.... A most important qualification should be added... *As long as they remain within the boundaries set by moral principles.* ..."[29] Raz adds another further important qualification: that this conclusion follows only "*if morality underdetermines* the principles concerning the form of government and the content of individual rights enshrined in constitutions."[30] This "underdetermination thesis" is one to which Raz subscribes and that was endorsed previously in our discussion of Honore's insights about the law's role in fleshing out the details of our moral blueprints. It is also, I added above, a thesis with which even a natural lawyer like Aquinas would likely be in agreement. Recall his theory of the "determination of common notions." In any case, these observations yield the following conclusion: Even if we might have chosen a different Charter were the choice made today, this does not mean that we do not continue to have very good reason to continue supporting the choice that was in fact made.

A third countervailing factor is this: Although precedent is always to some extent constraining on future decision makers, the usual common law powers of avoidance are always available. These, we observed, come in a variety of forms and with a variety of conditions under which these can be exercised. But under no sensible theory of common law reasoning would a contemporary Supreme Court be completely barred from overruling a constitutional precedent that was confidently believed (by the Court or by the political community) to have outlived its usefulness or its moral merit. Even the House of Lords, in its famous "Practice Statement," formally rejected the practice of considering itself absolutely bound by its previous decisions.

The common law approach... does not suppose that there is some independent value in adhering to past judgments that are by hypothesis wrong, which is to be compared to the value of making the right judgments.... [W]e should think twice about our judgments of right and wrong when they are inconsistent with what has gone before. We adhere to [precedents] not despite their wrongness, but because we might be mistaken to think them wrong. It follows that if, on reflection, we are sufficiently confident that

---

29 Raz, "On the Authority and Interpretation of Constitutions," in Alexander, ed., *Constitutionalism*, 173.
30 *Ibid.*

we are right, and if the stakes are high enough, then we can reject even longstanding [precedent].[31]

So if the dead hand of the past constrains us when we have a common law Charter, it will seldom do so in a way that seriously threatens the autonomy of a self-governing people. A Charter, so understood, permits the community to change its mind, make adjustments in light of improved moral knowledge and changing circumstances, and so on. It allows for the kind of incremental change, one hopes for the better, for which the common law, bottom-up method of legal regulation is celebrated. Unlike a Charter understood in the manner proposed by those fixed views against which the Critic continues to have a powerful case, a common law Charter is perfectly consistent with the ideal of *ongoing* self-government that lies at the heart of our commitment to democracy. Furthermore, it does not require us to view ourselves as the equivalent of a drunk in the pub from whom vulnerable individuals and minorities need protection. Recognizing our limitations, and the limitations inherent in the circumstances of politics and rule making, is something we can all do while perfectly sober.

Fair enough. Charters can be to some degree flexible and useful. And the extent to which they enable the dead hand of the past to constrain our choices need not overly concern us. But we are still faced with Waldron's question: Why opt for a *written* Charter instead of allowing public discourse, legislative debate, and – to some degree perhaps – judicial decisions framed within a common law of moral rights that is "free from the obsessive verbalism of a particular written charter"[32] to serve as our vehicle for rights protection within the public domain? If flexibility is important, then why not go for the most flexible option?

One reason is that Waldron's no-Charter option really isn't any more flexible – or at least it needn't be so. True, with Charters we are constrained to frame our debates in the abstract terms chosen to express its commitments. Americans, for example, have had to frame their discussions of expressive freedom in terms of "speech," not "expression." And this has on occasion proved somewhat awkward. As Waldron notes, it stretches linguistic propriety to think of flag burning and nude dancing as forms of speech, whereas it is quite natural to describe these as expressive acts. But there are a number of reasons why this poses no significant problem for the proposal under consideration. First, American courts seem to have managed, in their own ways, to come to much the same judgments as they would have done had the more general of the two terms been employed. Only those obsessed with the idea that Charters embody

---

31 David A. Strauss, "Common Law Constitutional Interpretation," (1996) 63 *U. Chi. L. Rev.* 877 at 896–7. Note the appeal to humility in the face of limited knowledge implicit in Strauss's characterization, a humility that is part and parcel of the common law theory of Charters for which this book argues.

32 *Law and Disagreement*, 221.

fixed points, established (in a way that is simply not possible) by the plain, literal meaning of the abstract terms employed, would reject the idea that it's the norms of political morality behind the linguistic expression chosen that are of paramount importance in such cases. In this instance, these are the individual and political values that argue for the need to recognize expressive freedom that we explored earlier when we examined Atticus's final reasons for not supporting the language law, of which freedom of speech is a species. In other words, the words constrain, but they need not do so to the point where the underlying values are ignored or sacrificed.[33] And if, at some point, the constraint does become too unwieldy or limiting, perhaps even irrational, there is always the option of constitutional amendment. Waldron complains that American debates concerning the death penalty have been unduly and needlessly hampered by the need to frame them in terms of whether the practice is both cruel and unusual. Perhaps this is an unfortunate fact of American constitutional history. But if so, it is one that could have been rectified by a constitutional amendment, if the difficulties truly were insurmountable. In short, the fact that drafters sometimes choose the wrong language does not show that we should abandon Charters altogether. It shows only that a better choice could have been made and perhaps still can be.

Charters need not be hampered by the need "to scramble around constructing . . . principles out of scraps of some sacred text, in a tendentious exercise of constitutional calligraphy."[34] But once again, we must ask: Why even run the slightest risk of this kind of unsatisfactory constitutional practice? Why not just abandon written Charters altogether and leave it to the courts, legislatures, and the general public to develop a flexible jurisprudence of rights? One important reason is that, notwithstanding the dangers of allowing words to constrain us in undesirable ways, we almost always do need, as Hart noted, to combine the desired flexibility with some measure of fixity. And with Charters we can achieve an acceptable mix. Charters are, after all, formally entrenched, written constitutional documents that solidify the commitments they represent in ways not always possible with less formal means. They also tend to be very well known among the general population. The average Canadian on the street,

---

33 In a number of early Charter cases, the Canadian Supreme Court embraced what is now known as the "purposive" approach to Charter interpretation. On this approach, the Court's aim is to decide in accordance with the moral norms for which a Charter provision is thought to stand, not the plain or original meaning or understanding of the provision, or its framer's "intentions." See, e.g., *R. v. Big M Drug Mart Ltd.* [1985] 1 S.C.R. 295, at 344, where the Court described the purposive approach as follows. "[T]he analysis is to be undertaken, and the purpose of the right or freedom in question is to be sought by reference to the character and the larger objects of the Charter itself, to the language chosen to articulate the specific right or freedom, to the historical origins of the concepts enshrined, and where applicable, to the meaning and purpose of the other specific rights and freedoms with which it is associated within the text of the Charter."

34 *Law and Disagreement*, 221.

for example, might not know many of the intricate details of how the Canadian Charter's provisions have been dealt with by the courts, but he often knows some of this legal history, and he is certainly aware of the Charter's more prominent sections, for example sections 5 (equality) and 33 (the "override" provision). Unwritten rules used to decide cases are, on the other hand, often more difficult to state and grasp, and subject to more controversy as to content than those embodied in written texts, particularly formally entrenched, constitutional texts. For these reasons, they can also, at least in some cases, be more easily avoided and finessed.

So there can be a kind of fixity in written Charters that is not always present with unwritten rules. Though there is much truth in this observation, it would of course be wrong to overstate it. Well-established unwritten rules and conventions, particularly those with constitutional status, are often as rigid and entrenched as written rules, if only because their elimination, alteration, or reinterpretation typically requires widespread changes in traditional attitudes, beliefs, and behaviour on the part of a wide range of political actors. And such changes can be as difficult to bring about as a formal constitutional amendment. They can also, given the right set of circumstances, be just as well known as written rules. Canadians, we noted earlier, are probably just as aware of the unwritten constitutional convention instructing the Governor General to appoint, as prime minister, the leader of the party with the most seats in the House of Commons as they are the requirement that no law shall abridge the right to life, liberty, and security of the person except in accordance with the principles of fundamental justice.[35] So if the case for Charters rested solely on the potential for a desired degree of fixity, we might agree with Waldron that we are better off without one.

Fortunately, there are other considerations in play. A second, perhaps more important reason for a written Charter is its *symbolic* value. This factor, though often cited in passing, is seriously underappreciated in discussions of judicial review. Charters help define and reinforce the character of the nation as one *publicly committed*, in its legal and moral practices, to the fundamental rights and values it includes. These public commitments can, of course, be expressed in other ways, for example, in the informal pronouncements of public authorities, or in legislative or judicial decisions that are sometimes publicly defended as a means of protecting the relevant rights. But Charters, as entrenched, foundational documents widely known, cited, and understood as embodying the nation's fundamental commitments to its constituent members, are a far more powerful means of expressing these commitments than most any other institutional or conventional vehicle. Ask an American for one feature of the American

---

35 *Paraphrasing the Charter*, sec. 7.

political culture of which she is most proud, and the answer will likely be the Bill of Rights. Ask a Canadian to name the one thing that publicly expresses the identity and commitments of the Canadian people, and the answer will likely be Hockey Night in Canada and the Stanley Cup playoffs. But the second most popular answer will be the Charter of Rights and Freedoms. The latter is seen not only as embodying Canada's commitment to rights protection but as expressing, in its commitments to such things as multiculturalism, group rights, equality before and under the law, and the mediating effect of section 1 limitations, an identity that distinguishes Canada, as a nation, from many other nations, including its more powerful neighbour to the south. This perception may, to some extent, rest on the faulty picture presupposed by the Standard Case. But Pierre Trudeau and Jean Chrétien were right on track when they invoked the symbolic value of the (then-) new Canadian Charter of Rights and Freedoms in heralding its adoption. Trudeau: "We must now establish the basic principles, the basic values and beliefs which hold us together as Canadians, so that . . . there is a way of life and a system of values which make us proud of the country. . . ."[36] Chrétien: "Now that our rights will be written into the Constitution, it will be a constant reminder to our political leaders that they must wield their authority with caution and wisdom."[37] These same sentiments were eloquently expressed by the American jurist Benjamin Cardozo, who, in his famous analysis and justification of judicial review, offered the following observations:

The utility of an external power restraining the legislative judgment is not to be measured by counting the occasions of its exercise. The great ideals of liberty and equality are preserved against the assaults of opportunism, the expediency of the passing hour, the erosion of small encroachments, the scorn and derision of those who have no patience with general principles, by enshrining them in constitutions and consecrating to the task of their protection a body of defenders. By conscious or subconscious influence, the presence of this restraining power, aloof in the background but none the less always in reserve, tends to stabilize and rationalize the legislative judgment, to infuse it with the glow of principle, to hold the standard aloft and visible to those who must run the race and keep the faith. . . . [W]e find its chief worth in making vocal and audible the ideals that might otherwise be silenced, in giving them continuity of life and of expression, in guiding and directing choice within the limits where choice ranges.[38]

---

36 The Right Honourable Pierre Elliott Trudeau, 1981, *The Charter of Rights and Freedoms: A Guide for Canadians.*
37 *Ibid.*, Preface, v.
38 Benjamin Cardozo, *The Nature of the Judicial Process* (New Haven, Conn.: Yale University Press, 1921), reprinted in Clarence Morris, ed., *The Great Legal Philosophers* (Philadelphia: University of Pennsylvania Press, 1959). The quotation is from the latter, p. 522.

Charters represent a potent, publicly accessible means for helping to establish the identity of the community and for solidifying its promise to each of its members – especially its minority members – that their rights count in fundamental ways. But they do so, under the common law conception, in a way that both expresses the requisite degree of humility and displays clear recognition of Hart's second fundamental need: the need to leave open, for later settlement by an informed (or at least better informed) choice, decisions that could not reasonably have been made in advance without the knowledge, moral and otherwise, that the unanticipated case brings to the fore. Judicial review should "preserve to the courts the power that now belongs to them, if only the power is exercised with insight into social values, and with suppleness of adaptation to changing social needs. . . ."[39] A Charter need not be conceived as declaring the following:

The Hubristic Message:

We know *which* moral rights count, *why* they count, and *the many complex ways* they count in the myriad circumstances of politics. Furthermore, we agree to tie ourselves and future generations of citizens and legislators to the mast of these commitments. We do this so as to counteract our (and their) natural tendency to become Hobbesean predators consumed with prejudice, greed, blind passion, fear and hysteria, and a willingness and desire to violate the moral rights of fellow minority members.

In fact, the message can be quite the opposite. A Charter conceived as the common law conception suggests says this:

The Humble Message:

We do *not* know, with certainty, which moral rights count, why they count, and in what ways and to what degree they count in the myriad circumstances of politics. What we do know, however, is the following. We know that the constellation of moral rights chosen for inclusion in our Charter constitutes, at least for the time being, a *reasonable* answer to the question of which moral rights deserve constitutional protection against government power. We further know that a reasonable answer to the question of why we should choose these and not some other collection of rights is that the chosen set contributes, in ways consistent with (though certainly not determined by) the demands of reason and morality, to the workings of a reasonably free, self-governing society which aspires to respect its members as rights bearers deserving of equal concern and respect. We further know that we are somewhat in the dark concerning the many concrete questions of rights which will inevitably, and in unforeseen ways, come to the fore when government power is exercised, principally, though not exclusively, through the introduction of general legislation. Although we do not know in advance what these questions will be or how they should be answered, we commit ourselves to asking them, and to acting on the answers arrived at by the relevant Court(s) in whose hands we agree to place the decision.

39 *Ibid.*

H. Waldron's Strategy

Recall that in Chapter 4 we distinguished, analytically, among four different questions: (1) What role is a Charter supposed to play in a constitutional democracy? (2) Is a Charter (serving that particular role) a good thing to have in a constitutional democracy, and if so, why? (3) Is judicial review on the basis of a Charter – that is, is judicial review – a good thing to have in a constitutional democracy, and if so, what form should it take? and (4) How should judges go about interpreting and applying Charters in the context of the judicial review of legislation? The Humble Message displays how the common law conception provides a framework within which to answer questions (1) and (2). And if we answer question (3) in the affirmative, we have a very promising framework in which to develop a detailed answer to question (4).[40] But we have yet to see a compelling reason for answering "yes" to question (3). One can imagine Waldron and his fellow Critics accepting Charters as the inspirational, symbolic, and yet humility-presupposing entities presupposed by the Humble Message. One can even imagine them adding that Charters can serve as a useful moral and conceptual backdrop within which public policy debates take place both inside and outside legislative chambers.[41] But by accepting all this, they needn't be taken to have signed on to judicial review. Again, nothing in the nature of a Charter demands its enforcement through the practice(s) of judicial review. New Zealand stands as an obvious counter-example to that assertion. And even if judicial review is chosen, there is, once again, no reason why it has to be in a form that provides the judiciary with final say on all questions raised by the Charter. Canada's section 33 override, to cite but one example, permits Parliament sometimes to substitute its own judgment for that of the Courts. In short, nothing here supports a strong practice of judicial review, even if the Charter is treated as the common law conception suggests. So we are still left with Waldron's question: Are there any good reasons for thinking that advantages would accrue were judges, not members of legislatures, handed the job of dealing with the complex, morally charged issues that would arise under a Charter conceived in the manner suggested by the common law conception? It is now time to address, head on, Waldron's formidable case against a positive answer to this question.

---

40 For example, we will be inclined to reject various forms of interpretive strategy, such as originalism, associated with fixed views.
41 Of course the symbolism can prove hollow if the political and legal cultures of the society in question fail to reflect the norms formally expressed in their Charter. And there is nothing to rule out the possibility of a society without a Charter possessing a strong culture of respecting the rights typically included in written Charters. The former Soviet Union is often cited as an example of the former, the UK an example of the latter. The only claim I make here is that within the context of a culture of rights recognition, the powerful symbolism of a Charter can enhance that practice.

In order to tackle that case properly, we need to begin by considering a key feature of Waldron's overall strategy that has, to this point, been largely ignored. Waldron's attack on Charters, judicial review, and the reasons usually offered in their defense combines a *stark realism*, concerning the prospects of agreement and pre-commitment in the circumstances of politics, with a professed *idealism* concerning the underappreciated possibilities of majoritarian self-government. The realism comes out, for example, in his rejection of Rawls's attempt to find a basis for agreement in an overlapping consensus of public reason.[42] The idealism comes out in his decision, early on in his critique of the Standard Case, deliberately to set aside or bracket many of the unattractive features of majoritarian rule to which Advocates tend to draw our attention and which serve as central elements in their case for Charters and judicial review. As we have seen, Advocates are fond of pointing out that majorities can often, in pursuit of self-interest, either ignore or under-appreciate the competing interests and rights of individuals as well as stable and transient minorities, and that they are easily swayed by factors like fear, insecurity, bias and prejudice, and the pernicious effects of campaign advertising dollars. We saw these sorts of factors in play when we investigated the dilemma faced by Atticus and his decision not to support the language law. Advocates are also fond of noting that political decision making in almost every constitutional democracy in existence today often amounts to little more than exercises in pure partisan politics. Waldron deliberately brackets such factors in developing his argument in favour of majoritarian decision making in order to counteract the undeniable tendency in much legal and jurisprudential scholarship to denigrate politics and legislative assemblies on the one hand and sanctify judicial reasoning and courts on the other. The former are often characterized as nothing more than a forum for the unprincipled clash of "deal-making, logrolling, interest-pandering, pork-barrelling, horse-trading, and Arrovian cycling – as anything, indeed, except principled political decision-making,"[43] while the latter is sanctified as the "forum of principle," the domain of cool, rational, objective, and impartial deliberation where reason rules and all are treated with the dignity and respect owed the bearers of rights. Bias in favour of courts, and hence judicial review, is, he thinks, the inevitable result, together with skewed jurisprudential theories and bad political philosophy. In order to counteract this imbalance in perspective, Waldron asks us to imagine what could be said in favour of politics and legislatures were they to *function well* – that is, were they to exemplify the ideals expressed by early modern democrats like Locke and Rousseau. We are asked to imagine a legislature, not as the forum of pork barrel politics but as a forum in which free and

---

42 This realism also underpins his critique of a range of other Advocates, including Dworkin, Freeman, and those who champion the ideals of "deliberative democracy" and "consensus politics."
43 *Law and Disagreement*, 30.

equal people, like our Atticus, come together, in common cause and the spirit of reciprocity, and bearing in mind the competing, contentious demands of justice and equality, to decide how they are to be governed in the circumstances of politics.

What I want to do is apply the canon of symmetry in the opposite direction. I want to ask: What would it be like to develop a rosy picture of legislatures and their structures and processes that matched in its normativity and perhaps its naivety, the picture of courts – "the forum of principle" etc. – that we present in the more elevated moments of our constitutional jurisprudence?[44]

In this light, he thinks, we'll begin to see not only the possibilities of democratic politics but also the hubris and unwarranted optimism involved in Charters and the insult to democracy and moral autonomy represented by judicial review and the Standard Case offered in its support.

So there purports to be both an element of realism and an element of idealism in Waldron's approach. He rightly refuses to allow Advocates to rest their case for judicial review on unwarranted assumptions concerning the possibilities of rational agreement and pre-commitment and the ability of courts, in the forum of principle, to hold us to these commitments. Here he stresses the stark reality of the circumstances of politics, the fact that it's disagreement all the way down. But when it comes to considering the possibilities of majoritarian politics as a means of dealing with these very same circumstances, we are asked to leave our cynicism at the door and share, at least for the time being, in a kind of idealism. But one can't help but ask: Is this a sound basis for addressing questions of basic institutional design? Should the same element of realism not apply to both sides of the argument? There is perhaps nothing amiss in considering how things might be in an ideal setting, but when the hard questions of institutional design are addressed, we had better reintroduce a good measure of realism into the mixture. And what do we find when we reintroduce these elements of realism? We discover not only a serious dilemma underlying Waldron's own argument in favour of majoritarian decision making but also a number of factors that add up to a pretty strong case for judicial review, despite Waldron's welcome warnings about not pushing that case too far.

I. Waldron's Cartesian Dilemma

Let's begin with the serious dilemma. As we noted, Waldron takes Rawls and others to task for presupposing a seemingly nonexistent consensus of judgments on fundamental questions of justice and equality. Here we are urged to be realistic in light of the circumstances of politics. But as many commentators

---

44 *Ibid.*, 32.

have pointed out, the deep disagreements of which Waldron's arguments make such heavy weather apply no less equally to the principles underlying his own case for majoritarian solutions. As a result, Waldron has given us no convincing reason to prefer *his* solution to the circumstances of politics (which rests on the procedural conception of democracy) over those offered by Advocates like Rawls, Dworkin, and Freeman (all of whom presuppose the constitutional conception). We might now add to that list the solution being proposed herein: the common law conception combined with some form of judicial review in which the standards appealed to are those of the community's constitutional morality. Joseph Raz, Tom Christiano, David Estlund, and Aileen Kavanagh all press this point home by noting the internal inconsistency that seems to underlie Waldron's arguments in favour of majoritarian solutions. As we saw earlier, much of Waldron's critique of the Advocates' position rests on the key premise that there is "disagreement all the way down." From this, we are told, it follows that we cannot agree on fixed points of pre-commitment that are presupposed by constitutional conceptions and that enable us to avoid the many objections to which Charters and judicial review are said to be susceptible. It further follows, according to Waldron, that we have no plausible option but to allow those with a stake in decisions about rights a continual say in their interpretation and application. We must, that is, affirm the fundamental "right of rights," to participate in decisions affecting ones own salient interests. And this, we are further told, rules out constitutional conceptions and judicial review. Yet if disagreement truly does go "all the way down," then nothing in Waldron's account rules out reasonable disagreement about "the legitimacy of the collective decision-procedures themselves in addition to the disagreement that animates the call for those procedures."[45] Advocates such as Freeman and Dworkin presumably have reasonable arguments to the effect that simple majoritarianism is inconsistent with democracy. Waldron, of course, disagrees, but surely he is not willing to say that the views of Freeman, Dworkin, et al. – and, we may now add, defenders of the common law conception – are all "unreasonable." If he is willing to press this charge, then he will be forced to recognize that his own views are open to this very same charge.

We seem, then, to be in a bind. It looks as though it is disagreement all the way down, so far as constitutional choice is concerned.... [W]e cannot use a results-driven test, because we disagree about which results would count in favour of and which against a given decision-procedure.... *[W]e cannot appeal to any procedural criterion either, since procedural questions are at the very nub of the disagreements we are talking about.*[46]

---

45 Thomas Christiano, "Waldron on *Law and Disagreement*," 520. Again, cf. Joseph Raz, "Disagreement in Politics"; David Estlund, "Waldron on *Law and Disagreement*"; and Aileen Kavanagh, "Participation and Judicial Review: A Reply to Waldron."
46 *Law and Disagreement*, 295, emphasis added.

Contrary to Waldron's claim that the right of participation demands that those whose fundamental interests are directly at stake should always be the ones to make the decisions affecting those interests, in some scenarios there can, as we observed earlier, be considerable plausibility in the opposing sentiment. Natural justice and the desire for sound, balanced decision making often combine to condemn situations in which individuals – reasonable and well intentioned as they might be – are permitted to serve as judges of their own cause. In many such situations, it is thought quite appropriate to assign the task of decision making to persons or institutions whose interests are *not* directly at stake. Independent arbitrators and judges are often appealed to in situations of this kind. We know, in situations like these, that the results of such a decision-making process – whatever these turn out to be – are likely to be better and more willingly accepted than if decisions were made by those whose interests are directly at stake. This is a perfectly valid "results-driven argument" that is in no way undermined by the fact that we cannot always agree on which particular decisions are in fact better.

It is quite plausible to think that an analogous results-driven argument can be used to defend judicial review. There is considerable plausibility in the suggestion that we should turn to judges to help us avoid the injustice and lack of wisdom of permitting unfettered stable or transient majorities to determine whether the government acts they support and perhaps demand unjustifiably infringe upon important minority interests and rights, contestable as these might be. We can know, as a general matter, that decisions made by individuals whose interests are not directly at stake, and whose official role is to be as fair and impartial as possible, are likely to be better than if such decisions were left in the hands of individuals whose interests are directly at stake.[47] We can know this even if we cannot agree in advance on what the right (or better) decisions will turn out to be – and even if we are very likely to continue to disagree on this matter after the decision has been made. Furthermore, we do not denigrate citizens' right of participation if we recognize that the most conscientious, reasonable, and well-intentioned members of majorities, concerned to assign fair weight to the contestable interests and rights of their fellow minority members, will sometimes fail, in light of the burdens of judgment, to achieve the desired balance. In light of this fact, they can reasonably support a practice that allows judges to reevaluate their decisions in light of an evolving understanding of constitutionally recognized moral rights. I say "reevaluate" because, as Waldron correctly notes, nothing in the nature of majoritarian, legislative processes rules out legislators themselves evaluating their proposed legislative measures to determine whether, in their best judgments, they do or do not violate

---

47 As noted in Chapter 4, we would be remiss were we not to acknowledge that judges do sometimes have a personal stake in the outcome of Charter decisions. But for the reasons outlined there, this need not be as serious a difficulty as might appear at first blush.

constitutionally entrenched moral rights.[48] Notice, once again, that nothing in the thoughts being developed here presupposes the image of a Hobbesean predator. There is nothing amiss in the idea of morally responsible bearers of rights recognizing their own burdens of judgment and welcoming the possibility of assigning the power to review their decisions, and the decisions of their elected representatives, to a body of persons less encumbered by those same burdens. There is nothing at all unflattering, or contrary to the legacy of human rights theory, in the alternative picture being defended herein. It would be foolish, of course, to push this point too far, as Critics of all stripes will no doubt continue to insist. After all, we must continue to remember that judges are themselves members of society, and that they are sometimes members of the very group whose interests are at stake in a judicial review. Yet as we saw, there are factors that often serve to mitigate this difficulty. These, combined with the requirement that judgments be publicly defended in light of constitutional principle, work against any political, moral, or self-interested biases to which judges might be subject.

So Waldron must surely admit that the reasonable disagreement he finds inherent in the circumstances of politics extends to his right of participation and the majoritarian practices and procedural conception of democracy he defends by invoking that right. Reasonable disagreement is to be found here too, leaving us, it seems, in a bit of a quandary. How are we to choose among the possible modes of decision making open to us without begging the question? If the response is that we can resolve the paradox by utilizing "higher order procedures that give everyone an equal say," then Waldron seems threatened by an infinite regress.[49] Why should we assume that there will be no reasonable disagreement about this higher-order procedure, that no one will dispute the claim that the higher-order decision procedure must be majoritarian?[50] Indeed, the fact that many Advocates put forward reasonable arguments in favour of a system incorporating judicial review suggests that we would be ill advised to make this assumption. Yet if there is reasonable disagreement even at this very elementary stage – which seems inevitable if disagreement truly does go all the way down – then how are we, ultimately, to decide? By fiat? In virtue of traditional practice? By way of a philosophical argument that has, as its conclusion, the one that Waldron seeks to defend? By an argument which suggests that we have to decide some way or other, and so it might just as well be by a procedure that gives everyone an equal say? But of course none of these strategies will work for Waldron. If one of these options is pursued, then sheer consistency and fairness – if

---

48 Indeed, some legislatures have staff whose primary role is to "Charter proof" proposed legislation – that is, advise the government on how to achieve its objectives in ways that are not likely to give rise to Charter challenges.

49 Christiano, "Waldron on *Law and Disagreement*," 520–1.

50 *Ibid.*, 521.

we could ever agree on what the latter means! – entail that it must be open to the Advocates as well. If unbridled majoritarianism is to be grounded in one of the aforementioned ways, despite reasonable disagreement about its soundness as a foundational principle, then there is nothing to disqualify others from positing their preferred starting points, despite the acknowledged fact of reasonable disagreement. There is nothing to prevent them from asserting, as their starting point, a constitutional conception of democracy, such as Dworkin's, that takes the defining aim of democracy to be a system of government in which "collective decisions [are] made by political institutions whose structure, composition, and practices treat all members of the community, as individuals, with equal concern and respect. . . . Democracy means government subject to conditions – we might call these 'democratic' conditions – of equal status for all citizens."[51] And we have not seen a compelling reason to rule out judges as a good choice for the task of helping to ensure that those particular conditions are met.

Waldron seems to have landed himself in a fix somewhat reminiscent of the one in which Descartes finds himself at the end of the first Meditation. Having pursued his method of doubt – which bars any proposition with respect to which there is any ground for doubt, however implausible that ground might be – to the point where even the rules of reason and logic must be rejected, Descartes turns around, in Meditation Two, and attempts to reason himself out of his predicament. He fashions arguments for the existence of a God whose benevolence guarantees Descartes' clear and distinct perceptions, including his perceptions of the rules of reason and logic. In other words, he uses the very methods – logic and reason – he is attempting to validate. But as Arnauld famously pointed out, this strategy is doomed from the beginning.

I have one further worry, namely, how the author avoids reasoning in a circle when he says that we are sure that what we clearly and distinctly perceive is true only because God exists. But we can be sure that God exists only because we clearly and distinctly perceive this. Hence, before we can be sure that God exists, we ought to be able to be sure that whatever we perceive clearly and evidently is true.[52]

The resulting circle robs Descartes' project of its foundation and its promised legitimacy. The moral of Descartes' story is that one cannot reject everything about which some meagre ground of doubt can be entertained, including the rules of reason and logic, and then try to *reason* oneself out of this fix. Something must be presupposed, something must be "given" before we can begin to reason about the world and what we can know of it. At the very least, we must accept, as a reasonable, provisional, and revisable starting point, propositions about which there are logically possible grounds for doubt. And this is so even

---

51 Dworkin, *Freedom's Law*, 17.
52 *The Philosophical Writings of Descartes: Volume II*, trans. John Cottingham et al. (Cambridge: Cambridge University Press, 1984), 150.

if an objector could reasonably disagree with one's chosen starting point(s). An analogous point seems appropriate in response to Waldron's valiant attempt to base his theory of institutional design on a solid foundation, one that is somehow invulnerable to the threat of reasonable dissensus upon which all other positions are said to founder. In Descartes' case, everything was subject to doubt, and nothing, as a result, could be proved beyond all doubt – the standard Descartes had imposed upon himself and to which he attempted, miserably, to adhere. In Waldron's case, everything in politics is subject to reasonable disagreement, and nothing, as a result, can be established that meets the "no reasonable disagreement" criterion, the standard that Waldron has set for himself and others and that cannot possibly be met. In short, Waldron's theory falls victim to his own standard of acceptable argument and institutional design. If, in response, he is willing, at some level, to privilege the supposed, but undeniably disputed, virtues of unadulterated majoritarian rule, then he is in no position to reject similar attempts by Advocates, who embrace Charters and their interpretation and enforcement via judicial review on the grounds that they all founder on the rock of reasonable dissensus.[53]

J. The Dignity of Legislation

So the element of realism at play in Waldron's critique seems to threaten the very foundation upon which he attempts to establish his own position. But the element of idealism at work is no less troublesome. Waldron is no doubt correct that philosophers tend to glamourize judging and denigrate ordinary politics, and that our theories should be sensitive to this tendency. But in attempting to correct the imbalance, he seems to have rigged the debate in the opposite direction. Waldron does us a great service in stressing both the circumstances of politics and the unreasonableness of the ideal pictures often painted of judges and their capacity to exemplify the ideals of Dworkin's ideal judge, Hercules. He also does a marvelous job reminding us of the possibilities contemplated by the democratic ideals associated with majoritarian decision making. But in attempting to restore reality to the judicial side of the equation and reinstitute the "dignity of legislation" by deliberately stressing the positive potential of the legislative process, he has left out many of the not-so-desirable features of the

---

53 There might also be a parallel between Waldron's position and the claim that if there is no moral truth, then we ought to allow each individual to decide questions of personal morality according to his own moral lights. Under such conditions, it is sometimes said, no one has the moral right to impose his own views on anyone else. Of course, if there is no moral truth, then there is no sound moral basis for this latter claim. Likewise, if we cannot agree on issues of political morality, then presumably one of the issues upon which we cannot agree is the question of whether we should, as a matter of sound political morality, allow the people affected by public decisions to decide for themselves. If we cannot agree on issues of political morality, then presumably there is no sound basis for this particular moral claim either.

latter, features with which the former might be well suited to deal. He has, in short, ignored important aspects of the circumstances of politics, over and above the fact of reasonable disagreement, and he has conveniently underplayed the ability of the courts to deal with those aspects effectively. Yet all those troublesome, unflattering elements of everyday politics that Waldron has us eliminate from the picture, so as to develop a more flattering picture of the possibilities of legislative politics and the workings of democracy, are as much a part of the circumstances of politics as the dissensus he cautions us not to forget. Let's put them back into the picture and see what results. Let's see what results from a comparison between judging and legislating in which these elements are also kept clearly in view.

We can begin by once again agreeing with Waldron and other Critics that judges are not Platonic Kings. They aren't smarter than the rest of us, nor do they possess a degree of moral insight and sophistication surpassing that of the average citizen or legislator. So we must completely agree that any attempt to justify a preference for judicial review over legislative supremacy premised on these idealistic assumptions is doomed from the start. If the role of the courts were simply to substitute, *under identical conditions of deliberation*, the judgments of a few heads (the court) for those of a greater number of heads (the legislature or the people), then there is no reason to think that the results would be any better. Indeed, if we accept Condorcet's jury theorem, Aristotle's arguments concerning the "wisdom of the multitudes," and the associated multiple heads principle, there is every reason to think, again as Waldron rightly points out, that we would probably end up with far worse results.[54] But all this rests on the key assumption that the contexts of decision are, in all relevant respects, identical to one another. But this is far from true. Let's consider a number of ways in which the contexts are quite different.

We should begin with the familiar point that judges are relatively insulated from the pressures to which legislators are inevitably subject. In Canada, all judges are appointed, not elected, as are all federal judges in the United States. This typical feature of the judicial office, coupled with the equally important fact of life tenure for many of them, provides judges with a kind of freedom to rise above the pressures to which legislators are either rightly or wrongly responsive.

A host of practical considerations are relevant, and many of these may argue forcefully for allowing an elected legislature itself to decide on the moral limits of its power. But other considerations argue in the opposite direction, including the fact that legislators are vulnerable to political pressures of manifold kinds, both financial and political, so that a legislature is not the safest vehicle for protecting rights of politically unpopular groups.[55]

---

54 See *Law and Disagreement*, Chapter 6.
55 Dworkin, *Freedom's Law*, 34.

True, things would be different if, when votes are cast, the following were the case: (a) members of legislative assemblies could be counted on always to bear in mind the constraints of justice and equality and not just vote in terms of the special interests or wishes of their constituents; (b) members also continued to bear in mind the "general good" of the wider community when deciding whether to support a measure that disfavours the interests or wishes of their own constituents; (c) members were not concerned to curry favour with special-interest groups upon whose support, financial or otherwise, their reelection depends; (d) members had the courage, sometimes, to break the bonds of party discipline when, in the members' best judgment, the party's measure is for some reason unjust or in violation of some other important moral right[56]; (e) members were willing to take a stand on an issue of principle upon which, in the members' best judgment, their constituents or backers are simply mistaken, perhaps because they have not thought through the issues in sufficient depth and are relying instead on "knee-jerk" reactions; (f) members were willing to stand up for the interests of oppressed minorities even when factors like prejudice, self-interest, or ignorance have led constituents to oppose a measure that protects the fundamental interests and rights (on any reasonable conception of those rights) of some minority group[57]; and so on. Under these ideal conditions of deliberation, there is considerable power in Waldron's arguments that the people, through the voice of their representatives, should be the ones to settle together, through majority vote, the hard questions of justice and equality that touch them all and upon which reasonable people of good faith and integrity disagree. But this is to ignore the wider circumstances of politics that Waldron's arguments have conveniently bracketed. Once those circumstances are reintroduced, the case for Charters of Rights coupled with some form of judicial review begins to emerge with strength.

So one crucial element of the circumstances of politics, bracketed by Waldron in his attempt to resurrect the "dignity of legislation," is that judges are largely removed from various pressures that often incline legislative members towards decisions favouring powerful majority opinion (however misguided) or towards opinions sanctioned by powerful elites. It would of course be unwise to discount entirely the courage sometimes exhibited by legislative members, some of whom will often be prepared to act as Atticus did and risk voting against a measure that is very popular among members of the relevant electorate. It would also be unwise to ignore the powerful, all-too-human desires for conformity and approval, which no doubt incline many judges towards maintaining

---

56 In Canada, many House members had to face this kind of dilemma on the issue of same-sex marriage.
57 A glaring example of this situation is legislation governing the rights of inmates to vote in elections. Courts and legislators who affirm such democratic rights are often pilloried in the press and in public discourse.

the status quo, or towards falling in line with widespread moral opinions even when, in the judges' best estimation, these are flatly inconsistent with the true commitments of the community's constitutional morality. No doubt it would also be unwise to ignore the views of those Critics who note the elite social backgrounds from which judges tend to be drawn. All these points must be kept clearly in mind and factored into decisions about how courts should operate and how judges are selected. For example, these points should play a prominent role in decisions concerning which groups, including those whose voices may have been overwhelmed or marginalized in public discourse and legislative debates, are to be granted intervener status in Charter cases. This last example illustrates yet another important respect in which the decisional contexts of judge and leg-islator are often relevantly different: For a variety of reasons, minority voices are often unheard or ignored in legislative contexts. They are drowned out by majorities and the powerful forces backing them up. A court is often the best, indeed only, institutional forum in which marginalized voices can successfully be heard and the expressed interests considered and given due measure. Judges may be the only persons who can provide minorities with the representation that majorities all too often take for granted.[58]

We should be careful not to push this point too far. And the reason is simple. No doubt these and other democratic deficiencies need to be rectified. But the solution can sometimes lie in reform of democratic procedures, not Charter supervision by judges. Citing what many now see as a "democratic deficit" within Western democracies, Canada's former prime minister, Paul Martin, at one point called for changes to legislative practices, changes that would, he claimed, have provided Members of Parliament with a greater ability to contribute meaningfully to the drafting of legislation and the freedom to break party discipline. Subsequent events, such as the requirement that all members of Cabinet vote in favour of the government's same-sex-marriage legislation or risk expulsion from Cabinet, led many to question Martin's commitment to dealing with the democratic deficit. But at least there has been public recognition of a problem. There has also been much talk, in Canada, of introducing some form of proportional representation to offset the perils of the first-past-the-post system, which has resulted in the inability of minority points of view (sometimes concentrated in provinces such as Alberta) to have much influence on the course of government policy. And then there are the frequent calls, in many different countries, for changes to the rules governing campaign financing, access by marginal parties to public airtime during election campaigns, and so on. Such changes, were they introduced, might have the effect of raising the level and quality of legislative (and public) debate. We should be cautious here, however:

---

58 Recall my earlier argument, in Chapter 3, that acting as someone's representative does not require election or choice on the part of the one whose interests, wishes, or views are represented.

The proposed changes could equally have the opposite effect. For instance, we must weigh against the virtue of allowing backbench legislators more freedom to vote against government policy the fact that there is strength in numbers, especially when a government's decision on a controversial, heated topic like the legal recognition of same-sex marriage meets with significant resistance within the general population. A legislator, no longer able to cite the imperatives of party discipline to escape the accountability that inevitably accompanies the liberty to vote one's own conscience, might well feel more pressured to fall in line with the misguided views of constituents. So the questions of institutional design are numerous and complex, and the answers uncertain, difficult, and significantly dependent on empirical evidence. But whatever our answers are, one fact remains: Though there may be democratic deficits that no doubt need to be addressed in all Western democracies, it does not follow that judicial review is the only or even the best solution to addressing that deficit. Better ways may be available, and many of these might involve reforming the legislature in some way.[59] Nevertheless, at the end of the day, and when all has been said and done – that is, when all the critical arguments outlined earlier have been duly answered in the manner suggested by the common law conception, and the Hubristic Message has been replaced in our thinking by the Humble Message – I hazard to suggest that such measures would not be enough. Were I forced to bet on which group, judges or legislators, is more likely to stand up to the relevant political forces at play in deciding the contentious issues that affect Charter rights, my money would be on the judges. Given factors (like life tenure) that to a degree insulate them from these pressures, judges will be better able to muster the courage to rule against powerful political and social forces that naturally incline legislators towards the easier, more popular route. And that more popular route can, again for reasons already explored, lead to violation of the community's very own constitutional morality and the commitments it represents. In particular, it can lead to the suppression of the interests and rights of minorities and vulnerable individuals.

K. The Circumstances of Rule Making

A further set of reasons for thinking that the judicial and legislative contexts are significantly different returns us, once again, to the circumstances of rule

---

59 A number of possibilities exist. For example, the deficit might be addressed by various familiar supermajority requirements in legislative processes, by election systems that favour minority interests (e.g., proportional representation, minority-sensitive districting, etc.), and by various constitutional designs that are not based on a constitutional Charter but on institutional checks and balances of the sort discussed in Chapter 2. So we must be careful not to dismiss the possibility that other institutions, besides constitutional Charters and judicial review, might work – perhaps sometimes even better – to achieve the purposes for which the latter are often heralded.

making. More specifically, it brings us back to the common law conception and to Hart's thoughts on the choices we face when attempting to implement the rule of law. As noted, we face two competing needs whenever we contemplate possible forms of legal regulation. On the one hand, there is the need for general rules that can be applied, at point of application, without fresh judgments about the relevant background considerations – that is, those considerations that (arguably) prompted creation of a particular rule and may (or may not) continue to justify the rule's existence. Such considerations are now commonly referred to as "dependent reasons."[60] On the other hand, there is the need to leave room, at point of application, for further consideration of dependent reasons. This is largely because unforeseen situations will inevitably arise, and these will bring into relief issues and questions – many of them moral in nature – that could not possibly have been appreciated and intelligently settled in advance. Hart suggests that there are a variety of techniques we can use to find an acceptable balance between these two fundamental needs. These include the employment, in drafting general legislation, of open-textured terms like "fair" and "reasonable." Yet another technique, one that Hart thought inevitable, is the exercise of discretion by judges. Judges must, he thought, be prepared to deal with hard, penumbral cases in which application of the relevant rule is unclear or indeterminate, or would for some other seem rationally or morally inappropriate. Perhaps application of the rule in the hitherto unforeseen circumstances would, to quote an old English legal phrase, lead to a "manifest absurdity or [moral] repugnance"[61] or would, as Fred Schauer put it, lead to "malignant results."[62]

Now one reply to Hart's suggested solution is that there is no necessity that decisions in such hard cases be left to the discretion of judges. After all, if we pursue the judicial discretion option, we face difficulties analogous to those cited by the Critics of judicial review: Judges are not philosopher-kings; the whole process is unfair to those who lose because of the discretionary decision made; decisions about what our rules should be, and about how these should be applied, even in unforeseen, troublesome cases, should always rest with the people, or with their elected and accountable representatives, and so on.[63] In

---

60 The phrase was first introduced by Raz. See, e.g., "Authority, Law and Morality" (1985) 68 *The Monist* at 295.

61 B. Parke in *Becke v. Smith* (1836).

62 Schauer, "Is the Common Law Law?" 455.

63 Dworkin's early criticisms of Hart's legal theory focused on the latter's theory of judicial discretion. Dworkin's criticisms, ironically enough, echo those of the Critics – those theorists who do not share Dworkin's attraction to judicial review in constitutional democracies. For Dworkin's early critique of Hart, see *Taking Rights Seriously*, particularly Chapters 2–4. For my response to Dworkin, see "Strong Discretion," *Philosophical Quarterly*, Vol. 33, no. 133 (October 1983), 321; "Herculean Positivism," *Oxford Journal of Legal Studies*, Vol. V, no. 2 (Summer, 1985), 187; and *Inclusive Legal Positivism*, Chapters 1, 2, 6, and 7.

light of these objections, one might be tempted to urge an approach to hard cases embodied in the French law of 16–24 August, 1790, title 2, article 12, which (in rough translation) reads: "Courts will address themselves to the legislature every time they believe it necessary to interpret a law," or in the French Constitution of 1790, article 256, which (again in very rough translation) reads: "When, after the Supreme Court of Appeal has quashed the decision of a lower court, a second decision on the merits is appealed on the same grounds, the issue cannot be discussed in the Supreme Court on Appeal until it has been submitted to the legislature, which enacts a law binding on the Supreme Court of Appeal."[64] Further appeal to the enacting body is always a logical possibility to deal with any hard case that arises when laws are applied to concrete scenarios. When the law's guidance runs dry, there is no absolute necessity that we turn to the discretion of judges.

There is obviously very good reason, however, why no contemporary political system (of which I am aware) actually pursues this early French model in dealing with hard legal cases. Legislatures must, of practical necessity, utilize the blunt instrument of *general legislation*. It is seldom possible to tailor legislation to each and every individual person and each and every situation that might arise within contemporary society. Of practical necessity, legislation deals, to greater or lesser degrees, of course, with *general* classes of individuals, engaged in *general* forms of conduct, in *generally* characterized circumstances. Owing to this fact, as we saw earlier, legislative efforts are always subject to under- or overinclusiveness.[65] Given this unavoidable feature of the circumstance of rule making, and of course the fact of unforeseeability that Hart was at pains to stress, a number of conclusions follow. Whatever general legislative solution a legislature were to propose to solve the problem raised in a hard case, it would likely meet with the same fate as the original legislation. That is, it would find its way back to the legislature, where a still further attempt to map out, in canonical, general terms, a solution to the complex array of questions which new, unforeseen hard cases bring to the fore would have to be made.

Take a case in which the "absurdity or moral repugnance" of applying a legislative rule involved a Charter value such as equality. Suppose further that, instead of choosing to specify an abstract right to equality before and under the law and then leaving further development of this norm to judges when they decide particular cases in which equality issues arise, the framers tried to be more specific. Imagine that they tried to outline, in concrete detail, how the value is to apply in any and all future cases that either could or are likely to arise. In so doing, they would have sought to provide more determinate guidance and to eliminate the need to resort to judicial discretion. The result would no doubt be further fuel for the objections of Critics, almost all of whom, we saw, view

---

64 I owe these translations to Michael Hartney.
65 Again, see Schauer, *Playing by the Rules*.

Charters as foolish, unwarranted attempts to create the kind of fixed points the legislators would here have been obviously trying to establish. Yet another result would almost certainly be a complete botch-up of the kind Reaume sketches for us in her critique of Canadian discrimination law. It is difficult to imagine intelligible, general rules that could somehow sensibly cover the wide variety of different kinds of particular cases and issues – many, once again, unforeseeable – and that will have to be decided in the name of a value like equality before and under the law, or comparable values like due process, freedom of speech, and so on. Any such attempt would almost certainly, for the reasons sketched by Hart, Reaume, and Schauer, meet with the same fate as Canada's discrimination law. The result, in short, would be unmitigated disaster.

But again, it doesn't have to be like this. One rightfully celebrated virtue of the common law method is its ability, owing to its inherent adaptability and facility for incremental change via case-by-case reasoning, to escape these troublesome features of futile attempts to follow the top-down model in inappropriate contexts. Precedents and judicial rulings, for all their "stickiness," do not represent attempts to settle issues once and for all, and in advance, by way of general rules whose exceptions are only those included within the rules themselves.[66] On the contrary, a precedent is typically said to stand only for the actual decision made on the concrete issue(s) raised and is recognized as provisional and revisable in light of developing case law and the new cases brought to our attention.

> The common law does not work from pre-established truths of universal and inflexible validity to conclusions derived from them deductively. Its method is inductive, and it draws its generalization from particulars. . . . The rules and principles of case law have never been treated as final truths, but as working hypotheses, continually retested in those great laboratories of the law, the courts of justice. Every new case is an experiment; and if the accepted rule which seems applicable yields a result which is felt to be unjust, the rule in reconsidered. . . . This work of modification is gradual. It goes on inch by inch.[67]

Through the kind of incremental, inch-by-inch change applauded by Cardozo, what often emerges, over time, is a body of law that, Bentham's hostility notwithstanding, exemplifies a level of practical reasonableness that top-down methodology struggles to achieve. This, the life blood of the common law, is something that the common law conception of Charters both allows and encourages at the level of constitutional practice.

So the circumstances of rule making in the kind of context we have been considering – for example, when Charter values like equality and due process are in play – are so complex in their particularity that they could not sensibly

---

66 The reference to the "stickiness" of judicial rulings and precedents is from Schauer's *Playing by the Rules*.
67 Benjamin Cardozo, *The Nature of the Judicial Process*, reprinted in Clarence Morris, ed., *The Great Legal Philosophers*. The reference is to the latter, p. 515.

be dealt with by the top-down model. Nor could they easily or sensibly be dealt with, on a case-by-case, bottom-up basis by an already overworked legislature. The latter would likely be swamped were it to assume, in addition to its already onerous duties, the additional responsibility to decide all unforeseen hard cases by reworking previously enacted general legislation to deal with them. This is one very good reason why modern systems of government opt for a division of labour between legislatures and courts: In some contexts, legislatures are asked to set the general rules and other normative standards to be applied, and courts are asked, not only to decide particular cases falling under the general norms but also to develop these norms using case-by-case, common law methodology. In these contexts, judges are assigned the task of dealing with the unforeseeable difficulties that come to the fore in cases involving the values the general rules seek to further. It is also, once again, worth noting in this context the extent to which, for much the same sorts of reasons, members of administrative bodies are empowered and asked to enact, interpret, and apply specific rules and guidelines pursuant to general legislation enacted by representative assemblies. And many of these individuals, we observed in Chapter 3, are unelected and not directly accountable to an electorate in the way that legislators are. Judges should be viewed as serving an analogous role. Indeed, this is the role theorists often have in mind when they refer to judicial discretion and similar powers of norm development as representing a kind of delegated, "quasi-legislative" power. In thinking of judges as quasi-legislators, we need not think of them as attempting to usurp the role of their legislative colleagues – a charge that is too often brought against judges when they engage in judicial review. On the contrary, their roles can be seen to be complementary and mutually supportive, not antagonistic. The one (the judges) is able to supplement the efforts of the other (the legislators). Each group, by making a good-faith effort to fulfill its role in dealing sensibly with the circumstances of rule making, can help contribute to an overall effort to secure the various benefits made possible by the rule of law.

So it is quite sensible (though admittedly not conceptually necessary) for legal systems to rely, at various points, on judicial discretion to help deal with unforeseeable issues and cases. But if this is true generally, then the Critic is faced with an obvious question: Why should we think things are different when the case or issue in question involves an unforeseen violation of a Charter norm? The norms with which judicial review deals are, after all, norms of the community's constitutional morality. Indeed, they are all norms thought so essential to a thriving constitutional democracy that they have been included within a community's entrenched Charter of Rights. Surely if judicial decision is relied upon when a rule of tort law leads to an unreasonable or repugnant result in an unanticipated case, the exercise of this same kind of judgment should also be possible when the conflict is with a fundamental norm of constitutional morality.

One reason for thinking, along with the Critic, that things might in fact be different when a Charter norm is in play – different in the sense that we should perhaps not here rely on judicial decision as a means of sorting things out for us – is the limited range and heightened significance of a typical Charter challenge. As noted in the previous paragraph, what is at stake is not just the wisdom of applying in some unforeseen case a rule whose application in that case threatens garden-variety, dependent reasons like reasonableness. Rather, what is at stake is a norm that is both of far greater moral significance and from a very limited range. We are, after all, talking about only *constitutionally recognized* rights and values of *very deep significance*. And these, as we have seen, are more often than not subject to deep political and moral disagreement as to their concrete implications. It would undoubtedly be completely unreasonable to send every hard case involving tort law, criminal law, contract law, and so on back to the legislature. The practical consequences for the workload of the legislature would be overwhelming. This fact alone provides more than enough reason to reject the proposal outright were it extended to all areas of law. But these consequences would not be nearly so severe were legislative referral restricted to cases involving constitutional norms. Surely, it might be said, legislatures can find the time to deal with *these* fundamental commitments of the community's constitutional morality! And surely this is the place where these commitments are best hashed out.

I'm not so sure. Consider, for example, the following fact. The number of cases in which, for example, the norms of the Canadian Charter figure is staggering. These include not only those landmark decisions that make the headlines and generate all the controversy. They also include, in far greater numbers, all those cases in which judges, carefully and deliberately, and without much fanfare, interpret and apply the Charter's norms to decide new types of cases previously unforeseen and unconsidered. We must also not forget all those cases in which judges interpret and apply, utilizing common law methodology, the more specific rules and precedents developed by earlier courts in deciding Charter conflicts under the Charter's general terms – rules like the "Oakes Test" in Canada, or the various free speech or due process cases in the United States.[68] Were all of these cases, with all their individuating facts and features,

---

68 In *Regina v. Oakes* [1986] 1. S.C.R. 103, the Supreme Court of Canada developed a set of guidelines for the interpretation and application of section 1 of the Canadian Charter. These are treated as binding on all lower courts. Oakes was charged with unlawful possession of a narcotic for purposes of trafficking. He challenged the "reverse onus" provision of section 8 of the *Narcotic Control Act*, which shifted the burden of proof to the accused. Once the Crown established simple possession, the accused was obliged to prove, beyond a reasonable doubt, that he did not possess the narcotic in question for purposes of trafficking. The Court, in ruling that section 8 violated the presumption of innocence guaranteed by sec. 11 (d) of the Charter, was obliged to determine whether this infringement could be saved under sec. 1, which provides that the Charter "guarantees the rights and freedoms set out in it subject only to such reasonable limits prescribed by law as can be demonstrably

in which some degree of moral controversy almost always exists, returned to the appropriate legislature for further discussion and decision, I suspect that the wheels of government truly would grind to a halt. As Hart stressed, and as defenders of bottom-up, common law methodology continually emphasize, life throws us many curves. This is one reason we opt for forms of legal regulation requiring fresh, better-informed judgments at point of application and one reason why, in most jurisdictions, we opt for the division of labour recommended by Hart. There is no cause to think that things will be different in the case of judicial review, where complex questions of political morality often hold centre stage.

There are some good, practical reasons, then, for not asking legislators to take on the task of applying and developing the norms of the community's constitutional morality in Charter cases, and for assigning that task instead to judges. That there are many more heads in a legislature is not a decisive factor in favour of the early French option. Indeed, the kind of case-by-case consideration of the hard questions of constitutional morality that Charter cases bring to the fore is, as noted earlier, is a task that judges are perhaps well situated to take on. A judge's legal training makes her in many ways an eminently suitable candidate for the job: The test of reflective equilibrium that judges employ in bringing common law methodology to bear in developing Charter norms is not that far removed from their more traditional tasks in developing, for example, tort law and the law of contract. In both instances, precedents and general norms must be reconciled with one another, and analogies must be drawn, distinctions must be made so as to distinguish cases, and so on. Charter precedents and the considered judgments of the community as a whole are somewhat like precedents and prior rulings in tort cases; the general moral norms to which Charters make reference and that represent the true commitments of the community's constitutional morality are analogous to the general norms governing legal concepts like "negligent," "foreseeable," and "reasonable" whose development we are often

---

justified in a free and democratic society." In fleshing out the contours of this general norm, the Court articulated what is now referred to as "the Oakes test" according to which: 1. the burden of proof is on the party, e.g. the Federal government, seeking to uphold the infringement; 2. the standard of proof to be met is the preponderance of probabilities; 3. the objectives to be realized by the infringement need to be sufficiently important as to warrant overriding Charter rights – they must be ones properly characterised as "pressing and substantial in a free and democratic society"; and 4. the means chosen to secure the relevant objective(s) must be reasonable and demonstrably justified. In judging whether condition 4. obtains, the infringing party must show that the means: (a) are fair and not arbitrary, that is, carefully designed to achieve the objective(s) and rationally connected to it (them) (the rational connection test); (b) impair the infringed rights as little as possible (the minimal impairment test); and (c) are proportional to the importance of the objective, that is, the more severe the infringement is, the more important the objective must be (the proportionality test). The Court ruled that section 8 failed the rational connection test insofar as possession of a small quantity of narcotic does not support an inference to possession for the purposes of trafficking.

prepared to leave to courts. What reason could we have, given these strong parallels, not to do the same in the case of judicial review? To all this we might add the following observations by Ronald Dworkin:

Obviously, on any theory of rights, decisions about rights are better if they are based on more rather than less information about a variety of facts. But I know of no reason why a legislator is more likely to have accurate beliefs about the sort of fact that, under any plausible conception of rights, would be relevant in determining what people's rights are. On any plausible theory of rights, moreover, *questions of speculative consistency –* questions that test a theory of rights by imagining circumstances in which that theory would produce unacceptable results – are likely to be of importance in an argument about particular rights, because no claim of right is sound if it cannot stand the test of hypothetical counter-example. But the technique of examining a claim of right for speculative consistency is a technique far more developed in judges than in legislators or in the bulk of the citizens who elect legislators.[69]

So there is reason to think that judges, with their facility for common law reasoning, are well suited to deal with the kind of issues of constitutional morality that Charter cases bring to the fore. The kind of bottom-up, common law method such cases demand is part and parcel of what it is to be a judge. The above reference to Dworkin suggests another point worth pondering. It is entirely possible not only that judges are well – perhaps even better – equipped than legislators to deal with the relevant issues in Charter cases, but that they are more likely to do so. In other words, they may be more likely than legislators to "take rights seriously."[70] As Joseph Raz observes, "we might have sufficient reason to believe that the legislature will not even try to establish what rights people have, or what restraint it should exercise, given the fact of disagreement over principles, whereas the courts, who are in charge of enforcing constitutional rights, will try honestly to do so."[71] This kind of abdication on the part of legislatures is all too common in societies hampered by the circumstances of politics.[72] Legislators, not wishing to alienate a constituency, are often prepared not only to compromise or deny constitutionally protected rights for the sake of placating a potentially resistant or even hostile electorate; they may opt not even to address the relevant issues of constitutional right. This has often been true in Canada, where, for close to twenty years now, Parliament has shied away from dealing with the contentious issue of legalized abortion. In its 1988 *Morgentaler* decision, the Supreme Court of Canada ruled that section 251 of Canada's Criminal Code was unconstitutional.[73] Section 251 had made it an offence to "procure

---

69 Dworkin, *A Matter of Principle*, 30, emphasis added.
70 The reference is to Dworkin's *Taking Rights Seriously*.
71 Raz, "Disagreement in Politics," 46.
72 So much for the Critics' charge that judges are involved in a naked power grab licensed by their role in judicial review!
73 *R. v. Morgentaler* [1988] 1. S.C.R. 30, 385.

a miscarriage of a female person" but then outlined a procedure that, if followed, would provide an absolute defence against the charge. The procedures
provided for a pregnant woman to petition a therapeutic abortion committee of
an accredited hospital for the termination of her pregnancy on the grounds that
its continuation would endanger her life or health. If that request gained the
approval of the committee, and the abortion were subsequently performed by
a qualified medical practitioner, neither the woman nor the practitioner could
be found guilty of an indictable offence. In its judgment, the Supreme Court
deemed these requirements unconstitutional, the principal ground being that
section 251 was thought to infringe a woman's section 7 right to life, liberty,
and security of the person in a way that was not "in accordance with the principles of fundamental justice." The main reason the infringement could not be
so justified was the fact that access to abortions varied considerably across the
country. Many hospitals simply did not provide abortions at all, while others
did so but imposed greater restrictions than others. For example, some hospital
committees were not prepared to authorize abortions for married women, while
others observed no such restriction. In any event, instead of attempting to draft
legislation to replace the impugned section of the Criminal Code, Parliament has
to this day chosen to remain silent. In place of the vigorous, open-ended debate
ending in a reasoned decision on legalized abortion of the kind envisaged by
Waldron, there has been a somewhat cowardly unwillingness on the part of Parliament to act, for fear of alienating large segments of the electorate. The result
has been a legal void, amounting to the *de facto* legalization of abortion without
restriction. By default, the opponents of legally regulated abortion have won the
debate that did not occur. I in no way mean to suggest by these comments that
those in favour of regulation should have won the debate had it taken place. The
point is that there never was the kind of vigorous, legislative debate idealized
by Waldron because there was no debate at all. Parliament displayed a similar
unwillingness to engage controversial issues of constitutional morality in the
context of same-sex marriage. Instead of taking a stand on the issue by drafting
legislation that either provided legal recognition to gay marriage or confirmed
the common law understanding that marriage must be between a man and a
woman, the Liberal government chose initially to offload the question onto the
Supreme Court. In its *Reference re: Same Sex Marriage*, the Court effectively
told the government to suck it up and fulfill its constitutional responsibilities
by passing appropriate legislation. Were the government to do so, the Court
intimated, it would then be perfectly happy to consider a Charter challenge to
the legislation passed should an adequate case for leave to appeal be forthcoming.[74] The government did, of course, eventually take up the Court's challenge

---

74 See *Reference re Same-Sex Marriage* [2004] 3 S.C.R. 698.

by introducing (and passing) *Bill C-38: The Civil Marriages Act*, which, in effect, rejected the common law definition of marriage and provided for full legal recognition of same-sex marriage.

So there is, as Raz observes, no guarantee that legislatures, if left with the task of protecting Charter rights, will in fact do so. Courts, on the other hand, owing in part to their insulation from the various political pressures discussed earlier, are (or at least can be) in a much better position to take constitutional rights seriously. It might be thought that a further reason for thinking that courts might be better suited to deal with issues of constitutional morality lies in the structure of adjudication. Unlike the legislative context, wherein any argument and any reason is open for consideration, adjudicative practices typically restrict judges to considering only the arguments and evidence advanced by the litigants. Furthermore, they restrict judges to a very limited range of questions. The question before a court is seldom "What does 'equality' mean in general terms and how can we devise a detailed scheme of legal regulation that accords with this understanding, and that is fiscally sound, and so on?" On the contrary, the question is almost always much more particular and focused: "Does denying this gay couple the right to civil marriage in Ontario violate their equality rights?" True, in issuing a ruling that answers the latter question, the court will have to answer a question of more general application: "Is denying gay couples in this sort of situation the right to civil marriage a violation of equality rights to couples of that sort?" But providing an answer to this general question is perhaps a far less ambitious task than attempting to draft general legislation that covers a much broader range of circumstances and that can be reconciled with the full gamut of reasons with which legislatures must concern themselves. If the structure of adjudication has this effect of narrowing down to questions of constitutional right, the scope and range of questions in need of answers, then there is reason to think that it provides a better forum than legislatures for the sensitive, informed development of the norms of constitutional morality that have found their way into a Charter.

As tempting as this line of argument is, there are reasons to be cautious in pursuing it. There are two main reasons. First, there is no reason why courts must narrow their focus in the manner described. As noted, they must, in providing reasons for their judgments, invoke reasons of a general or universal sort. They must, that is, explain not only why this particular couple should be married but also why couples of that sort in that type of situation must be afforded the right to marry. Providing reasons for one's decision forces one to generalize. And once one has gone down that road, there is, in theory, no limit to the range of relevant considerations. One might, in justifying a decision in favour of the right to gay marriage, invoke very abstract, far-reaching principles dealing with complex notions like autonomy, the good of human beings, and so on. Indeed, many of the landmark cases of constitutional law, for example the

American case of *Brown v. Board of Education* or the Canadian cases of *Butler* and *Andrews*, provide excellent examples of how far reaching the questions entertained in judicial review can actually become. And of course there is the point that most rights – even constitutional ones – must often be balanced against competing considerations, including less dramatic ones like the need for fiscal constraint.[75] It might seem as though one fails to take rights seriously in doing so, but the rights to equality underlying pay-equity legislation, for example, must sometimes be balanced against the effects such legislation can have on the overall economy. Such concerns can lead a court to side with a government whose pursuit of pay equity might not be as pure and extensive as some might like. Alternatively it can lead a court, as it did the Supreme Court of Canada recently, to declare such careful balancing to be within the purview of the legislature.[76]

A second reason why it is best not to stake the case for judicial review by judges on the more focused nature of adjudication is that there is no reason, in principle, why legislative debates could not be structured so as to introduce a similar focus. It is sometimes said that courts are a better vehicle for rights protection than legislatures because the former, unlike the latter, are restricted to arguments of principle. Unlike courts, legislatures are free – indeed, required – to concern themselves with societal goals, strategic considerations, and so on, that have little if anything to do with rights.[77] Courts, on the other hand, must take rights more seriously, thus excluding appeal to all other possible factors. But nothing in the nature of legislative debate precludes legislatures from observing similar limitations when constitutional rights are the topic of discussion. For reasons explored already, this possibility is perhaps not likely to be effective. Legislators who wish to placate the electorate may find it difficult, if not impossible, to restrict their thinking to matters of constitutional right. But the reason does not lie in structural differences between legislative debate and courtroom adjudication.

---

75 The Canadian Charter, by way of its section 1 "reasonable limits" clause, formally recognizes this important fact.

76 See *Newfoundland (Treasury Board) v. N.A.P.E.* [2004] 3 S.C.R. 381, where the Canadian Supreme Court was forced to deal with the issue of whether section 9 of the Public Sector Restraint Act of Newfoundland and Labrador violated the equality rights of women in the health care sector. The act deferred commencement of a pay equity scheme for these women to which the government had agreed in 1988. According to the government, the deferral was necessary in order to reduce what it claimed to be a crippling provincial deficit. One of the principal questions for the Court was whether this kind of consideration was enough to justify an infringement of equality rights under the sec. 1 "reasonable limits" clause of the Charter.

77 One Advocate who argues along these lines is Dworkin, who distinguishes between arguments of principle and arguments of policy. In Dworkin's view, judges should, and characteristically do, restrict themselves to arguments of principle. See *Taking Rights Seriously*, Chapter 4.

The foregoing cautions notwithstanding, practical reality suggests that we do well to assign courts a prominent role in shaping, through the process of case-by-case, common law development, the norms of the community's constitutional morality that figure in its Charter. We will not only have better decisions, we may well experience a rise in the level of public debate, bringing us to one final advantage of judicial review. It is a reason that undermines Waldron's objection to results-driven arguments. As Ronald Dworkin observes, "Even when the debate is illuminating . . . the majoritarian process encourages compromises that may subordinate important issues of principle. Constitutional cases, by contrast, can and do provide a widespread public discussion that focuses on political morality."[78]

When a constitutional issue has been decided by the Supreme Court, and is important enough so that it can be expected to be elaborated, expanded, contracted, or even reversed by future decisions, a sustained national debate begins, in newspapers and other media, in law schools and classrooms, in public meetings and around dinner tables. That debate better matches [the ideals of constitutional democracy] than almost anything the legislative process on its own is likely to produce.[79]

It would, of course, be foolish to push this argument too far. Along with Dworkin, I put forward only tentatively the suggestion that judicial review may provide a superior kind of public deliberation about issues of constitutional morality. It is put forward as yet another reason (a contestable one to be sure) among the many others considered throughout this book, for preferring that option. In combination with one another, these reasons are more than sufficient to warrant the conclusion that, in the end, we are very well served by a Charter understood as the common law model supposes – as one developed and applied by judges in partnership with other government bodies such as legislatures, and with the people themselves as they grapple with the complex, ever-changing nature of their true constitutional commitments. This idea of partnership is, once again, well worth bearing in mind. As repeatedly stressed above, nothing in the nature of judicial review yields a doctrine of judicial supremacy. Far too often, judges who strike down or otherwise alter legislation on Charter grounds are criticized for claiming superior authority over legislatures, and for engaging in a naked power grab. Yet as we have seen, this need not be so. The role of legislating general rules (whose moral consequences are sometimes unforeseeable) is fully compatible with the role (reserved for another body) of deciding – or advising – on what must be done in unforeseeable cases of potential conflict with the developing norms of constitutional morality. Seen in this light, judges and legislators need not be seen to be in *competition* with each other over who has

---

78 *Freedom's Law*, 30–1.
79 *Ibid.*, 345. This argument, not surprisingly, is thoroughly dismissed by Waldron as just another instance of an invalid "results-driven" argument. For his critique, see *Law and Disagreement*, 289–91.

more courage or the better moral vision. On the contrary, they can each be seen to contribute, in their own unique ways, from their own unique perspectives, and within their unique contexts of decision, to the achievement of a morally sensitive and enlightened rule of law. As noted in Chapter 4, some have taken up this idea and suggested that judicial review sets the stage for a "dialogue" between the courts and the legislature. In an effort to support this conception, Peter Hogg and Allison Bushell have argued that the role of Canadian courts in enforcing the Charter is best viewed not as an imposition that thwarts the democratic will but as one stage in the democratic process.[80] Hogg and Bushell show that Charter cases in which Canadian legislation is ruled unconstitutional are almost always followed by new legislation that accomplishes the very same objectives as the offending legislation but in ways that no longer violate Charter rights. The resulting effect is rarely to thwart the democratic will but to influence the design and implementation of legislation expressive of that will. They further argue Dworkin's point that judicial review often results in a public debate in which the Charter's moral rights assume a more prominent role in public discourse than they might otherwise have had absent the courts' intervention. This process indicates a thriving democracy rather than its suppression. In light of the arguments of this book, it can also be viewed as helping to establish and determine the requirements of the community's constitutional morality. And this may not be such a bad thing for democracy after all. Whether or not one wishes to call this a "dialogue" between the parties concerned, the fact remains that judicial review seems to promote interaction of a sort it would be foolish to ignore.[81]

L. Concluding Thoughts

We have come a long way in our quest to answer the Critic's challenge to judicial review. We have seen ample reason to reject the fixed views presupposed both in the Standard Case of the Advocates and in the arguments of Waldron and his fellow Critics. We should reject the view of Charters as confident, hubristic attempts to establish illusory fixed points of agreement and pre-commitment. We should view them instead as living trees whose roots are fixed by factors like precedent, the community's moral judgments in reflective equilibrium, and

---

80 Once again, see Peter Hogg and Allison Bushell, "The *Charter* Dialogue Between Courts and Legislatures (Or Perhaps The *Charter of Rights* Isn't Such a Bad Thing After All)."

81 The notion that judicial review provides an institutional vehicle for a "dialogue" between Parliament and the Courts has become popular in Canada and has even been invoked in many cases. But as noted in Chapter 4, that notion has been the subject of considerable controversy and dispute. For scholarly criticism, once again see G. Huscroft and I. Brodie, eds., *Constitutionalism in the Charter, Part I*. See also Christopher Manfredi, *Judicial Power and the Charter: Canada and the Paradox of Liberal Constitutionalism* (2nd edn.) (Don Mills, Ontario: Oxford University Press Canada, 2001).

the terms it has chosen (in its Charter) to express the fundamental commitments of its constitutional morality. But this living tree, though rooted in such factors, is also one whose branches should be allowed to grow over time through a developing common law jurisprudence of that same community's constitutional morality. If we take this view of Charters and judicial review we gain a number of significant advantages. We will have an entrenched commitment to moral rights within a stable, though flexible, framework for the day to day workings of law and politics. This will be a framework which restrains government power but does not allow the dead, possibly misguided hand of the past to constrain our current choices unnecessarily, or in ways which threaten our ability to engage in the ongoing project of flexible, though disciplined, self government. In short, it will be a framework of legal regulation which allows us to satisfy both of Hart's two fundamental needs, while at the same time living up to a self-image to which we should aspire – the image of a self-governing, autonomous people, respectful of moral rights, but, alas, fully aware that we do not have all the answers.

Bibliography

Ackerman, Bruce. *We The People: Foundations.* Cambridge, Mass.: Harvard University Press, 1991.

We The People: Transformations. Cambridge, Mass.: Harvard University Press, 1998.

Alexander, Larry (ed.). *Constitutionalism.* Cambridge: Cambridge University Press, 1998.

Austin, John. *The Province of Jurisprudence Determined.* New York: The Noonday Press, 1954.

Brest, Paul. "The Misconceived Quest for the Original Understanding." *Boston University Law Review 60* (1980): 204.

Cameron, Jamie. "The Charter's Legislative Override: Feat or Figment of the Constitutional Imagination," in G. Huscroft and I. Brodie (eds.), *Constitutionalism in the Charter Era.* Markham, Ontario: Butterworth's, 2004.

Cardozo, Benjamin. *The Nature of the Judicial Process.* New Haven, Conn.: Yale University Press, 1921.

The Charter of Rights and Freedoms: A Guide for Canadians. Ottawa: Publications Canada, 1982.

Christiano, Thomas. "Waldron on *Law and Disagreement.*" *Law and Philosophy 19* (2000): 513.

Christiano, Thomas (ed.). *Philosophy and Democracy: An Anthology.* New York: Oxford University Press, 2003.

Coleman, Jules. "Negative and Positive Positivism." *The Journal of Legal Studies 11* (1982): 139.

The Practice of Principle: In Defence of a Pragmatist Approach to Legal Theory. Oxford: Oxford University Press, 2001.

Coleman, Jules (ed.). *Hart's Postscript: Essays on the Postscript to the Concept of Law.* Oxford: Oxford University Press, 2001.

Coleman, Jules, and Scott Shapiro (eds.). *The Oxford Handbook of Jurisprudence and Philosophy of Law.* Oxford: Oxford University Press, 2002.

Cross, Sir Rupert. *Precedent in English Law,* second edition. Oxford: Oxford University Press, 1968.

Descartes. René. *The Philosophical Writings of Descartes: Volume II*, trans. John Cottingham et al. Cambridge: Cambridge University Press, 1984.

Devlin, Lord Patrick. *The Enforcement of Morals.* Oxford: Oxford University Press, 1959.

Dicey, A. V. *The Law of the Constitution*, tenth edition. London: Macmillan, 1965.

Dickson, Julie. *Evaluation and Legal Theory*. Oxford: Hart Publishing, 2001.

Dworkin, Gerald. "Paternalism," in R. Wasserstrom (ed.), *Morality and the Law*. Belmont, Calif.: Wadsworth, 1971.

"Paternalism: Some Second Thoughts," in Rolf Sartorius (ed.), *Paternalism*. Minneapolis: University of Minnesota Press, 1983.

Dworkin, Ronald. *Taking Rights Seriously*. London: Duckworth, 1977.

A Matter of Principle. Cambridge, Mass.: Harvard University Press, 1985.

"Rights as Trumps," in Jeremy Waldron (ed.), *Theories of Rights*. Oxford: Oxford University Press, 1985.

"Law's Ambition for Itself." *Virginia Law Review 71* (1985): 173.

Law's Empire. Cambridge, Mass.: Harvard University Press, 1986.

A Bill of Rights for Britain. London: Chatto and Windus, 1990.

Life's Dominion: An Argument About Abortion, Euthanasia, and Individual Freedom. New York: Vintage Books, 1994.

"Objectivity and Truth: You'd Better Believe It." *Philosophy and Public Affairs 25* (1996): 87.

Freedom's Law: The Moral Reading of the American Constitution. Cambridge, Mass.: Harvard University Press, 1996.

Eisenberger, Melvin. *The Nature of the Common Law*. Cambridge, Mass.: Harvard University Press, 1988.

Eisgruber, Christopher. *Constitutional Self Government*. Cambridge, Mass.: Harvard University Press, 2001.

Elster, Jon. *Ulysses and the Sirens: Studies in Rationality and Irrationality*. New York: Cambridge University Press, 1979.

Elster, Jon, and Rune Slagstad (eds.). *Constitutionalism and Democracy*. Cambridge: Cambridge University Press, 1988.

Ely, John Hart. *Democracy and Distrust: A Theory of Judicial Review*. Cambridge, Mass.: Harvard University Press, 1980.

Estlund, David. "Waldron on *Law and Disagreement*." *Philosophical Studies 99* (2000): 111.

Feinberg, Joel. *The Moral Limits of the Criminal Law, Volume 3: Harm to Self*. Oxford: Oxford University Press, 1989.

Feinberg, Joel, and Jules Coleman (eds.). *Philosophy of Law*, sixth edition. Belmont, Calif.: Wadsworth, 2000.

Freeman, Samuel. "Constitutional Democracy and the Legitimacy of Judicial Review." *Law and Philosophy 9* (1990–1): 335.

Gallie, William. "Essentially Contested Concepts." *Proceedings of the Aristotelian Society 56* (1965): 167.

Glendon, Mary Ann. *Abortion and Divorce in Western Law*. Cambridge, Mass.: Harvard University Press, 1987.

Rights Talk. New York: The Free Press, 1991.

Gray, John Chipman. "A Realist Conception of Law," in F. Feinberg and H. Gross (eds.), *The Philosophy of Law*, third edition. Belmont, Calif.: Wadsworth, 1986: 44.

Green, Leslie. "Are Language Rights Fundamental?" *Osgoode Hall Law Journal 25* (1987): 649.

"Internal Minorities and Their Rights," in Judith Baker (ed.), *Group Rights*. Toronto: University of Toronto Press, 1994: 100.

"Legal Positivism," in N. Zalta (ed.), *The Stanford Encyclopedia of Philosophy* (Spring 2003 edn). URL = http://plato.stanford.edu/archives/spr2003/legal-positivism/

Grey, Thomas. "Constitutionalism: An Analytic Framework," in R. Pennock and J. Chapman (eds.), *Constitutionalism (Nomos XX)*. New York: New York University Press, 1979: 189.

Hart, H.L.A. "Positivism and the Separation of Law and Morals." *Harvard Law Review 71* (1957–8): 593, reprinted in Joel Feinberg and Jules Coleman (eds.), *Philosophy of Law*, sixth edition. Belmont, Calif.: Wadsworth, 2000: 59.

Law, Liberty and Morality. Oxford: Oxford University Press, 1962.

The Concept of Law, second edition. Oxford: Clarendon Press, 1994.

Hiebert, Janet. "Is It Too Late to Rehabilitate Canada's Notwithstanding Clause?" in G. Huscroft and I. Brodie (eds.), *Constitutionalism in the Charter Era*. Markham, Ontario: Butterworth's, 2004: 169.

Hobbes, Thomas. *Leviathan.* Indianapolis: The Liberal Arts Press, 1958.

Hogg, Peter, and Allison Bushell. "The *Charter* Dialogue Between Courts and Legislatures (or Perhaps the *Charter of Rights* Isn't Such a Bad Thing After All)." *Osgoode Hall Law Journal 35* (1997): 75.

Hogg, Peter. *Constitutional Law of Canada*, fourth edition. Toronto: Carswell, 1997.

Hohfeld, Wesley Newcomb. *Fundamental Legal Conceptions.* New Haven, Conn.: Yale University Press, 1919.

Holmes, Stephen. "Precommitment and the Paradox of Democracy," in J. Elster and R. Slagstad (eds.), *Constitutionalism and Democracy*. Cambridge: Cambridge University Press, 1988: 233.

Honore, A. M. "Real Laws," in J. Raz and P. Hacker (eds.), *Law, Morality and Society: Essays in Honour of H. L. A. Hart*. Oxford: Oxford University Press, 1977: 112.

"The Dependence of Morality on Law." *Oxford Journal of Legal Studies 13* (1993): 3.

Huscroft, G., and I. Brodie (eds.). *Constitutionalism in the Charter Era*. Markham, Ontario: Butterworth's, 2004.

Kahana, Tsvi. "What Makes for a Good Use of the Notwithstanding Mechanism?" in G. Huscroft and I. Brodie (eds.), *Constitutionalism in the Charter Era*. Markham, Ontario: Butterworth's, 2004.

Kavanagh, Aileeen. "The Idea of a Living Constitution." *Canadian Journal of Law and Jurisprudence XVI* (2003): 55.

"Participation and Judicial Review: A Reply to Waldron." *Law and Philosophy 22* (2003): 451–86.

Kramer, Matthew. *In Defense of Legal Positivism: Law Without Trimmings.* Oxford: Oxford University Press, 1999.

Where Law and Morality Meet. Oxford: Oxford University Press, 2004.

Kymlicka, Will. "Individual and Community Rights," in Judith Baker (ed.), *Group Rights.* Toronto: University of Toronto Press, 1994: 17.

LaFollette, Hugh. *The Blackwell Guide to Ethical Theory.* Oxford: Blackwell Publishers, 2000.

Lee, Harper. *To Kill a Mockingbird.* Philadelphia: J. B. Lippincott, 1960.

Locke, John. *Two Treatises of Government*, second edition. Peter Laslett, ed. Cambridge: Cambridge University Press, 1967.

An Essay Concerning Human Understanding. Peter Laslett, ed. Oxford: Clarendon Press, 1975.

Mackie, John. "The Third Theory of Law." *Philosophy and Public Affairs 7* (1977): 3.

MacKinnon, Catherine. *Feminism Unmodified: Discourses on Life and Law.* Cambridge, Mass.: Harvard University Press, 1987.

  Toward a Feminist Theory of the State. Cambridge, Mass.: Harvard University Press, 1989.

  Only Words. Cambridge, Mass.: Harvard University Press, 1993.

Mandel, Michael. *The Charter of Rights and the Legalization of Politics in Canada.* Toronto: Thompson Educational Publishing, Inc., 1994.

Manfredi, Christopher. *Judicial Power and the Charter: Canada and the Paradox of Liberal Constitutionalism,* second edition. Don Mills, Ontario: Oxford University Press Canada, 2001.

Marmor, Andrei. *Positive Law and Objective Values.* Oxford: Clarendon Press, 2001.

  Interpretation and Legal Theory, revised second edition. Oxford: Hart Publishing, 2005.

Marshall, Geoffrey. *Constitutional Conventions.* Oxford: Clarendon Press, 1984.

Martin, Robert. *The Most Dangerous Branch.* Montreal: McGill–Queen's University Press, 2003.

Mill, J. S. *On Liberty and Other Writings.* Stefan Collini (ed). Cambridge: Cambridge University Press, 1989.

Montesquieu, Baron de. *The Spirit of the Laws,* trans. Thomas Nugent. London: J. Nourse, 1977.

Morris, Clarence (ed.). *The Great Legal Philosophers.* Philadelphia: University of Pennsylvania Press, 1959.

Morton, T., and R. Knopff. *The Charter Revolution and the Court Party.* Peterborough, Ontario: Broadview Press, 2000.

Parfit, Derek. *Reasons and Persons.* Oxford: Oxford University Press, 1984.

Pennock, J. *Democratic Political Theory.* Princeton, N.J.: Princeton University Press, 1979.

Petter, Andrew. "Immaculate Deception: The Charter's Hidden Agenda." *The Advocate 45* (Pt. 6).

Postema, Gerald. *Bentham and the Common Law.* Oxford: Clarendon Press, 1986.

  "Philosophy of the Common Law" in J. Coleman and S. Shapiro (eds.), *The Oxford Handbook of Jurisprudence and Philosophy of Law.* Oxford: Oxford University Press, 2002: 588.

Rawls, John. *A Theory of Justice.* Cambridge, Mass.: Harvard University Press, 1971.

  Political Liberalism. New York: Columbia University Press, 1996.

Raz, Joseph. "Legal Principles and the Limits of Law." *Yale L. J. 5* (1972): 823.

  The Authority of Law. Oxford: Clarendon Press, 1979.

  "Authority, Law and Morality." *The Monist 68* (1985): 295.

  "Authority and Justification." *Philosophy and Public Affairs 14* (1985): 3.

  The Morality of Freedom. Oxford: Clarendon Press, 1986.

  "Disagreement in Politics." *American Journal of Jurisprudence 43* (1998): 47.

  "On the Authority and Interpretation of Constitutions," in L. Alexander (ed.), *Constitutionalism.* Cambridge: Cambridge University Press, 1998.

  Engaging Reason: On the Theory of Value and Action. Oxford: Oxford University Press, 1999.

  Ethics in the Public Domain, revised edition. Oxford: Clarendon Press, 2001.

Reaume, Denise. "The Constitutional Protection of Language: Security versus Survival," in David Schneiderman (ed.), *Language and the State: The Law and Politics of Identity.* Montreal: Yvon Blais Ltee, 1991.

"The Group Right to Linguistic Security: Whose Right, What Duties?" in Judith Baker (ed.), *Group Rights.* Toronto: University of Toronto Press, 1994: 118.

"Of Pigeonholes and Principles: A Reconsideration of Discrimination Law." *Osgoode Hall L. J. 40* (2002): 113.

Rehnquist, William. "The Notion of a Living Constitution." *Texas Law Review 54* (1976): 693.

Rubenfeld, Jed. "Legitimacy and Interpretation," in L. Alexander (ed.), *Constitutionalism.* Cambridge: Cambridge University Press, 1998: 194.

Sager, Laurence. "The Incorrigible Constitution." *New York University Law Review 65* (1990): 893.

Justice in Plain Clothes: A Theory of American Constitutional Practice. New Haven, Conn.: Yale University Press, 2004.

Scalia, Antonin. "Originalism: The Lesser Evil." *University of Cincinnati Law Review 57* (1989): 849.

A Matter of Interpretation. Princeton, N.J.: Princeton University Press, 1996.

Schauer, Fred. *Playing by the Rules: A Philosophical Examination of Rule-Based Decision-Making in Law and Life.* Oxford: Clarendon Press, 1991.

"Is the Common Law Law?" *California Law Review 77:* 455 (book review of Melvin Eisenberger, *The Nature of the Common Law.* Cambridge, Mass.: Harvard University Press, 1988).

Shapiro, Scott. "On Hart's Way Out." *Legal Theory 4* (1998): 46.

"Law, Morality, and the Guidance of Conduct." *Legal Theory 6* (2000): 127.

Simpson, A. W. B. "The Common Law and Legal Theory," in A. W. B. Simpson (ed.), *Oxford Essays in Jurisprudence*, second series. Oxford: Clarendon Press, 1973: 77.

Simpson. A. W. B. (ed.), *Oxford Essays in Jurisprudence*, second series. Oxford: Clarendon Press, 1973.

Sniderman, Paul; Joseph Fletcher; Peter Russell; and Philip Tetlock. *The Clash of Rights: Liberty, Equality and Legitimacy in Pluralist Democracy.* New Haven, Conn.: Yale University Press, 1996.

Strauss, David. "Common Law Constitutional Interpretation." *University of Chicago Law Review 63* (1996): 877.

Strossen, Nadine. *Defending Pornography.* New York: Scribner's, 1995.

Sumner, Wayne. "Rights," in Hugh LaFollette (ed.), *The Blackwell Guide to Ethical Theory.* Oxford: Blackwell Publishers, 2000: 298.

Sunstein, Cass. *Legal Reasoning and Political Conflict.* New York: Oxford University Press, 1996.

Tocqueville, Alexis de. *Democracy in America.* New York: Schocken Books, 1961.

Tushnet, Mark. *Red, White and Blue: A Critical Analysis of Constitutional Law.* Cambridge, Mass.: Harvard University Press, 1988.

"Constitutional Interpretation, Character and Experience." *Boston University Law Review 72* (1992): 747.

Taking the Constitution Away from the Courts. Cambridge, Mass.: Harvard University Press, 1999.

"Weak-Form Judicial Review: Its Implications for Legislatures," in G. Huscroft and I. Brodie (eds.), *Constitutionalism in the Charter Era.* Markham, Ontario: Butterworth's, 2004.

Unger, Roberto. *The Critical Legal Studies Movement.* Cambridge, Mass.: Harvard University Press, 1986.

Waismann, F. "Verifiability," in A. Flew (ed.), *Logic and Language.* Oxford: Blackwell's Publishers, 1968.

Waldron, Jeremy. *Theories of Rights.* Oxford: Oxford University Press, 1985.

"All We Like Sheep." *Canadian Journal of Law and Jurisprudence XII* (1999): 169.

Law and Disagreement. Oxford: Oxford University Press, 1999.

The Dignity of Legislation. Cambridge: Cambridge University Press, 1999.

Waluchow, W. J. "Strong Discretion." *Philosophical Quarterly 33* (1983): 321.

"Herculean Positivism." *Oxford Journal of Legal Studies V* (1985): 187.

Inclusive Legal Positivism. Oxford: Clarendon Press, 1994.

"Legal Positivism: Inclusive versus Exclusive," in E. Craig (ed.), *Routledge Encyclopedia of Philosophy.* London: Routledge, 2001. URL= http://www.rep.routledge.com

The Dimensions of Ethics. Peterborough, Ontario: Broadview Press, 2003.

"Constitutions as Living Trees: An Idiot Defends." *The Canadian Journal of Law and Jurisprudence XVIII* (2005): 207.

Index